AMERICA'S BEST

By the same author:

ENJU

LYONS ON HORSES

and soon to be published
STANDARD MESSIAH

AMERICA'S BEST

a novel by

Sinclair Browning

For Karen —
1944 — your birthday
and a memorable time
in American history.
Happy 60th!
Fondly,
Zelle
AKA
Sinclair Browning

AMC Publishing
a division of
American Metro Company, Inc.

AMC Publishing, P.O. Box 64185, Tucson, AZ 85728
A Division of American Metro Company, Inc.

FIRST EDITION

Library of Congress Catalog Card Number: 95-77267

Browning, Sinclair.
America's Best / Sinclair Browning
        500 p. cm.
        ISBN 1-887037-00-4
1. World War, 1939-1945 - Philippines - Fiction. 2. World War,
1939-1945 - Prisoners and prisons, Japanese. 3. World War
1939-1945 - Personal narratives, American. 4. Santo Tomas
Internment Camp (Manila, Philippines). I. Title.

Printed in the United States of America
First Priniting: 1995
1 3 5 7 9 10 8 6 4 2

For memories of the dead,

of Mary Lou,

whose ashes lie scattered off of Newport Bay;

and of Mike,

who is buried in the South China Sea...

and for knowledge for the living,

for Ben, Courtenay, Logan and Chris

Prologue

It all really began the summer of 1929. On a dirt strip on the Arizona desert a young barnstormer and his middle-aged Navajo mechanic were thrown together with four others.

There was no way any of them could have known that their lives, connected that long ago hot summer day, would twist and come together years later.

Yet these average Americans, along with their countrymen, would face a battery of tests that would prove them some of America's best.

THE WAR BELL TOLLS

1

Baguio, Luzon
Philippine Islands
July, 1941

The dreams were back, haunting him. Some of them weren't so bad; the ordination dreams he called them upon awakening. He could remember kneeling before the archbishop, resplendent in his robes, surrounded by the glory of the Roman Catholic Church. The bishop had recited the Latin words over him and then he had become, in the eyes of the church, as well as in his own, another Christ. *Alter Christus*. He liked to think of himself in that way. Another Christ. And the ordination dreams were reinforcement for him.

But there were stronger visions haunting him this evening. Stronger than the holy church, stronger than the archbishop's blessing. Dreams of hell and fire and of demons prodding him. Telling him to kill. He struggled with the question *kill whom?* before finally awakening.

George Bendetti sat up, dimly aware of the sweat pouring off his body. He didn't have to retrieve his watch from the bedside table to know he was already late for the party.

❧

The Pines Hotel ballroom was decked out in twisted red, white, and blue paper streamers while a stern looking cardboard Uncle Sam joined the members of the combo who were elevated slightly above the diners by means of a sturdy wooden platform. The musicians had practiced for weeks and the result of their labor was evident as strains of *"She's a Grand Old Flag"* wafted throughout the cavernous room.

Miniature American flags were everywhere. Tables were scattered throughout the ballroom flanking the dance floor. On each was a metal holder with large white cards. There were no open tables.

Sky and Magda had little trouble finding Tom and Ellen Sullivan for General and Mrs. Douglas MacArthur were standing with them next to their table.

"General." Sky extended his hand to the American whom he had met on several occasions. MacArthur, over sixty years old, stood tall, his lean body impeccably clothed in a gray checked tropical suit with a white silk shirt. He had returned as a four star general from the United States Army three and a half years earlier and was now serving as Field Marshall for the Philippine Commonwealth. His work was cut out for him, building up the Philippine Army until it reached a total of four hundred thousand. The goal was a long way off but there was no question that the American military advisor was dedicated to the task at hand.

Sky bowed slightly before he introduced Jean MacArthur to Magda. The general's wife was a tiny little woman, younger than her husband. As she stood next to Ellen the two women looked as though they had been crafted from the same mold, for neither weighed over a hundred pounds.

"My pleasure," Jean MacArthur's Tennessee accent was apparent in her speech.

"Please excuse us, we must we going." The general said his goodbyes quickly.

"Cordial as always," Sky muttered to Tom. The MacArthurs were not known for their partying ways and the fact that he had come at all was noteworthy.

"Probably off to a movie," Ellen said, for the MacArthur's penchant for movies was well known.

"Sky," Tom interjected. "Meet Lord and Lady Chesterfield."

Taking the outstretched hand and listening to the clipped British voice, Sky smiled as he thought of the irony of an Englishman attending an American Fourth of July party.

"My wife is an American." It was as though Chesterfield had read his mind.

Sky turned to Lady Chesterfield.

"We've also met. Hello Sky."

Berringer's heart stalled. Kate Matthews, looking every bit as young and as fresh as the first time he had seen her in the Arizona desert years earlier, stood before him.

"Lady, Lord Chesterfield," his voice was hoarse, "Magda Masaryk."

"Well, this is a treat," Francis Chesterfield turned to Magda. He pulled out a chair for the Czechoslovakian as the others followed suit. When they were all seated one chair stood conspicuously vacant.

"Tom was just telling me about your escape," Kate said to Magda. "Were you in Prague?"

Magda's shoulder length hair swung from side to side.

"Strakonice. I worked in the munitions factory there."

Frank raised his glass of red wine. "Then you were there during the trouble?"

"I left right after. I was fortunate." Her hazel eyes clouded and they were all silent for a moment for they had all heard of the trouble in the munitions factory in Strakonice.

The Czechoslovakian president and foreign minister had been summoned to a conference with Hitler in March of 1939. There, under threats of a Prague invasion President Hacha and Dr. Chalkovsky had signed the Statute of Protectorate which had incorporated Czechoslovakia into the Reich. Although the country had fallen without the threatened invasion, thousands of Czechs had fled across the border. Over thirty thousand alone had fought with Poland when that nation had been attacked by Germany. Close to another thousand Czech aviators had fought with the British at Dunkirk.

The Czechs, although fallen, were a resistant lot. Some seven months after being taken as a German vassal state they had celebrated the anniversary of the founding of their Republic. To celebrate, many of them took the day off from work and proudly wore the national colors. Many were arrested by the Germans and tortured. The demonstrations were even larger the next day and finally the Protector demanded they abandon the colors and wear a badge showing national solidarity. The badges were dutifully passed out with the initials N.S., *nardoni sourvcenstvi* for national solidarity. The Czechs, ever resourceful, had promptly turned the badge upside down so they read S.N. Among themselves they connected these initials with *smert nemcum* or death to Germans.

Since then demonstrations and sabotage from the Czech slaves continued. Trains were derailed, cannons exploded, guns misfired and airplanes fell apart in mid-air. Sabotage in the factories was high and in an effort to curb it the Germans had arrested sixty workers of the munitions factory at Strakonice. They had all been executed.

"To a free Czechoslovakia," Chesterfield held his glass high as every glass at the table was raised in tribute.

It started as a whisper, tickling Ellen's soul. She tried to brush it away but it only became more urgent.

We should have left.

"To Britain, may she keep the Nazis at bay!" Magda Masaryk's toast shattered the spell as the Czech paid homage to the valiant island nation struggling to survive nightly bombings by the German Luftwaffe.

Ellen shuddered before raising her glass. She'd heard the stories of the British sending their children out of the cities to strangers on farms, places where their offspring would be safe from the bombs. The thought of entrusting her own two boys to people she did not know made her stomach roil.

The toasts continued as Kate Chesterfield saluted France, which had been occupied by the Nazis for over a year.

George Bendetti, his officer's uniform a sharp contrast to the white tropical jackets and pants the rest of the men wore, rushed in seating himself in the only vacant chair.

"Sorry I'm late, Tom." He fidgeted with the small silver cross attached to his starched clerical collar.

"No problem," Tom Sullivan shrugged, "I believe you know everyone here. Except for Sky's friend, Magda."

"Father."

The priest took her hand, giving her a scant glance as he reached for the glass of wine that had just been poured. He drank eagerly from it.

"But most of all to Russia." Sky Berringer continued the toasting.

"Good riddance." George set down his glass, refusing to drink to Germany's latest victim who had been invaded just weeks before. Although Russia had been a German ally, her vast resources of grain, iron and coal had proven irresistible to the covetous invaders.

"You've got to be an idiot not to drink to that." Sky's fingers were taut about the stem of his glass.

The priest stiffened but said nothing.

"We're on the brink of war," Berringer continued, "this will give us time to arm ourselves. At least the Russians will keep Hitler busy for a while longer."

"We're still a neutral nation," George sniffed, returning to his wine now that the danger of a disagreeable toast was past.

A Filipino waiter began serving dinner.

"We're selling defense bonds back home and running air raid black out tests in New Jersey. Roosevelt has frozen all Axis assets and those of the occupied countries. Do you honestly believe we're going to be neutral much longer?" Sky was incredulous.

"We're not ready for another war. I don't care what the president wants."

"I don't think we'll have a choice," Tom cut in.

Ellen shook her head. The war talk made her uneasy and only fed the voice inside that kept insisting *we should have left*. What was wrong with her? she thought. It must be the wine.

"Well I think we all agree that you can't do business with Hitler," Ellen offered, pleased that Douglas Miller's new book had already arrived from the States. Everyone was reading it. "Why don't we talk about something else?"

"Like religion?" Sky grinned and stared at the priest.

"Oh no! Say the selective service," she offered playfully.

"Something unprovocative."

The Selective Service Act had become law the previous fall. It was the first draft induction bill in the history of the United States, legislating that all young men between the ages of twenty-one and thirty-five register for the service. While the act had banned American draftees from serving overseas, President Roosevelt had initiated a campaign in June to drop that provision.

Even the rich and famous were serving their country. Both the young Henry Ford II and his younger brother Benson had been called up, as well as the pro golfer Ed "Porky" Oliver and the playwright Sidney Kingsley. Jimmy Stewart, found to be ten pounds underweight by the Los Angeles draft board, had gorged himself up to standard army weight. In January of 1941 Winthrop Rockefeller, grandson of the great John D., had been inducted into the army. a feat recorded by all of the major newspapers and newsreel photographers. Few were exempt; few wanted to be.

George laughed. "You're right. Ellen. I don't know what it is about your friend here. We can't agree on anything."

The priest's longing glances in Kate Chesterfield's direction had not been lost on the pilot. "Unfortunately that's not true, Father."

"George, I must say, I think you're wrong too," said Tom, turning to the clergyman. "America's got to get into this war."

"On the contrary," the priest argued. "We don't have to do anything. No one is challenging our borders, clamoring to take our cities."

Tom looked at the Chesterfields, embarrassed by the insensitivity of the priest's remarks. "And our allies?" His freckles were standing out more than normal.

George shrugged. "I'm sorry, sure I am. Kate, Frank, you know that. But it's not our war. Why should our young men die at Dunkirk?" He cut into his roast beef seemingly unaware of the pall he was casting on all of them.

"Or Cavite?" Kate raised an eyebrow. Cavite was the site of the only naval yard in the Philippines.

"It hasn't come to that." He argued.

"Yet." Tom shifted in his seat, fully aware of the pressure Ellen's leg was playing against his left knee under the table. There would be hell to pay later but he couldn't help himself. "You're sounding like a goddamned isolationist!"

"I am. Lindbergh's got the right idea about this thing. It's just a pity more people don't realize it."

Charles Lindbergh, the famous aviator, had formed the America First Committee as a vehicle for the isolationist view-point.

"I'm afraid I don't think much of your hero, sir." Francis Chesterfield's eyes grew dark. Lindbergh, in an April address to thirty thousand Americans attending a New York rally, had con-demned Britain for encouraging nations to fight with no hope of victory. Roosevelt had roundly condemned the aviator's speech and Lindy had resigned his commission as a colonel in the re-serves.

"Nor I," Tom chimed in, "I'm in White's corner."

William Allen White, a Kansas newspaper publisher, had started his own committee, The Committee to Defend America by Aiding the Allies. Like the Lindbergh group, White's support-ers were working hard to bring the American public around to their point of view.

"At least you both agree to stronger continental defenses," Sky offered.

"And you," Kate asked, "Sky, which side are you on?"

Berringer grinned, his dimples cutting deeply into both sides of his cheeks, just touching the dark moustache flecked with gray. "Neither."

"That's unconscionable. You've got to be on one or the other." Bendetti insisted on needling him.

"Is that the way your world works, Father? All black or all white? Thanks, but I'll sit this one out."

"Why Sky," Ellen said quietly, "that doesn't seem like you. It's so, so..."

"Un-American," the priest offered.

Sky bristled only slightly. He had heard all of the arguments before as most of the world news coming into the Philippines was bleak.

"I don't think so at all. Our involvement in the war is inevitable. Whether one is an isolationist or an interventionist isn't going to make any difference once we're in."

"Then if I follow your position correctly," Lord Chesterfield puffed to start his after dinner pipe, "you feel the Axis powers will directly attack America?"

Bendetti didn't wait for Sky's answer. "Somehow the sound of German storm troopers attacking Manhattan just doesn't ring true."

"No," Sky agreed.

"Then where?" Tom was interested in all of the war rumors and assessments.

"Here."

"You mean the Philippines?" Magda leaned closer, afraid to miss a word.

Ellen felt like vomiting.

"Or Guam. Or Pearl. Or Midway. But somewhere in the South Pacific. We're next. We've got to be."

"We're a long way from Germany," the priest challenged him.

"But not so far from Japan," Sky continued logically. "She can't afford to have us sitting here on the flank of her southern sea lanes. The Australian meat and grain are vital to England."

"Yes." Chesterfield nodded in agreement.

"Japan needs to take us along with Singapore to protect the Dutch East Indies."

"They're not hers," Tom reminded him.

"Yet. We'll see her in French Indo-China before long. We're a threat, there's no doubt about it. Japan knows we're not out here alone, that the Pacific Fleet in Honolulu would come to our aid in any prolonged conflict."

"Maybe we should have gone home after all," Ellen said, somehow relieved that the quiet voice that had been plaguing her for weeks was now out in the open.

"We'll be all right." Tom reached for her hand.

Ellen was still troubled. In February the United States had ordered all military dependents home, now only the civilian wives and children remained.

"What's the word at Benguet, Tom?" Sky asked.

Sullivan, chief engineer for the Benguet Consolidated Mining Company, was privy to a lot of corporate speculation.

"We've seen a lot of changes over there in the past year. They've taken down all the signs written in English and closed the cabarets. Hell, in their lust for baseball they've even invented their own phrase for 'kill the umpire'".

"They're not the most sophisticated people," Bendetti's disdain was apparent. "They smile when they're unhappy and write backwards."

"Don't underestimate them," Sky cautioned. "They've got six million men in the service, all veterans. They've been fighting in China for over four years now."

"But the army here is getting beefed up. That ought to account for something." Ellen suggested.

"Oh yes. MacArthur's a grand general, there's no doubt about it," Sky said. "But look what he's got to work with! Ten thousand United States army regulars and a ragtag Filipino army of Igorots, Moros and Tagalogs. They're untrained and untested."

"I thought you were supposed to be helping with that," Tom chided. Berringer had taken a job with the Filipino Army as a civilian aircraft instructor. "Sky's assigned to the Philippine Military Academy here," Tom said by way of explanation to the Chesterfields.

"That's the one patterned after West Point, isn't it?" Frank asked,

Sky nodded.

"I wasn't aware there was an air force here," Chesterfield continued.

"We'll have one next month, Eventually we'll end up with the 19th and 27th Bombardment groups," Sky explained, his eyes steady on the priest. Although Bendetti's orders posted him to the 27th Bombardment group until they arrived he had been assigned to the Academy on a temporary basis,

"The Academy's the general's baby," Tom added. "And Sky's."

Berringer grinned. "Can't deny it." He thought for a minute finally remembering where he had heard the Chesterfield name. "The speedboats!" He snapped his fingers. "That's it. MacArthur's boats."

"Yes, the Thornycraft PT's," Chesterfield replied.

"Frank's in shipbuilding, old sport. Sorry I thought you knew that," Tom apologized.

Douglas MacArthur's plan for the neutrality of the Philippine archipelago depended on a fleet of PT boats armed with torpedoes. The general called them quick, or "Q" boats. While Washington had thought his plan insane, they had eventually gone along with parts of it.

"How many did we finally end up with?" Sky asked.

"Three. We delivered them last December."

"Out of what was it, fifty?"

Frank nodded. "I'm afraid we've had to cancel the order, what with our being at war and all. Dreadful disappointment for the general. I'll be going back to London later this summer and I hope to resurrect something for your islands."

"That's it!" Ellen tapped her hands lightly against the table. "I'm tired of all of this gloomy war talk. Sky, will you dance with me?"

Without waiting for his answer the tiny blonde stood and extended her arm to the handsome aviator.

"You're looking wonderful, Ellen," Sky held her firmly as they glided into a smooth waltz. "How are Doc and Pete?"

"Driving me crazy, but fine. Doc's still into his crazy experiments," Ellen spoke fondly of her two children. "We had a party the other night and in the middle of it he walked through with a hammer and a saw, casually suggesting that he was off to build a lightning rod."

Sky laughed. The Sullivan boys charmed all who met them. Bright and quick they were not easily intimidated by their parent's friends.

"Of course I suggested that his invention could wait but then he insisted on debating me for another ten minutes."

They danced silently for a few minutes before she started talking again. "You know, Sky, all this talk scares the hell out of me. When Tom suggested I take the boys home I argued with him. But now, I think we should all go."

"Maybe you're right, Ellen. I think we're in for some rough water ahead."

"Tom won't leave. He says the Benguet people will tell us when it's no longer safe to stay. It is complicated, isn't it?" She laughed nervously. "But it's just not the same. This used to be such a nice place, now it's though...as though there's a pox on the whole thing."

"I wouldn't worry about it just yet."

"When the service wives left it was like geese heading south for the winter. Eery."

They were quiet for a moment before Ellen once again broke the spell.

"You and Charlie are coming for Doc's birthday next month, aren't you?"

"Wouldn't miss it for anything."

As they walked back to the table Sky was disappointed to see that Lord and Lady Chesterfield were missing.

"Kate and Frank said to tell you goodnight. They had to drive back to Manila." There was a smug note in Bendetti's voice. Sky stared at him.

Bendetti's full, pouting lips had always suggested inappropriate excesses for a priest. His blond hair, now streaked with gray, had always been combed a little too carefully for a man whose vows did not include vanity. The boyish features had coarsened, giving him the appearance of a bloated, middle-aged man. The hardened cast to his face was unflattering even in the soft light.

"I too am tired, Sky." Magda turned to the Sullivans. "Thank you both for a wonderful time."

Walking through the lobby of the Pines Hotel, Magda was drawn to a glass display case. There, inside, was a Red Cross appeal for funds.

"It may happen to YOU. You may benefit from Red Cross help," she whispered as she read the poster, her eyes fixed on a man handing out relief packages. An uncontrollable chill ran through her body as she sagged against Sky.

"I see pictures, awful pictures," her hands were pressing hard against her temples as though the pressure would erase what she saw in her mind. "Sky, we are all going to need their help."

As though taken with a sudden illness, the vibrant redhead was now limp and it took her concentrated effort to walk across the lobby and out the door.

Sky was silent as he helped her into the car. He had heard her talk of pictures before.

And she had yet to be wrong.

2

Empty boxes with strips of their gay wrapping paper still attached were strewn throughout the parlor in sharp contrast to the usual order. The houseboy, Irineo, a tiny middle-aged man, immaculate in crisp white pants and jacket, methodically stacked the books and metal cars and building sets in one corner. They were all new treasures, temporarily forgotten by their young recipient as he wrestled outside with a kite, trying to coax it into flight in the still afternoon.

Pete Sullivan sat quietly near the dining room door, intent on stippling Putt Putt, the family cat, with his brother's new oil paints.

"I can't believe this!" Ellen threw up her hands in mock despair, "I really should make Doc come back in and help clean."

"Why bother? He's only ten once," Kate was emptying ashtrays into a metal can, shielding their powdery contents from the breeze of the ceiling fans.

"Sometimes I think we have too much here," Ellen looked in Irineo's direction. "I worry that they'll get a distorted sense of values with all of this."

Kate picked up a carved jade statue of Kwannon, the goddess of mercy. "All of this doesn't affect you as a person or Tom or what the boys will become. They'll learn."

"I suppose so. But they'll be in for a big shock when they go back to the States and find out that not everyone has a cook, or a houseboy."

Kate smiled.

"He was pleased, wasn't he?"

"Doc?" Kate asked.

Ellen nodded.

"Wildly. That's what birthdays are for. Children. Christmas too. I think that's when I knew I was getting old. When the holidays weren't quite as exciting to me, when they didn't have quite the same spark."

Ellen picked up a picture, a charcoal portrait of Doc capturing all of his innocence and boyish charm. "This is really lovely Kate. Thank you."

She laughed.

"I think he was less than thrilled. I hope the tractor compensated for it. That was Frank's idea."

"He's such a dear."

"I'll miss him." Kate returned the statue to its resting place on the polished mahogany table. "But three months isn't such a terribly long time, is it?"

"Not at all. Besides with you here in Baguio we'll keep you busy with all sorts of things. With bridge and little theater and the mah-jong tournaments there'll be plenty of diversions."

Kate laughed. "And I thought Baguio was supposed to be a resort town."

"Oh it is. We can go hiking in the Benguets if that's what you want. We could start right now, by hiking out to the porch!" Ellen smiled. She hadn't been on a hike in fifteen years.

The porch, edged by a waist high whitewashed railing, ran the length of the house. An assemblage of mismatched rockers, one of Ellen's weaknesses, were scattered across the tongue and grooved floor. Some were heavy and wooden with arms wide enough to hold a drink; others were native rattan. Each had its own personality and feel, and all of the guests had been to the Sullivans enough times to have selected a favorite rocker. All were now rocking in them enjoying the pleasant August afternoon.

"Well, Charles I must say you are the first American Indian I have ever met. This really has made my day!" Francis Chesterfield patted the Navajo's burly arm.

Charlie grinned, showing white, even teeth. "Well Frank that makes us even."

"I say I hadn't thought of it that way at all. Yes, yes I guess that's right," he chuckled. "Sky tells me that you're the best mechanic in these islands. Is there any truth to that?"

Charlie shrugged.

"He's too modest," Sky interjected, "fact of the matter is Charlie can fix anything that moves. Including," he aimed a finger at Pete who was peeking around the corner, "you!" With a squeal the youngest Sullivan boy was off.

"That will come in handy I should think," Chesterfield said. "Even with your American factories on three shifts I'm told there's a lot of time involved before you get goods, parts and the like."

"Six weeks from the East Coast," Tom said.

"With luck," Sky added.

"And I dare say I don't think they're going to get any better."

"No, I'm afraid you're right." Tom was thinking of the practice blackouts that had started in Manila in July. "Sky, I guess I haven't had a chance to congratulate you."

"On what?"

"Japan's taking Indo-China."

"Oh that. I wish I'd have been wrong about it."

Although Japan had been in the north of Indo-China for some time she had expanded her control, taking over the entire country at the end of July. Her aggrandizement was roundly seen as a clear attempt to jockey into a better position from which to attack Malaya and the Dutch East-Indies.

"And our mutual friend, the general. What do you hear from him these days?" Frank asked.

"Very little," Tom replied. "He and Jean and little Arthur were invited to the party today but they couldn't make it."

"I'm not surprised," Frank said, "I have the feeling that your man Roosevelt is going to keep him pretty busy for a while."

In retaliation against Japan's Indo-China move, Franklin Roosevelt had taken several serious steps. He had frozen all Japanese assets in the United States and prohibited each Japanese from spending more than five hundred dollars per month. The freeze included all Japanese ships in American ports and made it mandatory for any Japanese to obtain a Treasury license to sell even a pound of silk. This step alone had created such a mass of paperwork in the Philippines that experts from the United States Treasury Department had already arrived to help the U.S. High Commissioner with the overload.

These restrictions were quickly followed by Britain and the Dutch government in exile. In effect, Japan had been cut off from many necessary goods including oil, scrap iron, and rubber.

Next the President had closed the Panama Canal to Japanese shipping. On the day of the closure ten Japanese freighters waited for their turn through the canal. But it never came for the Americans were fearful to allow even one ship flying the Rising Sun through, lest they blow up a lock. The Japanese were told the Canal was being repaired although other ships were allowed through. The Japanese freighters turned south for a nineteen thousand mile trip around Cape Horn.

The last step that Roosevelt had taken was to merge the American and Filipino troops placing Douglas MacArthur in the position of commanding general of the United States Forces in the Far East.

"I guess it was a surprise," Tom said. "In fact he was reading an unverified report about his appointment in the *Manila Tribune* when the war department cables arrived."

"Not too much of a surprise, I'll bet," Sky argued. "He's wanted that position for months now." He rose and walked into the house.

"I'm curious as to what you think about all of this, Charles." Chesterfield turned to Begay.

"I'll tell you what I told Sky months ago," the Navajo rocked slowly. "There are a lot more Japanese people in these islands than before. There are few women. Few children. But there are many young fishermen."

"And what, in your assessment, does that mean?" Chesterfield prodded.

"I think they are mapping the islands."

"Oh Charlie!" Ellen's hands flew to her open mouth. "That can't be."

"This is only the opinion of a tired old Indian. Maybe I am wrong," he shrugged.

"Or perhaps you're right," Chesterfield said in a glum voice.

"I think we're all looking at fishermen a little differently now," offered Ellen, thinking of the seventeen Japanese fishing boats apprehended off Hawaii just two weeks earlier. Each had been equipped with a radio transmitter, a camera and an officer of the Japanese Imperial Army.

"Amen," Kate agreed.

Frank puffed on his pipe in an effort to stoke it up. "I'm

afraid your Pacific will soon be in the same shape as our Atlantic."

"When are you heading back?" Tom asked.

"The first of the week. You will take care of my lady here," Frank said softly as he leaned over and patted Kate affectionately on her knee.

"Of course. Ellen's got her entire life mapped out at least through Christmas."

"Well, I hope to be back before then," Chesterfield said.

Charlie said nothing more the rest of the afternoon.

3

November, 1941

Tom held Doc's small hands in his own. He stared at them for a moment, marvelling at how they now almost filled his palms. The child he had started out in life calling his "baby man" would soon truly be a man. Still as he looked into his clear blue eyes, Tom was very much aware that this, his oldest man child, was still but a boy.

"Yes, Dad?" There was a catch in the boy's throat for he had been wondering about this quiet meeting. He looked to his father for an answer.

Tom cleared his throat, collecting his thoughts.

"Doc, you know I'm leaving tomorrow."

"Yes. General MacArthur told me that it's a very brave thing you're doing. Are you scared?"

Tom shook his head. "No, son. But I don't like leaving you and mother and Pete."

The boy was still, his blue orbs searching his father's face.

"And I kind of need some help from you."

"What kind of help, Dad?"

"I need for you to take my place for a while, Doc. You'll be the man of the family while I'm gone. Do you think you can handle that?"

"Does that mean I can stay up later?" Doc grinned as he tried to make a joke out of what he knew was a solemn occasion.

"It means you have to not only mind mother the very best you can," Sullivan knew this was a heavy burden for his rambunctious child. "But that you have to watch out for her and your brother. You have to keep them from harm."

"You mean like from the Japanese," Doc wrinkled his nose in distaste.

"Something like that. Just promise me you'll do your best to be good and to watch out for them."

The boy squirmed and pulled his hands away. He threw himself around his father's neck and squinted hard to keep telltale tears from spilling down his chubby cheeks.

"You can count on me, Dad. I promise. Don't worry about that."

Tom held his baby man tightly, slowly rocking back and forth in tune with the child's shaking body.

"Thanks, Doc. I knew I could," he whispered.

Although it was November the temperature was in the seventies that afternoon in Baguio as the occupants of the house were appreciating the fine day with the windows opened to a slight breeze. The faint smell of rain drifted in with the wind.

"We've got to be in this war by Christmas, George. There's no other way," Tom lit a cigarette and took a long drag. "There've been too many changes."

"Oh I agree," the priest played with the small silver cross on his collar. "There's no way Roosevelt can get out of this one. Or wants to."

America had indeed drawn closer to war. In August, Congress had cut off oil and aviation fuel exports to everyone but the British. Japan was now sorely feeling the pinch. In the fall,

Roosevelt had issued shoot-on-sight orders for the United States Navy patrolling the Atlantic. American merchant ships had been armed.

"At least we agree on war," Sky grinned. "Seems kind of irreverent, doesn't it, Father?" There was still something about the smug clergyman that Sky couldn't resist needling.

Ellen stood behind Tom's straight-backed chair, placing her hands on his broad shoulders. She leaned down and lightly kissed the top of his thinning red hair.

"Tell them your news, dear." There was a noticeable tremor in her soft voice.

Tom patted her hand. "It's confidential, but then I don't suppose any of you is a Japanese spy. General MacArthur has asked me to serve."

Kate set her wine glass down carefully as a chill ran through her body. "Serve? What do you mean serve? You're a civilian."

"Yes."

"He's going to help win the war," Ellen said. Although she was resigned to MacArthur's offer and Tom's acceptance, there was a bitterness in her voice. She was still sorting out in her own mind Tom's reluctance to refuse the four-star general. They had talked about it for hours last night and if he wanted to call it service, it was all right with her.

"I've been asked to go to Corregidor," Tom added.

Sky crossed to the parlor bar and helped himself to a stiff bourbon. His hand paused in front of the pitcher of water but he did not dilute the drink. As he took his seat again he could not look at either Tom or Ellen. He doubted whether any of them in the room, even Tom, knew just how serious the general's request was.

Berringer had been close enough to his military friends to know of the existence of the Orange Plan- the code name for the defense blueprint for the Philippines. In the event of a Japanese invasion, the plan called for all troops, American and Filipino alike, to withdraw into the Bataan Peninsula. Bataan would be the last stand and it was generally hoped that the troops there could hold out for at least six months until reinforcements could come from the United States.

Corregidor, an island fortress at the mouth of Manila Bay, held a critical part in the defense strategy. From the island, Allied troops would protect the bay.

"Because of the tunnels," Sky said.

"Yes."

The island was a labyrinth of tunnels and engineers would indeed be helpful, perhaps vital, on Corregidor.

"And you're going." Sky's question came out flat.

"Yes. I have to."

Sky looked at Ellen and felt a pang as he thought of Doc and Pete. MacArthur was asking too much of his old friend.

"Well, it's not all that glum," Ellen was making an effort to be cheery. "After all Corregidor isn't the end of the world. I'm even thinking of taking an apartment in Manila so we can see each other during his days off. Besides, Tom thinks he may be finished there right after the first of the year. That's not so bad now is it?"

Kate stared sadly at the two of them. "When do you go?"

"He's sending a car for me in the morning."

"I think it's damned cheeky of you to be off before Frank comes back. He'll be awfully miffed that he wasn't here to wish you well, you know." Kate, in spite of her resolve, dabbed at her eyes.

"Tell him I'm sorry I couldn't wait," Tom drained his glass.

"He left England last Monday. At least that's when he was supposed to leave," she prattled on in an effort to disguise her grief for the Sullivans.

"I've booked passage on the *President Polk* for Ellen and the boys. They'll be in San Francisco by Valentine's Day," Tom continued.

"But that's not until next year," Sky spoke softly trying to keep alarm out of his voice.

"It was the first passage I could get." Tom reached for a crystal decanter. "I should have sent you home by now," he whispered to Ellen. It was a rare admission for him. "Damn! I wish I had."

"It was no use. You tried, you really did. I wanted to stay." But *we should have left*, Ellen thought.

He put the decanter down and pulled her to him. "No one would have faulted you for leaving."

She held him tight. "I know, dear. Everything is going to be fine, you'll see." Her voice reflected an optimism she did not feel. Although a State Department directive had been issued urging all American citizens to return home, there were still many of them left in the archipelago.

"I'll take these," Ellen reached for the tray of drinks.

"I talked to a Japanese businessman at dinner the other night," Bendetti said. "He was a Konoye man."

They all paid attention. The resignation the month before of Prince Fuminaro Konoye, a member of the Japanese peacekeeping faction, and his replacement with General Hideki Tojo, a militaristic war hawk, had only accelerated tension between the two nations.

"He says the Imperial Hotel is swarming with Germans."

He paused to accept an offered drink from Ellen. "Hundreds of technicians, bringing all of their skills to the Japanese. Says they're even Gestapo agents teaching their tricks to the Home Ministry."

Ellen shuddered. "How awful!"

"Frankly I'm not surprised," Sky said, "Germany has been after Japan for a long time to throw in against the allies."

"But at the Imperial!" Ellen loved the old Tokyo hotel and found the idea of a German occupation distasteful.

"What do you hear in Manila, Sky?" Tom asked.

"MacArthur's being lobbied to move the planes."

Nine Boeing B-17's, known as the "Flying Fortresses", had been delivered to Manila. Sky had worked on the Model 299 prototype to the airplane while at Boeing in Seattle. Once the heavy B-17's arrived, he had been transferred to Manila.

The delivery of the Flying Fortresses, and the promise of more, had caused General MacArthur to issue orders to expand the landing strips at the two major airstrips on Luzon that were capable of handling the large airplanes. Additionally he had ordered Del Monte on the southern island of Mindanao expanded to accommodate the B-17's.

"Move them? Where?" George was pacing, a trait that he had picked up in the past few years and one that only added to his already nervous demeanor.

"Del Monte."

"But why?" Ellen asked. "It's so far. They're not going to give us much help down there." The Del Monte airfield was five hundred miles south of Manila.

"But they'll be out of range of the Japanese." Sky explained.

"Oh." Ellen shook her head sadly and took a long drag on her cigarette. She resented having to know any of it- the military terms, the politics, the strategy.

"Mama, Mama!" Pete came running in from the front porch. "Uncle Charlie is telling us the best stories about Coyote!"

Ellen smiled, welcome for the break in the conversation. She had listened to the Navajo tell her children the Arizona stories.

The Indian myths, rife with the antics of Coyote, Frog Man and the wisdom of Changing Woman, the goddess of the earth, were as fascinating to her as they were to the boys.

"You should give Charlie a break. Let him join the grownups," she suggested, for Begay had been with the boys for over an hour.

Sky held up his hand. "You ought to know better by now, Ellen. He's doing just want he wants to do. He enjoys sharing his stories with them."

"I know," she mused, "sometimes I wonder if we wouldn't be better off telling each other fairy tales."

Pete piled a plate high with mangoes, pineapple and bananas before retreating to the porch. Three of the dissimilar rockers were clustered together and he eagerly retook his seat to listen to more of the Coyote tales.

Begay paused in his storytelling as he watched the government car come slowly up the drive. Stopping in front of the house the driver stepped out of the vehicle, wasting no time in opening the rear door of the car. A young lieutenant, a man Charlie recognized as a member of General MacArthur's staff, exited the vehicle. He was crisp in his army uniform as he took the porch stairs two at a time.

"Good day, sir," he addressed the Navajo politely. "Could you direct me to Mrs. Francis Chesterfield. I was told I might find her here."

Charlie nodded. "Do you want to go inside?"

The lieutenant suddenly seemed less crisp. "Are there many in there?"

"I will get her."

A moment later Kate faced the young officer.

"Yes?" She was clearly puzzled by his seeking her out.

"Sorry to disturb you ma'am," he removed his cap," but the

general sent this message." He handed her a stiff white envelope. "He said to tell you he's sorry he wasn't able to deliver it personally."

Kate rolled the formal envelope over and over in her hands. She tried to hand it to Begay, who shook his head.

"It is best if you open it."

"Yes, I suppose so. Besides," she laughed nervously, "It's probably just an invitation to some silly party or something."

The Navajo and the lieutenant remained silent.

"Still," she began to slowly unseal the gummed flap, "I can't imagine why the general would go to all this fuss."

She withdrew a single sheet of paper and began to read.

"Oh my God!" A scream ripped from her throat, bringing Sky and Tom on the run. The paper fell from her hands as she slowly crumpled to the porch floor, saved from a nasty fall by Charlie who caught her limp body. Carefully, he propped her up in the nearest rocker.

"What is it? What on earth has happened?" Ellen ran to the unconscious Kate. "What is it?"

Sky had retrieved the offending paper and he quickly read it. "It's Frank," he said softly. "He's been caught in an air raid in Liverpool."

"Caught?" Ellen did not understand.

"Killed." There was little emotion in the aviator's voice.

"Dead? Dead? No!" Ellen swayed in disbelief, throwing her weight into Tom. "Dear God, where will all of this end?"

4

Kate sat on the porch, a woven afghan wrapped around her knees. Ellen was beside her, quietly knitting.

"The boys will be home soon," Kate remarked dully.

"Yes. I always view Fridays with mixed feelings."

Doc and Pete attended the Episcopalian Brent School. Their studies took the major part of each weekday with weekends off.

"It's so peaceful now. We'd better enjoy it." Ellen offered.

"And yet so strange." Kate looked terrible. Dark bags hovered under each eye and her long brown hair was unkempt and dull looking. "I can't believe it's been almost two weeks, El."

The small blonde patted her friend's leg. "I know, dear."

"And even today," Kate gestured limply with a free hand, "It's a beautiful day. The sun is shining, the skies are clear, and yet there's no joy here now, is there?"

"It will come later, Kate. It takes time."

"No, no," she waved impatiently. "It's not just Francis, although God knows that is a lot of it. It's everything."

"Yes." Ellen looked down the full run of the porch, thinking not for the first time how empty things seemed.

"And now Tom's off to Corregidor and George has gone

off with his group." The 27th Bombardment Group had been put on twenty-four hour alert in Manila and although he had tried, the priest had been unable to change his orders.

"And Sky's at Clark Field," Ellen said. "Things are getting tight down there." There was no sense shielding Kate. She would have to be strong.

"It isn't good at all, is it, El?"

She shook her head. Both women had been following the news reports. The Phillips radio had been on day and night to catch the war news.

Sky had told them that on the twenty-fifth of November Washington radioed all the commanders in the Pacific to expect Axis movement from any direction. The directive suggested that possible targets might be Guam or the Philippines.

A week after Tom's arrival on Corregidor, General MacArthur had put all troops there on full alert, cancelling any leave time that had accrued. In the last week there had been many confirmed reports of unidentified aircraft sighted near Clark Field, the Lingayen Gulf and along the Luzon coast. There had been at least one known instance of the American P- 40's encountering Japanese airplanes over Iba Field.

"You know," Kate attempted humor, "I think I used to like Baguio better before it got so popular."

"Or at least things didn't seem so imminent then," Ellen agreed.

The summer had been a busy one in Manila. A constant stream of notables and newsmen had come through, looking for stories. Henry Luce and Clare Boothe, Ernest Hemingway, Ralph Ingersoll- the list went on and on. All acting on a tip that the unprepared Philippines would be sitting ducks for the Japanese. Most of them had gone home long ago.

Now Baguio was under siege as a higera of civilians had come up from Manila leaving the strategic military locations- Cavite, Nichols and Clark Fields, Stotsenberg- behind in favor of the mountain sanctuary. The summer homes and all the hostelries in the mountainous community were packed with the emigres. The people of Baguio, unprepared for the onslaught, were handling the influx the best they could. Already, food supplies were short.

The phone rang twice and stopped. Irineo stepped onto the porch. "It's Mister Sky, for you," he nodded to his mistress.

Ellen was not in the house for long and when she returned her worried look was apparent to Kate.

"More bad news?"

"Yes," Ellen's voice dropped to a whisper, a trait she'd had since high school when she feared losing control. "More Japanese planes were spotted over Iba. General MacArthur's doubling the guards at all the fields. They're dispersing as many of the planes as possible."

Kate stood, her eyes more alive than they had been in two weeks. The afghan, forgotten now, fell in a wad on the floor. "El, how much food do we have in the house?"

Kate and Ellen spent a nervous weekend, watching the sky for the feared Japanese invaders. In spite of their vigilance, Saturday and Sunday passed without incident.

The candles were flickering, almost melted to the crystal bobeches that prevented their wax from dripping onto the polished wooden table. Ellen pulled the glass decanter to her. Slowly she filled Kate's crystal snifter half full with the amber liquor.

The table had been cleared, the boys shuffled off to bed by their *amah,* and now the two women were relaxing, enjoying the quiet of the late evening.

"You're very lucky to have them," Kate's eyes misted. "That's a sadness in my life. That Frank and I couldn't have children."

"I can imagine," Ellen sipped her brandy. "Still I suppose we could all go crazy looking back. I've been trying not to."

"You?" Kate was surprised.

"The whole thing with Corregidor. I wish now I'd have raised holy hell over his going." It was a confession she could make to Kate and few others.

"You couldn't do that, El."

"No, I suppose not. It seems so unfair. But it was something he felt he had to do and there's no escaping that now, is there?"

Kate nursed her brandy. "No."

"Was I wrong not to stop him?" Torture dulled Ellen's blue eyes. This was obviously something she had been wrestling with for a long time.

"I don't think so. We all have to do what is important to us. I don't think Tom would have been happy saying no to General MacArthur."

"No. Well!" She twirled the snifter between her palms, "This is cheery talk for a Sunday evening. Tell me, aren't you sorry now you didn't accept Sky's fine invitation opting to spend the weekend with a spoiled, brooding woman instead?"

"You're neither. Besides it's too early for parties." The aviator had invited Kate to a party the Twenty-Seventh Bombardment group was throwing that evening for Major General Lewis Brereton, commander of the Far East Air Force under General MacArthur. Twelve hundred fliers, including the crews of the B-17's, had been turned loose in the Manila Hotel for the evening. Sky had told her that they stalled their orders for Mindanao so they could attend the grand affair. Still, the young widow declined the invitation, preferring the quiet of Baguio.

The shrill ringing of the telephone startled both women. Ellen looked at her watch. It was after eleven, too late in the evening for a social call. She rose from the table.

"I'll have to get that. They've all gone to bed."

A moment later she returned, her face ashen.

"It was Sky again. The night patrols have picked up some more unidentified planes over Clark Field," Her eyes met Kate's. "He doesn't think I should send the boys to school tomorrow."

A SHATTERING OF LIVES

5

Bendetti's silver cross was askew as he stumbled down the steps of the Manila Hotel. Really not fitting, he thought. He was more than tipsy. He was on the verge of passing out since he'd had more than his share of whiskey at the Brereton party. The guest of honor had left early in anticipation of his morning flight to Java. Undaunted by the general's departure, the fly boys had toasted many a round in his absent honor and the priest had matched them one on one.

He stood at the curb trying to stand as steady as he could. That was important, he knew, not to give the appearance of having had too much to drink. Most of the time, if you just kept still and didn't say much, no one would know you were as drunk as you really were.

He smiled. He liked to drink. It helped him forget he was involved with the goddamned army. And it helped blur the memories of that incident in Arizona so long ago. That's why he had signed up. Not out of any sense of duty but to escape.

Censure, if not excommunication, would have been imminent if he had been found out.

The voice was his problem.

That goddamned voice. Teasing him, goading him on, instructing him in things he knew were wrong.

After the incident he had even gone so far as to see a psychiatrist in Tucson. There had been three visits and he had kept his appointments all three times. When Dr. Meirhouser had started using technical terms like deviant sexuality symptomatic of obsessive reactions, Bendetti had become frightened. Could the doctor associate his patient with the story that had appeared in the *Arizona Daily Star*?

He had taken no chances. He made another appointment which he never kept. And he was thankful that he had had the foresight to visit the doctor under an assumed name.

There had been no doubt that his bishop suspected him. Stripped ecclesiastically without the support of the head of the diocese, he was given a choice by Bishop Argyle. Censure and exile to the Alexian Brothers Institution for errant priests or enlistment in the United States Army.

Two days after he had missed his last scheduled psychiatric appointment he had enlisted. It had never occurred to him that obedience in the service could be a problem. But the church indoctrination had taken its toll and where he would have gladly served his church superiors, he had trouble with the army officers.

Although he'd been concerned about the psychiatric evaluations for the army, he had sailed through them. He concluded that Dr. Meirhouser had been wrong in his diagnosis. A conclusion that was substantiated by the stilling of the inner voice since he had come to the Philippines.

He tried to focus his eyes on his watch, luminous in the early morning light. Two-thirty. Too late to call for a car. He would walk home. That would do. He stared at the wristwatch again. Only a little over five hours until he had to be at Our Lady of Lourdes in the walled city of Intramuros to celebrate the Feast of the Blessed Virgin.

He hesitated on the curb, trying to collect his thoughts before walking out into the night.

The slapping of leather pounding against the pavement caught his drunken attention. A young soldier was racing up the street. As he ran to the curb, his heel caught the edge of it and he bumped hard into the clergyman.

"Sorry Father," he apologized, pulling the unsteady priest up.

"Say, wait a minute," Bendetti reached out and caught the youngster's sleeve. "What's the hurry?"

The soldier pulled back, eager to escape the range of the priest's rank breath. "I'm looking for Major Davies, sir."

"Well you won't find him in there," George said thickly. He waved a hand across the sky, "he's gone. They're all gone. I'm the last to leave."

The soldier's eyes grew wide. "My God. Excuse me sir, but it's Pearl Harbor. She's been bombed by the Japs, sir."

"Pearl Harbor?" Bendetti shook his head. It did not make any sense to him. "You mean Thai?"

"No sir. Pearl."

"But it's, it's so far," slowly he was coming out of his drunken stupor. "And it's the middle of the night."

"Not in Hawaii, sir. It's almost nine o'clock there."

"And yesterday." The time and day differences due to the International Dateline had finally sunk in.

6

By 4:00 a.m. most of the partying boys from the Twenty-Seventh Bombardment group had been alerted by their superiors. Few of them had yet gone to bed.

The Japanese had pulled a tactical coup. Taking advantage of the Americans' love for holidays and weekends, they had deliberately chosen a Sunday morning for their surprise raid when most of the servicemen would be spending a leisurely day at home or attending church services with their families.

Hitting Pearl Harbor at the unlikely Sunday hour insured minimum crews at battle stations. Few servicemen are behind anti-aircraft guns, ammunition boxes are found locked, and there are no torpedo nets up to protect the fleet.

Swooping in on Honolulu at 7:55 a.m. over four hundred airplanes come off of six aircraft carriers to attack the Pacific Fleet anchored at Pearl Harbor. Sea vessels including two battleships, destroyers, tankers, two heavy cruisers and a fleet of midget submarines (none over eighty feet long) are also engaged.

Although President Roosevelt and his government advisors, fearing widespread panic among the American people, will withhold the extent of damage at Pearl Harbor, the losses are major.

In six separate attacks all of the nine United States battleships anchored in the harbor are hit. The twenty-six year old *Arizona* explodes taking over 1,100 men with her to the bottom of the harbor. The obsolete *Utah* a target-training ship long out of combat, the *West Virginia* and *California* are all sunk. The *Oklahoma* capsizes, and the *Nevada* miraculously manages to get underway but is hit and has to be beached. The *Maryland*, *Pennsylvania* and *Tennessee* are all damaged.

The U.S. Navy's program of heavy dependence upon the battleship is capsized at Pearl Harbor as most of the battleships are rendered unserviceable. The Japanese bombing of battleship row will turn the navy toward the aircraft carrier, a position that will eventually undo Japan.

The destroyer *Shaw* explodes. Two others go down. A mine layer is lost along with countless other ships that are destroyed or damaged.

Because many of the aircraft are parked wingtip to wingtip, over one hundred and eighty-eight airplanes are also lost in the raid.

By a stroke of extraordinary luck, the three United States aircraft carriers connected with the Pacific Fleet are all absent from the harbor at the time of the attack. Oil storage tanks escape unscathed. The American submarine base escapes attack.

The five Japanese midget submarines, deployed to sabotage the harbor, are all destroyed by the American Navy.

As quickly as they appear, the Japanese are gone, leaving behind fifty-five of their kinsmen to twenty four hundred dead Americans.

Pearl Harbor is a tactical success for the Japanese aggressors.

7

The sun was beginning to filter through the mountain mist as Kate strained to pull her elbows up to her bent knees.

"Sixty-three," she muttered, more to herself than to anyone else. The words came out just as the elbows touched their target and she flattened her back against the woven mat before pulling herself up to the next sit-up. It was part of a new routine she had begun the week before, one of strenuous calisthenics. She found that as her body began tightening up, her mind was quickly following.

The windows to the kitchen were wide open and the Phillips radio was blaring.

Ellen came out carrying a tray with a coffee carafe and two thin china cups.

"I don't know, sometimes I wonder if electricity is a boon or a bust." The radio was a sore point with her. The Filipino servants insisted on the high volume so they could follow their beloved KMZH in Manila, regardless of their location in the Sullivan house.

"Seventy." Kate sat on the mat collecting her breath, relieved that she had finished, having done five more sit-ups than the previous morning.

"Well," Ellen began pouring the coffee, "nothing too ominous yet, is there?"

Kate sat in an empty chair next to Ellen and reached for the coffee. "A day out of school won't hurt anything."

Suddenly the music on the Phillips stopped. There was thirty seconds of silence across the airwaves before Don Bell's familiar voice came over the air. He sounded strained and harried.

"We interrupt this broadcast to bring you a special news bulletin," he began.

The two women froze.

"Pearl Harbor has been attacked by the Japanese. We repeat, Pearl Harbor has been attacked by the Japanese. This is not a drill. Repeat, this is not a drill."

"Oh my God!" Ellen's cup shattered against the brick paving of the patio. "Tom!"

Kate didn't hear her, drawn as she was to the outer wall of the garden. Squinting into the morning sun she could see an obscure mass on the horizon. As she watched, transfixed, the mass began to rise and within minutes she could hear the steady droning of powerful aircraft engines.

Ellen, as though in a trance, joined her friend.

"What are those?" Although she whispered there was a note close to terror in her voice.

"Airplanes, El."

"Ours?"

"I can't tell. Damn! I wished I'd paid more attention to that kind of stuff."

They didn't have long to wait. Soon the airplanes, seventeen bombers bearing the sign of the rising sun on both sides of their sleek fuselages, flew overhead.

Hypnotized, the speechless women turned, their eyes following the path of the airplanes, watching them drop low. As they dropped, a long raggedy sound, not unlike that of someone ripping a starched sheet, split through the morning air. Black smoke and earth exploded into a cloud above the target.

"John Hay. It's got to be," Ellen could tell from the direction of the smoke. "It's the only thing worth hitting out there."

"Yes. But why?" The camp was not a large military or civilian installation. Its bombing and strafing didn't make much sense, even to Kate's untutored military mind.

"Quezon. MacArthur." Ellen explained. Irineo had brought home the news the day before. President Manuel Quezon and the American High Commissioner Francis Sayre had been in Baguio for an emergency meeting with the general. Quezon was still in town.

The minute Kate wondered how the Japanese could have known about the meeting, she remembered Charlie's warning. "Those goddamned fishermen."

The air raid sirens started whining now as both women ran for the open kitchen door. They could hear the telephone ringing and as Ellen dashed for it, she was surprised the appliance was still working.

"Hello." She was breathless.

"Ellen, it's Sky. Pearl Harbor has just been bombed."

"Yes, we know. The radio is on."

"I'll get up there as soon as I can but it's a mess down here. General Brereton's been trying to get the go ahead from the General to send the Clark bombers to Formosa. He's having trouble getting past Sutherland." Richard Sutherland was MacArthur's unpopular chief-of-staff. "They're talking about evacuating Sayre and the government to Baguio although President Quezon thinks the islands can remain neutral, that Japan won't hit them."

Ellen laughed caustically into the mouthpiece. "They've just bombed John Hay."

"Jesus! Is Kate there with you?"

"Yes. The boys too."

"Stay inside. Away from windows. I'll try to call you later." With that the line went dead.

Berringer put his field glasses on the porch railing of the wooden communications building and looked at all of the airplanes parked at Clark Field. He shuddered. They were sitting ducks. A mass of confusion and indecision had resulted in the scene now before him. Major General Brereton had been asking MacArthur's chief-of-staff all morning for permission to at least place bombs in the bays of the B-17's.

Finally orders had come from Washington to disperse the aircraft at Clark as radar screens had depicted unidentified aircraft flying into the Philippine air space. Eager for action, the Air Force commander had sent his fighters up to thwart any attack. All but one of the B-17's was sent up to circle and cruise at Mount Arayat so they would not be caught by the Japanese bombers if they were indeed on the way.

The radar screen had gone empty, signalling a change of mind on the part of the unidentified aircraft. Brereton continued to push for the bomb placements. Finally General MacArthur called his air commander back agreeing to bombing missions later that afternoon. The B-17's were called back for arming and the fighters were called back for refueling.

Now Sky watched as servicemen loaded bombs into the bays of sixteen of the huge flying fortresses while fuel hoses snaked pumped gasoline into the smaller P-40's and the obsolete P-35's. In fact, all of the fighters were on the ground.

Although the mission, scheduled for later that afternoon was known to most of them, Sky shook his head sadly. He didn't like seeing all the planes down at the same time. Under the circumstances, he considered it to be courting disaster.

He looked at his watch. It was noon. Many of the fliers and maintenance men were taking off for lunch, seemingly unconcerned as they knew many of their tasks could be performed after the midday meal.

"Hey Sky!" Berringer turned, as a signal corpsman stuck his head out the door. "Get a load of this. Don Bell says there's an unconfirmed report that Clark Field's been hit!" The man, not waiting for a reply to his gossip, walked away, chuckling to himself as he retreated back inside the building.

Three of the heavy B-17's were taxiing into position, preparing for their runups, eager to take off on a reconnaissance flight over Formosa. They followed one another down the runway.

Sky looked to the north, noticing for the first time, what appeared to be a huge rain cloud moving in. Reaching quickly for the binoculars he held them to his eyes.

"Holy Christ!" He muttered softly under his breath recognizing the V formation of the Mitsubishi bombers. Before he could sound an alarm, a low rumbling noise filled the air. Entranced, the few servicemen on the field stared at the dropping black cloud of the Japanese Eleventh Air Fleet. Combat-green, the gun crews stared transfixed at their first glimpse of the enemy they had trained so hard to face.

Suddenly they raced into position, eager and terrified to test their newfound skills. Gunners took their places at their anti-aircraft weapons as fighter pilots raced for the P-40 cockpits. Only four fighters made it off the ground, for the Mitsubishis bellies had opened and were dropping their heavy bombs on the three B-17's readying for takeoff. The mess truck, having just served many of the men lunch, exploded into bits, taking its faceless driver and his assistant with it.

The low flying Zeroes, providing support for the bombers, were crisscrossing the field, strafing mercilessly as their tracer bullets ripped men and equipment apart. Fuel tanks burst open pouring great oily clouds of black smoke into the sky. Airplanes, in wingtip parking formation, exploded and shredded apart in the black air.

Sky watched an anti-aircraft gunner catapult out of position, his body sailing through the air like a weightless projectile in slow motion. Hesitating only seconds, Berringer raced for the gun, almost reaching it before a Zero dropped, smashing the machinery to bits with a well-aimed strafing run. Sky's hands flew to his face to offer protection from the flying bits of metal. He retreated to the side of the field now, aware that there was nothing a man could do to combat the onslaught without benefit of gun or airplane.

By 1:30 it was all over.

Not a hangar stood. The P-40's and B-17's of which General MacArthur and Major General Brereton had been so proud, lay in scattered ruins across Clark Field, their blackened bones a grim tomb for the fliers trapped inside. Nothing remained of military order. Men raced to quiet the growing flames of the headquarters building.

Bodies were strewn carelessly across the runways and the screams of the wounded and dying gave macabre testament to the terror that had just taken place. Overhead the sky was thick with oil and death. The two hundred Japanese planes had done their job well, leaving a broad wake behind them.

The priest stared in horror and disbelief. The dead were all around him now and he knew he should be offering the last rites to the men who were close to meeting their God. But still he stood, rooted to the same spot he had occupied for fifteen minutes now, unable to move.

A sergeant from the 26th Cavalry dashed from the closest building to the back of an open jeep. Quickly he reached in and pulled out a submachine gun, checking its clip. Satisfied the gun was loaded, he threw it onto the passenger's seat and started up the engine. As he pulled the jeep around he caught sight of the transfixed Bendetti.

"Father," his Southern drawl was apparent even over the noise of the jeep's engine, "if you think you might want to do some praying, come along."

It was the impetus Bendetti needed and wordlessly he hopped into the open car, cradling the loaded gun between his knees.

The sergeant drove past the end of the field before taking a hard right. The jeep bumped and jerked along the dirt road for a mile or so before stopping in front of Good Joe's, a bar popular with the enlisted men.

Without explanation, the sergeant retrieved the gun from the priest and went inside the tavern, Bendetti on his heels. It was empty this afternoon except for a barmaid perched on one of the stools and a man drinking a beer behind the bar. His beer bottle stopped in mid-air when he saw the armed sergeant. Regaining his composure he reached under the scarred top of the bar.

"Get them up, Bernardo," the sergeant waved his weapon at the barman, "or lose 'em."

Obediently the man placed the palms of his hands flat against the bar.

"You." The soldier motioned to a scared waitress. "Where's Joe?"

Terrified she pointed to a wooden door at the back of the bar. "In the office," she whispered.

The sergeant pulled a .45 Colt out of his waistband and handed it to Bendetti. "Ever use one of these?"

The priest nodded.

"If that son-of-a-bitch so much as twitches, let him have it," he said softly.

The sergeant took the room in several strides. There was no hesitation as he kicked open the flimsy wooden door with his heavy leather boot.

Inside sat the smiling Filipino who had befriended so many American and native soldiers. The man who had so willingly extended credit to them, who had provided liquor and women and gambling for all of them, sat fumbling with the dials of a powerful short-wave radio transmitter.

The crash of the door startled him as he half turned in his seat, a broad welcoming smile ready for the intruder.

Before he could say a word, the soldier opened up the submachine gun. The bullets exploded in a rhythmic pass over the tiny room splattering face cartilage and bits of bone and blood and brain all over the radio gear. Joe slumped forward, his blood spilling onto the sheets in front of him that he had been so eager to transmit.

Before the bartender and waitress had time to think, the sergeant was back opposite the bar. "Stand back, Father," he said grimly as he again let the tommy gun go.

The mirror behind the bar was shattered so it could not reflect the jerks and spasms of the dying man and woman.

As they left Good Joe's, George found that he did not feel like praying in the least.

8

Overnight, the peaceful life the Americans had enjoyed in the Philippines became disrupted and changed irrevocably.

War preparations were uppermost in everyone's mind. Schools were dismissed as every available body helped store water, hoard food and dig shelter. Meals became hurried affairs, sandwiched between bandage rollings and the construction of sandbagged barricades, as well as a host of related activities, all intended to keep the dreaded Japanese at bay.

In the days that followed, the years of spying in the Philippines paid off handsomely for the Japanese as they destroyed target after target. Planes from the Japanese carrier *Ryujo* hit Davao.

Tarlac and Iba Field were both hit. Nichols Field, under blackout but outlined by red flares put out by Japanese spies quickly joined the growing list of devastated targets.

By the tenth of December the Japanese had taken Guam, Tarawa and Makin Islands. The naval base at Cavite on Manila's south harbor was in ruins having been pounded heavily by the Japanese bombers. The Olonongapo naval repair station was wrecked. Even as the enemy bombed and strafed the Philippine archipelago, they dropped leaflets for the Filipino people assuring them they were bringing independence to the islands.

Finally the Japanese landed on Luzon at Aparri on the northern coast and at Legaspi in the south.

The squeeze for Manila was on.

9

"How about these?" Kate was carrying a handful of books which Ellen recognized as an 1899 leather bound Funk and Wagnall's edition of Shakespeare's plays. Bought from an antiquarian book dealer years ago, they were one of her favorite possessions. She hesitated only momentarily before shaking her head.

"Too heavy. Besides we can't eat books."

"No, I suppose not." She looked around at the montage of household possessions scattered around the floor. "I suppose everyone's going through this."

"Uh huh," Ellen wiped an already damp handkerchief across her forehead, "It does make you look at things in a little different light though."

The two women were sorting through the Sullivan's personal possessions in anticipation of a trip to Manila. Culling only those items essential to their survival, they watched in disbelief at the growing pile of discards they had once thought so necessary. Pots, dishes, heavy canned goods, brass picture frames (although Ellen had rescued and insisted upon packing some family photographs), books and small appliances sat in the expanding heap.

"It really is amazing, how little we really need when we get right down to it," Kate mused as she folded a lightweight cotton blanket. "Should we take linens?"

"I don't think we'll have room. They said everything should fit into a suitcase. I've thrown in a towel. The clothes are all ready," Ellen nodded to still another pile.

She ferreted through her own and the boys' wardrobes taking only those things that were absolutely necessary. Only the most comfortable, practical clothing had been included. Good sturdy walking shoes, suntan protection cream and insect repellent for the hotter Manila climate, a single bar of soap, toothbrushes. Ellen threw three hats on a chair. They would offer protection from the blistering sun should they have to do any walking. She shuddered at the thought.

Opening a heavy scarred wooden chest she pulled out a long slender brushed velvet case and withdrew an ornate silver dinner knife. All of her sterling rested in the chest and she thought of the many dinner parties where she had proudly displayed the fine antique silver flatware and flawless Limoges.

The sterling had belonged to her grandmother. Quickly she threw the knife back into the chest, not bothering to take the time to even replace it in its sheath. The silver, while a family heirloom, was only metal. Heavy, useless metal that would quickly become a burden and was inedible in nature.

"Irineo!" She called and the Filipino was at her side, still drying a glass from the kitchen. "Take this," she waited until he put the glass down before handing him the heavy chest, "and bury it out in the yard, behind the rose garden. In fact, dig a large hole. We may bury a lot of things."

Kate gave her a curious look.

"Well," Ellen shrugged, "I don't know whether we'll ever come back. But I sure don't want the Japanese eating off of grandmother's silver!"

The day had been long. Now with the suitcases packed, Ellen felt better knowing they could move out with little notice. It was with a good deal of relief that she sank into one of the rattan rockers. Irineo brought both women a glass of wine.

"When do you think we'll have to go?" Ellen asked.

Kate's eyes followed an old pickup truck making it's way slowly up the drive.

"Probably pretty soon," she offered as the women watched Sky park the ancient vehicle. As he climbed out of the cab he turned back to scoop up an armload of brightly wrapped packages off the front seat. Ellen jumped up and helped him with his parcels.

"Sky what is this?" It seemed incredible that he would remember the holiday in the middle of the war.

"Merry Christmas," he bent low to give her a quick kiss. "Hello, Kate."

"Sky." It was the first time the three of them had been together in weeks.

Pete came tearing around the house, howling with indignation.

"Mother!" He yelled as he ran. "Doc's dying again! Make him stop."

"I am not, you big tattletale!" Doc, as if on cue, strolled casually around the corner at a much slower pace. "I'm not going to play war with you any more if you act like a big sissy." He studied his fingernails with deliberate nonchalance.

"Doc," Ellen warned. She had talked to the boys before about their war games. Fascinated by the bits and pieces of the war news they overheard, both Doc and Pete had amused themselves for hours with their inventive war play.

"Oh boy!" Pete spotted the packages. "Are those for us?"

Sky nodded and shifted the packages in his arms before climbing the porch steps.

"Can we open them now?" The younger boy was next to Sky, his eyes straining to read the tags on the gifts.

Ellen laughed. "No, Peter. It's not Christmas yet. Four more days."

Sky sat the presents on the porch floor and bent down to talk with the boys at eye level.

"I'll tell you what. You go in the house and play for," he glanced at his watch, "fifteen minutes and I'll see if we can't work something out."

"Oh boy, oh boy," Pete raced for the front door with Doc at his heels, both of them filled with the anticipation of an early Christmas.

"Mind if I fix myself a drink, Ellen?" Sky was already headed for the bar at the end of the porch.

"Is it that bad?" Kate stood at the porch railing looking down on the valley.

"It's not good," He poured himself a stiff bourbon. "You're all right up here?"

"Except for the air raid sirens," Ellen said.

"They're not working?"

"We hear the planes long before the sirens."

He nodded. "It's that way in Manila, too."

"Then it's as bad as we hear?" Kate asked.

"With Clark and Nichols gone most of our bombers and fighters are out. There's no question about who's flying around up there," Sky looked at the ceiling of the porch, "so if you hear a plane and no siren, take cover because it isn't us."

"Without airplanes I guess it's kind of hard to do your job, isn't it, Sky?" Kate asked.

His dimples cut deep into the sides of his mouth.

"Difficult, but not impossible. Our boys were great," there was an animated glow in his gray eyes. "Three of them took on twenty Zeroes and lived to talk about it!" There was obvious pride in his voice. "They shot down three airplanes and sent a fourth home with his tail between his legs."

"Those damned Japanese," Ellen wrinkled her nose in distaste.

"And the Germans, dear lady."

"The Germans? They're not here," Kate's voice ran cold as she remembered the horror stories that had permeated Europe for years.

"Not in force," Sky explained, "But a few Messerschmitts were seen over Manila."

"Messerschmitts?" Ellen was unfamiliar with the term.

"German fighters. Some of our boys reported in that even some of the pilots in the Zeroes were white. Apparently the Japanese had some help from their friends. Out at Clark we found some bombs that had been dropped that were duds. Do you know what was stamped on them? Frankfurt 1916!"

"Then the Germans will come," Ellen's voice dropped to a whisper.

"No. There's no need for them to. They've got their hands full in Europe and the Japanese seem to be getting things under control here. There's talk of MacArthur's withdrawing into the Bataan Peninsula until help arrives from the States."

With the annihilation of his air force, a critical part of General MacArthur's defense plan had been lost. Recognizing the weakness of his ground forces, the general had counted on defending the Luzon coast from the air. With his planes gone, the only viable part left of his plan was a retreat into Bataan, leaving the coastline relatively undefended.

"Brereton's pulling what's left of the Far East Air Force out of here on Christmas day."

"Pulling out. But where?" Ellen asked.

"Australia. What's left of our B-17's at Del Monte will be going."

"Then you'll be leaving us," Ellen whispered, destroyed at the thought of losing Sky as well as Tom.

"No," Sky reached over and patted her hands which were clenched together in her lap. "I'm not going. I'm staying here in the islands. In fact, I'll even be in Baguio for a few days. There's a lot of unfinished business up here. Have you talked to Duggleby?"

Ellen shook her head. Al Duggleby, head of the Benguet Consolidated Mine, was a good friend as well as Tom's boss.

"The gold's already being shipped to Manila." In fact, the gold from all of the Baguio mines had been sent down in an effort to keep the assets from the Japanese. "I promised Tom I'd take care of some things for him before he left for Corregidor."

"I think you mean us," Ellen smiled weakly.

"Yes. But there are chores at the mine, too. Then the bridges and the fuel supplies."

The enormity of what he was saying was beginning to sink in.

"It's inevitable, isn't it, Sky? The Japanese are coming."

"Yes." Time was too short to sugarcoat anything for them. "They landed on Davao two days ago."

It had been a tactical move for the Japanese to land on Mindanao for it was a valuable link in a chain around the Philippines. Davao, along with North Borneo, would give the Japanese a detour around the narrows guarded by Allied submarines in the South China Sea.

"We heard a rumor," Kate said, not bothering to burden him with the fact that there had been no newspaper or mail delivery for days now.

"The *Stingray* spotted a heavily guarded fleet of troop transports off Luzon." Sky's voice was calm, belying the gravity of the report.

"And that's why we should have an early Christmas, isn't it, Sky?" Ellen asked.

"Yes. It's happening all over. Even your friends the MacArthurs are celebrating early."

"Can it wait until morning?" She was exhausted from the day's packing.

"No, I'm afraid not. Tell me where things are though and I'll help you get ready." Sky had read her weariness and was sad that he couldn't delay yet another task. He was so sorry for her. The children could be a mixed blessing. They might keep her strong, yet he suspected that their futures would gnaw and eat at her before this was all over.

"No. Sit. I'll get the presents," Ellen said woodenly.

※

Ellen opened the last present as a tear dropped on the silk scarf she held in her lap. The boys, having opened all of their presents in a matter of minutes, were off running through the house in Pete's new wagon. Ellen had seen Doc throw his new football several times indoors but she had ignored him, not really caring or seeing what difference it would make if he broke something that was left behind.

"I feel so odd about this," Ellen was slowly unwrapping the scarf for there was something inside it. "A present from Tom. He must have bought it before he left. But silk!"

Irineo had produced the present for Ellen as Tom had entrusted it in his care before leaving for the island fortress.

Kate remained silent. She knew mixed feelings were haunting her friend. With the enemy threatening their very existence, the Japanese scarf somehow seemed tainted.

"Oh!" Ellen had opened the small square box inside the colorful fabric. Inside, nested on jeweler's felt was a large diamond solitaire. "Oh." She removed it from its slot and held it up. In spite of the dim parlor lighting the exquisite faceting of the flawless stone was apparent.

"Diamond Lil!" Kate offered. Even from the distance she could tell the ring was well over a carat.

"Tom always said he was going to get me a diamond," Ellen slipped the ring, a perfect fit, over the third finger of her left hand. It nestled comfortably on top of her thin gold wedding band.

"It's beautiful," Kate was beside her now, holding her hand and admiring the stone. "Really beautiful."

"We were so poor when we got married," Ellen was dabbing at her eyes with the corner of the offensive scarf. "He'd just gotten that job with the county engineer. Do you remember?"

Kate smiled. She remembered. The simple wedding. Tom's disappointment that he couldn't buy Ellen an impressive engagement ring. It had been years ago and now the irony was a ring given by an absent husband. She watched as Ellen, caught in her own memories, twisted the silk scarf around and around her hand. It reminded Kate of a fishing lure. Bait used for prey to be taken. Involuntarily she shivered.

The boys dashed through, terrifying Putt Putt, the cat, whom they had placed in the bed of the new red wagon. The speed of the vehicle, combined with Doc's swift recapture of her every time she tried to escape, contributed to her feline terror. As the wagon veered too sharply around the coffee table it fell on its side, finally releasing the frightened animal who took off like a shot.

"Enough." Ellen stood, her moment of depression gone. "It's time for bed, boys. Run in and get your pajamas on and I'll be in to tuck you in."

"Hey guys, I've got an even better deal for you," Sky grinned. "Just because today is a very special day, being almost Christmas and all, just because of that you can sleep in your clothes tonight. What do you say to that?"

"Yippee!" Pete squealed as he dashed off, the metal charms dangling from a Christmas beanie as he bobbed his head. He ran off fast, not waiting for his mother to contradict Sky's offer.

"And I suppose, Sky," Ellen folded the scarf carefully and placed it back in it's box. "Just because today is a very special day that Kate and I get to sleep in our clothes too?"

"Yes, you do."

The significance of his offer had not escaped them. They could be rousted in the middle of the night for Manila. Without having to change into street clothes, they would be that much closer to escape.

"May I use the phone?" Sky asked.

The women gathered up the ripped paper.

"What wasted effort,"Ellen looked at the tidy parlor. "We may even be out of here tomorrow."

Sky came back into the room.

"You will be."

"Tomorrow." Ellen's lower lip trembled only slightly.

"We've confirmed reports that the Japanese are landing in Lingayen Gulf." Sky's voice was steady.

"Lingayen? But it's so close!" Kate was surprised, for the landings would be within sight and earshot of Baguio.

"How will we get to Manila?" Ellen asked, suddenly re-membering that the car had been commandeered ten days earlier.

"There's a bus leaving at five a.m. You and Kate and the boys will be on it." He had already made the arrangements.

※

It was still dark outside when the boys were awakened. They were grumpy from their lack of sleep as Ellen explained to them that the time had come to leave for Manila.

Pete swung out of bed pulling on his new beanie before he padded to the corner where he had carefully parked his shiny new wagon. He pulled on the tongue and the vehicle followed him into the parlor. His mother, her heart aching, knew exactly what he intended. She followed him into the large room and watched him park the wagon next to the two suitcases.

"Peter, "she came up behind him, her hands on his narrow shoulders. "Sweetheart, we're going to have to leave the wagon. It's too big. They won't let us take it."

Although she had expected a fight from him, she was surprised when he turned to her, tears streaming down his face.

"I know, mom," his voice was full of resignation as his little boy body crumbled into her own.

Doc took advantage of the moment to stick his favorite new possession, a Benjamin Super Shot air pistol into the waistband of his shorts. Quickly he covered it with his shirttail.

"Hey we can share the football. It's not too big, is it, mother?"

"No dear." Ellen was blaming herself for buying Pete such big presents.

Pete brightened, comforted by the thought of sharing his older brother's presents. "And the b.b. gun, too, Doc?"

Doc squirmed, feeling the cool metal against his stomach.

"Are you taking your b.b. gun to Manila, Doc? Don't you think that's best left behind?" Ellen's voice was calm and gentle, belying the pressure she felt to get her boys to the bus. The leave-taking of the only home her boys had ever known was too important to short change.

"Well, yes. Yes Mother, I am taking it with me," he pulled his shirt up, displaying the weapon secured against his flat little belly. "I think it might come in very handy. I told Dad I'd take care of you and Petey and this will help me do it."

Ellen gathered Doc in her free hand, taking care not to release Pete. She kissed him softly on his forehead.

"Thank you darling. That's very kind. But we'll be staying at the Bayview Hotel. I don't think we'll be in much danger there, do you?"

"Well, if it's all the same to you Mother, I'll take it with me," Doc covered up the gun again.

Putt Putt, interested in the unusual morning activity, came into the sala, and was rubbing against Ellen's legs as she held the two boys.

"Putter!" Pete squirmed out of his mother's grip and gathered up the furry cat kissing and stroking her.

Doc looked at his brother holding the cat. He looked at the suitcases. Suddenly he was suspicious.

"We didn't pack any cat food."

Ellen knelt.

"No Doc, we didn't."

Pete, instinctively knowing what was happening, clutched the beast tightly to his chest.

"Nooooo!" A long thin wail, coming deep from inside of him was released in the still room. "We can't leave her Mom!" He was sobbing now. "We can't leave her. The dirty Japs will eat her!"

"No Peter, the Japanese won't eat her," Ellen held his small face in her hands, "She'll be happier here with Irineo and Gambino and the rest. You know how cats hate to travel and this is her home."

"It's our home too and we're leaving," Pete argued.

"I know darling. But we'll be back. Putt Putt will be here waiting for us. You'll see her again," she injected a note of optimism she did not feel.

Sobs racked the younger boy's body as Doc reached over and patted the cat that had been such an important part of their young lives.

"Yeah Petey," Doc said bravely, fighting to keep the tears from coming. "She'll be happier here. Besides there are all those cars in Manila. You wouldn't want her to get run over would you?"

Kate, standing in the doorway, remained silent, damning the Japanese for the wrenching tableau in front of her.

"Besides," Doc offered, "everyone knows the Japanese don't eat cats. They like fish."

"It's time," Kate said quietly.

"Yes, I guess it is," Ellen held Pete tightly.

"May I see you for a moment, El?"

"Boys, go tell Irineo and Gambino goodbye," Ellen stood, straightening her dress, wet from Pete's tears, as the boys ran off, lugging Putt Putt with them.

"El, would you hate me," Kate hesitated, uncomfortable with what she had to say. "Could you ever forgive me if I didn't go with you to Manila?"

"Not go? What are you talking about? You've got to go Kate. You don't want to stay and be ravished by the Japanese, do you?"

"I don't know what I want to do. I feel like a rat not going. I know you'll need a lot of help with the boys and all but I don't want to leave just yet."

"You may not get another chance. You heard Sky said they're blowing up all the bridges today."

"Yes. I could walk if I had to." Clearly, Kate had thought it through.

"A hundred and twenty miles? That's a healthy stroll, dear."

"There are a lot of people staying and I just think I'd rather."

"Maybe we all should." For the first time Ellen was having misgivings about the safety to be found in Manila.

"No. Go to Manila. You'll be closer to Tom there."

"Why did you wait to tell me?" There was no accusation in Ellen's eyes, only tired despair.

"God I don't know, El. I've been thinking about it off and on, I really have. But I only decided for sure in the middle of the night. This is right for me now. I know it."

"Have you discussed this with Sky?"

"No and I don't intend to. He'll insist that I go with you. You don't mind my staying here in the house, do you?"

"Not at all. I can't promise that Irineo will look after you and cook or that he'll even stay."

"It doesn't matter," She hugged Ellen, "you will forgive me, won't you?"

"You silly thing, of course." Ellen gripped her hard.

"Now get the hell out of here before I become a crying old poop," Kate ordered.

There were no empty seats on the bus bound for Manila as small children sat on their mother's laps and six people squatted in the aisle. One elderly man sat on the steps at the front of the bus for the entire five hour ride to Manila despite the fact that younger women had offered their seats to him.

Ellen and Pete sat together and Doc was on an aisle seat across from them. The early morning hour and the solemnity of the trip was not conducive to conversation and there was little noise on the packed bus during the first hour of the journey.

By mid-morning as the vehicle continued its descent from the five thousand foot altitude, windows were dropped so the fresh morning air could come in. The air, choked with dust from the unpaved road, offered a little breeze to the frightened travelers.

Children, already bored with the trip began to whine and cry while the women shared rumors and speculation. Baskets of fruit were passed and rooming arrangements discussed. Most of them had already made plans to stay in hotels or with friends once they arrived in the city.

The first half of the trip was marred for the Sullivans when Pete insisted on changing seats with Ellen. He had been seated for only a few minutes when he began to fiddle with the window. A sudden rush of air lifted his prized Christmas beanie from his head, dangling charms and all, and sucked it out onto the open roadway. He had cried and carried on for the better part of a half an hour over his loss.

Soon the pine trees and mountain mists were left behind and the country smoothed out into a vista of sugar cane fields. The trip became much more pleasant when the dirt evaporated into the comfort of asphalt and the bus began to make better time.

Pete had settled down now and he sat quietly beside Ellen, content to draw pictures of the scenes he was leaving behind.

Doc, who had to be reprimanded at least hourly, was up and down the aisle of the bus, checking in with old friends and making new acquaintances. He had already shown the b.b. gun to three envious schoolmates. In all it was a glorious adventure for the children and their heads were filled with the glamor and excitement of their destination.

The war.

10

Sky was sweating in spite of the cool day. He mopped his brow with an already wet handkerchief and then placed his forehead against the rough log in front of him, waiting for the bridge to blow.

Right on schedule the concrete structure obliged as the deep rumbling of the exploding dynamite filled the mountain air. This was the second one today. There were three more to go on the penciled diagram that Tom had given him. Next to the sketches there were brief instructions as to the most strategic placement of the explosives for each bridge.

He felt the ground beneath him vibrate with the repercussion of the blasting and was reassured by it. At least the troops on the eighty Japanese ships that had been spotted landing in Lingayen Gulf wouldn't have an easy time getting to Manila.

Berringer, like the other men who had stayed behind, worked like an animal all that long Monday. The Naguilian trail had been destroyed as well as Kennon Road after the bus filled with American wives had passed. The railroad was in ruins. Some of the men, he knew, were working on irrigation breaches which would clog the land with mud, making travel even more difficult. All the tactics were delaying ones at best for there was little doubt that the Japanese were indeed coming.

By mid-afternoon, charges had been set off in the mine and after the dust and smoke had cleared, a huge camouflaged tarpaulin was drawn over the mess in an effort to disguise its location. The huge fuel tanks, so necessary in the day-to-day operations of the mine, had been destroyed and now black, thick oily smoke filled the valley. Supplies were set on fire and those vehicles not destroyed were sabotaged as sugar was poured into their gas tanks, spark plugs were pulled and thrown away, and tires were slashed.

Sky was thoroughly exhausted when he climbed the porch steps to the Sullivan's house late that evening. While he had forgotten to ask Ellen about staying, he knew that Irineo, if he had stayed, would let him sleep there.

The lights were off as he entered the house. Relieved to see that the rattan bar was still in the corner he poured himself a drink and sank onto the overstuffed sofa, pulling at his mud encrusted boots. He was as bone tired as he had ever been.

A sudden noise near the kitchen startled him as he quickly rolled off the sofa, reaching for the .38 he had started carrying two days earlier. He slid the weapon out of its holster. It was probably ridiculous, he told himself, knowing the Japanese had not had time to reach Baguio. Still his heart pounded as adrenaline fed his unnamed fears.

Kate appeared at the kitchen door.

"Hello," there was a slight tremor in her voice.

"Don't shoot," Sky warned as he slowly rose from the floor, forgetting that the gun was still in his hand.

Kate laughed with relief. "It's you!"

Frowning, he crossed the parlor floor, holstering his gun as he did so. Reaching her he shook her shoulders roughly.

"What in the hell are you doing here? Goddamnit you're supposed to be in Manila." He looked around fully expecting Ellen and the boys to come bouncing out of their bedrooms. "They're gone. So is Irineo. I'm the only one left."

"Don't stab me." For the first time he noticed the meat cleaver that she was holding by her side. She, too, had feared an intruder. "And next time, lock the door," he said gruffly.

"You're not happy with me."

"I don't think you know what you're in for. The Japanese are at this very moment pouring men ashore at Lingayen. It's just a matter of days before they get here. They could be here as early as tomorrow."

"I know. And then, within days, they'll be in Manila. So what difference does it make if I'm here or there?" She poured herself a drink. "At least it's more pleasant here."

"So if you're thrown into a prison camp you'd rather be up here with people you don't know than down in Manila with those you do?" Sky laughed rudely, "That's fine reasoning, Katie, if I do say so myself."

Tears came into her eyes and although she tried to stop them they escaped down her cheeks. "That's pretty cruel, Sky."

"Cruel?" He laughed again. "It's the goddamned truth. What? You think they'll say 'ah nice pletty lady can cook and clean for us in fine palace?" He was untouched by her tears. "And now all the goddamned bridges have been blown so you can't drive down, even if you could find a car."

"I have no intention of going."

It was as though he had not heard her.

"You can walk. That's it. There's a group of men from the mine that are starting out early in the morning to join their families in Manila. You can go with them."

She shook her head. "Sorry Sky. I appreciate your concern but it's my decision and I'm the one who will make it."

"Baguio's been declared an open city. You know that, don't you?"

"No," she hesitated, "what does it mean?"

"The authorities have agreed that it won't be defended. They're giving it to the Japanese."

Her eyes widened. Although there were only two companies garrisoned in Baguio she had thought there would at least be some resistance.

"But on the positive side, the Japanese, if they follow the Geneva War Convention won't be dropping any more bombs here. It should be a fairly easy transition."

"You're staying too?"

He shook his head. "I'm not eager to live behind wire any sooner than I have to."

"But where else is there to go? They'll be all over the islands, you said so yourself."

"It's a big place, Katie. There are a lot of hiding places in the Philippines."

"And that's how you'll spend the war. In hiding?" The disgust was evident in her voice.

"What are my choices? Get killed on Corregidor as Tom is going to be? Or mince around giving hypocritical spiritual advice as your friend Bendetti is probably doing right now. No thanks."

"Can't they arrest you or shoot you for desertion?"

"Sorry to disappoint you but my contract expired months ago. Besides I'm still a civilian. Not that that matters any more. The fliers are trained and the Aussies aren't short on instructors."

"It's a shame the rest of them aren't in your shoes," Kate said trying hard to keep the sarcasm out of her voice.

"There'll be new orders coming down any day now. Our servicemen may be given the choice of surrender or heading for the hills. There are a lot of us who aren't ready to roll over and play dead."

"I'm going with you."

"You're not invited. You have a choice too. You can stay here in Baguio and be interned or go to Manila and be interned."

"Thanks, dad," there was real sarcasm there now, "but as you said it's my choice and frankly neither of your options appeal to me. I think I'll head for the hills," she drained her brandy.

Sky looked at her steadily before responding.

"You're a fool, Kate. You're as childish as Doc and Pete, thinking this war is a game. What do you know about the jungle? You won't survive five minutes out there. How do you feel about pythons? Ever eaten a lizard? Had leeches suck your arms and engorge themselves on your blood? Malaria? Blackwater fever? All those wonderful things your government told you about and inoculated you against before you came over here. They're all out there Katie. Waiting for you. Waiting for the bones and blood of an Englishwoman."

"American, Sky. I'm an American. Frank was the Englishman." She looked at him steadily, unfazed by the anger she saw in his eyes. "And I don't need you. I don't need you to tell me what to do or to take my hand and lead me through the jungle or to teach me how to eat lizards. I'm going to survive this thing, by God. And I can do it alone if I have to."

He knew he was beaten, that he couldn't leave her.

"All right, goddamnit. We'll leave at first light."

✈

Lingayen Gulf, visible to their naked eyes, was far below them now for they had been climbing all morning. Although they were too far above the activity to hear the noise and excitement of the Japanese landings, the air was punctuated occasionally by a Japanese airplane flying over and providing unnecessary air support.

Kate, tired but determined not to complain, and Sky sat on a decaying log looking down at the sea of activity below them. Pulling a pair of binoculars from his pack Berringer studied the scene.

Japanese troop transports, large even from the distance from which they were viewed, peppered the gulf. Cruisers and destroyers were further out, apparently relaxing now that they had seen the transports safely into Philippine waters. Smaller boats could be seen ferrying the enemy troops to the beach.

While General MacArthur had committed two of the Filipino Army divisions to beach defenses, they were gone now and the only thing delaying the Japanese from reaching land any quicker was the size of the large waves cresting and crashing against the sandy beach. The breakers were playing with the landing craft, tossing and even overturning them occasionally. Still the troops kept landing. They had been at it since two that morning.

"It looks like they solved that problem," Sky handed the glasses to Kate.

"What problem?" She held them to her eyes, fumbling with the focus.

"Water's shallow down there. That's why their transports are anchored offshore."

Kate soundlessly returned the field glasses.

General Masaharu Homma would land 43,000 troops at Lingayen Gulf. By afternoon they would begin marching down Route 3 toward Manila. Another large force would land at Atimonan, southeast of the capital city. Together, they would form the pincer movement for Manila.

Sky broke off a piece of cheese, one of the few perishables they had brought with them. He handed it to Kate.

"Want to go back?"

She shook her head furiously.

"OK, let's hit the road, Katie girl." In a single fluid movement he was on his feet. " We've miles to go before we sleep."

SINCLAIR BROWNING

11

Doc carefully unrolled the broad adhesive tape, his small fingers having trouble keeping the band from sticking to itself. Stretching it along the window he patted it as he worked, smoothing out any wrinkles. This was his first paying job and he was eager to do it the right way. Señor Gerardo was paying him hand-.somely, a dime for every window.

Things were different now in Manila, even the ten year old boy knew that. Señor Gerardo wasn't alone in his efforts to comply with the blackout regulations. All along Dewey Boulevard merchants were taping up their storefront windows and stacking sandbags around their entrances in order to provide a safe haven for both their merchandise and their clientele. It was the price they all had to pay for having lost the air to the Japanese as the enemy bombers flew over unchallenged. Only occasionally could a lonely anti-aircraft gun be heard.

The United States High Commissioner's office had formed an emergency committee to counsel the Allied civilians. Directives were coming out of the office with suggestions as to what procedures to follow in the event of a Japanese occupation. So far the committee members couldn't seem to agree on whether or not the civilians should stay in one place together or stay in their own residences.

The bombing had taken its toll too. Water supplies throughout the city were suspect. Fearful of an epidemic, many of the Americans had been inoculated just the day before. While the tetanus shot was not something that Doc had looked forward to, he had delighted in torturing his younger brother with tales and measurements of the length of the needle.

Even at home in their room at the Bayview Hotel there were taped windows. In the lobby, Doc had helped sweep up the dirt and grit from the sandbags which was tracked all over the smooth tiled floors.

In the havoc created by war, looters were becoming increasingly common, and some of the merchants had foregone the taped windows, preferring to board them up, making access to their wares more difficult for the drunken pillagers.

Although most of the private vehicles had been commandeered by the Philippine Army, those that were driven at night, whether by civilian or serviceman, were fitted with special blackout shields. The Philippine Constabulary had set up stations around sandbagged outposts in order to catch any vehicle not so equipped.

Everywhere signs of communal living were evident. The jai alai pavilion had been converted to a hospital, and groups of civilians banded together day and night in preparation for the travail to come. Winding and cutting gauze to make bandages and gas mask filters, cooking and planning meals for dozens, hauling, saving and purifying water, the mundane survival tasks filled the long hours.

War discussion stifled every conversation, and in the course of his eavesdropping, Doc had added a new word to his vocabulary. Fifth columnist. Spy.

While most Filipinos had thrown in with the Americans, there was no denying that there were still many who had opted for the other side. Secret flares were set nightly to guide the deadly bombers to their blacked out prey. Operating with long fuses, many of the Japanese sympathizers escaped by the time the signals finally went off.

Doc looked at the large wall clock on Señor Gerardo's wall. It was eleven o'clock. Time to go. His mother and Petey would be back from the store. They went every day now buying as much food as they could, for it had become an obsession with Ellen and many others. She had already installed a padlock on the bathroom linen closet where she could store her canned goods safely.

Ellen had consented to Doc's job under the condition that he would be back at the Bayview every day by eleven fifteen. While Manila had been bombed almost daily since Pearl Harbor, the one constant that could be counted on was an air raid at mid-day. Right around noon the Japanese bombers, usually in a formation of twenty-seven airplanes, would swoop into Manila Bay. While they had long since destroyed most of the boats in the harbor they were now systematically obliterating warehouses and piers.

And while it could be argued that Doc was just as safe inside Gerardo's shop as in the sheltered, sandbagged lobby of the hotel, Ellen wanted her oldest son with her during the most dangerous times.

"Sorry Señor Gerardo, it's time for me to go now."

The tiny Filipino looked at his gold pocket watch and compared the time he found there with that on the wall. He patted the tow headed boy on the head, hoping for luck. Fumbling in his pocket for two dimes-a feat in itself for the Filipinos were latching onto the hard silver coins making pocket change a rarity- he handed them to the boy.

"All right, Doc. I'll see you tomorrow."

"Not tomorrow Señor Gerardo. It's Christmas!"

The shopkeeper looked to the wall again, his eyes squinting against the small print of the calendar hanging next to the clock.

The boy was right. It was so easy to lose track of the days now.

"You're right, Doc. Have a merry Christmas," he said warmly.

"Oh, it'll be all right. But we already celebrated it." The boy was off, skipping down the sidewalk.

*

"The Japs are coming, there's no denying that, my friend," the American soldier pulled on a plug of tobacco and slid it into his grizzled cheek. "You best be making miles between here and your very own body, *padre*."

"What?" Bendetti looked at the stranger as though he had not heard him or the bombs that had been exploding in Manila all day. "What do you hear?"

"Villasis," the soldier looked over the priest's shoulder as he talked to him, his eyes riveted on the black oily smoke that hung like a shroud over Manila. "Jap troops are landing there right now. Ship after ship. And there ain't no one there to try to stop them."

Villasis was eighty-five miles from Manila. The enemy was closing in.

"Thanks, soldier." George walked past him and headed for the waterfront. He needed to go to the Bayview to see Ellen and Kate. First though he would check at the dock and see about the chances of getting passage on a ship for all of them. Destination at this point was unimportant. Just out of the Philippines, or even Luzon, he thought. That would be enough for now.

It was late afternoon when he arrived at Pier Seven, touted to be the largest in the world and nicknamed the Million Dollar Pier. The pier was empty, not a ship docked. Two inter-island steamers the *Don Esteban* and the *Mayon* bobbed their gray bodies at the next pier. They were the only vessels in sight as a number of people milled around the two steamers. Probably bartering passage, George thought, hurrying his pace so he, too, could get in on the act.

As he drew nearer, he recognized the tall, trim figure of General MacArthur. A small, slight mestizo, bent over in occasional fits of coughing, he knew was Manuel Quezon, President of the Philippine Commonwealth.

George was running now, entering the mouth of the pier. As the wharf narrowed, a fence cut across it and a soldier stood, blocking his way at the wire gate.

"Pass, sir?" The soldier cradled a heavy Enfield rifle in his arms.

"Pass?"

"Sorry, sir. No one's allowed down without one."

"But I'm a priest." George caught himself fumbling for his rosary beads, stopped, aware that his uniform supported his admission. "What's going on?"

The soldier debated with himself for a minute and then decided there was no way the clergyman could spread the news before the general and his party were gone.

"Manila's being declared an open city."

The news did not disturb the priest. He had, in fact, hoped for it. That way the civilian population, including himself, would be spared. "And they're leaving."

"Doesn't make much sense for them to stay, does it?" The soldier had caught the jealousy in Bendetti's voice.

George watched as Quezon, his wife, son and two daughters were put on the *Don Esteban*. While the whole affair was taking place in full view of the Manila Hotel, no one seemed to be paying much attention to the exodus.

Mrs. MacArthur and young Arthur were helped onto the steamer. Then the High Commissioner and Mrs. Sayre. Clearly, the government was being relocated.

"How far can they get?" Bendetti knew the harbor was ringed with Japanese. The only thing that had saved the bay itself from enemy takeover had been the troops garrisoned on Corregidor, Fort Drum and Fort Hughes, the islands guarding the mouth of Manila Bay.

"Corregidor." The soldier's answer was obvious.

Six Filipino soldiers, guarded by an equal number of armed escorts came down the pier toward the President's Landing. George stepped aside as they pushed a platform cart with heavy metal trunks in front of them. Stamped on all sides was the certification "Property of the Philippine Commonwealth."

The men hurried through the gate and below General MacArthur stepped aside to allow the soldiers to unload their precious cargo. The trunks contained the last of the gold and silver of the Philippine government. Once loaded, the soldiers saluted their President and their General before retreating up the walkway.

MacArthur took one last look before stepping onto the *Don Esteban*.

A dockhand pushed off from the pier as he tossed the gnarled, mildewed rope back on the dock. Slowly the two steamers chugged out into the bay.

As the *Don Esteban* left, a lone soldier on board could be heard singing a few strained stanzas of *"Silent Night."*

On the way to the hotel, Bendetti stopped beneath an electric cigar sign. Visible for miles, it had been a Manila landmark for years. Now in the blacked out city where even the Malacanyan Palace was dark, the Alhambra sign was glowing in curious defiance to the municipal order. There was a lot of activity centered around the commercial beacon. Everyone seemed to be looking for the magical switch that would turn off the huge sign before the

Japanese realized it was on, offering yet another target to the capable Mitsubishi pilots.

A jeep full of American soldiers pulled up beneath the sign. One of them pulled out a machine gun, slipped in a clip and, after hollering his intentions to anyone foolish enough to be standing behind, near or under the sign, began firing. Soon the other soldiers began discharging their weapons at it. Within another minute even the few armed civilians took potshots at the electrical quarry. Finally the Alhambra Cigar sign sputtered and popped, and the sky was dark again.

George climbed back into the truck he had stolen and headed back to town. As he made his way to the Bayview Hotel he was grateful for the bright moon filled evening. With the blackout, travel after dark was a lot more difficult. Traveling at night was not a safe undertaking in the war torn times and traveling without the benefit of streetlights, headlights or flashlights made the task even more dangerous.

"Who is it?" Ellen had taken to asking the question of her few visitors before opening her door.

"It's George, Ellen."

She opened the door and hugged the priest. "I'm surprised to see you. I'd heard the 27th had left."

Bendetti ignored the question. In the confusion of the Bombardment Group's departure, he had deliberately stayed behind.

"Hello boys," he nodded to Doc and Pete who were playing marbles on the floor. Doc gave him a passing glance, not eager to offer his cheek for any of the priest's wet kisses.

"Father George! Father George!" The exuberant Pete jumped up and hugged Bendetti around the knees. Just as quickly, sensing his older brother's disapproval, he sat back down on the floor again, snatching the shooter from Doc and taking his turn.

George took the room in with one quick glance. A small hot plate and refrigerator were in one corner and the two day beds and cot were evidence that they were all living in the single room.

"Where's Kate?" He asked apprehensively.

"In Baguio."

"What?" His disbelief came out high and shrill.

"She didn't come with us. It was all last minute, really. She didn't feel it was something she wanted to do. "

"He made her stay," the priest's voice had dropped now and was threatening.

"Who, dear?"

"Berringer." The word came out like venom from his lips.

"No," she patted his arm to reassure him. "Sky wanted her to go. In fact he thought she did. He was already gone the morning we left."

George sank onto one of the day beds.

"Do you have any coffee?"

Ellen nodded as she put the pot on the burner.

"How long have you been here?"

"Since Sunday."

"I'll head back up there tomorrow and bring her down."

"I don't think that will do any good. She really didn't want to come. Besides, I don't even know if she'll be in the house."

"Why wouldn't she be? Where else would she go?"

"Well I don't know, dear. I just think in these unsettled times we all have to do what is right for us and I think that is what Katherine is doing. We mustn't judge her by our standards."

"Just like the Japanese, right Mother?" Doc shot one of his brother's marbles across the room.

"Yes Doc." Ellen smiled. She had been trying to make the boys understand that the Japanese were doing what they felt they had to do although it seemed to be at the expense of the Americans. Apparently some of her lectures were sinking in.

Bendetti stood.

"Forget the coffee, Ellen. I'm going back to Baguio. I'll be back later in the week or as soon as I can."

"But that's insane, George! She won't come. Besides the roads are all gone. They blew the bridges the morning we came down."

"I know," resignation was apparent in his voice, "I can walk."

"Why, that will take you weeks." Ellen was all too familiar with the deep mountain gorges and steep trails on the way to Baguio. Without bridges the distance would be much rougher.

He bent and gave her a wet kiss on the cheek. "Keep the coffee warm for me."

There was a glazed look in his eyes and for the first time Ellen wondered if he was all right.

Sometimes there was just no reasoning with him.

12

"You will be going soon," the Filipina said as she massaged the back of Charlie's neck. "The soldiers are coming."

"Yes."

"Where will you go?"

"With our soldiers. Into the peninsula." He looked to the door where his pack awaited him. "Do not worry."

She shook her head, a gesture Charlie felt rather than saw.

"I am not concerned. Only curious."

Begay stood and stretched. He rubbed his belly and grunted. Patting down his stout legs he felt the sheathed knife hidden just inside his cowboy boot. It was the only weapon he had but it was one that had served him well.

"I am ashamed," the woman said simply.

He turned and looked at her. "There is no shame in this for you."

Isabel shook her head again. "That you have to leave. That you are not safe in my country."

He drew her to him and wiped the corner of her eye with the tail of his shirt.

"Sssh. We are healthy and we have our strength. You have no control over this thing."

"I am sorry it has come to this."

"Our paths will cross again," he held her to his chest for one last minute feeling the racing of her heart. With that he was out the door.

☙

The Japanese troops were all over the countryside now. Although the bridges had been blown up and the trails destroyed, they seemed to be having little trouble navigating the rugged mountain terrain.

The priest had kept the army truck and had driven it as far as he dared. While the road had still been sound when he abandoned it, he had seen little foot traffic and instinct told him that the Japanese were close. After pulling the vehicle off the road and a weak attempt at camouflaging it with loose brush, he had walked for a couple of hours before encountering his first Japanese soldiers. Luckily he had heard their approach before they had seen him and now he kept to the underbrush, having given up traveling the road as too dangerous.

Although it was just past noon, Bendetti had already sought cover four times this morning. His nerves were on edge as he discovered the Japanese were also in the underbrush as well as on the road.

He was out of shape for this kind of thing. His body had gone soft and even as his heart pounded in his ears he thought, for the first time, about the possibility of his having a heart attack. He lay next to a huge pine log and in an effort to still his thrashing heart he thought of Kate.

Kate made the effort worthwhile. Rescuing her was more important than his army commission, than saving souls, then any thing he could imagine. He had never met anyone like her and it was a great sadness to him that he had finally met her only in his last years in the seminary. Maybe if she had only come into his life a few years earlier. Even during his junior years when he could have left without fear of recrimination. But by the time he had met her, late in his last senior year, right before the novitiate, it had been too late. The years and years of intellectual and religious indoctrination had taken their toll.

Perhaps if Kate had given him any encouragement, things would have been different. But she had been content to keep their friendship on a light, almost impersonal basis. The seminarians were discouraged from any contacts with the opposite sex, other than those of family. All incoming and outgoing mail was thoroughly read with any dubious missives from women confiscated and the recipient punished.

All through their seminary years the young men had been taught that women, beautiful vessels though they might be, were the devil's tools set on earth to test the chastity of men. Unfortunately, the arguments against the fair sex were not always persuasive, and for this reason, the young Franciscans would retire to their rooms, cells really, three times a week. Alone, they would strip and reach for the knotted whip hanging from the back of every door. Chanting the haunting verses of the 50th Psalm, the *Miserere*, each seminarian would flog his own flesh until any thought of sex was indelibly removed. None of them thought to question this self flagellation, for by that time they were all committed to a lifetime serving their vows of poverty, chastity, and most importantly, obedience. To insure that none fell by the wayside, the Superior strolled up and down the hallway, pausing momentarily in front of the closed doors until satisfied that the proscribed beatings were, in fact, taking place.

Though they never discussed it, George had often wondered whether any of his fellow seminarians had figured out a way, as he had, to service himself while keeping the rhythm of the self flagellation.

The combination of the beatings, fastings and censored mail were enough to discourage George from continuing his fledgling friendship with Kate. And then he had gone into his novitiate year, exchanging his christened name for that of one of the saints, as they all did to signify their new, spiritual lives. Shaving their heads, their bodies clothed in hooded robes fashioned out of irritating wool, their shoes replaced by sandals, they entered the six year novitiate phase.

Then, finally, ordination and a commitment to a life of *Cura Animarum* the saving of souls and devotion to vows. The archbishop had solemnly told all of them "Thou art a priest forever."

After that there had been no question of turning back. Until he had come to the Philippines and had run into Kate again, without fear of censored mail or self-flagellation or any of the horrors that had so haunted him during his years at Santa Barbara.

With his ear against the ground, George could feel a vibration that didn't belong to the quiet forest. He froze, not daring to even breathe. His eyes closed tightly as he lay immobile, feeling the vibration grow stronger. Gradually realizing he could not hold his breath indefinitely, he slowly exhaled, the very tempo of his released air frightening him, causing his heart to pound louder and louder, in an alter rhythm to the footsteps that were growing stronger.

He prayed he would not be discovered this time. He had not taken any special precautions in his choice of a resting place, but now he was grateful that at least he had the cover of the heavy log next to him. Slowly, as though he feared the very act would draw attention to his hiding place, he opened his eyes. There was a shaft of light separating the misshapen log where it touched the forest floor and the priest, his cheek ground into the mud, peered through this peephole.

He waited, knowing by the feel of the ground that the vibrations were very close now. A flash of boot came into the light shaft, blacking it out. Suddenly it was like a fixture with an electrical short in it as it flashed on and off, on and off, interrupted by the footfalls of the Japanese soldiers passing by. Bendetti again held his breath, encouraged by the fact that at the first flash of darkness a saber had not been thrust through his heart. Maybe he was safe. There was light again and he stared at it for a long time as he felt the vibration against his muddy cheek dim and fade.

He waited for at least twenty minutes before he sat up. His left side was caked with the heavy mud and forest debris, and his body ached from having maintained one position for so long. He rolled his neck around on his shoulders and stretched his arms in an effort to restore circulation in his stiffened body parts. Although he was dying for a cigarette, he knew the risk was too great to have one.

Finally the total fear of what he had just been through hit him and he bent forward, barely in time to avoid hitting his own feet, and retched onto the log. As he watched the physical evidence of his terror drip and roll off the felled tree and into the mud, he was struck with self-realization. He didn't have the courage to continue.

Resigned, he backed away from the log and turned back toward Manila.

General MacArthur had started the army withdrawal into the Bataan Peninsula. There, according to the Orange Plan, his troops would hold off the Japanese while waiting for American reinforcements to come.

One of the major problems with the retreat, which the general preferred to call a retrograde maneuver, was the fact that his forces were split. The men of the Northern Force, some twenty-eight thousand strong, and the fifteen thousand of the Southern Force, had been over a hundred and fifty miles apart when the maneuver had first been ordered. It had taken no small amount of coordination to bring the two groups together. On a military map the entire stratagem had looked like a dangerous game of leap-frog, played backwards. One force would fight, the other would pivot around.

To the troops the orders read much like "stand and fight, slip back and dynamite." And dynamite they did. By the time both forces reached the Calumpit Bridge, they had already covered their retrograde maneuver by blowing up over one hundred and eighty bridges.

Charlie stood looking at the Calumpit Bridge, aware that since the two highways, Three and Seven, met ten miles east of the structure, the road across the bridge was the only one into Bataan. Although he had been on Luzon for twelve years, Begay had never come this close to the Bataan Peninsula. He had seen the tongue of land from Manila Bay and the thick jungle growth had not appealed to him. Now as he stood staring at the bridge, he knew it was the only thing separating him from a commitment to Bataan. He could still turn back. To Manila and Isabel.

The bridge, a twin spanned affair with railroad tracks on one side, stretched across a deep gorge. Deep below, the Pampanga River thrashed and roared, a formidable body of water to cross without benefit of the bridge.

Pedestrians struggled across the tracks, seemingly oblivious to the thought that a train might come along, leaving them stranded with no place to go to avoid being mowed down. But it was the road side of the trestle that was a real mess. Jammed with cars, *calesas* pulled by tired horses, vividly painted buses, rusty trucks, bicycles, jeeps sporting official government decals, the bridge was a swarming mass of humanity.

Army troops and equipment now vied with civilians for the chance to cross into Bataan. Every possible vehicle had been called into service to ferry people and supplies from one side to the other. MacArthur's South Luzon Force had arrived at the Calumpit Bridge and they were now streaming across, along with still more supplies from the quartermaster. Begay had never seen so many people in one place together in his life. For the second time he thought about returning to Manila.

Just then an elderly Filipino man who was driving a rickety *calesa* about to cross the bridge, tumbled face first from his cart. Begay jumped in front of the tired horse and grabbed his bridle, preventing the animal from getting away. Had he thought about it, the impossibility of that event would have occurred to him for hordes of people were entering the head of the bridge, making the beast's escape impossible. Inside the *calesa* a young Filipina crushed her two wide-eyed children to her breast.

"Here, hold him." Charlie shook the reins of the horse, indicating that the woman should take them. She shook her head, burying her face into the top of one of the children's shaggy heads. The Navajo shook the reins again. Finally she got his drift and she nervously gathered the loose reins in her small hands.

Charlie struggled through the traffic jam to reach the fallen man. Although there were people everywhere, none stopped to help, preferring to sidestep his unconscious body. Charlie tugged at him in an effort to raise him to his feet but the man was limp. Finally he lifted him and placed him into the *calesa* next to the frightened children. He pointed to the other side of the bridge. The woman shook her head. Holding the horse for a minute was one thing but she could not drive him anywhere.

Charlie walked to the animal's head and grabbing his bridle he pulled on his mouth, leading him across the Calumpit Bridge.

A narrow lane of the bridge was guarded by soldiers. In spite of the masses pouring into Bataan, they were keeping the lane open for vehicles traveling back to the Manila side. Begay now saw that many of the vehicles were returning empty, except for their drivers. They were ferrying people back and forth.

They had reached the other side now and quickly the Filipina jumped down, gathered her children and her bag, and without so much as a nod, left Charlie standing at the horse's head. He led the animal off to one side, allowing those behind him room to pass.

As he lifted the still unconscious man from the *calesa* he saw his dull brown eyes staring back at him. He did not have to feel in the hollow of the man's neck to know he would not find a pulse there. Charlie shuddered. He did not want to touch the man. His people had strong feelings about the dead. They would not touch them, would not say their name after death, and would even burn a dead man's hogan with all of his possessions in it. Begay hesitated a moment before carefully putting the dead Filipino on the matted grass. A taste of ashes invaded his mouth as he did so.

"Hey, you!" A beefy looking sergeant addressed the Indian. "Let's turn that rig around and head back over."

Without hesitation Charlie led the horse back across the bridge.

EXODUS

13

The army orders had been very clear. Nothing that could be of military benefit to the Japanese was to be left behind intact. Fuel supplies, locomotives, cars and jeeps, warehouses and any of the military installations unharmed by the Japanese bombers had been blown up or set on fire.

Cavite had been torched Christmas night. Supplies were still being ferried across Manila Bay to Bataan and Corregidor, and rumors had it that over three hundred barge loads had already been sent to Corregidor.

The Manila railroad, normally a conduit to move supplies, was now useless, deserted by its civilian crew. While American troops had offered to put the train back into operation, permission had still not been granted by the Philippine government and now the train stood still, frozen on its tracks by lack of a crew.

The countdown was near, anyone could tell that just by watching the Manila sky. It was black and dense with oil filled smoke. When the Pandacan oil storage tanks were blown, there was a tremendous explosion that had shaken the city. Fires were everywhere and the flames from the great Pandacan fire could be seen for miles.

Oil slicks burst into flames and drifted down the Pasig River setting smaller fires as they touched here and there along the shoreline. Fires could be seen in the east too, for the storage tanks at Fort McKinley had also been blown up.

Looking out through the criss crossed adhesive tape of her window, Ellen did not have to be told that she was watching hell. The stench of burning petroleum and cordite was apparent, even through the paned window. It hung over all of them, an unrelenting shroud of stench and death. It reminded her of a time when she had been a girl on a campout. There had been a great bonfire and when she had gone to bed that night her hair, her clothes, her very being, reeked with the odor of smoke. It had been a great relief to her then to be able to return home and bathe. But there was no solution to avoiding the odors that assaulted her senses now. There was no getting out of it. No escape. She closed her eyes and said a silent prayer for her boys.

Doc and Peter sat playing cards. The fascination of watching the fires was gone for them and as Pete had so articulately said earlier in the evening, "you see one dumb fire, you've seen them all."

"Gin!" Pete grinned as he threw his hand on the table.

"I'm bored with this," Doc's cards were thrown quickly on top of Pete's making an accurate score more difficult. "What's happening out there, Mother?"

Ellen quickly drew the curtains, not wishing the boys to see how much worse the sky had become since they had looked an hour earlier. "Not much, dear."

"Let's read Peter Rabbit," Pete suggested his favorite story.

"That's a baby story," Doc argued, "I know. Let's make New Year's resolutions. After all, tomorrow is going to be a brand new year!"

Ellen walked stiffly to the desk and withdrew two sheets of paper and two pencils and handed them to the boys.

"You too, Mom," Doc insisted, "you've got to make your new year's plans too."

Silently Ellen returned to the desk.

"I think I'll sit over here," she said, taking another sheet of paper from the drawer. Her back was to the boys so they could not see the tears running down her cheeks.

Charlie was bone tired from working throughout the night.

He looked at the scrawny Philippine horse and wondered how many more trips the poor beast could make before it dropped dead of exhaustion like so many others before him. He had lost count of the times they had crossed the bridge. At least the animal never had the burden of Charlie's weight for the Navajo had made every trip on foot, leading the horse behind him.

In the light of dawn he could see that there were few people left. Many of the private limousines and Pambusco buses were now disabled on one side of the bridge or the other having run out of gasoline hours earlier. Still, many of the animal drawn conveyances continued to work.

The Twenty-sixth Cavalry Regiment of the prestigious Philippine Scouts had started to cross the bridge. They had waited until the end, guarding the retreat into Bataan. The Scouts, a group of veteran soldiers begun by General MacArthur's father in 1901, were so elite that the only entrance into the regiment was by legacy. They would repeat their vigil again and again in the course of the next few months.

The road junction just above Calumpit was guarded by army tanks for the Japanese were expected at any time. They had been in position for the last three days. As Charlie headed back over the bridge, he saw that the first of the tanks was heading over on the railroad side of the Calumpit. The last trip over would be made very soon before the bridge would go, he thought.

There were no women and children left on the Manila side. Charlie noticed a priest waiting. He wondered about the men who waited for rides when they could walk. While many of the men were disabled or elderly, he had refused rides to many able, healthy men, preferring to use the horse's little remaining energy on those who really needed help in getting across.

"Hey, over here." The priest was waving his hand.

Charlie approached him. The man's back was turned, out of the slight breeze, so that he could light a cigarette. When he turned back, Charlie found himself looking into the cold, hooded eyes of George Bendetti.

"You!" The priest said accusingly.

"Do you want a ride?" Although Charlie had never liked the priest, he knew they didn't have long before the bridge would be demolished.

"I'll walk."

"Suit yourself," the Indian started to turn away, "they're blowing it in fifteen minutes."

Bendetti looked across the span. Surely he could make it safely across by then. Still he was weary, not in shape. He licked his full lips. "All right, I'll ride."

Pat Casey's engineers, civilians like Tom Sullivan, were working hand in hand with the Army Corps of Engineers. Many of them had been working for years with the mines in the Philippines and they had dynamiting down to an art. Working with tremendous courage, for many of them would be working in full view of Japanese troops and tanks, they put their extraordinary talent to use.

At six fifteen in the morning on the New Year of 1942, the Calumpit Bridge which had served in connecting the Bataan Peninsula to the rest of civilization so well, exploded.

Tons of steel and masses of twisted metal, signifying years of planning and construction, fell uselessly into the raging torrents of the Pampanga River.

General MacArthur's retrograde maneuver had been a success. His forces were united, all eighty thousand of them. Together with twenty six thousand civilians, they had evaded the Japanese forces for the time being. Now the problems they faced were a little different. They would have to learn to cope with the jungle.

And starvation.

14

"What's an enemy alien?" Pete's innocent blue eyes were trained on Ellen.

"That's what we are, dummy." Doc's reply was quicker than his mother's.

"Is that true, mother? I thought the Japanese were the enemy." Pete refused to believe his brother.

"They are, dear." Ellen patted his smooth soft cheek. "But the Japanese are in charge now. And to them we're the enemy."

"The monkeys are in charge of the zoo," Doc grumbled.

"Doc!" Ellen warned. She had been after him all week on the monkey business. It had started when some older boys had convinced him that the Japanese were descendants of a group of shipwrecked Chinese who had mated with monkeys on the Japanese island of Honshu. "They are people just like we are."

"No they're not. They're meaner," her eldest son was not one to give up easily.

"Since we're their enemy, then that's why we have to live in this place?" Pete scratched his head. None of it made much sense to him.

"Yes, darling." Ellen reached for her knitting needles, thankful that she could continue her hobby even in captivity.

The Japanese had arrived in Manila during the second night of January. At dusk the next day they had driven through the city in cattle vans with the dung still in them, using a bullhorn to broadcast that all civilians would be taken in for questioning. Instructed to take their passports and a change of clothing only, they had been crushed into the filthy trucks.

They were driven to the fifty acre University of Santo Tomas, a large Catholic university whose opening in 1611 gave it the distinction of being the oldest university "under the American flag." After the bombing of Clark Field, classes throughout the islands had been suspended. When Manila had been declared an open city, the American Emergency Committee of the Red Cross, foreseeing the possibility of internment of Allied citizens, requested, and received, permission from the Santo Tomas administration to use the university facility as an internment camp.

A central committee, composed entirely of male members, had been formed to deal with the problems of internment. Sixteen committees coordinated specific tasks ranging from labor and finance to family aid. While confusion seemed to be the order of the day for the first few weeks, things were now settling in at Santo Tomas. Everyone was assigned a job of some sort.

Positions included those in sanitation and health, in construction, in educational and medical areas, in the kitchen and in the vegetable garden. Jobs held on the outside held little or no meaning here. The toilet attendant had been, before the war, the president of a large firm; society ladies cleaned the women's latrines, and the chore of washing out filthy mosquito nets, crawling with bugs, fell to a former bank manager.

Jobs had also been assigned to the Sullivans. Ellen would teach in the lower grades and Pete had secured a job as a messenger. Already he was hard at work making a little wooden wheelbarrow out of scraps so that his delivery duties could be expanded. Doc, never eager to help with the dishes at home, landed one of the most prestigious jobs of all, cleaning the kitchen pots and pans.

While Ellen and the boys had been in the first contingent of three hundred civilians interned at Santo Tomas, the population had now swelled to thirty three hundred people of varying nationalities. As the days passed, they felt somewhat comfortable among their old friends and classmates. Although there had been talk of the internees being responsible for their own meals- a frightening, if not impossible task- the Philippine Red Cross committee had gotten down to a routine and now at least coffee and soup were being served daily.

"I just delivered a message to the administration building. They're putting up sawali on the front fence," Pete volunteered his news to his mother.

"What?" Discouragement was evident in Ellen's voice. The open iron fence was their only contact with the outside. It had come to be a conduit for those inside. Servants, along with those of neutral or Axis nationalities, would stand outside the wrought iron fence with signs sporting the names of those they wished to contact. Food, ranging from bananas to fish, had been squeezed through the bars along with medicines, clothing and small household necessities. The conduit operated under the good graces of the Irish priests of the Malate Church, for it was a well known secret that they were using the confessional there as a message center. "Where?"

"In the front, along Calle España."

Ellen left the building and hurried to the front fence joining a group of stunned internees who were gathered there. Japanese guards were rolling out the bamboo matting and attaching it to the metal railing. On the other side she could see a group of Filipinos with their placards and packages. Communication between internee and free man had suddenly become much more difficult.

"Mrs. Sullivan?"

Ellen turned in the direction of the vaguely familiar voice. A tall buxom redhead was offering her hand. "Magda Masyryk. I met you with Sky Berringer last summer."

Ellen returned the firm handshake. "Of course."

"I thought I saw you with your children a few days ago but I couldn't reach you in time."

"Well, I'm glad our paths crossed again," Ellen said. "Of course I don't mean that I'm glad you're in here." She laughed uneasily, hoping the Czechoslovakian woman would not misunderstand her.

"No." The woman waved her hand. "We are all alike in here, no? Well, maybe if one was a Panamanian or something outrageous like that!"

Ellen laughed. The last she had heard there were thirty-seven nations at war throughout the world. Those numbers alone had practically destroyed the League of Nations.

"They're getting tougher," Ellen nodded in the direction of the sawali.

"Yes. But then hopefully we won't be in here long before your American friends come."

"Hopefully," Ellen repeated the word, wishing she shared Magda's optimism.

"Your husband and Sky. They are in here too?"

Ellen shook her head.

"Tom's on the Rock."

"I'm sorry to hear that." Magda, like most of the Santo Tomas internees had heard that the MacArthur and Quezon families were on Corregidor. The island had been subjected to daily bombardment.

"I don't know where Sky is. The last time I saw him he was in Baguio," Ellen offered.

"So many changes." Magda shuddered in spite of the stifling heat. "There are many things now to deal with, are there not?"

"Yes. Where are you staying?"

"The main building. And you?"

"The annex. It's crowded but at least there's a roof over our heads." Ellen felt immediate guilt. The main building, she knew, was even more crowded than the annex. Even the classrooms were being converted to makeshift dormitories. "I must be getting back now." She left the Czech watching the last of the bamboo matting obliterate the view of the outside.

Ellen hardly noticed the drone of a lonely fighter as she made her way back to her children. In just a few short weeks she had become a veteran of aural detection of aircraft. The Zero, she knew, was just making a lazy pass and had no intention of strafing a camp under Japanese control. As she passed the administration building, her stomach turned as she saw the flag with the rising sun flying there.

※

Charlie's eyes were cast to the ground as he walked through the cogon grass. He had surprised a huge python in the same vegetation just last week and he was not eager to repeat the experience. The snake had reinforced all of his doubts about the Bataan peninsula.

The twenty-five mile long strip of land was as unlike his native Arizona as a place could be. Two extinct volcanoes, treacherous roaring rivers cutting deep gorges in rock canyon walls, thick whiplike vines that seemed to snake out and grab a man's ankles before he knew they were there, jungle growth that exhausted all of a man's energies before he could move ten feet- all the exotic tropical elements were here, and Charlie quickly discovered that he cared little for them.

General MacArthur apparently cared little for them either, judging from his one brief trip over from Corregidor when he had met with General Jonathan Wainwright. Charlie had heard about that meeting for the bamboo telegraph was quick to spread any news to the remote areas of Bataan. Dressed in sweat stained khakis, Wainwright, the charismatic cavalryman who was in charge of the Bataan forces, had asked the immaculate MacArthur to chat with some of the beleaguered troops. Morale was low and he suggested that a visit with MacArthur could raise the men's spirits. MacArthur had refused the request and returned to Corregidor that same day. Since then there had been several messages from General MacArthur, each promising that United States troops and airplanes were on their way.

Charlie crossed the cogon grass and eased his thinning bulk down against the thick trunk of a giant banyan tree. Shaded by its leaves, he took off his doughboy helmet, a World War I leftover given to him by an army captain, and closed his eyes.

It was nice to be alone, he thought. With more than one hundred thousand people shoved into Bataan it was sometimes hard to find solitude.

The steady growl of an airplane interrupted his wandering thoughts. He had no need for further cover, protected as he was by the grove of banyan trees. Besides, there was no advantage to the pilot's selecting one man for a target, unless, of course, that man was General MacArthur. But then the general was still secure on Corregidor, three miles off the coast.

Charlie watched the Mitsubishi fly in low, low enough to make out the rising sun on its sleek body. The plane was dropping paper, this time, not bombs. It was all part of a propaganda campaign aimed at the defection of the more than sixty-five thousand Filipinos that were in the army. There were only fifteen thousand American servicemen on Bataan and the Japanese, if they could get the natives to defect, would score a heavy military advantage.

The leaflets were pretty insulting to the Navajo's way of thinking. They were ingenious enough, he thought, although none of the arguments they had presented had tempted anyone he knew to go to the other side. The pamphlets struck at every possible nerve. They showed beautiful women and suggested that the Filipinos should return to the comforts of life in Manila. Others were more ominous with pictures of skeletons advising surrender before it was too late, and offering the holder the choice between life or death.

The chattering of a band of monkeys overhead caused Charlie to freeze. The rumbling in his stomach reminded him of his mission out here and he held very still. In the palm of one hand he held a piece of a canned peach. The piece of fruit had been saved for ten days now. When it had begun to shrivel, he rehydrated it by soaking it in water.

He sat still for ten minutes. The chatter of the animals died down and he knew that they were considering taking a closer look at him. He imagined, as he sat there frozen into position, that the animals may have been spooked by hungry men looking for food.

General MacArthur had ordered all of the men on half rations the minute they had destroyed the Layac Bridge. Safe temporarily from the Japanese, they had faced the possibility of starvation and the half-rations had since been reduced even further. Now everyone on Bataan was hungry. Sitting around at night, after a few ounces of rice, they talked of food. Although it was a tortuous exercise, it had kept the men entertained and held out the hope of better times.

Animals were beginning to get scarce on the peninsula. There had been wild chickens and pigs, but the last of them had been eaten over a week ago. Most of the clumsier, slower lizards had also disappeared and even the ever present rats that nested in the wild bamboo were getting rare.

Two young monkeys skittered down the tree and made a wide half circle around Charlie. They talked to each other while keeping wary eyes on the human slumped against the banyan. Charlie was barely breathing. He tried hard not to think of the large red ant that was crawling up his forearm, for he knew if he so much as twitched, the animals would be out of sight, and reach, within seconds.

The smaller of the two monkeys came in closer while the more cautious primate scolded it.

Just as the smallest one moved in to take the peach the other started screeching wildly. The distraction gave Charlie enough time to grab the creature by its tail. Hanging on tightly to the appendage, the Navajo scrambled to his feet as the monkey climbed up its own tail and sunk its teeth into the fleshy part of Charlie's hand just below his thumb. Blood gushed from the nasty bite as Begay swung the animal around, bashing its brains into the bark of the banyan tree.

The animal twitched and was still.

Charlie shook it roughly, making sure the monkey was really dead, before he dropped it on the ground and held his throbbing hand to his lips. He sucked on the wound, spitting out his blood.

Finally satisfied that the wound was as clean as he could make it, he gathered small twigs and made a fire.

Taking his knife from his boot, he carefully skinned the creature, taking care to leave the carcass intact. Without its fur the monkey resembled a baby, and as Charlie worked he ignored comparisons. He whittled a stick and pierced the animal's body with it, and after rigging up a secure wooden stand he began toasting the meat over the fire.

He pulled the meat from the stand and took his first bite, instantly sorry that the cramping in his stomach had not allowed him time to boil his meal before roasting it. As he sat against the tree tearing into the strong monkey meat, he thought of his ancestors. Was this really so different from the mule they had been so fond of? Then, with a sadness, he knew that soon he too would be eating mule, for there was already talk of slaughtering the cavalry animals.

✠

"Sir, could you come over here?"

Bendetti looked up. A young American private was hurrying up to him, carrying a shovel.

"There's something over here that I'd like you to take a look at, sir."

George rose with some resentment. Hunger was constantly gnawing at him and it had done nothing to improve his disposition.

"What is it?"

The soldier led him through the jungle. A dark cloud hovered over a clearing just ahead.

"Fire?" He sniffed the air, trying to detect the smell of smoke.

The private shook his head.

"Flies."

As he walked into the clearing, the priest felt bile rising in his throat. Scattered across the damp earth, were eight dead Japanese soldiers, all in varying stages of decomposition. The heat had swollen the bodies three times their normal size. Bluebottle flies were everywhere, feasting on the dead flesh.

"Why do I need to see this, soldier?" Bendetti's full sensuous lips were chapped and dry, and he was trying hard to mask his anger.

"Father we thought we ought to bury them. And we just supposed, we just thought, that is, that you might want to say a few words or something. I mean they are soldiers and all. We thought that if it were our guys we'd want them taken care of."

George reached for the soldier's khaki collar and pulled him roughly up to him, amazed that the boy was so light.

You're wrong, soldier. I wouldn't say 'horseshit' over those heathen bastards." George spun the open mouthed boy away from him as he left the clearing.

15

Rain began to fall. It was a light and misty drizzle, only furthering the men's misery. Leaving them damp, in air thick with so much moisture they sometimes had trouble breathing, it soaked their rations and their spirits and, in its wake, left mold and mildew on everything.

Charlie slushed along behind his captain on the southwest coast. Strange coalitions were being formed throughout Bataan and this night patrol was typical of the new hybrids. The captain wasn't an infantryman at all, but a displaced Air Force pilot whose planes had been sent to Darwin, Australia along with all but a few P-40's that were left at Kindley Field on Corregidor.

Charlie, although a civilian, had volunteered to go on patrol with the captain's detail. Many of the soldiers on Bataan were down with dysentery and the captain had been pleased to add Begay to his group. Strays were everywhere now- pilots without planes, shipless sailors, cooks with guns, ragtag groups of displaced soldiers all attempting to pool their resources.

Concessions were being made with uniforms, too. The army nurses who had come to Bataan from the Sternberg General Hospital were quickly finding that not only did their crisp white uniforms get filthy, but they made lovely targets from the air. The women were issued drab green army uniforms, most in size 46. With the help of a Chinese tailor the uniforms had been cut down into coveralls and these were serving them well. Sailors had discovered a similar problem with their whites and they quickly soaked them in strong coffee, turning them an earthen shade.

The patrol walked silently in the drizzle, as they followed their leader. They had come to trust him for in addition to being a pilot, he had been raised in the hill country of Kentucky and his backwoods instincts had proved infallible on more than one occasion.

The full moon, combined with the falling mist, gave an eery cast to the jungle growth as they hacked their way through it. The rugged coastline, jagged rocks appearing as specters, loomed ahead. They were dropping now as they headed for the sandy beach, the only possible landing point for several miles. The unoccupied shore could be made out below and even through the steady downpour the cresting of the waves against the wet sand could be heard.

The captain stopped and held up his hand. In spite of the sound of the rain and the ocean, the steady drone of motor boats could be heard. Even as they froze, listening to the sound, the boats were coming closer. With a wave of his up lifted hand, the pilot instructed them to break into two groups. Charlie followed the Kentuckian to a break in the dense brush. Peering through the greenery the Navajo could see six barges silhouetted against the horizon.

The captain held a radio to his lips.

"Base, this is B patrol, do you read?"

"B Patrol, this is Base."

"We've got one hundred C rations." He used the agreed upon code.

"Roger. Give your position."

The captain gave the proper map coordinates and put the radio away. He swung his Springfield rifle around, checking to insure the safety was off. His men quickly followed suit.

The barges were coming in to land. Suddenly a harsh noise broke through the drizzle and the ocean and the sound of the boats. An airplane was breaking through the overcast sky. There were two of them, P-40's, and as they flew into view, the captain pulled a flare gun from his belt, pointing it in the direction of the barges. Instantly the air was light, exposing the position of the enemy troops.

Surprised by the sudden exposure the Japanese troops opened fire on the bank, but the captain's men were well hidden and easily returned the fire. Caught between the airplanes and the infantrymen, their barges already in shallow water, the Japanese had no choice but to attempt a landing. As the planes dropped and began strafing, the enemy soldiers began pouring over the sides and onto the beach.

It was a bloodbath. The captain had often told his men that fighting the enemy was like rabbit hunting. Now the Japanese were sitting ducks. The only thing saving them from total annihilation was the mist created by the rain. Charlie braced his rifle against a heavy vine and calculated carefully, making each shot count. Two of the barges were listing badly and a third had already sunk. The sea was churning with the dying Japanese. Protected as they were by the dense underbrush, the Americans had the luxury of time to place each shot and they did this very well.

The last barge, the only one that had not made the fatal error of coming in shallow too fast, was pulling out now and heading south down the coast. Chasing them on foot on shore was out of the question.

"Damn!" The captain muttered to himself as much as to anyone else. "Now we're going to have to put up with their shit."

Charlie remained silent. The Japanese had already taken Abucay, forcing the troops halfway down the peninsula. After the Abucay-Mauban line had been lost, the Allies had retreated to the

Bagac-Orion area. Now the Japanese were not only pressing the new defense lines but they were starting amphibious landings along the coast. Eventually there would have to be an end to what the senior officers were calling the retrograde maneuver.

Heading back to their base position, the men walked in silence, alert to the possibility that some of the Japanese soldiers from the sixth barge, may have already landed and could be close.

The captain stopped abruptly, straining to hear foreign noises against the rain. The men, accustomed to his woods wise ways, waited for his direction. Again he held up his hand and motioned for them to split into two groups. He indicated they were to remain in position while he went on ahead. Charlie followed.

They moved slowly through the brush, knowing that with the thick growth, they could easily stumble upon the enemy. Their caution was rewarded, for not twenty yards in front of them eleven Japanese soldiers were squatting on the ground. Charlie could see, as he peeked through the brush, that one of them was holding a canteen to a wounded man's lips. Four enemy soldiers, guns drawn, walked in circles around the squatters. Like their American counterparts they too were straining to hear foreign noises.

The captain reached into his belt and pulled out a twenty-three year old grenade. He pulled the pin and threw it. The grenade rolled to the side of where the men were resting. Nothing happened. A dud.

The rain was against them. They had learned weeks ago to test the obsolete grenades. They would pull the pins, release the spoon, and tap them hard against the heel of their boots, not releasing them until they heard the snap of the pin inside. Tonight, the sound of the rain precluded this test.

The captain reached in his belt for a second grenade. This time the Japanese saw it coming and they opened fire even as they scattered. But Charlie had one too, and it was his grenade, the third one thrown, that finally detonated. Japanese soldiers and parts of them were thrown everywhere.

Quickly the rest of the patrol moved in. They were efficient in stripping the Japanese soldiers of their coveted rations. Their rice cakes and fish balls seemed like a feast to the starving men of Bataan.

The rain finally stopped as the captain walked up to the first of the grenades and stood over it sadly shaking his head.

"How in the hell do they expect us to win a war when we don't even have decent weapons?"

It was a rhetorical question; one that was echoed throughout Bataan. Weaponry, much of it old and obsolete and left over from the first World War, was unreliable and defective. On some occasions eighty percent of the grenades failed to explode. The water cooled 30 caliber machine guns, model 1911, would jam every time a misfire came up. And misfires in all the weaponry were common, for the ammunition had been stored for years in the tropical climate. Verdigris, a green deposit that thrived in the tropics, covered many of the brass shells. At times the mold was so thick the shells were unable to fit into their designated chambers.

Mortar shells could never be taken for granted. In one platoon it had gotten to be a game, they had actually started keeping records, instigated by an encounter in which only five out of fourteen shells had been good ones. It was a deadly game though, as the normally reliable World War I Springfield and Enfield rifles failed to fire they were no match for the newer, reliable weaponry of the Japanese Imperial Army.

"It's one bitch of a way to fight a war," the Kentuckian grumbled as he walked off.

16

Whatever romance Tom Sullivan held for Corregidor was gone.

With a total land area of less than three miles, shaped like a giant tadpole facing the China Sea, the island was almost solid rock with lush foliage. It was a veritable flower garden with its wild orchids, bougainvillea and frangipani defying its nickname "The 'Rock."

Corregidor was the South Pacific's answer to the Rock of Gibraltar. Guarding the mouth of Manila Bay, Corregidor's acreage was varied. The widest area of the tadpole, the head, jutted six hundred feet into the sky while the acreage known as bottomside, a gentle sloping area just a few feet above sea level, hosted the docks and piers. The west shore, sporting steep, inaccessible cliffs was nearly impregnable, while the beaches on the south side were easily approachable.

Philippine legend has it that The Rock got its name, Corregidor, from two illmatched lovers. The daughter of a wealthy Spanish family fell in love with a young Filipino. The family, disapproving of the union, sent the girl to a convent. One moonlit night she escaped the cloister and secretly met her lover. They fled to the closest island at the mouth of the bay. When her parents discovered her flight, they sent a magistrate, or *corregidor*, to retrieve the pair. Thwarted in their love they were taken back to Manila, the girl astride a horse, the boy on a carabao. There the daughter became a nun, or *la monja*, her lover a *fraile*, or monk.

In addition to Corregidor, four smaller islands clustered in the bay guarding Manila's harbor. Caballo, Carabao, La Monja and El Fraile- all names stemming from the eighteenth century tale.

Tom loved the story when he had first heard it. Since he'd been on Corregidor for over two months he was beginning to wish he had never heard of the legend, or the island.

Fifteen thousand people were now living on the island fortress. At least two thousand of them were civilians. Few were combat trained. Food and supplies were already getting scarce.

As Tom rubbed his left cheek, his hand caught a lump of healing scar issue, a grim reminder of his first air raid. It had happened on the first day The Rock had come under Japanese attack, on the twenty-ninth of December.

Standing on the northwestern plateau, an area known as Topside, he had caught a piece of flying metal from one of the wooden buildings that had been bombed. Later they had all been warned of the danger of flying metal for the corrugated roofs, once exploded, became bombs themselves, scattering dangerous, piercing parts of metal in every direction.

Still and all there could be worse places to be during the war, Tom thought, for Corregidor was indeed a fortress. Buttressed by huge guns on all sides, the island boasted three tiers of defense, with a labyrinth of underground tunnels connecting all of the positions. While other islands hosted resorts or fine beaches, Corregidor's claim to fame was her defense fortifications and they were vast. Even before the first World War the Americans had spent a small fortune, some said as much as one hundred and fifty million dollars, to make Corregidor a bastion.

Miles of barbed wire had been strung along likely landing areas to discourage unwelcome visitors. Mines had been laid, tank traps built, and trenches and foxholes dug. Twenty-three batteries accommodated fifty-six guns, ranging from three inch guns to twelve inch mortars. Although some of the guns dated from the Spanish-American War of the late 1800's, they were still formidable weapons. Their one weakness was that their original positioning was to defend against naval attacks. Emplaced in an era before the airplane, the guns were open to the sky and vulnerable to air raid. Aware of this weakness, five additional batteries now housed anti-aircraft guns.

Corregidor's current charm, despite the romanticism of the Philippine legend, was her invulnerability. General MacArthur had not been kidding when he had said after the fall of Manila, "They may have the bottle, but I've got the cork." The cork, was, by all indications, secure.

While Corregidor had been heavily bombed right before and after the Japanese had taken Manila, the enemy had eased off now, leveling everything they had at the Bataan Peninsula. Still the Mitsubishis could be counted on for daily attacks at sunrise and sunset. The two most beautiful times of the day, Tom thought ironically. Also the two times when the Corregidor gunners would be at a tremendous disadvantage trying to target the enemy bombers flying out of the sun.

The day felt good. Tom broke into a little jog but stopped, only a few yards later, panting and gasping for breath. He was out of shape. As he held his ribs in an effort to dissolve the side stitch developing there, he could feel how close his bones now rested to his skin. Although the food was reputed to be better and in greater abundance than that on Bataan, the rations on Corregidor had been cut, and now the diet was anything but balanced. Canned salmon and rice. That was it.

The jungle was silent these days. Tom had heard some of the men who had been garrisoned there before the war talk of small deer and monkeys that had lived on the island. Now they were gone. Eaten by the starving people on Corregidor.

Tom squinted his eyes toward the sky, trying to make out the airplane he had heard. It flew unhampered over the Corregidor airspace.

"Photograph Joe from Tokyo," Sullivan mumbled to himself as he flipped the finger to the faraway plane. This particular plane, the Dinah, came over daily on its reconnaissance missions. Flying high over the Bataan Peninsula photographing troop placements, it would report back and the deadly white Mitsubishis would return later in the day and blast the discovered quarry. Tom shook a fist at the plane and as he shouldered a imaginary bazooka to shoot it down, he noticed with surprise that the aircraft was indeed falling.

She was dropping fast in altitude and circling overhead. For one brief paranoid moment Tom thought the plane was coming in after him. He shook his head. He looked around. His presence was indiscernible.

Tom pushed through the overgrown vines toward the beach. There, floating on the water, was the Dinah's prey, a crippled Star sailboat bobbed on the water, trying to limp into shore.

"Eeeeha!" Tom yelled. He hoped the anti- aircraft gunners on the North Shore had also spotted the plane. Pushing and plowing through the thick undergrowth, he made his way onto the sandy beach. The sailboat was a little closer now as the Dinah dove low, strafing the water. It was a game, Tom thought, a god-damned game. The greedy Japs can't stand the thought of a single vessel afloat in the bay.

He ran to the barbed wire cutting off the beach. He was in luck for not twenty feet from him there was a break in the wire.

Rolling under the nasty fence he ran to the shoreline and without a thought of removing his shoes, he waded in, fighting the pressure of the water as he struggled to reach the boat. Looking up he saw the plane make another pass and knew there wasn't much time.

But the Star was sitting high in the water and when he reached it his hands slid off the slippery bow. For the first time he doubted if anyone was inside it.

"Hey, come on," he pounded his fist against the side of the wooden hull.

"Amen, brother!"

With that a body rolled out of the boat making a large splash as it hit the water. The sailor was stronger than Tom and he hit the beach running fast for the wire.

"No! This way!" Tom dashed to the cut in the fence, "through here."

The Dinah was in low again and as they rolled under the fence the bullets pounded into the sand urging them through and back onto their feet. Without looking back, they raced into the jungle.

Tom collapsed, exhausted. The rescue effort had taken more energy than he had expended in a long time.

The new arrival rolled over on his back, arms crossed on top of his chest as he fought for air. After a few minutes his breathing had slowed down and, without embarrassment he reached over and pulled Tom to him, delivering a kiss on his cheek.

"You just saved my ass, boy. Do you know that?" Just as quickly as he had grabbed the older, surprised Tom he released him.

"Son-of-a-bitch! That bastard wanted to reel me in and set me out to dry." He pounded Tom on the back. "Thank you sir, I do thank you."

The sailor was sitting up now, patting his wet clothing. From his left shirt pocket he retrieved a soggy cloth case. Pulling out a harmonica, its metal dull with use, he shook the water out of the instrument.

"And I still have old Tunes here!" Quickly he put the harmonica to his lips and blew through it, further clearing sea water from the valves. Tom stared at him in amazement. There were few men left on Corregidor who had the robust vitality of the man he had just helped out of the water.

"Tom." He tried to break the spell as the man began playing the instrument. "Tom Sullivan."

He held out his hand as the man slipped the harmonica back into his pocket and encased Tom's hand in a bear paw of his own. For the first time Sullivan noticed how big the man really was.

"Theodore Barkley. My friends call me Bark."

"All right, Bark."

"Gunner," it was another way of explaining his nickname, "looks like they could use a few around here."

"I don't know what happened up there," he waved his hand in the general direction of the closest anti-aircraft battery, "they usually go after them if they're down that low. Which isn't often."

Bark stood and stretched his muscle hard body.

"God this is a pretty sight. Never thought I'd make it. I was out there for two days."

"Manila?" Tom asked.

"Cavite. I was one of the lucky ones, I found a boat. Of course oars were another thing." He grinned and paddled his arms.

As they walked back to Malinta Tunnel, Bark brought him up to date on the Manila news. Tom had borrowed high-powered binoculars and watched much of the fall of the capital. Angry and physically ill when he had seen the American flag pulled from the pole at the Manila Hotel and replaced by the Rising Sun, he had sat for hours watching the activity across the bay, wondering about Ellen and his boys. Now Tom listened in horror to Bark's tales of civilian internment by the Japanese.

As they approached the east entrance to the tunnel, they threaded their way through angled walls and heavy cables set up to prevent any enemy bombs from skipping in.

"Very nice," Bark offered his approval as he was led through the maze.

Tom gave him a sidelong glance, remembering the distaste he felt the first time he had come to Malinta. Now they were assaulted with a battery of unpleasant odors, urine and unwashed bodies, sweat and filthy clothes, blood and excrement and over all the faint lingering odor of disinfectant. The stench was the simple result of too many people inhabiting too small a space.

But Bark said nothing, watching in amazement as they walked through the main tunnel.

Forty-eight laterals branched off three tunnels. Malinta Tunnel alone held twenty-five laterals, all with a specialized purpose. The walls, of reinforced concrete, and the ventilation system, were the two things that made the tunnel safe and liveable, Tom thought. But just barely. He was supposedly one of the lucky ones, having been assigned a cot inside. Although the confinement drove him crazy, he did as he was told. Even General MacArthur had refused to stay in the tunnel, preferring to take his chances, sleeping outside.

As they passed the hospital lateral the dim sounds of men in pain wafted out, muted, almost, by the bustle of people talking and working together in the cramped quarters. Branching off from the main tunnel, twelve smaller laterals ran off of it. Wards, operating rooms, nurses quarters, hospital supplies and a mess hall could all be found off the hospital lateral. The hospital, originally located at the vulnerable Middleside, had been moved into Malinta weeks earlier.

"Mining cars?" Bark pointed to the pair of steel tracks running along the floor.

Tom shook his head.

"Trolley cars. Great for moving supplies." The main tunnel was thirty feet wide and they were quickly finding that they needed every inch.

A little boy, almost four years old, came roaring at them, running at his top speed. He skidded to a halt, adjusted his miniature army cap and saluted them. This mission accomplished, he turned away from them, humming the *"Battle Hymn of the Republic"* as he left.

"Kids?" The surprise was evident in Bark's voice. "You've even got kids in here?"

"The kid," Tom replied with a twinge. Seeing young Arthur MacArthur always made him think of his own two boys.

"Arthur?" Even Bark had heard of the apple of MacArthur's eye.

Tom nodded, as a tall blonde, her khaki coveralls doing little to hide her almost flawless figure, walked by. Bark's head whipped around as he watched her disappear into the hospital lateral.

"What was that?" The pupils of his eyes almost covered the brown there.

"That, my friend," Tom explained, "is what we in Arizona call a nurse."

"Christ! Even women!" The blonde had confirmed to him the wisdom of his coming to Corregidor.

"Army nurses. The ladies MacArthur, Quezon and Sayre. And a few others. Home sweet home." Tom grinned and in the artificial light of the tunnel his boyish freckles were even more apparent than in direct sun.

The light was dimmer as they turned into Lateral Number Three, the communications center. Wires snaked across the floor as nervous men consulted maps and adjusted radios. Bark was surprised to hear the ringing of telephones as they squeezed into the busy center. Five men waited in line at the drinking fountain, one of the few luxuries in Malinta Tunnel.

"Busy place," Bark said.

"Always is. Day or night," Tom led him down the center aisle, not an easy task, for Lateral Number Three was much more narrow than the main tunnel and the desks were set at odd angles to accommodate the aisle.

"I'll leave you here," Tom stopped at a desk at the end of the tunnel. "Colonel Sutherland will want to talk to you." As he looked up he could see MacArthur's tall, thin chief-of-staff working his way through the communications center. "When you're done, come out to the west entrance and we can talk if you like."

Bark extended his huge hand. "Thanks, Tom. I'd like to do that. I'd like to know more about the man who saved my life."

As he left, Tom felt more optimistic than he had in weeks.

17

The *USS Trout* arrived in the middle of the night. Her presence was cause for celebration, for she had not only evaded the Japanese ships, but she had brought in welcome anti-aircraft shells. Unfortunately they were not the high altitude explosives that had been requested.

"C" Battery had the highest elevation and the guns there used twenty-one second powder trained fuses. The noses would be turned a certain distance and the turning would set the number of seconds before the missile would explode. Their maximum altitude was 24,000-27,000 feet. It had take the Japanese little time to discover this ceiling and they had merely flown higher.

The submarine had been unloaded earlier, and Tom and Bark were now watching the soldiers load heavy boxes into the *Trout*.

"Can't be food," Bark speculated.

"No," Tom agreed. "Gold."

"Gold?" The Oklahoman had trouble believing it. "We're hungry and they're worried about gold?"

"Protection. We can't let the Japanese have it."

The transfer of the Philippine wealth was just another of a growing number of signs that the fall of Corregidor was imminent. The gold from the Baguio mines had been transferred to Manila right after Pearl Harbor. Then to Corregidor. And now it was on it's way to Australia.

Tom pointed to barges, barely visible out in the bay. "See those?"

Bark shaded his eyes, straining to bring the boats into his vision.

"Yeah."

"Our guys. They're dumping silver out there. Also in the water between Caballo and the Rock."

Tom had seen the coin details leave every day with their loads of silver. In the beginning they had needed the barges to ferry the coins out and the boxes were manually thrown over the side. He had heard one soldier tell how much fun it had been for the first ten minutes. After that it had become a tedious and back-breaking task for each box weighed well over three hundred pounds.

"Shit." Bark was intrigued. He wondered how long the war would continue and how long it would be before a man could re-turn and dive for the sunken treasure.

⚔

Even through the reinforced concrete, Tom could hear the Mitsubishis flying over. Moonlit nights, once so popular, were now damned by all of them, for they gave the Japanese just one more excuse to pound The Rock.

There was a full moon this evening and the enemy was tak-ing full advantage of it.

Tom rolled over on his side trying to get comfortable on his cot. As he did so, he saw that Bark, lying on the next litter, was staring at the ceiling. The overhead lights were flickering and sud-denly they failed completely, plunging the tunnel into suffocating darkness.

"Better turn over, Bark, "Tom suggested quietly. Although

the tunnel was never quiet, all of the men tried to speak softly during the evening hours.

"Why?"

Just as Bark asked, the tunnel heaved and vibrated and falling dust from the concrete ceiling fell into his open eyes and mouth. He sat up abruptly sputtering and spitting the chalky substance onto the floor.

"Shit." He spat again, suddenly aware of the stillness in the tunnel. "Aren't those damned ventilators working?"

"No," Tom said quietly, "they have to shut them down when the bombers come so they won't suck smoke in. Sorry." Tom knew how terrible the dark, still tunnel was the first night.

"This is, without a doubt, the shittiest hotel I have ever stayed in. Man can't sleep in here."

There was truth in Bark's words. Everything echoed throughout the tunnel. No conversation or misery was private. Even the moans and groans of the wounded in the north hospital laterals could be heard throughout Malinta. Packed with people sharing toilets, scarce food and secrets, nothing belonged to one man alone any more. Even the seductive lilting tones of Tokyo Rose could be heard drifting from the communications lateral.

"Come home. The 4-F's are having a good time with your sweethearts," her soft, sexy voice wooed all of them. Although her broadcasts came from Japan, the Japanese had wasted no time in making use of KZRH in Manila. The woman who had called herself Orphan Annie, had been nicknamed Tokyo Rose by the Americans. She continued with her broadcast telling them of the enthusiastic Filipino cooperation.

"Slant-eyed bitch," another engineer, a few cots away, responded with the same comment every night.

Rose, born in the United States and one of U.C.L.A.'s more infamous graduates, was in rare form tonight.

"Yes, Douglas MacArthur is with us, my friends," she was caressing them all with her words. "He is talking to us. Telling your secrets. And he will be justly rewarded. They are planning his execution right now in the Imperial Plaza."

Her silky voice could have been convincing, had they not known that the general was working down in the communications lateral and that little Arthur and his mother were asleep in the ladies' quarters.

A loud hacking cough pervaded the tunnel, drowning out Tokyo Rose. The coughing went on and on, and the air was choked with the man's trying to gasp for air while at the same time he tried to expectorate whatever was irritating his lungs.

"Jesus! Is that one man?"

Tom rolled over and faced Bark.

"It's President Quezon. He has tuberculosis."

Another bomber flew over and great billowing clouds of dust filled the tunnel. Everyone began choking and coughing on the dry, pervasive powder. When the universal struggling had stopped, the lone hacker dominated the night air.

"Can't they give him something?" Bark asked.

"They do. Morphine, when they've got it. His doctor's here too," Tom explained. "The dust is terrible for him, he goes outside every chance he gets."

Bark did not have to be told that supplies were running low. He had seen evidence of that fact everywhere.

"You know, Bark. He's a fine man," Tom thought about Manuel Quezon. He had been an example for all of them. "He had his second inaugural here in the tunnel. You know what he said? They're going to fight with us no matter how bloody this thing gets."

It had been an endless source of inspiration to the engineer that the Filipinos, wooed by the Japanese with talk of co-prosperity and guaranteed immunity, would throw in with the Americans despite great personal cost.

Bark's snoring was just another sound to keep the rest of them awake.

⚔

Thomas Henry Fletcher. Henry Edward Weeks. Blakey Borthwick Laycock. The names were all etched in their minds. They were the first casualties. The examples for all of them.

On February 11, 1942, the three men, sometime after evening roll call, had scaled the wall at the University of Santo Tomas. A short three miles north of camp they had been caught by Japanese soldiers.

"Have you heard?" Magda had come into the classroom and was whispering to Ellen while her pupils labored over their problems. Mathematics was one of the few subjects Ellen could teach, as American history and geography had been strictly forbidden.

"Yes, they caught them." Ellen nodded. There were few secrets of that magnitude in the camp. Besides the Japanese commandant had insisted that all the internees be told that the men had been captured and that the entire Santo Tomas population would suffer for the escape.

"No," Magda lowered her eyes, "they are to be executed!"

"No!" Ellen half stood before sinking back in her chair. It was too much. Just too barbarous.

"Here?" She looked at her young charges, sickened with the thought that they might have to witness a public execution.

"We do not know yet. There will be a statement read tonight at roll call."

» 127 «

The day dragged. Ellen found it hard to keep her mind on her work and not for the first time did she wonder if things were any better in Baguio. She had already heard that the civilians there had been interned in Camp Holmes.

Evening came. A camp spokesman, one of the executive committee, came to the women's annex. After roll call the man stepped forward and read in a stiff monotone.

"The Japanese Commandant has ordered that the internees of this camp be informed that the penalty for attempted escape from this camp is death by shooting, and that the three internees who recently attempted to escape have been tried by military court martial and sentenced to death."

He went on to read that the Executive Committee had submitted a written petition to the camp commandant requesting reconsideration of the sentence. The petition argued that the men had had no idea of the consequences of their action.

Ellen tossed and turned all night. Nightmares of firing squads plugging bullets into twisting, spasmodic bodies haunted her sleep as she struggled to shield her boys from the vision.

By Sunday afternoon, the entire camp buzzed with the news of the execution. The chairman of the Executive Committee, along with two other room monitors, a reverend and an interpreter, had gone to the Manila South Police Station. From there, accompanied by the three prisoners, they had adjourned to the Manila North Cemetery. After being read their sentence, along with some comforting words from the reverend and the camp officials, Fletcher, Weeks and Laycock were taken to a common grave dug by the Japanese.

Ordered to sit with their legs dangling into the hole, they were quickly blindfolded. Japanese soldiers stood a few feet in front of them and, when the Camp Commandant gave the appropriate signal, each man was shot in the head. There would be no public execution.

It was with a mixture of sadness and relief that Ellen heard the news.

18

Kate, bundled up in an old army fatigue jacket that Sky had somehow managed to scrounge up, sat shivering at the edge of the fire, oblivious to the smoke that was permeating her hair and clothes. She stared in amazement at the Ifugao men in front of her. Dancing clad only in red and white g- strings they seemed totally unaware of the cold. She knew nothing of these people, although she and Sky had been living with them for five days now. Maybe if she danced, that would warm her up, she thought before immediately dismissing the idea.

Carlton Melton walked around the fire and held out a steaming mug.

"What's this?" Kate reached eagerly for the brew.

"Don't ask." The friendly anthropologist handed her the vessel, "it's really better not to know."

"Oh." Kate sipped the thick concoction, thankful for it's warmth.

"Fascinating, aren't they?" The white haired Australian nodded to the dancing men.

"Yes. I can see why you've made them your life's work." The anthropologist had lived with the pagan tribe for over twenty years. "What I don't understand," she lowered her voice to a conspiratorial whisper, "is why you still have your head."

"Oh, that," Melton sipped from his cup. "Luck I guess. It's certainly not because they're discriminating. Just about anyone will do, you know."

Although warmer now, Kate shivered. It was like drinking from the mug. Better not to think about it.

"Actually it's really quite interesting. They select their victim and then spring from behind," Melton rose and crossed to a tree, picking up a head axe that rested there. Returning to Kate he continued with his lecture, "pinning the poor devil's head down."

He held a small wooden axe, not over two feet in length, it's finely honed metal blade sporting two evil looking thin blades, a wide one and a fine razor sharp thinner counterpart. Wielding the axe deftly, evidence of his hours of practice with the weapon, the anthropologist pantomimed the taking of a head. Grunting as he held his hand firmly against the notched wooden handle he pried up on it as though popping a head off a neck.

"It's over very quickly."

"I'm sure." Kate looked nervously around for Sky. The Australian seemed too interested in his work. Maybe the years living among the Ifugaos were taking their effect.

"But they're really a very friendly people." Melton smiled widely showing bright red pointed teeth and stained gums. Their first night with him he had told them that he had taken up the pagan's stimulants. Wrapping the betel-palm nut in leaves and sprinkling it with lime juice, he had chewed on the mixture, encouraging them to join in. One look at his teeth, as well as those of their hosts, had discouraged the Americans from taking part.

An Ifugao woman, her arms tattooed up to her shoulders and her hair tangled up with red and white beads, passed a basket of rice to them.

Ignoring the bugs in it, Kate scooped out a handful before passing it to Melton.

"So what's happening here tonight? Are they getting ready to eat us?" Seeing his pained look, she immediately regretted her attempt at humor.

"Oh no. This is a *canao*. A rice feast. They're asking the gods for a good crop yield."

Kate smiled, thinking of her first visit to the Banaue Valley. Paddy after paddy had been reinforced by rock walls hosting green stalks of unharvested rice. It was a testament to the farming and engineering skills of the Ifugaos, for some of the rock walls towered as high as fifty feet without the benefit of mortar. She had been so enthralled with the terraced rice paddies that she had done several watercolors of them.

Sky startled them, coming up from behind the way he did, both of his hands clasped tightly around a steaming wooden bowl. Sitting crosslegged against the cold ground, he held out the bowl. Kate shook her head even as Melton took a long broad leaf and pushed the sloppy stew onto it, using the axe blade as a utensil. Sky followed suit. Soon his fingers were sloppy and wet and he licked them before wiping them on his pants.

"It's good. Are you sure you don't want any?" He held out the leaf to Kate who again declined.

Although she tried to ignore his poor table manners her unease was not lost on him.

"Sorry," he grinned.

She shrugged. She really was not finicky about such things now. They had hiked for days before she had had her first spit bath. They had grubbed and sweated and stunk together and she doubted whether after two and a half months together, living in the wild, there were any personal habits left to hide from each other.

Sky pushed his bowl aside and yawned. He stood and held out a hand, pulling Kate to her feet.

"It's been a long day. Will you excuse us?"

"Certainly." The anthropologist was agreeable as he continued to mop up the stew. "Goodnight."

The one room house was not grand by any means. Slightly elevated on stilts to discourage insects and snakes from coming inside, its rough wooden floor and thatched roof at least kept the rain off their heads. Kate had been embarrassed when Melton had told them that the house, the finest one in the village, belonged to the Ifugao chieftain. After weeks of sleeping outside, they had tried to insist on not taking the quarters but the Australian had assured them that to decline would have served as an insult. Not eager to incur the wrath of the headhunters they had willingly taken the offering.

"We'll be leaving in the morning," Sky offered as he dropped onto a mat.

"All right," Kate smoothed her own mat out, inspecting it carefully for bugs, an almost impossible task in the dim light.

"You could stay here if you'd rather."

"God, no!" She had yet to tell him about the incident with the headhunter's axe.

"We could probably sit out the whole war up here and never be found. But I wouldn't be happy with that."

"No." She was tired. She had learned in the last ten weeks to trust his instincts. He had taken her through things that she knew she would not have survived alone. He had taught her to eat things that she would have sworn would have killed her.

His lessons had included hunting and catching small animals, listening for strange sounds that did not belong to the jungle. How to keep warm. But most of all he had kept her free. Away from the Japanese.

"I told you it wouldn't be easy."

"Yes, you did." She was untying her shoes now, shivering, fighting the tears that were welling in her eyes. She was just so damned cold and hungry. Now she wished she had accepted some of the stew.

"But if we go toward Manila there's a chance of meeting up with some more people like us. There are a lot of military people who didn't give up. We just have to find them."

"Really, I'm fine." She squeezed his hand as he pulled her to him.

Her shivering had not gone unnoticed by him.

"I think I know a way we can warm you up," he volunteered as his hands fumbled under her jacket.

Outside, the headhunters danced on.

✦

The leaflets were really beginning to irritate him. There were all kinds. Some of them were informative, telling the Filipino soldiers that all of the Manila banks were under Japanese control and that the wages the Americans were paying for their military service were useless. This one was a surrender ticket offering amnesty to the bearer. It gratuitously added that "any number may surrender on one ticket." Charlie crumpled it and threw it to the ground.

The airplane that had dropped the leaflet had circled and was coming back now. This time, instead of leaflets, beer cans with paper streamers attached, fell from the cargo bay. The Navajo watched them float down and when one hit not far from where he was standing he grabbed it. An empty. He smiled at the shallow tactics of the Japanese. It probably would have made more sense for the enemy to drop full cans, scattering their precious contents as they hit. That would have demoralized the men more than the empty cans.

There was something inside the can though and he shook it until a corner of the paper was visible just inside the opening. Pulling it out he unfolded it and saw that it was a message addressed to General Wainwright and addressed to "Your Excellency". Another surrender message. Charlie dropped the beer can and the paper to the ground.

He was tired of it all, and not for the first time did he question his wisdom in coming to the Bataan Peninsula. But he was here now and there was no escaping that fact. His clothing hung loosely from his body, a constant reminder of the fact that, for the first time in his life, he was skinny. Still, he was faring much better than some of the city people. For a while there had been papaya and breadfruit. Now they were all digging for roots and chewing the leaves from the mahogany trees . Even the constant chirping of the night insects, which had kept so many of them from sleeping at first, was dimming as more and more of the starving men gathered up the crusty beetles and crickets for a pathetic meal.

Mosquitoes were everywhere, piercing, sucking, spreading their diseases. There were no mosquito nets to be had. No shelter halves. And the men suffered for it. Struggling on three-eighths rations they were getting weaker all the time. Unable to do even half of the work they had done before Bataan, they grabbed snatches of sleep through the relentless Japanese shelling. They drank contaminated water. Slowly they came to the realization that America was not coming to save them, regardless of the encouragement that their officers gave them.

The soldiers, American and Filipino alike, were prime for the diseases that set in. And they did. Malaria. Scurvy. Vertigo and pounding hearts. Dengue Fever. Beriberi. Pellagra. Hookworms eating into their intestines. Amoebic dysentery. Under normal conditions, most of the soldiers would be declared unfit for combat.

Even on the reservation Charlie had never seen so many sick people in his life. He was weary with the smell of urine and vomit, spittle and shit. The stink of death was everywhere, for men were dropping continually, their pitiful, decaying bodies thrown into hastily dug graves by the few that were able-bodied enough to complete that task in a reasonable amount of time. Still they kept fighting.

Led by their beloved General Jonathan Wainwright, known by Skinny a nickname given to him at West Point, the men followed without question. He seemed to be everywhere at once, praising them, threatening them, talking to them. He thought nothing of sharing his last cigarette with them and more than one farmboy soldier had talked horses with the general. The front lines held no fear for Skinny Wainwright as he walked up and down, giving encouragement to his men. His attention was richly rewarded with unfaltering loyalty from the men he led. They would follow him into hell. And had.

The Bataan Peninsula was pounded daily now. The men did not have to be told that the Japanese were losing face for every day that Bataan held. Taking the peninsula and then Corregidor was vital to controlling Manila Bay. Japanese ships sat off shore waiting for their entrance to be granted and that task was impossible without control of Bataan and the island fortress.

While the trip over from Corregidor was only a short, five minute hop in one of the few remaining PT boats, General MacArthur had not returned to Bataan. Charlie did not need a vision from Changing Woman to tell him why. While rumors raged that Allied help was coming from Australia, Charlie did not believe them. The Americans weren't coming. He knew it. Felt it in his Navajo bones. MacArthur could not come back over and lie to his men again. Rather than tell them the discouraging truth, he stayed on Corregidor.

It hadn't been easy for any of them. Their leader had a new name. Dugout Doug. General Douglas MacArthur. Now immortalized in song. With lyrics sung to the music of the *"Battle Hymn of the Republic"*, his tired starving troops would sing:

> Dougout Doug is ready in his Chris-Craft for
>   the flee,
> O'er bounding billows and the wildly raging
>   sea
> For the Japs are pounding on the gates of old
>   Bataan
> And his troops go starving on.
>
> Dugout Doug MacArthur lies ashaking on the
>   Rock
> Safe from all the bombers and from any sudden
>   shock
> Dugout Doug is eating of the best food in
>   Bataan
> And his troops go starving on.
>
> Dugout Doug's not timid, he's just cautious,
>   not afraid
> He's protecting carefully the stars that
>   Franklin made
> Four star generals are as rare as good food
>   on Bataan
> And his troops go starving on.
>
> We've fought the war the hard way since they
>   said the fight was on

All the way from Lingayen to the hills of old
    Bataan
And we'll continue fighting after Dugout Doug
    is gone
And still go starving on.

Charlie leaned against the mahogany tree and thought of Isabel. She was a good woman, a strong woman, and he knew that her nationality as well as her sex, would offer her some protection in Manila. She had kept her job at the cement factory. They had agreed on that before he left and he knew that she would have enough money to keep her going. If there was one thing the Japanese were going to need, it was cement, for repairs had to be made in the military installations and airstrips. When Manila Bay was finally opened to the Japanese, cement would be needed to repair the bombed piers and docks. No, Isabel's economic future was as secure as one's could be given the circumstances of war.

A group of soldiers from the Thirty-First Regiment were marching into the clearing now. In front of them, hands posed on the top of his head was a young Japanese soldier. He was a straggler from the Battle of the Pockets and the Battle of the Points. The battles had been fought two days earlier and had wiped out the last of two enemy battalions which had landed on the west coast.

The Americans motioned for their prisoner to sit in the middle of the clearing. Dragging with exhaustion the soldiers visibly relaxed once the enemy was seated. They dug into his pack in search of cigarettes, rice cakes, any crumb that might have been left there.

The enemy soldier waited until they were well at ease before slowly drawing his knees up to his chest. As Charlie watched he reached into his shoe and withdrew a long, thin knife. Charlie thought about warning the soldiers but he remained silent, knowing they were in no danger.

Suddenly the prisoner's posture stiffened and without hesitation he drew the knife high in the air before plunging it into his own stomach, twisting and wrenching it about in one fluid motion. Silently he watched with surprise as his insides began to ooze and spill over onto his uniform. The pain must have hit him then for he raised his head in a gesture of training, signifying his head was ready to be taken to avoid the agony. But there was no second there to accommodate him and the only noise of the deed was a soft thump as his body hit the earth, his guts and blood spilling out onto the dry soil.

The soldiers jumped and ran to their prey but it was no use. The man had started dying the minute he had pulled the knife.

Charlie pulled a piece of bark from his pocket and broke it into small pieces. The smallest one he popped into his mouth, chewing it thoughtfully. It was not the first time he had seen the rite of *hara-kiri* performed. Many of the Japanese, once taken, preferred the suicide option to the humility of captivity.

Charlie chewed slowly, trying to retrieve whatever dim flavor the bark held. He did not understand it. There was only pride in this thing. How could one learn by one's mistakes?

19

Lateral Number Three was, as always, a sea of confusion. A naked overhead light bulb cast eery shadows against the concrete walls. Civilians, soldiers, General MacArthur, they were all there, squeezed into a space designed for half as many, hovering over radio sets. And the radio was the hub of the communications lateral. Although it was late morning, many listened to William Winter on San Francisco's KGEI. He was giving a six p.m. newscast, first in English, then in Tagalog.

An intelligence officer, fluent in Japanese, listened to another hookup, monitoring the Japanese air traffic out of Manila. It wasn't much, but it let them know with some degree of accuracy, when bombing missions would hit Corregidor.

Off in a corner, a signal corpsman sat quietly reading serial number after serial number to the United States Treasury Department in Washington. The numbers on his list all corresponded with digits imprinted on the American currency on Corregidor.

At still another desk Carlos Romulo, MacArthur's press aide, sat poring over one of his news broadcasts. Quickly known as the Voice of Freedom, Romulo was on the air three times a day, playing swing music and offering encouraging newscasts to the beleaguered men.

Bark delivered the message that had come in from Kysor Battery. He had not read it. There was no need, for he knew what it said. Night blindness again.

The men, stressed not only with a lack of food, but also with a lack of vitamins, were having trouble picking out enemy airplanes in the dark. The problem, unfortunately, was not peculiar just to Kysor, for all of the gun crews on the coastal batteries were complaining of the same inadequacy.

Tom squatted beside a crate just outside the hospital wing. He was not alone. Men perched on crates and on the floor, waiting for treatment. Bloody dressings attested to their wounds, and stained pants evidenced their dysentery. The tunnel reeked of sweat and excrement.

Water, always short, had been brought over from Bataan in barges. Now the Japanese had hit a water tank on Topside and it had been days without showers or laundry. Even the drinking water stank. Men scratched themselves until their skin was raw, so absorbed were they with the prickly heat.

"Outside?" Bark asked.

Tom nodded and followed his friend through the labyrinth of tunnels to the west entrance. They walked a short way before stopping to share a cigarette. Every smoke they put in their mouths was precious.

"It's pretty grim in there," Tom offered, inhaling deeply on the cigarette.

"Or, as my daddy used to say, it's like making love to a skunk. You ought to stop before it's too late." It was Bark's turn with the butt. "They're opening up another well so we'll be all right by evening." He handed the cigarette back and reached for his harmonica. As they walked he slowly played *"Yankee Doodle"*.

Tom stopped and reached for his arm.

"Bark?"

His response was a longer note than usual as he continued playing.

"I walked out to the cemetery earlier," Tom said. It was on the tail of the island and the two of them had gone there before. Silently they would sit and stare at the rows of graves marked with crude wooden sticks and dog tags. "It's filling up fast."

The smell of smoke caught their attention and they followed the odor. Soldiers stood around a large oil drum, laughing and chatting as black smoke curled from the container. Bark and Tom watched in disbelief as pile after pile of United States currency was fed into the hungry flames.

"Shit." Bark pounded Tom on the back. "Do you believe that?"

Twenties, fifties, hundreds, all were gobbled up by the greedy inferno.

"Things must be getting bad," Tom mused. "That's a lot of money."

"The Filipino money's next," the soldier closest to them offered.

"How much are you guys torching here?" Bark asked.

The soldier shrugged. "Couple of million."

"A couple of million dollars," Bark repeated slowly, "What I could do with a couple of million."

"What *they* could do with a couple of million," Tom corrected.

⚜

The horses hadn't worked for weeks now. Like the men they were weak from malnutrition. As Charlie stroked the tall blood bay he could feel just how close the animal's bones were to his skin. There was no fat on the thoroughbred now.

They had asked him to help out and it was a task he was not looking forward to. They had made the mistake, thinking that because he was an Indian, he knew about horses. Actually he had been on one. Once. He did not think about that this morning for the horses of the Twenty-sixth Cavalry would not be ridden again.

"Good morning."

Charlie turned to face the tall, thin soldier. Grief was etched into his well worn face.

"Is the quartermaster here?"

"He's getting ready, sir." Charlie recognized General Wainwright immediately.

The general stroked the white star on the face of the tall gelding. The horse nuzzled him in recognition and Wainwright buried his face in the familiar brown neck, breathing deeply of the horsey odor there.

"Well, Joseph Conrad, we've seen some good campaigns together, haven't we?" The general's voice was hoarse now as he fought to conquer the emotion he was feeling.

As though he could understand, the bay pushed against his owner.

"You know," Wainwright talked to Charlie, but kept his face away from him so he could not see the tears forming in his eyes, "I brought this horse over here from the States."

Charlie nodded. One of the men from the Twenty-Sixth had already pointed out the general's prized jumper.

"Goodbye, old friend," Wainwright gave the thoroughbred a last pat. "He'll be first," he said tersely to Charlie before walking off.

Joseph Conrad was the first horse of the Twenty-Sixth Cavalry to be killed to feed the starving men on Bataan.

The sun was falling fast in the west as Tom and Bark sat on the steep bank which dropped sharply to the dock below. The earth, once lush and green, now stood scorched and torn, a constant reminder of the toll of the Japanese bombers. Not a blade of grass remained anywhere near the battle ravaged dock.

They had noticed the PT boat moments earlier and they sat wondering where in the hell it had come from. There were a few left over at Sisiman Bay on Bataan, but it had been a long time since they had seen one anywhere near Corregidor. Now they sat waiting to see what purpose the lonely boat would serve.

They didn't have long to wait.

General and Mrs. MacArthur quickly appeared. Young Arthur, clutching a worn stuffed rabbit in one hand and his *amah*'s hand in the other, trailed his parents.

Quickly the crew of the PT-41 helped them on board.

"The rats are leaving the ship," Bark quipped.

Not three weeks earlier, the Quezons and the Sayres had left on the submarine *Swordfish*. The war correspondents had left shortly after that on the inter-island *Princess de Cebu*. Carlos Romulo, rumor had it, had been offered a way out but had refused to take it.

"It looks that way," Tom agreed, fighting the churning in his stomach.

"Shit. He's even taking the kid's nurse," Bark observed. While some of the men on Corregidor revered the general, it was a devotion he did not share.

"They'd probably kill her if she was left behind," Tom offered.

The waves outside the small bay were high now, dangerously high, showing white caps.

"Shitty night anyway for a boat ride," Bark said as he walked back to the tunnel.

Pete licked his lips in anticipation as he crept up on his prey. Raising the rolled magazine high over his head, he crushed the fat, black fly. Carefully scooping it up, he deposited the insect in the tin can he was carrying. Already the can was half full and the contest had just started!

Peter and Doc had both become charter members of the Junior Swat-the-Fly Club. Besieged with the nasty things, the Executive Committee had initiated the Swat-the-Fly contest, putting the children to work at a task that would benefit the entire camp.

"Hey Doc, I got another one!" Pete chortled to his big brother who was intent on filling his own can.

Prizes were going to be awarded to the three youngsters with the most flies.

"Mom!" Pete yelled, "this is really fun. Kind of like hunting for Easter eggs!" touchy about the morality of the camp now. In spite of the heat, they had forbidden the women to wear shorts. Handholding among married couples had also been outlawed.

She reached for the grocery bag string and knotted two short pieces together. She would use the string like yarn, knitting it into a surprise of some sort for the boys.

"You have fine sons," Magda said.

"Thank you."

"And you are handling this very well." The Czech lowered her voice.

"Handle? What choice do I have?" Ellen laughed wryly as she unrolled more string.

"You had servants before the war, yes?"

Ellen nodded.

"I see many of these women in here. They have to learn how to take care of their own babies." Disgust was evident in Magda's voice.

"Well, dear, we all do what we have to do," Ellen said. That their pampered lives had drastically changed had not been lost on her either. Many of the American women, charmed with cooks and *amahs* before the war, were now having to learn how to fend for themselves. There had been a funny story told about a young mother who did not know how to change her son's diaper without sticking him. Unfortunately it was true.

"Besides, it shouldn't be much longer now." Ellen mused. "Help will be here in two or three months." It was an optimism shared by most of them, for with the Americans holding Corregidor and Bataan, help could not be far off.

"I am sorry you have not heard from Tom." Magda said, regretting her words as she saw a dark look pass across the American's face. They heard the daily shelling of the Bataan Peninsula and knew that Corregidor was also under bombardment. "But I want you to know he is all right." She offered it as an afterthought, a consolation for even bringing up the subject.

Ellen's face brightened. "Why do you say that?"

"It is very strange and I do not like to talk about it. But I see things here," Magda touched the middle of her forehead in the area between her two eyes. "He is thin but his health is good."

Ellen smiled. She did not believe in psychic predictions, but still it made her feel good to hear someone say that Tom was well.

"And Kate?"

Magda concentrated for a minute.

"She too is well. She is not far from here. With Sky."

"Hmmm," Ellen knotted some more string as she watched her boys dart back and forth in search of the elusive flies. "And the future, Magda. What is to become of all of us, dear?"

"That is one thing I do not talk about unless I can help. Besides," the redhead shrugged, "the future can change so quickly. It is man's free will."

"And we have little of that in here," Ellen agreed, looking to the fence and the armed guards.

"Mother, look!" Pete came flying across the grass holding his tin can high in the air. Just before reaching them he stumbled and the can flew out of his chubby hands, spilling it's precious contents all over the grass.

"I'll never win the contest now!" He wailed as he stared at his treasures, black dots nestled in the green grass.

"Sssh," Ellen wiped his cheeks with the tips of her fingers, "here, we'll help you."

With Magda's help she began picking up the dead flies and putting them back into the can.

20

"Captain!"

Although it was the dry season, the rain was pounding steadily
.down. Charlie, only yelling to the next foxhole, found his already
weak voice further diluted by the drizzle.

A Zero swept in in the wake of the Mitsubishi that had just
skirted the jungle clearing. Hanging low, the airplane's guns peppered the area. Even in the falling mist Charlie could see a man
not fifty feet away, jerk high into the dense air before collapsing in
a twitching, dying mass. The Zero was pulling up now, in an effort
to gain altitude before making another sweep.

"Captain!"

Still there was no answer.

Dragging his exhausted body from his own foxhole, Charlie
inched along, his belly flattened against the moisture soaked ground.
He edged up to the captain's hole and peered inside.

"We're the battling bastards of Bataan, no momma, no pappa,
no Uncle Sam. "The man was delirious, using all of his strength to
get the words out. "No pills, no planes, and nobody gives a damn."
In his delirium he was scrambling the verses.

"Captain, we've got to get out of here." The bombs had

been falling fast. Their target, one of the few tanks left on Bataan, was in the center of the clearing. Of course, the Japanese had no way of knowing that the tank was out of gasoline and had been immobile for days.

The captain was limp in his foxhole, his glazed eyes staring out beneath his helmet. There was no indication, none at all, that he had heard Charlie. Suddenly his whole body shook and trembled with yet another malaria attack. Even the falling rain did little to dispel the stench emanating from the hole, an all too familiar blend of sweat and the bloody mucus discharge that was passing for diarrhea. The assault on the captain's body, just one more in his month long battle against starvation and amoebic dysentery, had devastated him.

As Charlie looked at the shell of the man who had led him on so many maneuvers, his heart filled with sadness. There was nothing left there. All that remained was a shaking, shriveling piece of humanity who was quaking in the manmade excavation, unable to gather the strength, or the will, to get to safer ground.

The Navajo raised into a squat, his ear straining to hear the rumble of the returning airplanes. Reaching in, he pulled the captain's limp hands over his helmet and reached under his soggy armpits. His face strained with the effort as he half pulled, half dragged the man from the hole. Now afforded the luxury of space, the army captain tumbled over on his side retreating into a fetal position, tucking his knees up high under his chin. This achieved, he closed his eyes again.

Charlie nudged him, but again there was no response. The man was frozen in the neonatal posture. He could hear the planes as he pulled the man into a carrying position. But the weeks of food deficiencies, the days of sharing one can of rations, the fact that the last can, tomatoes, was eaten two days ago and shared with three others, all these things, coupled with his own dysentery, had taken their toll. He no longer had the energy to hoist the emaciated man and carry him to safety.

Pausing only seconds, he grabbed the heels of the captain's leather boots. As he did so, one of them slipped from the man's leg, for he had lost weight even there, and fell into the mud. Ignoring it, the Indian pulled and strained to drag him through the resisting muck.

When he reached the edge of the jungle he continued to drag his human cargo until he was some distance from the clearing. Gasping for breath, Begay was startled as he realized that the great rasping sounds were coming from his own lungs. Exhausted, he fell against an ipils tree, letting his body mold against the trunk as he slithered down it and onto the muddy ground. He closed his eyes for only seconds, listening to the returning bombers. This time they were successful and even from the distance, Charlie could feel the heat of the exploding, useless American tank.

The weakness was frustrating. The last of the two hundred and fifty cavalry horses and mules had been eaten weeks ago. The water buffalo, used to pull the heavy 155 mm guns were long gone. General MacArthur's earlier plan to defend the coastlines was coming back to haunt his men. The quartermaster supplies on the central plain were now either gone or used by the enemy while the Americans and Filipinos trapped on Bataan were starving to death. With the failure of that part of the general's plan, there had been little time for preparation for a long stay on the isolated peninsula.

Charlie closed his eyes again, oblivious to the rain or to the dying man beside him. He tried hard to think of what day it was.

Concentrating and counting days past on his fingertips he determined that it was April 5, 1942. That had to be correct, he thought, remembering that the Japanese had started blasting the frontlines at Mount Samat on the third. Yes, that was right. It had been going on for two days now. How could he have forgotten Good Friday?

On that sacred day, the Japanese had done their heaviest fighting yet. Man to man. The Japanese had proved formidable opponents, screaming and stabbing with their bayonets. Wave after wave of enemy troops had assaulted them, leaving the entire area reeking with the scent of their aggression- cordite, blood, burning flesh.

Familiar pains tore across Charlie's guts as his hands dropped involuntarily to his lower right side. Although he knew his hands would not alleviate the wrenching, he massaged the area even as he felt his body double over with the pain. Stumbling to his feet he dropped his pants just in time to let the poisons exit. He was standing, too weak to assume the classical pose. Finally done, he pulled his muddy trousers up and pulled at the captain, trying unsuccessfully to rouse him into consciousness.

Closing his eyes for a moment as he asked Changing Woman for the strength to do what had to be done, Charlie knelt and finally gathered the frail captain in his arms. He stumbled through the jungle, not daring to think of anything but getting the soldier to the hospital.

The Japanese bombers ignored the white sheets staked out on the hillside identifying the hospital. Frenetic in their hunt for the Americans, they were dropping bombs all around Hospital #1. The hospital had already been moved once from Limay to Little Baguio. The sophisticated operating rooms and facilities left behind had been replaced with a few wooden buildings that had previously lodged motor pool vehicles.

Hospital #1 was where they all came at first. The surgeons were here. Then, if a man made it through, he was moved on to the second hospital. That one was less sophisticated, with its open air wards set under the dense foliage of the mangrove trees. The sky was the roof and canvas tents served as operating rooms in Hospital #2.

Charlie and the captain had made it to the first one. Overflowing to capacity, the men who were able to sit up were slumped against the frame walls, while others were brought in on litters and on their comrade's backs. Bloody bandages hung in tatters from field dressed wounds and wails of the wounded filled the air.

Nurses, their khaki coveralls stained with blood and various other body fluids, scurried back and forth trying to prioritize the constant stream of wounded humanity. Just outside, more men were being cut down by the flying pieces of shrapnel.

Charlie entered the crowded building with the captain draped across his once broad shoulders. He set him gingerly down against a wall in the corridor and hurried after the retreating back of a harried nurse.

"Excuse me," he touched her arm lightly, "I have a friend over there who needs medical attention."

The nurse nodded wearily.

"Yes, they all do."

"If you could just give him a shot or something. Something to get his fever down."

She stopped and faced him.

"Malaria?" It was a good guess, for over seventy percent of the troops on the front lines were suffering from it.

Charlie nodded.

"I'm sorry, there's just nothing left. The quinine ran out days ago. We're even out of cinchona leaves." In the absence of quinine they had turned to the bark of the Filipino tree from which the miracle drug was derived. "I'm afraid he'll just have to do it on his own."

Charlie's heart sank. The captain had regained consciousness now and was mumbling.

"Is there nothing I can do for him?"

"Stay with him. Give him liquids." It was not much to offer, they both knew that. "Oh, we're putting the malaria victims outside now."

Charlie could not blame her. Everywhere he looked there were men in need of attention, their gaping wounds, their blood smears staining the hospital walls where they had slouched against them in an effort to be supported, their glazed eyes and delirious looks and slack, dry, pleading mouths screaming silently for care.

Charlie turned back to the captain. He was stretched out with one of his legs sticking awkwardly into the hallway. People hurried past him, stepping over the offending limb. Charlie pulled him together and cradled him in his arms.

"Mary? Mary, is that you darlin'?" The captain dropped into a Kentucky twang Charlie had never heard him use before, "Oh, I can see your pretty face, it's you, Mary, it really is. Your sweet lips." The soldier's rough fingers were clawing at Charlie's mouth.

"Are the radishes in yet? She didn't mean anything to me, you know that Mary darlin'" The captain was now stroking Charlie's unshaven cheek.

"God you're beautiful. Oh, sweet Jesus!" With one awful shudder, the captain stiffly arched his back and collapsed.

The Navajo bent his head to the man's chest. He could not hear the familiar rasping that had been so much a part of his life over the past weeks. The dead glassy eyes stared accusingly at him. Tenderly, Charlie pulled the lids over the staring blue orbs. He stood, collecting the man in his arms. He walked down the hallway until he found a medical corpsman.

"He must go outside." There was a catch in the Indian's throat. He had to get the captain outdoors, where his spirit could escape.

Without bothering to look at the dead man, the corpsman waved a hand toward the rear of the frame building. "They're all out back. We've been wrapping them in woolen blankets. You can see if there are any out there."

"Will they bury him?" It was important for the Navajo to know that his friend would be taken care of properly.

"Tonight. They don't want the Japanese to know how many casualties we have."

Charlie stepped outside, relieved to be in the rain again, free of the hospital horrors. There, lined up in row after row were the dead. Some were wrapped in the army blankets, many were not. The falling rain fell against their features, frozen in death masks.

Charlie looked for a blanket, but there was none. He walked to the end of the line and put the captain's warm body on the sodden earth. Reaching into his own pocket, the Indian pulled a dirty rag out and smoothed it out the best he could before placing it over the soldier's face. Only then did Charlie Begay shudder with fear.

It was the second time in his life he had ever handled a dead person. The Filipino at Calumpit had been the first. Corpses were something that the Navajo people avoided at all costs. The Sun and the Moon, with their daily demand of a human life, would be happy today, Charlie thought as he looked upon the rows of dead.

Briefly, he wondered if the captain would get a proper burial. He shuddered again. If not the soldier's ghost would return. Charlie shook his head trying to get rid of the Navajo teachings that were harbored there. One thing was for sure.

He would never repeat the dead man's name again.

21

George Bendetti struggled with the 155 mm cannon. There were twelve of them working on it. They were thankful it had been dry for a few days now, for if the rains had continued they would have been unable to move the heavy machinery in the mud. Grunting and pushing with their weakened bodies, the men shoved it a little closer to the edge of the ravine. They stopped, not daring to use energy to talk as they panted and gasped for breath.

George tugged at his shirt collar, bereft of the little silver cross that had rested there. He had removed it earlier in the day. There had been too many calls to give extreme unction, last rites, and he found that it was impeding his progress to Mariveles. Still, even passing as an ordinary soldier, he had been called into service.

"Let's try her again," the balding lieutenant ordered.

They strained and pushed some more, taking care not to get too close to the edge. With a final effort the heavy gun capitulated and went tumbling over the side, giving off sparks as its metal scraped and hit the sharp rock outcroppings on its way down.

"That's one gun those Jap bastards won't get." The lieutenant spat in the mud. "Let's go again."

It was happening all over Bataan. As the enemy came closer and closer, the Allied supplies were being sabotaged and destroyed so they would not fall into Japanese hands.

George waited until he could safely fade from the group. Exhausted and hungry, he joined the hordes of men on the trail leading south to Mariveles. The air was clogged with dust kicked up by the tired men limping and scraping along to the little port town.

Cut off from the rest of Luzon by the approaching Japanese army, they found themselves shoved toward the sea and Mariveles was the last link to Corregidor. Like a taunting Lorelei, the Rock stood three miles off the point of Bataan. Corregidor seemed a refuge to the battle weary men for the Japanese bombardments against the island fortress had slowed considerably while they threw everything they had at the Bataan Peninsula.

The road was jammed with retreating soldiers, buses, trucks, Filipino civilians, and hand pulled carts. Many of the vehicles were stalled and left where they stopped, creating additional barriers to the desperate travelers. A pall of smoke hung over all of them, for the ammunition dumps and supplies had already started to be blown up. Communications were all but gone and there was more than one breakdown in command. The dead were deserted along the side of the road.

Overhead, the Japanese Zeroes ducked and dived, strafing the retreating forces. Squeezed into the mass of exhausted humanity, retreat to the jungle was often impossible.

Bendetti trudged along the side of the roadway consumed with reaching Corregidor. It had to be safer there, he thought. General Jonathan Wainwright had inherited MacArthur's command and had been on the island since the twenty-first of March.

In turn, Major General Edward King was now leading the Bataan troops. Any place that Wainwright was, George figured, had to be safer than Bataan.

As he neared Mariveles, he reattached the cross to his uniform. It couldn't hurt, he thought.

Reaching Corregidor burned in his mind. It was the one thing that kept him going, kept him walking just a little faster than the rest of the weary troops.

※

"Goddamnit," Bark complained, "we can't even fight them." Now that so many American and Filipino troops were grouped on the tip of Bataan, General Wainwright had ordered a cease fire.

Bark was stationed at Battery Hanna and his frustration was shared by many of the gun crews. They could see the heavy pounding the peninsula was taking from the Japanese yet were unable to fight back for fear of hitting their own troops.

Tom studied a hairline crack in the cement ceiling and wondered, for the hundredth time, about the engineering skills that had gone into the planning of the tunnel.

The seductive voice of Tokyo Rose was lilting through their lateral. She was again assuring all of them that General MacArthur was in the custody of the Japanese and would soon face a public execution. The men on Corregidor had already been told that their commander had made it safely to Darwin, Australia. News of his landing speech, including his intention of organizing the American offensive from the island continent as well as his promise to return, had already been duly reported.

"Let's take a walk, Bark," Tom rolled off his dirty cot, "the night air will do you good."

They walked in silence through the tunnel listening to the moans of the injured.

"Come on, I'll show you my place of employment," Bark brightened as they walked into the night air.

Although Battery Hanna was a good walk away, the Japanese were ignoring Corregidor tonight and there was little danger to the island pedestrians.

They walked quietly along the path, dodging pieces of buildings, rocks and trees that had been scattered about during the bombardments. The remnants of Middleside Barracks, once hailed as indestructible, littered the old parade ground, next to the shell of the now evacuated quarters.

They passed Batteries James, Rysor and Rock before coming up on Hanna. At each of the emplacements a few men stood guard, ready in a moment to use their skills should the order be given. Bark pointed out the three-inch guns to Tom.

"They're the babies," he explained, "we got them ranging all the way from this little fellow," he patted the cold tube of one of the two guns, "up to the twelve-inch mortars."

Tom inspected the gun with what he hoped was enthusiasm, but his mind was on the sounds that were carried across the water.

Even from the distance, they could see the fires burning on Bataan. Men were screaming for help, for salvation, and their pleas drifted across the still waters of Manila Bay. The two men stood and silently listened to the comrades they could not help.

A tear rolled down Bark's cheek.

"My drill instructor never told me it was going to be like this," he said helplessly as he broke into sobs.

⤱

Tiny Mariveles was flooded with American and Filipino soldiers. They had all been pushed toward the seaport. There was no place left to go, for Mariveles was on the tip of Bataan. Like lemmings, their next step could only be into the South China Sea.

George Bendetti made his way into the water. There, rocking on the churning water, were two rickety boats. Through the smoke and haze he could see the outline of Corregidor just off the coast.

Making his way to the water's edge, he stopped an armed infantryman. The man's pants were wet from wading back and forth between the boats and the shore.

"I need to get to Corregidor." He fiddled with his insignia hoping to emphasize his clerical position.

"Sure, Father. We all do." The soldier turned away from him and motioned to a nurse who was standing behind him. "Come on sweetheart."

The nurse, one of the few who would be evacuated before nightfall, held her shoes in one hand as she waded into the water.

Bendetti sloshed through the water after them.

"I've got to get out there. I have a message for General Wainwright."

The infantryman helped the nurse into the wooden boat.

"Sure you do." He had heard it all before. Men had been pleading with him all day for one of the precious seats in the small boats.

"Got one more, Pete." He yelled to a man on the shore who motioned to another waiting nurse.

"God, man, you don't understand," Bendetti fumbled in his pocket for money.

The soldier gripped his wrist and looked him in the eye.

"Oh but I do, Father." He gave the priest a rough shove before returning to the beach.

Bendetti looked at the occupants of the boat as the five women averted their eyes. He looked to the other waiting boat. It was half filled. Wading through the waist high water he half swam, half walked toward it. Its bow was pointed toward Corregidor and a soldier sat in the stern, his Garand rifle resting across his knees. When he saw the priest, he cradled the gun in his upper arms. It was not the first time he had been approached today either.

"I have to get to Corregidor. I have a message for the general," he tried his spiel again.

"Last I heard we still had radio communications." The soldier's skepticism was apparent. "Let me see your papers."

It was useless. The boat was sitting too high in the water to offer any hope of getting the gun away from the man. The priest turned back to the beach.

Just as he reached the hard packed sand, a group of Zeroes came over, flying in perfect V formation as they peeled off their pattern to strafe the beach. Bendetti dove for the sand, feeling the earth vibrate underneath him as the plane's missiles hit all around. There were cries and confusion as people, caught in the open, tried to figure out which way to run. The planes were circling and they came in again. George buried his face in the coarse sand feeling it invade his eyes and mouth. He rolled to one side and squinted. He was comforted by the fact that both boats were still sitting on the water.

The armed man who had been guarding the first boat was now slumped heavily into the wet sand, just yards from Bendetti. Moving quickly he rolled over to the wounded soldier. A gaping black hole was pumping blood down the back of the man's neck.

The priest rolled him over, ignoring the pleading eyes that stared at him from the soldier's speechless face. He wrenched the rifle out of the soldier's arms, an easy task, for the man's strength was ebbing as his life forces stained the damp sand.

He waited a minute longer to make sure the Japanese were not returning. Then he stood, taking advantage of the confusion, and walked once again to the water's edge. He was trying to be casual, as he backed into the water, his eyes darting here and there to make sure that his theft had gone unnoticed. But the man who had been helping the Bataan nurses had spotted him.

"Hey you! Father, you can't go out there."

George held the rifle straight out from his waist as he backed into the water, not bothering to answer. As the soldier began advancing on him, he raised the gun swinging it in the man's direction. It was enough to freeze the soldier in position.

Charlie had helped the last nurse into the boat and was heading back to shore. The man walking backwards into the sea caught his interest. There was something vaguely familiar about him.

"Don't do it!" The soldier's attention was still riveted to the priest. "You'll never make it."

Bendetti ignored him, as he continued his backward retreat. Suddenly the rifle flew out of his hands as a heavy force hit him hard from behind. Half turning, the priest's hands became talons, clawing out for his attacker's face, as he was dragged beneath the water.

He gathered his feet and shoved off his attacker's leg shooting to the surface. He gasped for breath just as he was pulled under again, salt water stinging his open eyes. Sand churned all around them now, thrown up by their struggle, making visibility impossible. He could only see a dim outline of the man who had hit him from behind.

He lashed out again with his legs, trying to hit the other man's groin but the pressure of the water deflected his blow. A powerful hand clamped down on his shoulder and before he could stop it he was spun around, his arm twisted painfully high above his back. The man from behind gripped him hard around the back of his neck and wrenched his body half out of the water. Bendetti gasped and sputtered spitting the salt water out of his bruised mouth.

Charlie grunted with exhaustion and pushed the priest to the water's edge where the infantryman stood waiting for them. The Indian shoved his captive hard onto the packed sand. As the priest came to his feet, recognition crossed his face.

"You!" All of the hatred and venom he harbored for the Navajo came out in the one word.

Before Charlie could speak, the soldier stepped forward and with one solid punch knocked the priest out.

⚓

The men were strewn out everywhere near Mariveles. Many of them clutched white flags fashioned out of filthy handkerchiefs, pieces of sailors' uniforms, used dressings. It was as chilly as it was going to get at six a.m. and the men huddled together for companionship more than for warmth.

That the end was near had been the main topic of conversation for days, yet now that the inevitability was close at hand, few words were given to it. Instead, the troops talked about food, and home, and the effects of an earthquake that had hit the peninsula earlier that morning.

There was a lot of speculation as to whether the Japanese would take them prisoner at all. The few officers who had studied the subject, the ancient Japanese code of *Bushido*, were reluctant to discuss it, although it was known by all of them that the enemy thought little of surrender.

General MacArthur had sent a radiogram to General Wainwright stating his opposition to any type of surrender. He had also ordered them to execute an attack against the enemy, a suicide mission at best. An attack by the wounded, sick, starving men could only result in their own annihilation. Attrition, from wounds, illness, starvation, had already taken close to ten thousand troops.

General King, now in charge of the troops on Bataan, ignored the orders to attack. He had left his men, under the protection of a white flag, to meet with General Masaharu Homma, the Japanese officer who had so doggedly pursued the Americans into Bataan. And King's starved, diseased, crippled troops now waited in the early morning hours to hear the results of that meeting.

Two hours later, the word spread that General Homma had not met with the Americans. Colonel Motoo Nakayama, a senior operations officer for Homma, had served as his emissary, demanding an unconditional surrender. After assuring the Americans that his countrymen were not barbarians, he had taken General King prisoner, while letting the American aides return to their own lines.

Charlie Begay sat along the Mariveles road quietly praying. He was not alone.

Bark was on his gun, his right foot twitching, eager to hit the trigger should the signal be given. It was impossible though, he knew from the sounds drifting across the water. There was no way the three-inch guns could be fired at the enemy without hitting the American and Filipino troops. Unhindered, the Japanese had already started placing their 75 mm guns on the beach at

Cabcaben. Soon they would be able to reach Corregidor.

Dusk was falling and Bark squinted in the dimming light, mesmerized by the sight and sounds of the exploding ammunition dumps just across the water. Even from the distance he could make out the flashing S.O.S. signals on the peninsula.

Tom sat on a wall near the gun. Silently he held out a cigarette to Bark. It was a kind of grim ritual, this taking of two separate cigarettes instead of sharing them as they had in the past.

"Romulo's gone," Tom said.

"Good. I hope the poor bastard makes it. His life won't be worth much if they catch him."

"No," Tom agreed. He cocked his ear, straining to catch specific sounds from Bataan. "Tell me something, Bark. Is it worth it?"

"Bataan?"

Sullivan nodded.

"You bet your ass it is." Bark took a long, deep drag on the cigarette. "They've held those bastards at bay for more than three months now."

"But why?" Tom was tired. He was an engineer, not a military man.

"Look at it this way, they've kept the Nips out of somebody else's hair. Those tanks and troops and guns could have been in Arizona by now."

"Or Oklahoma."

"Or Oklahoma. And I'll tell you another thing. King's all right in my book," he spat on the cement beside the gun. "Those sons-a-bitches behind desks don't know anything about what's really happening out here. It's not the war game they think it is."

"No, I guess not," Tom agreed.

"One thing's for sure, my friend," Bark stood and stretched in the darkness.

"What's that?"

"Them rules we've all been taught are all over now."

✦

Longoskawagan Point was a madhouse. The men, fully aware that the Japanese troops were approaching, panicked. The beach was littered with clothing, duffel bags, and weapons, as men stripped and raced into the water in a desperate quest for Corregidor. They had made the choice of the long swim, over surrender.

Some made it. Most did not, falling prey to their own exhaustion and to hungry sharks. The Japanese thwarted the planned escape of many of their anticipated prisoners as they bombed and strafed the bay.

With the cession of the seventy-five thousand Battling Bastards of Bataan, General Edward King had effected the largest surrender of troops in American history.

SURRENDERED LIVES

22

Ellen's sore shoulder was testament to the fact that her Leica was still safe, secure in the custom made case that a Manila camera shop had designed for Tom over a year ago.

The box, large and square, resembled an overnight bag and because of that similarity it had escaped inspection months ago when they entered Santo Tomas.

Even then food had been the uppermost thought on everyone's mind. Three days after they had been interned the Japanese had posted a sign on the main building- "INTERNEES IN THIS CAMP SHALL BE RESPONSIBLE FOR FEEDING THEMSELVES." With that caveat, the camp authorities had seemingly refused to take responsibility for feeding their charges.

Confined behind walls, without food or money, the internees had been struck with the helplessness of their situation.

Providing food for the camp had fallen to the Philippine Red Cross. While many of the foreign Red Cross officials had been interned, their Philippine counterparts were still free, and willing to find food for the more than three thousand internees.

Although a vegetable garden had been planted in mid-February, the fruits of that labor were just now beginning to be seen. There had been cause for rejoicing, when the first nine basketfuls of talinum, a leafy spinachlike vegetable, had been harvested just last week. The bounty, however, had only been sufficient for the hospital patients.

Ellen had heard stories from the men on the garden committee. Working in the middle of the warmest season, the workers had quickly become exhausted. Water had to be hauled large distances twice a day to nurture the struggling plants. No, she thought, it would be some time before the fruits of the garden would be enjoyed by all of them.

In the meantime she was doing all she could to trade with the Japanese guards for food. They were all doing it. Scraping together what little they had, in the hope it could be exchanged for something edible. Her jewelry was still hidden and for now she thought the camera, bulky and expensive, was her best barter choice.

She walked nervously to the bamboo watchtower at the back of the camp. The guard at the base she recognized from morning roll call. Relieved to see that it was Tejiro, and not the sadistic Lieutenant Abiko, she approached him. Even this was risky business, she knew, for many of the guards would take the offered goods without return payment.

Pulling the Leica out of the bag, she pantomimed her desire to part with it. Tejiro took the camera and shook it once before inspecting it. Although there was film inside, Ellen did not even think of its exposure. Soon, hopefully, the film, along with the camera, would belong to Ajiro. Without opening the camera, the guard nodded his approval. Ellen waited. He went inside the shack and returned with a small sack of rice.

She held her breath and shook her head. The camera was worth hundreds of dollars and she had hoped for more. Tejiro disappeared inside and added six cans of food to the rice. Ellen handed him the camera case and, balancing the cans on top of the rice, wondered all the way back to the women's dormitory where she would hide it.

☙

The fine, powdered dust was everywhere, there was no escaping it. The town of Mariveles, was jammed with soldiers of both sides, tanks, trucks, cars, buses, all stirring the dust and creating a huge brown cloud that hovered over the tiny town. The gritty powder that settled on everything and everyone only added to the hideous occasion.

Confusion reigned, as neither the Japanese nor the Americans knew what was going on. Men marched back and forth, poked, prodded, stole from one another, but still there seemed to be no master plan.

In fact there was one.

It had been complicated by the numbers that General King had surrendered. General Homma wanted his prisoners off the Bataan Peninsula as quickly as possible. He had planned on taking the captured troops to Camp O'Donnell, an unfinished American airfield that would serve as a POW camp, over sixty miles away.

The plan called for the men to walk from Mariveles to the rail line at San Fernando, and from there they would be freighted to the camp. The problem had come when Homma realized that the anticipated forty thousand prisoners was, in fact, nearly twice as many. While the Japanese troops had had the benefit of steady rations and medical supplies, the Americans and Filipinos had not. Exhausted, sick, beaten, many without shoes, they were in no shape to conform to the Japanese general's plan.

The steel tip of the bayonet poked harshly against Charlie's ribs, catching his immediate attention. A Japanese lieutenant jabbed him hard again and motioned for him to get up. Standing directly behind the infantryman was a little cadre of Americans, and he barked loud staccato orders at them in Japanese. When it became obvious they did not understand him, he motioned to a corral beside the road.

Begay led the group through the gate and into the confines of the corral. Two more enemy soldiers joined them, as the lieutenant motioned for his prisoners to strip.

Charlie began unbuttoning his shirt. A young signal corpsman, no more than nineteen stood next to him, and although they were not touching, the Navajo could feel the boy's trembling. He was rooted to the spot, too terrified to move.

"Take your clothes off," Begay whispered.

The whisper had been caught by the lieutenant and his rifle butt came crashing into Charlie's midsection as the Navajo crumpled in the dust. The enemy soldier gave him a swift kick in the side, and the Indian felt one of his ribs sag with the weight of the boot. Quickly realizing he was an easy prey as long as he remained on the ground, Charlie scrambled to his feet and began undressing. The signal corpsman was now almost nude.

The Japanese worked quickly. They emptied the pockets of the fallen trousers, taking what appealed to them. They stripped the wrists and fingers of the men, wrenching off wedding rings and wristwatches. Within minutes, Charlie's knife was taken. In one of the pockets of a dusty shirt they found a package of Japanese cigarettes.

The lieutenant turned in rage to the man whose shirt he held. Sputtering rapidly in Japanese, he slapped the man hard twice across his face before shoving him against the wooden fence. He feigned walking away from the terrified prisoner and then suddenly spun back driving the bayonet hard into the man's belly, slicing and ripping it up like a ripe watermelon. The American soldier, stared in disbelief, as his body followed his innards onto the dry ground.

Charlie was aware that the boy next to him had just wet himself.

Content that their countrymen had thus been avenged, and that there was nothing left to steal, the soldiers abruptly left the corral, leaving their naked prisoners alone in the dust.

The men silently dressed, averting their eyes from the unlucky American lying next to the wooden fence.

"Thanks mister," the boy held out his thin hand. "Tennessee Parker, 228th Signal Operations. You just saved my life."

Charlie nodded as he looked into the boy's innocent blue eyes.

"I can't believe they did that over a pack of lousy cigarettes." Parker pointed in the direction of the dead man.

"They kind of figure how he got 'em," a sergeant offered.

The men were standing in a circle, their mutual experience creating an unwanted fraternity, unsure of how to continue.

"Where do we go from here?" The sergeant turned to Charlie.

He shrugged. "They've been heading them up the road. Maybe if we start walking we can do it alone." He had already seen groups leave Mariveles, some were accompanied by the Japanese soldiers, some were not.

They began walking through the dust shrouded town. All Americans. All, save Charlie, soldiers. That natural division would cause them little suspicion, for the Japanese were separating the soldiers from the civilians.

They had not gone more than a half a mile, when a Japanese soldier stepped in front of them. He prodded them over to a group that was standing by the side of the road.

"You wait here," he said in broken English.

"What's going on?" Parker asked an Army major whose insignia ranked him the highest officer in the group.

"You got any water?" The major stood.

The boy shook his head. "They took my canteen the first time."

The major looked to the rest of his new arrivals. "How about the rest of you?"

Charlie nodded. His canteen was half full. He had been looking for an opportunity to fill it all morning. Several of the others still had their canteens, but they were empty.

"It's going to be a long walk," the major said, sitting back down alongside the road.

The Japanese soldier returned. "You go. Now." He pointed his rifle north. The men stood, and he poked them and prodded them until they were in a rough formation, in lines of four abreast. "Soldiers watch you." He warned.

The men moved out. They were in luck, for a Japanese guard was not going with them. All morning and for the next several days the scene would be repeated, as Americans and Filipinos were set on the move in groups ranging from fifty to one hundred. The military would all be thrown together- airmen, Filipino Scouts, cooks, infantrymen, the officer and the private- all would be ordered up the road on the long walk to San Fernando.

Some would be accompanied by anywhere from one to four guards, some would go alone. The sick, the wounded, the crippled and the weak, all hungry, would be ordered up the road. There were no exceptions.

They were just out of Mariveles, when they noticed a group of excited Japanese soldiers grouped around a Japanese man who, judging by the American fatigues he now wore, had been one of the few Allied prisoners. As the Americans walked by, the soldiers placed the man against a tree and three of them raised their guns, shooting him again and again, even as his tortured body jerked and twisted against the bark of the mango tree.

"Jesus!" Parker whispered loudly, but still quietly so the enemy could not hear him. "Why in the hell did they do that?"

The major's eyes were on the road ahead. "They don't believe in prisoners. The code of the Samurai says it is honorable to die in battle. That failing, one must commit *hara-kiri*."

"Jesus!" Parker repeated, his blue eyes quickly losing their innocence.

"Their families don't get paid if they're taken prisoner. If they kill themselves, the family gets some kind of pension."

It was only one of the major cultural differences which would make the Bataan Death March a hell on earth, for the Japanese were eager to show their contempt for those who surrendered.

"Major!" A cook had broken their formation and had come to the head of the column. "It's Fred, sir, he's having a hard time."

The group continued walking, as the major went to the rear. The man called Fred, supported by two thin men looked up, aware that his commanding officer was there.

"Sir," it came out like a hiss, issued as it was between teeth gritted in pain. The man's right pant's leg was tattered and bloody, and pieces of his flesh dangled from his leg, sticking out here and there through the torn trousers. Blood oozed from his knee and dribbled weakly onto the dust.

The major reached for him, pulling his left arm up and around his own neck. "Give me a hand with him," he ordered the other man who supported his other side. Lagging with the extra weight, the men slowly made their way to the head of the column.

"We'll do it this way," the major said. "Anyone who is physically unable to walk will come to the front of the columns. We'll support them as long as we're able to and then pass them back through. That way the burden will be shared."

"Sorry, sir," the man hissed again.

"Save your strength, soldier."

They walked and walked. Those with water would sip slowly, ever so slowly, from their canteens, offering a drink to those without. The sun beat down on them unmercifully, blistering their skin, pickling their brains. Many of them were shoeless, and their feet, far from being toughened, were blistered and aching, as they poured their concentration into putting one raw foot ahead of the next.

As they passed through a small farming settlement, they saw a well to one side of the road. The major pulled his group up and indicated to a soldier guarding the water that they would like to fill their canteens from the artesian spring. The guard sneered at them, displaying his yellowed, decaying teeth. Pointing his bayonet at their leader, his intent was clear. There would be no water for them from that well.

They walked on, exhausted but afraid of stopping for fear they could not continue. Fred was in the rear again, having been passed through the group for the first time. Spread out now, the weaker soldiers had fallen behind.

"I think if I had a helmet, it wouldn't be so hot," Tennessee said, offering his first conversation in over an hour. "Doesn't it bother you?" He turned to the Navajo. They were both still in the front of the column.

"Try not to think about it," Charlie suggested.

"Still, if I only had a hat," Parker mused. Many of them were without hats, and water bubbles were popping up on their cheeks, noses and foreheads. Sun poisoning would not be far behind.

The heat was taking its toll. Those who passed out from heat prostration, or were too weak to continue, were left with what little water could be spared, sitting in the shade with the hope, however ridiculous, that medical help would be on the way.

Fred was back up front again, struggling along on his shattered leg, trying hard not to lean too heavily against those who supported him. He should have been left behind miles ago, but as long as he kept struggling, kept trying to march, they continued to help him. His will to live was an inspiration to all of them.

They were passing up stragglers from the groups that had set out ahead of them. The dead and dying were littering the sides of the road, and yet the group marched on, knowing that any one of them could be next. When they had gone about six miles, they overtook a group that was under Japanese guard. It was the end of their unescorted journey, that much was made clear when the guards motioned that they were not to continue on without them.

They moved into a clearing and fell down, exhausted. There was no water left in any of the canteens and their tongues were thick and fuzzy from thirst. The guard lounged against a large wooden box, with a spigot sticking out of it, steadily dripping clear artesian spring water. The Americans licked their swollen, crusted lips in anticipation of the water.

The major asked the guard for permission to drink. Before answering, the Japanese soldier played with the faucet, increasing the volume of water coming out of it. He splashed his face with the fresh artesian water and then offered a drink to the major. The American drank thirstily from the offered liquid.

Slowly he straightened and held up a hand to his men. The guard grabbed his hand in mid-air and shook his head, pointing with his free hand to a stream just beyond the well.

The water was green and murky, and even from the distance the major could see the dead Filipino bodies, bloated and blackened from the cruel sun, floating there. He tried to argue with the guard but the Japanese would have none of it, jamming his rifle butt hard into the major's stomach, now engorged with water.

He returned to his men.

"I guess it's the stream."

The men stampeded for the polluted water. Dropping to their hands and knees, they drank greedily from the stream hosting the dead. The relief from thirst would soon be replaced with dysentery for the few who did not yet have it.

They drank their fill. Canteens were filled to the brim with the brackish water.

"Charlie, look." Parker's voice was low as he showed the Indian a helmet he had retrieved from one of the dead men in the water. As he rolled it over, a swarm of maggots squirmed as the sunlight hit them. "Of course I've got to clean it up a little," he said.

They were ordered to sit in the clearing in the hot sun. As they waited, they watched other tired, thirsty groups march by.

Occasionally, a truck bearing Japanese troops would come through and they watched the soldiers lash out with their rifle butts, hitting the heads of the marching American prisoners. Some wore steel helmets, many did not. Even with the helmets, sometimes the blows were hard enough to send the victims rolling in pain on the ground. Charlie made a mental note to try to stay in the center of the column to lesson his chance of a casual attack.

The suffocating dust was worse now, aggravated by the increasing traffic. The guard stood, wrapping a dirty handkerchief over the lower part of his face. They fell into their familiar four columns and wearily headed north again.

But their pace was not good enough for their escort. Poking and prodding the major, he indicated that they were to do double time. Somehow they managed it. The pace continued, mercifully, for only a short distance for it finally occurred to the guard that he, too, was too tired to keep up the rapid trot.

They passed Cabcaben and Charlie saw that the Japanese had completed their military entrenchments. The guns there were firing at Corregidor, secure in the knowledge that those on the island would not return the fire for fear of hitting their own soldiers.

Night was falling, creating visibility problems in the dust.

"Shit!" Tennessee had moved to the outside of the column and now, for the second time since the sun had set, he had run into another road marker. The concrete posts, marking the distance from Manila, were on the side of the road, and in the dim light they were almost impossible to detect.

They passed other groups sitting in clearings or caged in corrals, but their exhaustion and fear was such that they did not exchange information with each other. There was no need. They were in hell and they all knew it.

Charlie followed the rest of his group into the tiny school

house. By the time he was herded into the second, and last, room it was apparent to him that the structure was much too small to support the hundred or so men that the Japanese guard was cramming in.

But still they came. Charlie edged as close to the wall as he could, but still the sweaty, smelling bodies pressed against him. He could feel a man's breath on his neck. He fidgeted trying to get more space.

The men sat down. There were too many of them to allow any kind of sleeping position. There was no room to lie down, and finally Charlie pulled his knees up to his chest and rested his tired head on top of them.

Just before falling off to sleep, he remembered that he, like most of the others, had not eaten a thing that day.

23

At first light, the schoolhouse door was opened and the men stumbled out into the bright sunlight. The Japanese guard, rested from his night outside, prodded them back onto the road.

The day stretched out as the water from the stream of the dead had caught up with most of them and they were all dysenteric. They relieved themselves as they walked, pulling their pants down if they had the chance. After the first few times, the horror of what they were doing soon passed and they relegated themselves into that animal state that follows instinct.

Their morning walk was punctuated with occasional shots from behind them. It had not taken them long to figure out that the Japanese were killing those too weak to continue. The road, littered with the shot and bayonetted bodies who had faltered, offered constant encouragement to keep walking.

They walked for a few kilometers, when the rumbling of yet another Japanese troop transport was heard. They split into columns of two, hugging the side of the road, so the vehicle could pass. A large Japanese soldier, carrying a long, black snake whip, sat on the tailgate of the truck.

As he passed, he lashed out with the weapon, its wicked leather catching an MP, unfortunate enough to be in the front of one of the columns.

The American struggled and clawed at the burning leather and even as he did so, his pace quickened, as he realized that he was being pulled along by the truck.

The Japanese laughed heartily as he pulled his prey along; the soldier's eyes grew wide as his oxygen supply shortened. The American stumbled, then fell, in the dust. Charlie watched as the man was dragged along. Finally the truck stopped and, given the slack, the Japanese soldier was able to flick and twist and unwind the whip from the MP's neck.

Charlie wanted to run to the fallen soldier and offer him aid, but he was just too tired. His muscles burned and twitched. It took every effort to just plod one foot after the other and he was simply not up to it. They would reach the fallen American in time.

The man's body was twisted into a distorted position and, even before they reached him Charlie knew he was dead. Without stopping, the men walked around him following the road out of Bataan.

They passed a group of their own soldiers, hands on top of their heads, as they posed next to a piece of American artillery. The Japanese guards, at the suggestion of the *Domei* news service cameraman, positioned and posed the prisoners for a propaganda film.

"Watch out!" Begay grabbed Parker. Just as he pulled him to one side, a large metal pipe swooped across the column, knocking three men into the dust.

A cheer came from a cadre of Japanese soldiers resting in the shade of a tree. For sport, they had tied the heavy pipe onto a branch taking turns swinging the metal into the columns of exhausted prisoners.

Charlie helped one of the felled Americans to his feet. An ugly welt from the impact of the pipe was already beginning to swell his cheek.

"Lousy bastards," the soldier's fingers explored his injured face.

"Save your strength," Charlie turned him toward the head of the column. "Get your revenge. Live."

As they passed Hospital #2, just fifty yards off the road, the wounded and dying were lying on cots, too weak to sit up and watch their fellow soldiers march by.

The columns split again as another tank came upon them. A patient, struggling on crutches and disoriented, stumbled out of the protection of the mangrove. Barefoot and clad only in a long shirt, he stumbled into a guard who reached out and held him by one thin elbow. The patient's eyes were glazed. He had no idea where he was.

The tank grew closer. Just before it reached the guard, he slammed the patient out into the cobblestoned road. As he rolled onto his side, the marching Americans could see that his skin had been peeled off by his skidding across the stones on his face.

The tank was very close to the fallen man now and suddenly, awareness crossed his bleeding features. Without his crutches he was lost. He tried to crawl away from the tank even as the tracks effortlessly rolled over him, imprinting his body into the cobblestones.

"Fucking bastard!" Parker sagged against Charlie's side, sobbing. The Navajo, exerting strength he did not think he had, pulled the boy in close to him, offering what little comfort he could.

The guard, ignoring the man he had just murdered, motioned for them to move out again. The group walked in silence passed the flattened body.

Time and again they passed groups that were standing at attention in the grueling sun. There was no sense to it at all. The

Japanese would line them up and make them sit. For hours. It was, Charlie thought, just another way of making the Americans suffer for their heinous crime of surrender.

The major's group marched on. It was growing smaller now. Many of the men who had started at the head of the columns, had now been passed back and the men in the rear, as weak and exhausted as any of them, were leaving more and more soldiers by the side of the road. Miraculously, Fred, with his mangled leg and will to live, kept hobbling on, doing the best he could and trying hard not to drain the strength of his comrades.

They walked all day, sustained only by what little water they carried that was left from the stream of the dead.

Finally, at dusk, the guard herded them into a corral at Lubao, although there were other men already confined there. The pen was small, no where large enough for the over three hundred men it now held.

The corral, with its three strands of barbed wire for confinement, had been used before by the groups ahead of them. Now, in addition to the manure from the cattle, human excrement and vomit was everywhere. As they walked into the pen, the human and animal wastes came up over their feet and ankles.

They were lucky. The groups that followed them, that would use the same pen on the sixth or seventh day, would have the muck halfway to their knees.

The flies and maggots were everywhere, their greedy little mouths constantly working. There was no sense in trying to brush them away. The effort took too much strength and there were too many of them.

Charlie and Tennessee made it to the edge of the pen. While there was no more room there, at least they could look out. Lying down, even if any of them wanted to in the filth, was again out of the question. They stood, sleeping on their feet, listening to their fellow travelers groan and struggle to make it through the night.

By morning, three more were dead. Two had fallen in the muck, face down, and whether or not they had just died or had drowned in the filthy mixture, no one knew. The third man was draped across the barbed wire, eyes glassed, looking out toward the freedom that had escaped him.

The third day wore on, and got hotter as they turned inland. Images began to burn in Charlie Begay's brain. They were licking their own sweaty skins now. Anything for moisture. Finally thousands of men were allowed to line up at an artesian well and fill their canteens from the slow drip, drip, drip coming out of the narrow rusted pipe. His group had waited in the sun for over four hours before they were done and ready to move on. Not one man complained, for they had learned to cherish the times they were allowed to drink. Too many times they had seen thirsty men shot, or bayoneted, as they broke rank and ran for water.

The Japanese guards had their own rations and were unconcerned about feeding their captives. The starving prisoners passed the swamps of Orion with its healthy green rice stalks waiting to be harvested.

Death was common. Slain Americans propped up against trees, cigarettes dangling from their mouths, dead fish eyes staring at the passing travelers. Grim reminders that the Bataan march was a game to their Japanese captors. A deadly game. The road was littered with personal possessions as the thirsty, hot men dumped everything they could in an effort to lighten their loads.

Their hunger pangs had all but dissipated, for many of them had been without food for a week now. When the priorities were sifted through, water came out on top. The hot sun created that craving, as well as one for salt. Few had the energy any more to discuss food, or to talk much at all, for every ounce of their strength was centered on survival. On walking. On making it to wherever the Japanese were taking them. On doing what they had to in order to live.

On the fourth day, they stumbled into Balanga in the midst of thick dust. They had passed many flattened bodies on their march, and now many of them did not exert the strength to walk around them. It was better not to think about it. To walk over the figures that bore little resemblance any more to human beings.

Charlie trudged on. He looked down. There, just ahead of him, was the flattened form of a man, pounded very, very thin by the tanks and trucks and troops that had passed over him. His very essence had now become part of the cobblestones. The Indian was struck by the form of the man for one of his hands was stretched over what had been his head, reaching for something. Deliverance? Charlie made the effort to walk around him.

A little further was another flattened form. This one was drawn up into the fetal position and had either been a very small man or a Filipino child. He walked around this one too.

"They're going to feed us," Parker's voice cracked. "Rice."

They marched into a pasture, which, in spite of the dry weather, was wet and slimy with the human wastes of the thousands of prisoners who had already passed through. They sloshed through the filth and formed a line.

Japanese soldiers stood over a rusted gasoline drum, stirring the boiling rice.

Tennessee Parker, following the lead of the man in front of him, held out his two hands while a Japanese officer ladled the steaming rice into them.

"Yeow!" The hot rice caused the signal corpsman to jerk his hands apart and now some of the precious grains had fallen to the soggy ground.

Parker bent to retrieve the fallen rice from the slop. An enemy soldier, his rifle butt aimed at the boy's head, stepped forward just as Charlie grabbed Parker and pulled him to his feet. The jerking motion caused Tennessee to spill an entire handful of rice.

"Goddamn you!" The boy's eyes turned to animal fury. Tears welled in his tired blue eyes. Charlie gently pushed him to the other side of the drum as he held out his own hands for his meager share of the rice.

A Filipino stood off to one side, dribbling salt over the rice as the prisoners passed by. Charlie again got his share before he went looking for Tennessee.

He was sitting on the side of the road, staring at his one full hand and crying softly. Charlie sat next to him. Wordlessly he reached for the boy's right hand and carefully dribbled the rice from one of his hand's into the boy's own.

Parker looked at him in amazement, tears and snot mingling and running together down his cheeks. He didn't have a free hand now to stop them.

"No," he shook his right hand gently, fearful of spilling still more rice. "It's yours. You take it." He held out his hand to Begay.

The Navajo shook his head. "I do not need it." He carefully took a few grains into his mouth, savoring the taste of each one.

"I'm sorry," the boy was really blubbering now. "The guys told me you saved me from getting my head bashed in. I didn't see him."

The Navajo watched some of the troops plod by, raising dust that covered them as they marched past.

"Forget it."

They finished their meal in silence and then it was time to walk again.

Shortly after noon they passed through another Filipino settlement. The natives lined the streets sadly staring at the defeated soldiers. The Americans had been in the Philippines for a long time. Many had married into Filipino families, and all along the march the Filipinos had tried to help where they could. Sips of water, rice wrapped in banana leaves and crude sugar rolled into hard little balls were passed or thrown to the prisoners as they walked by. And when they had no food, they offered encouragement by crossing themselves and praying as the groups marched by.

It was a deadly charity for, when caught, the Filipinos found themselves at the wrong end of the Japanese bayonets.

Fred was at the front of the line again, sandwiched between Parker and Charlie. The blood soaked rag around his leg was green now with the infection leaking out of his body. His leg was swollen three times its normal size and the soldier could hardly walk. He had quit talking the day before.

"He's going," Parker's voice was hardly a whisper.

"I know," Charlie looked back over his shoulder. There were no guards there now but he could see the rising dust of a group not far behind them.

A stout Filipina, her long skirt dragging the ground, clucked to them. Charlie hesitated only a moment, before dragging the wounded Fred to the side of the road.

Silently the woman hiked her hem to her plump hips and Charlie shoved the feverish American in next to her heavy legs. Quickly the woman dropped and adjusted her skirts, the soldier invisible now.

Parker and Begay returned to their columns.

"How long will she have to stand there?" Tennessee asked.

"Who knows?" They had and seen the Filipino women perform the magic act before. "At least he has a chance there."

They were into the river country now, and that sapped their drained energies even more. The American engineers had done a good job going into Bataan and they had blown bridge after bridge. While the Japanese were in the process of repairing the blown structures, frequently the prisoners had to slip and slide down the banks and scramble up the other, rugged sides. Men were lost, unable to navigate the challenge of anything other than the now familiar cobblestoned road. One saving grace was the rivers were now shallow and tame thanks to the dry season.

It was late afternoon and there had been no water since noon. The men, even those lucky enough to be suffering only from malnutrition and dysentery, were staggering and stumbling. Shots from behind were common, a grisly signal of the day's toll.

The Japanese guard held up his hand. He pointed to a carabao wallow off to the side of the road. The men stampeded, stumbling and falling against one another in an effort to reach the brackish water. They dropped to their hands and knees in the slimy manure and gorged themselves on the green scum.

Something caught Charlie's ear and he tugged on Parker's sleeve.

"Get up."

They faded into a small group standing some distance from the green slime just as a Japanese officer lifted his Arisaka and, without a warning, fired the heavy rifle into the group of drinking men. Bodies slumped and fell in the wallow as men scrambled to get away from the gunfire.

It was over in seconds, as the angry officer emptied his clip into the mud hole. He walked to the guard who had allowed them to drink and slapped his face hard. Clearly there had been a difference of opinion.

They hit the road again. The trucks were coming faster now and it seemed as though every few minutes they were stepping aside for the vehicles to pass. It had slowed their already laggard journey. The dust hung like a thick brown cloud over all of them.

Suddenly, stirred by a slight breeze, the dust became even thicker, its grit getting into their ears, eyes and mouths even as they turned their backs on it. The back of the truck that had just passed was invisible. Out of his squinted eyes Charlie was dimly aware that the Japanese guard had crossed to the far side of the road to avoid the swirling soil.

Everyone froze. Movement was impossible for visibility was nil. The dust invaded all of them.

Charlie groped through the dusty fog for Parker. Feeling what he thought to be his arm, he pulled the boy to him. He dragged the boy, jostling and pushing his way through their frozen companions, to the side of the group.

He looked back to the center of the column and could only faintly, very faintly, make out the men huddled there. He was sure the Japanese guard was still on the other side, his canvas cap flaps folded down to protect his yellow neck from the onslaught of dust.

If I can't see him, Charlie reasoned, then he can't see me.

Tennessee Parker gripped Charlie's hand, knowing that they could easily become lost from one another in the dust storm.

The Navajo groped straight ahead now, praying he would not run into another guard. They were yards away from the cobblestoned pavement and if the dust suddenly cleared, their intent would be clear.

He felt some growth, and ran his free hand along it. It was waist high and fairly thick. They followed it and when his hand felt a blossom, he picked it and held it to his clogged nostrils as he continued to walk. Even through the dust and grit he could still detect a faint odor. Gardenias. It was a gardenia hedge.

Yanking and pulling on Parker, Charlie crashed their way through the sturdy branches. The dust storm still raged, as they quickened their pace. They trotted through the haze and just when Charlie was beginning to think they might have a chance, his heel caught in a slippery bank and they went tumbling into a marsh. Their hands were separated now and they coughed and sputtered as the dust assaulted their startled, open mouths.

"You all right?" Charlie whispered.

"I think so."

The dust was thinning now and the Navajo could see his young friend.

"Jesus! I can't believe we did it!" Charlie heard hope for the first time in Parker's voice.

The Indian held his fingers to his lips. They had to be quiet. He motioned to the bank, and the two of them sloshed through the marsh to the other side. Charlie pointed to a thicket of undergrowth and the two of them crawled through the spiny branches into it.

It was not a large space and they curled around one another and drew their legs in tight.

And waited.

24

"*Qhayo gozaimasu,* " Ellen tried to catch the difficult words in her throat. "*Qhayo gozaimasu,*" she repeated, this time with more confidence.

"Good morning?" Magda questioned her greeting for it was now early evening.

"Practice, practice." Ellen explained, as she sat on the steps leading into the women's dormitory. "I'm not sure I'll ever master this."

"Ya." Magda agreed. She had heard her friend practice her lessons before, and thought it curious that she somehow spoke Japanese with a French accent.

Once the educational program for the children had been instituted, the Central Committee had put together a curriculum for adult education. Spanish, French, Japanese and Tagalog were taught, along with mathematics and astronomy. Seminars in physics, geology and chemistry had been offered. Then accounting, typing, shorthand, and music appreciation were added. Although interned, the enemy aliens were not content to let their minds stagnate.

"I am not sure I ever read 'The Three Little Pigs' in English," the Czech offered, "but now in Japanese!"

Ellen laughed. It had been a good day. A reasonable portion of rice had been served for dinner. There had been no bad news or disturbing rumors, and her children seemed to be thriving under the direction of B.G. Leake, the Boy Scout advisor who had been put in charge of all the young boys.

"And now, no toilet paper!" Magda rolled her eyes.

"Those old magazines can still serve a purpose, dear."

"Ya, but when I get out of here, that will be first on my list."

"I think I'll stick with cheese." Ellen mused. It was the one food she really missed.

"You want to walk?"

Ellen stood. "Yes," she glanced at her wristwatch, "we only have thirty minutes."

"That is a bother. I hear the committee is asking that it be extended."

They walked quietly down the streets and paths of the University. Past the main gate.

"They've taken it down," Ellen noticed.

A ragged, hand lettered cardboard sign had been hanging from the gate for the last two days. It had borne two words. "Bataan Fell."

"Feel," Magda held out her right hand, reaching for Ellen's with her left. She took the American's finger and ran it along the inside of her thumb and forefinger. "Callouses."

"The sewing?"

"Ya. We're busy. " Magda had been assigned to the Red Cross sewing unit. Most of every day was spent on repairs and alterations. "Mostly reductions here," she pulled out the waistband of her own skirt.

"And baby clothes?"

She shook her head. Although there had been eleven babies, all girls, born since internment, the unit was not sewing baby clothes. Yet.

A Japanese guard standing at the base of the bamboo tower motioned for them to return in the direction from which they had just come. Almost simultaneously, the loud speakers came on advising that curfew was on and for all internees to return to their quarters.

"That's odd," Ellen looked at her watch again, "I have seven twenty. They're early tonight."

Magda checked her own wrist. "That is also the time I have."

Jasper Farnsworth, a young Englishman, rushed up to them. "Have you heard the news?" He asked.

The women shook their heads.

"We've bombed Tokyo. That is, you've bombed her."

"The Americans?" Magda was stunned.

"Yes. Luther just heard it over the guard's radio. That's why they're calling early curfew."

Luther Kozalczyk, an elderly Russian Jew, joined them.

"It is true," he said.

It was just one of many rumors that would come into Santo Tomas. In this case it was a rare one, true. Sixteen United States bombers, led by Lieutenant Colonel Jimmy Doolittle had taken off from the carrier *Hornet* and surprised Japan in a daring daylight raid.

※

George plodded one foot after the other. How he was doing it was beyond his own understanding, for two days ago his feet had sprouted thousands of tiny little bubble blisters and now they had all burst, leaving raw, exposed skin.

He was numb to all of the bodies along the road. He had fought bile rising in his throat all that first day, but now, after five days on the march, it was as though the bloated, stinking, decomposing bodies were rocks by the side of the road. He could not think of them as people, for he could not bear to be reminded of his own mortality.

He had kept to himself on the march. There was no use taking on someone else's problems, he thought, for it taxed all of his energies just to take care of himself. Had there been some who were noticeably stronger than he, than perhaps he would have considered a partnership.

He had tried, in the beginning, to talk to the Japanese guards, but they changed at least daily, sometimes more frequently. After one had punched him in the stomach with the end of his rifle, Bendetti had given up trying to curry their favor.

Water was constantly on his mind. He had drunk from carabao wallows and polluted streams and from rusted buckets with manure caked on the bottom of them. It seemed as though the more he drank, the more he needed. Even now he could feel the effects of the contaminated water, for as he walked, his body excretions oozed from his backside and trickled down his legs. He was numb to that too.

"The railroad's not far from here." A captain from the Thirty-First Infantry sidled up next to him. "We'll be shipped out on that."

"Railroad?" It was music to Bendetti's ears. "Then we won't have to walk the rest of the way."

"I think it's going too slow. Even for them," the captain nodded in the direction of the closest guard, "they expected us to be healthier."

"What's healthy?"

"Right." The captain tugged on his penis and relieved himself as he walked, trudging through the dust he had just dampened.

"Where will we end up?"

The infantryman shrugged. "Who knows? Manila?"

"Anything's better than this."

They walked in silence for another hour, before the guards herded their charges through a fenced off area. They poked and prodded them into a large, tin *bodega*. A sign over the front entrance of the warehouse proclaimed it property of the National Rice and Corn Corporation.

The captain pointed to the sign, "maybe we'll get lucky."

It was not to be. Others had preceded them. As they walked through the slop and human waste, they quickly became aware that the only thing left in the steamy building was their own group of sick and dying men.

The Japanese were tugging on a steel cable, shoving and pushing their prisoners away from it, as they strung it taut.

"They're locking us in!" Bendetti yelled, as the heavy tin doors were pulled closed. There were no windows and darkness descended on all of them.

There was no room to move around or sit, as the men, like tin soldiers stuffed in a too small box, shuffled and pressed next to one another. Intimate body contact was inescapable in the dark, steamy enclosure. The tin warehouse had been roasting in the sun all day long, and now, with its doors closed and its innards packed with men, the temperatures quickly soared to over a hundred degrees.

The priest jockeyed into position, trying to get more space for himself. As he squirmed, his footing gave way on the slime beneath him. He started to fall in the muck and as he did so he clawed out for the first thing he could reach. It was an emaciated young soldier, and Bendetti grabbed him as though he were a drowning man. Tugging and pulling on the exhausted youth, he used him like a rock, half crawling, half climbing on top of him to avoid his own plunge into the mire. In so doing, he exchanged places with the young man, who was now groveling in the feces and vomit left by earlier inhabitants of the bodega. The young soldier, too tired to try to fight his way to the top, collapsed in the filth.

They stood that way all night, with the slop and slime of their own bodies sloshing up above the tops of their shoes. The still humid air only magnified the stench of their malodorous anatomies.

Morning finally came.

As the great tin door was opened, the men staggered and stumbled out, squinting their tearing eyes as they tried to shield them from the bright early sunlight.

The men who were able, were forced to stand in the fenced clearing as the Japanese guards entered the bodega. They exited quickly, dragging the bodies of those without the energy to withdraw on their own. They tugged these unfortunates over to a large hole in the earth. Without ceremony, they threw them over the side and into the earthen cavity.

"God, they're not all dead."

Bendetti turned, recognizing the voice of the captain he had talked to the night before.

As they watched, a soldier, who suddenly realized what was happening, attempted to pull himself out of the common grave. A Japanese guard viewed his struggle for a few minutes and then hit him hard on the head with his shovel.

Still, the dead and dying were pulled out of the bodega and thrown into the hole. The grave was getting full now and it was apparent that many of its occupants were not yet dead. The few with the strength to try to climb out, were quickly discouraged by the flat heads of the strong steel shovels and by the stout butts of the Japanese rifles.

The guards began shoveling earth into the cavity, even as muffled sounds kept coming from it.

"They're burying them alive," the captain's eyes were now glassy.

"Yes." Bendetti agreed. "Poor bastards."

The grave was quickly covered and the men began to march out again. As they walked past the fresh mound, George was aware of a hand sticking out, its fingers clawing for freedom.

They marched all that day and slept in a cattle pen in Guagua. Halfway into the following day they reached San Fernando.

The cockfighting pit they were put into there was a great improvement over the tin *bodega*. At least there were open ends to the shed, allowing what little breeze that came up to blow through.

By late afternoon they were herded to the railroad. The steel boxcars were narrow gauge, with each side sporting sliding wooden doors. One hundred men were packed into a little over two hundred square feet. Many boxcars carried more.

As the heavy doors slid closed, there was no opportunity for escape and little chance of fresh air. It was a repeat of the night in the *bodega*. Crammed into the airless cars, the men freely vomited and shat upon one another. There was no salvaging any of their clothes and many of them were half naked now anyway. They went crazy with the confinement. They suffocated. They wailed and swore and prayed and died. The dead and the living alike stood, for there was no room to fall.

George Bendetti could feel the urine, feces, sweat, mucus and vomit of the collective, roll and slosh around in his shoes. He was dimly aware of his own body's contributions to the filth, as his head pounded and tears rolled down his cheeks. Soon he began hearing the nagging, silent inner voice that had been still for so many years.

The twenty-five mile ride to Capas took almost three hours. The narrow gauge finally stopped, and the men were let out into the sunlight and forced to sit on the ground while they were counted and the dead were piled in stacks on the ground.

Bendetti pulled off his shoes and watched the slop inside of them drip onto the ground. He was not alone. The men who were fortunate to still have shoes, were all cleaning them the best they could.

It was a good thing to have done, Bendetti thought, as he fell into a column for the last eight miles to Camp O'Donnell.

The Bataan Death March was finally over when the last group of American and Filipino prisoners reached O'Donnell.

It had taken sixteen days to get the various groups to the final destination and had claimed the lives of ten thousand men.

25

"Watch it! Don't let his head get near you!"

Kate jumped back from the large thrashing lizard. He was clearly in his death throes, and she had been morbidly drawn to his struggle. In her fascination, she had stepped very close to the lizard's head.

"Their bites leave nasty infections," Sky explained.

They waited quietly until the lizard quit flopping.

Berringer nudged the reptile with his boot. There was no response. Kneeling beside the huge lizard, he drew out his knife and began skinning the creature. He peeled off a long strip of hide and held it suspended from his knife.

"Want a piece?" He dangled it in Kate's direction.

She shuddered. "No."

"It's supposed to be an aphrodisiac." Sky's dimples could hardly be seen now for the thick beard he was wearing.

"Thanks anyway."

He worked fast. It had been a week since they had tasted meat and the lizard, although stringy, would be very tender. He had eaten it before in Borneo.

He carefully gutted the animal and held out the gall bladder for Kate to take.

She shook her head.

"I'm not asking you to eat it. Hang on to it. We'll dry it."

She reached for it, her mouth shriveled into a distasteful grimace.

"We'll make it into tea later. It's supposed to give strength," Sky began cutting great chunks of meat from the animal, laying them carefully on a broad flat river rock. "We can render the fat and mix it with herbs. It's a good balm."

"Versatile little devil, isn't he?" Kate, as always, was amazed at the breadth of Berringer's knowledge.

"Yep." He grabbed two large chunks of meat. "How would you like it? We have fried water monitor, stewed monitor, broiled monitor or grilled monitor. Perhaps you're willing to wait for smoked monitor?"

Kate laughed, in spite of her growling stomach. "Quick monitor sounds best."

"Very well," Sky bowed low, almost dragging the lizard steaks in the dirt. He had started the fire earlier, and the coals were glowing. Deep in the jungle, they were not too concerned with the Japanese. As for the natives, the few Filipinos they had run into had been genuinely glad to see their American faces.

The meat was cut thin and cooked quickly.

Kate sat on a log, tearing the meal apart with her fingers. It was juicy and stringy. "Delicious." She licked the lizard's juices from her fingers. "My compliments to the chef."

"Tasty aren't they? You know there are restaurants where they serve them. Sometimes they're a real delicacy. They keep the babies and give them water but don't feed them. Then after a couple of weeks they drown them in an herbal mixture and brandy. Makes a tasty liquor."

"Ugh." While the baby lizards did not appeal to her, she

was so hungry that she did not stop eating as she listened to the gruesome culinary practice.

"They're carnivores you know."

"What?" She looked at him, unsure whether he was teasing her or not.

"Sure. They eat carrion. Not too particular about it either. On Komodo, those giant monitors have been known to go six feet into the earth to get at the dead."

"People?" Now she did stop eating.

"Uh huh. On Bali they put baskets over the corpses. Then a member of the family stands guard until the lizards show up and eat the body. That means they've gone on to the spirit world."

Kate was turning pale. "God, I think I liked you better before the lizard lore."

"Well you need..." suddenly he rolled off the log and onto the ground. He held a finger to his lips, indicating she was to remain quiet. It was an exercise they had been through many times in the past few months. Kate froze.

Sky rolled into the brush and disappeared while she sat very still on the felled tree.

There! There it was. She could hear it now. The sound of footsteps falling on the soft jungle floor. They were close. Petrified, she sat, waiting for Sky's instruction. The sound of her own pounding heart sounded like an alarm to her. How could the approaching intruder not know where she was?

A Filipino, his bolo drawn, stepped into the clearing. Kate's eyes riveted to the sharp blade of the knife, before they traveled up to his face. He was not a large man.

He looked quickly around the clearing and then back to her. "You alone?"

She was relieved to hear his English. "Yes," she lied, aware that she was still holding the lizard.

His eyes dropped to the ground and widened with the realization that a half eaten piece of meat was lying there. But the knowledge came too late as Sky pounced on him.

He grabbed the smaller man around the neck, choking him with the crook of his elbow, while his right hand chopped him hard on his lower hand. The hard strike caught the Filipino by surprise, causing him to drop his bolo. As Sky half pulled, half dragged the man back from his weapon, Kate quickly retrieved it.

"The pack, Katie. Get the gun out of the pack."

The intruder's eyes were bulging as the pressure against his neck had not lessened.

Kate pulled the .38 out and pointed it at the Filipino.

Berringer released his grip on the man and shoved him hard, pushing him to his knees, before walking to Kate and taking the gun from her. He sat back on the log, pointing the weapon at the fallen man.

"Who are you?" Sky's gray eyes were cold.

"Jesus Christ, man, you could hurt somebody with that kind of routine," the Filipino rubbed his bruised throat.

"You could be a lot more hurt if you don't answer my questions. Who are you?" Sky repeated.

"Faustino," the man was now rubbing his arm, "Faustino Tapay. May I reach in my pocket?"

"Carefully."

"Hey, man," he held up his hands, "I'm a friend." He reached in his rear pocket and withdrew a torn leather wallet. He spread it before them, taking great pains to move very slowly. He pulled out a card and threw it to them. It landed a few feet in front of Kate.

She picked it up and studied it, looking back and forth from the card to the man, comparing the face on the card to that of the Filipino.

"He's a schoolteacher," she said handing the card to Sky.

"And you're playing hooky today?" Sky relaxed a little. He doubted whether he would have to worry about a teacher. Usually they weren't lethal.

"I'm unemployed, haven't you heard?"

"Why don't you tell me about it." Sky was clearly now enjoying the break in their usual routine.

"The schools never reopened after Pearl Harbor. Quezon's closed them all. He doesn't want those murdering dwarfs indoctrinating our kids."

Kate smiled. The Filipino wasn't that much larger than the Japanese she had seen.

"He's closed all the schools?" She repeated.

"That's right. Things aren't so hot right now in Manila in case you haven't heard."

"We've heard," Sky waved the gun at him. "What are you doing out here?"

"Going home."

"You're heading in the wrong direction."

"To San Alberto. My parents are there," he was still rubbing his arm. "Man you got some kind of chop there."

Sky ignored him.

Faustino's eyes darted to the cooking meat. It was a glance that was not lost on Kate. She looked at Sky and he nodded.

"Well Katie, I guess we'll have to trust this little bastard." He tucked the .38 into the waistband of his pants.

"Hey man, that's great, " Tapay stood and walked toward them just as Sky reached across the log and grabbed his bolo.

"We'll hang on to this a while longer," he explained.

Kate held out a piece of cooked meat strung on the end of a stick. Faustino took it eagerly, and tore into it for he, too, had not had meat in days.

"I take it you're not into co-prosperity?" Sky waited until he finished the meat.

The Co-prosperity sphere, a program initiated by the Japanese, promised the Filipinos joint cooperation for mutual economic gain.

"Prosperity begins with a job, and since they arrived I seem to have lost mine," Tapay explained. "The dwarfs have grabbed our trucks and boats and put us out of work. This is prosperity?" He accepted a second piece of meat from Kate.

"How long are you out of Manila?" Sky asked.

"Three weeks. I got a little nervous. They're rustling everyone up and are throwing them into camps."

"Oh no!" Kate's hands flew up to her mouth.

"It's happening all over the islands," Tapay wondered for the first time where she had come from. "Manila's a real zoo. It's supposed to be business as usual, but the Japanese walk around distrusting the Filipinos, the Filipinos hate the Japs, and everyone is wondering who is real and who's a spy." He shook his head.

"Can you use that thing?" Sky pointed to the bolo.

"Old Ernest? Sure."

"You're free to go," Sky was trusting his instinct now. He was also sure he could blast him with the .38 before he could kill both of them.

Tapay sheathed the knife.

"You're a pretty good cook," he said to Kate.

She shook her head and pointed to Sky.

"May I ask you something?" she asked.

"Sure."

"Why do you call that," she pointed to the knife at his waist, "Old Ernest?"

"After Hemingway," Faustino's teeth gleamed like pearls.

"Oh." She said, not understanding at all.

"I'm an English teacher. Literature. And this guy's written a couple of books I like." He said. "Thanks for the meat." He waved a hand at them and crossed the clearing. He stopped, hesitating only a minute.

"If you like, I'll take you to San Alberto. You'll be safe there."

Kate looked at Sky. They had been on the run for so long that a village sounded appealing.

"How far is it?" Berringer asked.

Tapay looked to the sun. "Day, day and a half."

Sky mulled it over in his mind.

"Hey man, it's up to you." Tapay was eager to be on his way.

Wordlessly, they gathered their things and followed the young Filipino out of the clearing.

26

"Thick slices of smoked ham smothered in red eye gravy. Grits. Black-eyed peas."

"No, no," argued Tom. "Green corn tamales, cheese enchiladas, frijoles."

"Would you settle for a nice juicy hamburger?" Bark rolled over on his side and grinned at his friend. "I'm not all that hard to please, Sullivan."

They were resting on their cots, trying to take advantage of the unusual lull in the bombing. General Homma had desperately wanted to deliver Corregidor to Emperor Hirohito on the twenty-ninth of April, the Emperor's birthday. The general's disappointment at not making that self-imposed deadline was now apparent as the Japanese pounded the island. From the sound of the shelling, Batteries Geary and Crockett on Topside seemed to be their prime targets.

"Fried shrimp," Tom said.

Restricted to a scant forty ounces of food every day, nutrition and meal planning had become a vital part of their lives.

Tom wrapped his left hand around his right wrist and was not surprised when his middle finger and thumb touched one another.

"Hey Bark, I made it." He held his encircled joint in the air.

Bark struggled with his own, but he was still three quarters of an inch short.

"Shit, you just have tiny bones."

They were trying hard to distract each other from the fact that radiomen were working around the clock to transmit to Washington all of the names and serial numbers of those on Corregidor.

Tom reached in his pocket and withdrew his gold pocket watch. He snapped it open, looking for the third time that day at the faded black and white of Ellen with Doc and Pete. It had been taken on a picnic in the mountains and the wind was playing with their hair. Ellen looked like an angel to him, with her gossamer flaxen tresses fanned out around her face. The boys looked like strange hybrids, crosses between clowns and cherubs, as their hair blew wildly and they wrestled with one another, each insisting the other behave. They had all thought the picture horrible and to tease them he had put it in his watch. Now, it was the only photograph he had. He put it softly to his face, the glass cool against his lips. God, how he wished he had insisted on their going home last year.

"Chocolate sodas." There was a dangerous catch in Bark's voice and without explanation he rolled back over and faced the concrete wall.

After Bataan fell, the Japanese had leveled everything they had at Corregidor. The newly emplaced Japanese guns on the tip of the peninsula pounded the batteries and topside guns of the Rock. The attacks had done their job, for Batteries Rockpoint, James and Hamilton had all been knocked out by the middle of the month. Because of the open positions of the anti-aircraft guns at Kindley Field on Corregidor's tail, those emplacements had been abandoned. Under the constant barrage of gunfire, most of

Corregidor's giant searchlights had also been put out of commission and night bombings had increased. Few buildings remained on the island and nearly all of the shore craft and motor vehicles had been destroyed.

Two days after the fall of Bataan, the cease-fire had been lifted. Now the ancient Batteries Geary and Way, comprising a total of ten twelve-inch guns, were still in operation and their crews were enthusiastic in their efforts to knock out the Japanese guns across the water.

The damage from the shelling and bombing could be seen everywhere. The wounded were stacked up in triple bunks in the hospital laterals, as welders worked into the night joining still more of the metal beds. Bloody dressings were used and used and used again. Although the island afforded some protection from malaria, the quinine was nearly depleted. Frustrated by their lack of supplies, haggard doctors and nurses worked around the clock to administer to the wounded.

The shell shocked were yet another fraternity needing care. Some were in hysterics, wandering aimlessly through the tunnel, doing little to help the overall morale. It was also becoming harder to get some of the soldiers to leave Malinta now. The tunnel rats insisted on the stifling security of the concrete tunnel to the risk outside. Many stayed inside, refusing to leave, defying their officers.

Water supplies, now that the barges to and from Bataan were out of commission were also dangerously low. Showers had ceased to exist.

Although the bombing today had been heavy, Tom willingly followed Bark to Battery Crockett. There was little for them to do these days, other than to wander around and see where they might be of help. Malinta was crammed with people and both

Bark and Tom were willing to risk the enemy shellfire just to get out occasionally.

Battery Hanna had already been knocked out and Bark's spirits plummeted with the loss of his gun. He offered to fill in on the other crews, but none of the soldiers had been willing to forfeit his opportunity to strike back at the Japanese. Now they were at Crockett to see if there was any chance of relieving one of the gunners.

"Hey Bark! Over here!" A skeleton of a man standing near the magazine waved his arms.

Bark turned just as a tremendous blast shook the island. He was dimly aware of his body flying up in the air before it came down hard against the earth. His jaw caught the hard dirt and he realized with disgust that he had just bitten into his tongue. The ground beneath him reverberated with the shock as he collected his wits.

Tom, who had been just a few feet from him before the explosion, was now ten yards away crumpled in a ball in the dirt. Bark struggled to his unsteady feet and wobbled over to the unconscious engineer. He rolled Sullivan over gently and inserted his fingers in his mouth checking to insure he had not swallowed his tongue.

Tom began to groan as he reached for his head. A welt was beginning to grow there.

"What happened?" Sullivan's eyes flew open. "You all right?" He looked at the blood dribbling out the side of Bark's mouth.

"Just my tongue." He stuck it out. "Still there?"

Tom checked his friend's mouth. "Yes. It's a gash though."

All around them, men were getting to their feet. Miraculously, none of them had been hit by shells or bomb fragments.

"It's Geary!" One of the gunners pointed to a huge roll of

black smoke to the northwest. "Sons-a- bitches got Geary!"

They did not have to guess what happened. It had been an ill kept secret that the crews at Battery Geary had hoarded their shells waiting for the end to come to give the Japanese a big surprise. Although the commanding officer had ordered the magazines emptied, the task had not been completed. Now the Japanese had scored a costly hit on the center magazine.

"Let's see what we can do," Bark was off in Geary's direction with Tom on his heels.

Geary was a purgatory of burning fires and screaming men. Twenty-seven had been instantly killed. The six firmly anchored mortars, weighing over sixteen tons each, were scattered about like misplaced toys. One gun had flown through the air over one hundred and forty yards, finally coming to rest on what was left of the golf course.

"Shit. I guess I can knock old Geary off my list." Bark was furious as he ripped off his shirt, not even taking the time to unbutton it. He grabbed the first bleeding soldier within range.

"Come on." He wrapped the shirt around the soldier's torn, bleeding head. Instantly the fabric was blood red. "We'll take you to Malinta." Although the huge man struggled to carry the smaller soldier, he was unable to do it on his own. Together, Tom and Bark cradled the wounded man and began carrying him away from the rubble that had been Battery Geary.

"How bad is it, Bark?"

The gunner looked over his shoulder at the smoldering ruins. "We've got Way left. And the beach defenses."

Tom shifted the weight of the wounded soldier and grimly walked with Bark back to Malinta Tunnel.

The submarine *Spearfish* had arrived in the night and had taken out a few more key army and navy personnel as well as twelve nurses.

Somehow, impossible as it seemed, the shelling had intensified now. The effect inside the tunnel was like a giant continuous earthquake. The smoke and dust, combined with the odor of the unwashed and the dead and dying, made the air almost, but not quite, intolerable to breathe. The lights in Malinta were flickering, and there had been no water coming out of the tap for hours. Some laterals were completely darkened with power failures and for the people huddled in them the terror of falling dust and claustrophobic quarters was magnified by the added handicap.

Outside, the island was changing forever as artillery and bombing missions altered it. Cliffs crumbled, landslides filled canyons and gullies, trees and jungle growth disappeared as though they had never existed. The manmade structures, the roads and concrete buildings, were blocked and disintegrated by the debris of war. Stripped, raped, scarred and mutilated, the once beautiful island that had been a military masterpiece, was mutated into a wasteland of death and destruction. In many ways it was a testament to General Wainwright and his men. For President Roosevelt had given them the choice of surrendering along with Bataan or fighting it out on Corregidor. The evidence was everywhere that they had opted for the latter.

The fourth of May was, for everyone on Corregidor, the beginning of the end.

"All right Sullivan, this is it." There was a sparkle in Bark's eyes that had been absent there for some time. "We're cutting loose."

"A final defiant Okie act?" Tom raised a skeptical eyebrow. He did not see how they could stand much more. There were only three 155mm guns left along with the mortar in Battery Way. It was not much of a defense.

"I'm going to Way. If you want to come, I'd be glad to have you," Bark reached for a steel helmet. "It's still raining out there." His reference was to the shells and debris pouring out of the sky, "So if you want to stay, I understand."

"What the hell." Tom reached for his helmet, a soldier's legacy.

They darted and dashed to Battery Way, driven on by the reassuring sound of its big gun. It was the only one left and it had become a symbol to all of them. The crews simply refused to give up and the big gun was firing every five minutes. The Japanese barges were barely visible as Battery Way kept systematically knocking them out, despite huge losses of her own crews.

It was a mad relay race. As each man was killed, a new one stepped in to replace him.

"The fighting fools," Tom muttered. It was a nickname given to the men at Battery Way.

"God bless 'em!" Bark turned to his friend and grabbed him by the shoulders kissing him on both cheeks. Tears were streaming freely down his cheeks. "Sullivan I've found a spot. Do you mind if I don't walk back with you?"

Tom hugged him tightly, wishing not for the first time that he had had the military training to be more helpful. Bark was running for the gun now.

"Take care, Theodore Barkley, you hear?"

But Bark didn't hear, for he was eagerly approaching the standing cadre of men fervid to take his part.

Darkness had set in and still there was no sign of Bark. Tom tried hard not to think about it as the shells pounded Malinta. There was too much exposure out there for the men at the remaining battery. The Japanese were not fools and they were leveling everything they had at the last working mortar, knowing it was the only thing between them and the taking of the island. The American casualties were high, some said they were approaching seventy percent at Battery Way alone, and Tom watched nervously as the wounded were brought in.

He looked at his watch in the flickering light. It was almost ten p.m. He walked to Lateral Number Three, knowing if there was any news it would be there in the communications sector. The tunnel was a hub, as men hovered and whispered and pointed at maps on the concrete walls. Tom stood for a moment, listening. He stayed long enough to hear that anti-aircraft sound detectors had picked up a large noise approaching the island. The Japanese were coming in on motorized barges.

As he stepped outside the east entrance, he could hear the popping of rifles and small arms.

The Japanese were coming ashore.

27

Tom tried to run, but a crablike shuffle was all he could manage in his emaciated state. It was over a mile and a half to North Point and he stumbled along, fueled by his own adrenaline. The dark night closed in on him as he kept on in the direction of the gunfire.

The Fourth Marine Division had done a good job in anticipating the enemy landing. The fifteen hundred marines, supplemented by twenty five hundred non-combat troops, nestled in their foxholes in the cliffs above the beach. Aided by powerful searchlights, they had a bird's eye view of the Japanese barges. As the first wave of enemy soldiers came ashore, they were picked off by the American machine guns and artillery fire.

While the Japanese had intended on landing on Corregidor's northeast shore, the strong currents of Manila Bay forced a landing at North Point, bringing them right into the Americans' hands. As the moon began to rise, visibility became even better.

Tom flattened out, his belly pressed against the packed earth as he looked at the scene below him. At least three of the barges were listing badly and would soon be under. Bodies floated on the surface of the water and under the lights he could tell, even from that distance, that the sea was churning with Japanese blood.

It was a shooting gallery, yet still they came ashore. Wave after wave, stumbling and falling over their own dead who littered the beach. Even with astronomical losses, they kept charging onto the island. The few who made it were attempting to scale the cliffs now, but the marines had prepared for that too. Artillery shells slid down the bluffs, exploding as they hit the sand taking with them still more of the Japanese soldiers.

Tom's heart pounded against the earth. There was no stopping it, he could see that. Although the enemy were losing over sixty percent of their landing craft and an equal number of their soldiers, there were simply too many of them. They had the numbers to overwhelm the Corregidor defenders. It was only a matter of time. The engineer inched his way back from the edge of the cliff, before rolling over and onto his feet.

He began walking back to Malinta, for he knew that was where the last stand had to take place.

Tom walked through the tunnel and out the west entrance. Men were busy stacking sandbags around it, in preparation of a Japanese assault. He helped haul a heavy bag and dropped it into position, just as a litter came in with Bark on it. Sullivan dropped the sandbag and ran to his friend, relieved to find him conscious.

"Are you all right?" Tom walked along the litter, knowing the carriers could not stop. Bark needed what little medical care was available and the soldiers needed to free their stretcher as soon as possible, so they could return to the wounded.

The gunner rolled his head in Tom's direction. He was holding a dirty, blood soaked bandage to his left eye, but his right was shining and clear.

"You should have seen it Sullivan! Everyone's pitching in out there. Way's killing them. " His voice was weak. "Aren't any gun crews left but she's still firing. Cooks, Sullivan! Can you believe it?"

"Easy." Tom patted his friend's arm, thinking he was delirious. He had never heard of a cook firing a twelve-inch mortar before.

"It's true," one of the carriers had seen the incredulous look cross his face. "Motor pool guys, typists, they're all keeping Way going."

"How is he?" Tom asked.

Bark pulled the bloody rag down, exposing a large gaping throbbing mess running just above his eyebrow to the middle of his cheek. Ruptured blood vessels and pieces of bone hung from the mangled flesh, hiding the eye.

"Am I gonna lose it?" Bark's hand grabbed him.

"No, no you're going to be fine," Tom lied. There was no way he could tell. "They'll take you back there and the doctors will clean you up. I've got to go back to work, but I'll see you later."

Bark's face was badly swollen but somehow he managed a crooked grin. "Give 'em hell for me, Sullivan."

Tom reached the sandbags just as a marine came running up.

"They've pulled three goddamn tanks on shore. They've already got half the goddamned island!" The marine was a runner, for communications all across Corregidor had broken down.

Tom did not have to be told that the Japanese were advancing. The sounds of the small arms fire were getting closer and closer. Clearly Malinta Tunnel was the next target.

By mid-morning Battery Way was silent. The crew had stopped only long enough to help their wounded commander, but the pause was enough to freeze the breechblock on the ancient gun.

"It's so quiet, Sullivan. Am I hallucinating?" Bark whispered.

"No."

"God, it hasn't been this still the whole time I've been here," the bloody bandage was still covering half of Bark's face. He was one of the lucky ones. He had been given a pain killer and the effects of the medicine were saving him temporarily from the agony of his wound. "It's so eery. What's happening?"

Tom squeezed his hand. "Wainwright's ordered a cease-fire. They're drawing up the surrender right now."

"Shit." Bark licked his parched lips. "It had to come to this?"

"We don't have a choice. The Japanese are close." Tom didn't add that he had heard General Wainwright had already signed the surrender document, insuring that it would go into effect in the event he was killed. "They're destroying everything right now."

Operation Pontiac was in effect. It was a repetition of the exercise first seen in Manila, then on Bataan, with the Americans destroying any war materiel that would help the enemy. The Fourth Marines had burned their colors, codes were being fed into burning oil drums, the few remaining boats were sabotaged and sunk, fires were purposefully set.

"They'll begin broadcasting any time now," Tom explained, "we shouldn't have long to wait."

The broadcasts would begin in English at ten thirty that morning and would be repeated in Japanese. The message promised that a white flag would be displayed on a prominent position on Corregidor at noon.

Irving Strobing, a young army signal corpsman, sat hunched over his telegraph key. He had been transmitting to Honolulu all morning and he still held his contact. Quietly he began tapping out a message on his radio key. It was one that would be heard around the world:

"THEY ARE NOT NEAR YET, WE ARE WAITING FOR GOD ONLY KNOWS WHAT. HOW ABOUT A CHOCO-LATE SODA? ...NOT MANY. NOT NEAR YET. LOTS OF HEAVY FIGHTING GOING ON...

WE HAVE ONLY GOT AN HOUR TWENTY MINUTES BEFORE...WE MAY HAVE TO GIVE UP BY NOON, WE DON'T KNOW YET. THEY ARE THROWING MEN AND SHELLS AT US AND WE MAY NOT BE ABLE TO STAND IT. THEY HAVE BEEN SHELLING US FASTER THAN YOU CAN COUNT..."

The surrender broadcast had been running for well over an hour.

"WE'VE GOT ABOUT FORTY-FIVE MINUTES AND I FEEL SICK TO MY STOMACH. I AM REALLY LOW DOWN. THEY ARE AROUND SMASHING RIFLES. THEY BRING THE WOUNDED IN EVERY MINUTE. WE WILL BE WAITING FOR YOU GUYS TO HELP. THIS IS THE ONLY THING I GUESS THAT CAN BE DONE. GENERAL WAINWRIGHT IS A RIGHT GUY AND WE ARE WILLING TO GO ON FOR HIM. DAMAGE TERRIFIC. TOO MUCH FOR GUYS TO TAKE. ENEMY HEAVY CROSS-SHELL-ING AND BOMBING, THEY HAVE GOT US FROM ALL AROUND AND FROM SKIES..."

Smoke was thick in the tunnel. Although the ventilators had been turned off hours ago, the black smoke from the shelling was mixing with falling dust.

"FROM HERE IT LOOKS LIKE FIRING CEASED ON BOTH SIDES. MEN HERE ALL FEELING BAD, BECAUSE

OF TERRIFIC STRAIN OF SIEGE. CORREGIDOR USED TO BE A NICE PLACE. BUT IT IS HAUNTED NOW. WITHSTOOD A TERRIFIC POUNDING...

"JUST MADE A BROADCAST TO MANILA TO ARRANGE MEETING FOR SURRENDER. TALK MADE BY GENERAL BEEBE. I CAN'T SAY MUCH. CAN'T THINK AT ALL. I CAN HARDLY THINK. SAY I HAVE SIXTY PESOS YOU CAN HAVE FOR THE WEEKEND. THE JIG IS UP...EVERYONE IS BAWLING LIKE A BABY..."

In spite of the smoke and fear the tunnel was still quiet.

"THEY ARE PILING DEAD AND WOUNDED IN OUR TUNNEL. ARMS WEAK FROM POUNDING KEY LONG HOURS. NO REST, SHORT RATIONS, TIRED...

"I KNOW HOW A MOUSE FEELS. CAUGHT IN A TRAP WAITING FOR GUYS TO COME ALONG AND FINISH IT UP...GOT A TREAT...CAN OF PINEAPPLE OPENING IT WITH SIGNAL CORPS KNIFE...

"MY NAME IS IRVING STROBING. GET THIS TO MY MOTHER MRS. WINNIE STROBING, 605 BARBEY STREET, BROOKLYN, N. Y. THEY ARE TO GET ALONG OK. GET IN TOUCH WITH THEM AS SOON AS POSSIBLE. MESSAGE. MY LOVE TO PA, JOE, SUE, MAC, GARRY, JOY AND PAUL. ALSO TO MY FAMILY AND FRIENDS. GOD BLESS 'EM ALL. HOPE THEY CAN BE THERE WHEN I COME HOME. TELL JOE WHEREVER HE IS TO GIVE THEM HELL FOR US. MY LOVE TO ALL OF YOU. GOD BLESS YOU AND KEEP YOU...LOVE, SIGN MY NAME AND TELL MOTHER YOU HEARD FROM US.

"STAND BY..."

It was the last radio broadcast the Americans would make from Corregidor for several years.

The American flag had been burned and a thin white flag, actually a bedsheet, now hung at the west entrance to Malinta Tunnel. Although the Americans had been ordered to cease-fire, there was no let up, for the Japanese were still shooting.

Tom looked at his watch. Twelve thirty. Something had gone wrong and now, with their weapons destroyed, they had no way to defend themselves.

"Sullivan?" Bark's voice was getting weaker and Tom knew that he was struggling to stay awake, to see the end.

"I'm here, Bark."

"Why hasn't it stopped? They're still shooting at us, aren't they?"

"I don't know. A surrender team went out a little while ago. We shouldn't have long to wait." It was a phrase he would repeat all day long.

The peace team met with Colonel Moto Nakayama, who insisted that General Wainwright himself come to the Japanese lines. When Wainwright complied, he was surprised and disappointed not to find General Homma. He insisted on seeing the Japanese officer.

They took Wainwright to Bataan. The afternoon wore on and still General Homma did not show up. Propaganda pictures were taken of the American general and his captors. Soon copies of them would be found throughout the archipelago.

Homma finally arrived late in the afternoon and the negotiations began. Threatening to kill everyone on Corregidor, the Japanese general demanded the surrender of all American and Filipino troops in the islands. Wainwright informed him that his command included only those troops defending Manila Bay and a few garrisons in Northern Luzon. He explained how General MacArthur had kept command of the Philippines and how he had split the authority for the various areas, but Homma was having none of it. He left the meeting in an angry huff, vowing that General Wainwright would regret his decision.

They returned to Corregidor. The formalities were now over and General Wainwright was forced to wade ashore.

As they approached the east entrance to Malinta, Wainwright noted wryly that the Japanese had taken advantage of the truce and were now within three hundred feet of the tunnel. The American commander insisted on seeing the Japanese officer in charge of the Corregidor invasion. When he met with him, it became quickly apparent that the Japanese troops had continued pressing in on Malinta, even after the white flag had gone up.

With visions of wholesale slaughter of his brave men haunting him, General Jonathan Wainwright was willing to meet the demands of General Homma. Quickly, he surrendered to Colonel Gempachi Soto.

※

"It's so still." Bark had been drifting in and out of sleep all night.

"Yes," Tom whispered. He was exhausted. The waiting had taken its toll on all of them. In some ways, the surrender was a relief. The inevitable had been met.

"What time is it?"

"Just after midnight." Even the wounded were quieter tonight.

General Wainwright was at that moment signing the surrender document prepared by the Japanese Army commander.

Men were openly crying now. They had heard the news and now the only thing that was left, was waiting for the arrival of their Japanese captors. Personal weapons were quietly torn apart and smashed against the concrete walls. Pictures of loved ones were hidden. Prayers said.

The Japanese soldiers entered the Navy Tunnel, ready with hand grenades and bayonets. Their relaxation was apparent when they found no resistance there. The Army Tunnel must have scared them more, for they came in with tanks and flame-throwers. Again, they met no resistance. Systematically, they began looting the personal belongings of the American soldiers.

"Has he left yet, Sullivan?" Bark was afraid of missing any of it.

"No. Soon." The rumor was that General Wainwright would soon be leaving The Rock to go to Manila to broadcast the surrender. The terms were very specific and assembly points for the American and Filipino troops would be given, so that the Japanese Imperial Army could take custody of them more easily.

There was a shuffling now in the tunnel.

"Sullivan," Bark's grip tightened on the engineer's hand, "help me up."

"Stay quiet. There's nothing to see."

"Help me up." There was anger in his voice.

"Bark, you've lost a lot of blood. You're weak. Stay tight," Tom pleaded with his friend.

"Goddamnit," the gunner struggled with his weakened body, rolling it off the cot and falling to his knees. Tom reached for him, pulling him up by his wet armpits. He could feel the trembling muscles and exhaustion there, but still Bark was trying to stand.

An amazing thing was happening. All along the corridor the wounded, the weak, the exhausted and the dying were struggling to get on their feet.

General Wainwright, with tears streaming down his face, was walking down their corridor and to a man they were giving it their all to stand for their beloved commanding officer.

Tom felt Bark stiffen as the general walked past them. He turned to his friend. Tears were streaming from his good eye as he gave his general a last crisp salute.

General Wainwright would not return to the Rock. Corregidor had fallen.

In the beginning, the Americans had been expected to last five days. They had stood five months.

THE WIND BLOWN

28

The ocher yolk of the broken egg dribbled down Tennessee Parker's peach fuzzed cheek.

"Delicious." He swiped at his face with his napkin as he devoured his third egg. "Ma'am this is the best meal I've ever had."

Isabel smiled. "They're called *baloots*. These are only a week and a half old."

"*Baloots*," he repeated the name, although his mouth was full. "That a kind of chicken?"

"Duck."

"Usually they let them ripen for two and a half weeks before cooking them," Charlie explained the fertile duck eggs. "Then they boil them up."

"Tennessee was studying his own plate more closely now and he imagined he could see the outlines of baby ducklings there. "I think I'll have some more papaya if you don't mind."

They had arrived at Isabel's the evening before, reeking of two weeks of unwashed travel. They bathed and collapsed into bed.

Charlie had started out curled up next to Isabel in the soft warm bed but it had been so long since he had slept in one, that he found himself opting for the floor in the middle of the night. She said nothing when she awakened in the morning and found him there. Charlie and Tennessee had slept for fourteen hours and now they were beginning to feel like human beings again.

"You heard about the island?" Isabel asked.

"No." They had heard that fifth columnists were everywhere and they had not dared trust any Filipinos they had seen. For this reason they avoided all people in their flight from the peninsula.

"They surrendered day before yesterday. General Wainwright was on the radio."

"Have you heard anything from my friend?" Charlie reached for another egg. He had given Isabel the aviator's name a long time ago.

The tiny Filipina dragged a wooden stool over to her kitchen counter. By stepping on it and standing on her tiptoes, she was able to reach a coffee tin on her highest shelf. Taking it down, she shook the precious coffee crystals onto a ceramic plate until the tin was half full. Reaching inside, she withdrew a small piece of paper and handed it to the Navajo.

He read it quickly and then walked to the stove and reached for a box of wooden matches. Striking one, he watched the flame for a few seconds before lighting the paper. He dropped the burning message into the sink.

"You'll be leaving again." The woman's eyes teared.

"Yes. There's no need endangering you any longer than we have to."

"I am not worried of that."

"Is your friend safe?" Parker asked.

"Yes. He's north of here." "

"I have to go now. To work." Isabel was apologetic. "There's plenty of food. Help yourselves."

Charlie stood and reached for her.

"Fortunately the cement plant is still at work." She hugged him, not wanting him to see her tears. "I am so ashamed."

"Ssh." Charlie wiped her cheek with a rough brown finger. "Can you get me a knife?"

She pulled away. "A knife?"

"Like the one I used to have."

She nodded. "You will be here when I return?"

"Yes. For tonight."

"Don't answer the door." She cautioned.

"No."

A loud crash startled both of them. Tennessee Parker's head had fallen onto the wooden table. He was asleep again.

"Guests of the Emperor," the tiny, almost miniature, Japanese man was standing on a wooden platform to give him the stature he did not have. "You will be considered guests of the Emperor."

The lecture had been going on for some time, and sweat streamed off George Bendetti, and the thousands like him who were seated on the sandy ground with the blazing sun beating down upon them.

The priest was playing with the sand, picking up handfuls and letting it trickle through his fingers. As he went for another fistful, he felt something hard. He pulled it up carefully, looking around to see if anyone was watching. Satisfied that his find went unnoticed, he pulled on the hard object.

It was a fan. A Japanese fan. The instant he realized what he uncovered, he dropped it back on the sand as though it had stung him. Quickly, he shoved it back into the hole he had dug and brushed sand over it. His hands were shaking, his heart pounding as he looked around again. But no one had seen him. A soldier had obviously buried the souvenir, not wanting to get caught with it.

"Geneva Agreement not in order here." The commandant continued, noting with perverse pleasure that the exhausted men were now paying more attention to him. "Japan never signed."

"Lying bastard." An older man, his insignia missing from what was left of his tattered army uniform, muttered under his breath.

He was one of the few men there who would remember that, in fact, the delegation from Japan had indeed signed the articles at the 1929 Geneva Convention. Unfortunately the agreement had never been ratified by the Japanese government.

Although the commandant had been talking for over an hour, there had been no mention of medical attention or of food. Bendetti was beginning to wonder whether the omission was a deliberate oversight.

"You have left many comrades behind you." The man's sing song, scratchy voice was irritating to listen to and would have been so even if the words coming from his mouth had been comforting. "You sorrow over them and feel they were unfortunate to die. You will soon see they are lucky ones." The tiny man spun on his heel and left the elevated stand.

A coldness was gnawing at the bottom of Bendetti's stomach. If the familiar urge to disgorge came over him, there was no place he could do it with any degree of privacy. He fought back the feeling.

The guards were moving into the crowd, prodding and poking them with their bayonets, indicating their dispersal.

Men wandered around looking for their friends. George stood, rooted in the sand, not in the least bit disappointed that he had no one to look for.

Camp O'Donnell had originally been an American airfield and was only partially completed by the time the war had broken out in the Philippines. When the Americans and Filipinos had engineered their retreat into the Bataan Peninsula, the water supply at O'Donnell had been one of their prime targets.

One water spigot remained working and it seemed no matter how early in the morning that Bendetti awakened, there were always hundreds of men standing in line before him, waiting for their turn with the precious liquid. The long waits were necessitated by the need to allow the pump time to rest. Because of the numbers, filling the canteens was out of the question. A half a canteen per man. That was it. Showers were nonexistent.

Men were dropping daily. Exhausted, sick with beri-beri, pellagra, malaria, emotionally beaten, many were heading quickly toward death. Camp O'Donnell would soon make the death statistics from the Bataan Death March pale.

Now, two weeks after their arrival, they were taking twenty dead Americans and one hundred and fifty dead Filipinos out of the gates every day. Judging from the numbers and the conditions, things could only get worse.

The ten men had quit moaning the day before. Now they were silent, their bodies still and untwisting under the brutal sun.

"Someone's got to give them water. They'll never make it without it." A Filipino soldier remembered that Bendetti was a Catholic priest. "Can you do it, Father?"

"They'll shoot anyone who tries," he said coldly.

"Then we should kill them."

The priest thought for a moment. "To do so would be a sin. It is in God's hands."

Caught while trying to escape, the men had been strung up by their thumbs on a simple wooden rack, their feet clearing the sandy ground. For the first day or two, their moans had been heard throughout the camp. Now there was nothing but silence.

"They are probably all dead by now," Bendetti suggested.

"No, Father. That one," the Filipino pointed a finger to a young American, "the second one from the right. I walked by him a while ago and he whispered to me. I heard it with my own ears."

"He's still alive?" The priest was incredulous that a man could hang like that for four days in the hot sun without water.

"Yes, Father."

"God bless him." Bendetti crossed himself before walking off.

On the sixth day the men were cut down from the wooden framework. The second one from the right was still, miraculously, alive. The Japanese wasted no time in shooting him through the head.

✗

Pete's forehead was blistering to the touch. Even as Ellen cradled him and felt the fever within his small body, there was no doubt that her youngest child was not getting any better. She looked at her watch. Over an hour since the aspirin and still no change in his temperature. The small boy's body was racked with coughing spasms and as he pulled away from her to catch his breath Ellen could hear the ominous rumblings in his thin chest.

"I got it." Magda came in and squatted beside the bed holding out a piece of paper. "The Committee went to work on it right away." She handed the paper to Ellen.

"And the Germans?"

"They will direct you when you leave. Do you have everything?"

Ellen nodded. She had already packed a few things for Peter and herself in the hope they would be granted an outside pass. Dr. Wolverschmidts, patriarch of an old German family living in Manila, would be able to give Peter the medical care that was impossible to receive in Santo Tomas. It would be expensive, but she had also packed some of her finer pieces of jewelry.

"You are to wear these at all times." Magda handed her two red armbands.

Ellen nodded. She had seen them before. They were to alert outsiders that those who wore them were Japanese prisoners.

"And Doc?"

"I will watch him. Mr. Leake will too."

Ellen frowned. She did not like splitting up her family. But there was no point in wasting time. She bundled Pete up and noticed with alarm that he was too weak to protest her carrying him. In spite of her own slight weight, she swept the boy into her arms.

"Can you manage?" Magda stood, wanting to help.

"I'll have to," Ellen replied as she walked outside with her sick child.

※

The woman was oblivious to Kate's sketching her as she sat by the river pounding her clothes with a small wooden paddle. She gave the Americans little notice now for they had been here over a month.

Kate had thrown a few sketch pads and pencils into her

back pack when she left the Sullivan's house. Settling into a routine at San Alberto had agreed with her and now, for the first time since she had left Baguio, she was returning to her artwork.

"That's good." Sky sat next to her admiring the sketch, "looks just like her."

"Thanks," Kate mumbled with her number three pencil in her mouth.

"Did you bring a lot of paper with you?"

"Mmm huh."

"Save it."

She removed the pencil. "For what?"

"Reconnaissance. Plans, diagrams."

"For our guerrilla band?" She laughed. It was a joke between them for there had been no guerrillas at San Alberto.

"No. America. There's a lot going on in these islands that they're going to have to know about. The more information we can get to them, the easier their task will be in taking back the Philippines."

"Oh." She had not considered that before.

"In fact, Katie darling, your skills are going to come in very handy." His hand slid down the bridge of her sunburned nose.

A low long note startled both of them. Sky pulled a conch shell tied to his belt. He turned the shell over in his hands, before finding the hole on the side and blowing into it. The result was another long, low note, very similar to the one they had just heard. The Filipina had stopped washing her clothes and was now watching the two Americans with interest.

The sound was returned and within minutes Faustino Tapay came into sight. Sweat poured off his face.

"You know, man, I'm not sure I'm cut out for this kind of work," he offered. "Even when I know it's you, that just scares the shit out of me."

Sky laughed. "How'd you know we weren't a real bojong bird?"

"Hey, the birds don't bother me, it's the dwarfs." His heart was pounding, as he admitted his fear. Having just come from Manila, he had had his share of close calls. "The whole place is crawling with them."

"Did you get into Santo Tomas?" Kate asked, eager for news of Ellen and the boys.

He shook his head.

"I walked around the fence but it's tight. They weren't letting anyone in without a pass and I couldn't get my hands on one of them. It looks all right from the outside. Though I hear there's a lot of pellagra and beri-beri in there but they're trying to take care of it. Sorry." He shrugged in apology.

"What other news did you pick up?" Sky's impatience was obvious. He was disappointed that he could not have been the one to go to Manila, but they had all agreed that for him to have done so would have been sheer stupidity. At least Faustino was a Filipino and could pass for a peasant. His Tagalog was also more fluent than Berringer's.

"Corregidor's fallen. They say Wainwright has asked all Americans in the islands to surrender."

Sky rubbed his forehead. He had been to Corregidor before the war and he had wondered how long a small garrison of men could hold the bay.

"And are they?"

"Some of them. Some are heading for the hills. They say a lot of the commanding officers are looking the other way and giving their guys a day or two."

"Good," Kate muttered softly.

"The *Tribune* had a charming story," Tapay said. The *Manila Tribune* had been taken over by the Japanese and was now serving as a propaganda vehicle for them. "Seems as though you bombed Tokyo."

"Oh?" There was real interest in Sky's voice.

"Some guy named Doolittle. Anyway it really pissed the dwarfs off. They massacred over a hundred families in China because they thought they helped him out."

"Did they?" Kate asked.

"Who knows?" Faustino shrugged. "Oh, and MacArthur made it off Corregidor completely. Took his whole damn family and most of his staff and the dwarfs never even saw him. They made it to Australia. He's going to direct our liberation from there."

Sky stood and slapped Tapay on the back. "Good work, Faustino. That's good news. Now, my friends, we really will have something to work for."

"There is one more thing," the Filipino offered. "I ran into a good friend of mine down there." He placed his bag on the ground and rummaged through it. "Jack Daniels." He grinned as he unscrewed the bottle of whiskey.

"They're coming! They're coming!" Doc was bouncing up and down with excitement, for a week had passed since he had seen his mother and little brother. Magda peered through the heavy wrought iron gate, encouraged when she saw that Pete was now on his own two feet, walking slowly, but on his own regardless.

Within minutes, they entered the camp showing their outside pass to the guard on duty who promptly took it from them.

Magda reached for Pete's forehead, relieved to find no heat there. "Ya, he's much better."

"Yes." Fatigue was evident in Ellen's tired blue eyes. "Let's get him to the hospital."

Later, after Pete was tucked into his own hospital bed Ellen and Magda went for a walk. Magda's large brown eyes were shining with excitement.

"I have something for you," she whispered when she was sure there were no guards around.

"For me?" Ellen was surprised. Gifts were almost nonexistent in Santo Tomas.

Magda reached inside her brassiere and withdrew a tiny block of paper. It had been folded many times, until now it was no larger than a thick dime. She handed it to Ellen.

"What on earth?" She turned the paper over in her hands and started to slowly unfold it. Tears flooded into her blue eyes as she recognized Tom's almost illegible handwriting.

"Where did you get this?" She grabbed Magda's arm and squeezed it harder than she intended.

Magda smiled. "It came the evening you left. I was walking on our rounds and someone brought it to me. There was a whole packet of them brought in by one of the Filipino priests."

"I don't understand."

"Guerrillas," Magda explained, "they're handling our mail now."

"My God." Ellen sat on the ground and began to read Tom's letter.

> Darlings:
> It's been five long months since we've seen each other. They have passed with disappointment, despair and worry. The shooting part of this war is now over and we are entering a new phase which holds for us only God knows what.
> To cover my doings since the surrender on May 6. We surrendered at noon and I was picked up by the

Japanese on May 7th about 10:00 a.m. We were moved down to a place called the 92nd garage near the sea and it was a petiole with hor rible sanitary conditions. We did swim to keep partly clean. We all became ill with prickly heat and Guam blisters. Of course dysentery broke out and we lost a number of men then and there.

On the 23rd of May we were marched to the dock and loaded on cattle boats for Manila. We were in deed happy to leave The Rock. We were put on the beach at the end of Dewey Blvd. and marched from there to Bilibid Prison where we stayed until the 26th , then by train to Cabanatuan. The next day we marched 20 kilo meters east to a P.I. Army camp where we are now interned.

News from Manila is scarce but we do hear that you are still interned and getting three meals a day. Our diet on Corregidor was deficient and here it is onion soup and rice three times a day. Some days one quarter of a carabao for fifteen hundred men and today, for the first time, some squash in our soup. We all have beri-beri which is a worry unless things improve.

I've met a great guy called Theodore Barkley. We call him Bark. He has been a godsend to me through all of this.

Ellen darling, out of this war and our separation and hardship one good will come and that is it will teach us how to live and enjoy life. I pray God allows us to live and rear our two sons to become the fine men that we can make them through our love for one another. After this life I want only you, Doc and Pete near me every minute. Money has lost its importance and value to me and my one and only effort will be to live a happy, simple life and to make all of you as happy as possible. I am going to fight to live, my darlings, for all of you.

With deepest love,

Tom

"Good news?" Magda asked.

"Oh yes," Ellen wiped her eyes, "he's alive!"

29

The young marine had celebrated his eighteenth birthday just days before. He had, for the first time since he entered the service, finally told the truth about his age. Not that it would matter now, for there was, unfortunately, no way of kicking him out, of sending him home.

He doubled over again, rolling his wasted body into a fetal position. The cramps were cutting across him once more, eating and tearing at what was left of his insides. He had tried to get rid of them, to think them away, for the medicine, if it had ever existed at O'Donnell, was now long gone. But thinking about the cramps didn't help. The only thing a man could do was to ride them through, knowing that every journey took a terrible price. He was desensitized now, to the point of not even knowing when he evacuated the watery, bloody mucus that seemed to constantly ooze from his whimpering body. He reeked with the fetid odor of his amoebic dysentery.

The cramps were easing and he squinted, trying to focus on the barracks, not twenty yards away. The burning sun beat against his naked back, as the shade under the wooden structure beckoned. If he could only make it there, he thought, it would be so peaceful. He would not have to suffer the heat from the noonday sun.

Slowly, painfully, he began inching his way across the sandy ground, concentrating all of his strength, his very essence, on making this last mission. He reached the steps. No one came in, or out, as he rolled onto his side and into the welcome shade of the building.

Gasping for air, he continued his inching, until he was directly under the building. It was cooler here. The moisture of the paths of excrement and bloody mucus of the men who had crawled under before him was comforting. In a way it was like coming home, he thought, a fleeting smile played across his face as his soft cheek settled into the pile of waste left by other human beings.

He closed his eyes and a peace came over him. It was so cool. So restful here. Somehow, blissfully, this spot was filling some primal need deep within him.

Slowly his thoughts turned back. To a time when he was six years old and his cat, a beloved tabby named Arthur, had gotten hit by a car. When he had tried to reach his pet the animal had spit and hissed at him and had run under the old house. To die.

Too late the comparison came to him. He raised his head only slightly and looked at the bright sunlight just feet away. But he was too tired to go back out. Besides, there were others under here. This couldn't be such a bad place, after all. He reached out and touched the man beside him, marvelling at how cold and refreshing his skin felt. No, he would stay. Where he was safe. Where it was peaceful.

It was three days before the carriers climbed under the barracks, crawling through the muck and filth to retrieve the scores of men who had crept, like wounded and dying animals, under the building to die.

Tom shifted his weight and felt himself sink deeper into the mud. It was everywhere, for the rains had been constant since his arrival in Cabanatuan. The adjustment to hell was made all the more difficult by the draining sky.

It had taken a few days, but Tom had finally stopped staring at his fellow prisoners. The first time he had seen the men from Bataan, he was shocked at the walking skeletons. Their skins were yellow and stretched tight over bones that seemed to jut out at awkward angles. He could tell which of the men had come from Bataan and which had been on Corregidor. Just by looking. The island soldiers were in better physical shape. More meat on their bones. The bony structures that haunted Cabanatuan were testament to the rigors of the Bataan Death March.

"Used to be an agricultural station, you know," the skeleton in front of Tom offered.

"That's comforting," Tom searched the man's face, wondering whether he had been handsome before Bataan. Now it was impossible to tell, with his sunken eyes and skull-like appearance.

"A United States Agricultural station," the man continued. "Corregidor? When'd you come?"

"Last week. You?"

"Bataan. I hear we're getting more in. Some guys from O'Donnell. That's the shits. Less food for us."

As if on cue, Tom's stomach started grumbling. He sank in the mud again, shifting the three canteens he was carrying.

"Can you see the water yet?"

"Yeah. At least that means we're getting closer. Damn thing just drips. System ain't very efficient."

"What is?" Tom asked, as he looked at the hundreds of men behind him, waiting to fill their canteens. He had been standing in line for over three hours. It was worth it, for each of them were only allowed one canteen of water each day.

"My best friend died this morning," the man said, no emotion crossing his gaunt features. "Just up and died."

"Sorry. That happens in here."

"But the funny thing was he wasn't awfully sick or anything like that, you know? He just stopped eating."

Tom grunted. He had seen it before. Although the rice was often sour and contaminated, most of the men had gotten over any queasiness about eating it. Food was too scarce. Some men though would refuse to eat and in so doing just got weaker and weaker until they finally died.

"Lost the will to live," the man nudged Tom in the ribs, a gesture he did not appreciate, "you believe in that?"

"Sure." Tom felt a twinge as he thought of Bark, left behind in the barracks with his wounded eye.

"You got to learn to hate something in here, I'm convinced of that. That's the only thing that'll get us through this shit. Hate."

"Hate?" Suddenly Tom was thinking of love. Of Ellen and his boys. "What's the matter with love?"

"Oh it's all right. Hey, I got a wife and kids just like the next guy. But that won't see me through this. If I can just remember all these Nip bastards done to me then I'll make it because I'll have to get even."

"Well that's an interesting theory," Tom said. He had heard the philosophies before. Some men added two more things to their formula for survival. A belief in a God of some sort and a sense of humor.

"John. John Case. That was my friend's name. He just

couldn't hate. Do you know what I did this morning?"

Tom shook his head as he moved up in line.

"Right before he died. See, I could see it coming. Well, I got me a big stick and I started pounding him with it, I mean slapping him real hard all over, like I seen the medics do." Tears were now swelling in the man's sunken eyes. "I screamed at him. Told him if he died I was going to go home and fuck his wife and you know what that lousy son-of-a- bitch did? He died." The man wiped his face with a grimy hand. "He couldn't hate. He just couldn't hate and I couldn't give him the will to live."

Tom remained silent. There was nothing that could be said. He moved up in line.

The canteens, once filled, were heavy and Tom could feel his strength failing as he hauled them back to the barracks.

He and Bark had realized from the start that the only way to survive in Cabanatuan was to band together in a tight little group where each man would look out for the next. There was too much theft in here. And death. A man alone was asking for it. You needed friends to see you through. Of course there was the draw-back mentioned by the man in the water line. One risk. Sometimes they died and left you alone.

Bark was writhing across the bamboo slats that served as beds, holding his face, as Tom entered the barracks. The engineer unscrewed the top of one of the canteens and poured some of the fresh water on a filthy rag.

"How you doing, Bark?"

"Did you get the medicine? Did Tully get it?"

"No, he's still looking." Tully, a medical corpsman, was part of their group. He had run out of medicine a long time ago and was now out searching for more. "Let me clean you up with a little water."

"No!" Bark shrieked. "It hurts too goddamn much to have you touch it. I think I'd rather die, Tom, I really do."

"Goddamnit, Bark. Don't talk like that." Tom grabbed him by one thin shoulder.

"Could you kill me Sullivan? I mean if I asked you to do it, do you think you could?" Pain twisted the good parts of Bark's face. "I'm not asking you now, you understand. But could you?"

"Shut up, Theodore Barkley."

Tully arrived in time to hear the gunner's request. The bald corpsman had little patience for those eager to die. "I got some medicine for you."

"You do?" Bark half rose off the cot.

"Course we've all given up smoking as of this moment," Tully grinned at Tom. "Now, hold still and let's see what I can do for you."

Tully had cleaned Bark's face a few days earlier. It was so hard to get anything really clean in Cabanatuan. Everything was dirty. Used. The bandages, such as they were, were put on and then taken off and rinsed out, rarely sterilized. Medicine was almost to the point of extinction. It was by sheer luck that Tully had run into another medic with a nicotine habit stronger than his urge to cure. He had gotten taken on the trade, but it was worth it if he could save Bark.

"Can you hold him?"

Tom nodded.

"You don't need to do that." Bark squirmed, as Tom's hands came down hard across his shoulders.

Tully carefully pulled the bloodstained bandage off the gaping, crusted wound. A gasp involuntarily escaped from Tom as he pinned Bark tighter to the bed.

"How's it look?" The gunner whispered, afraid to hear their answer.

"Fine. You're going to be just fine, Bark. Now shut up and hold on. This is going to hurt some." Tully began carefully wiping the eye cavity.

"Jesus Christ!" Bark writhed under Tom's weight, wincing with the pain of the pressure against his injured orb. "What in the hell are you doing to me?" He gasped, his voice wrenched with pain.

"Hold still. I'm wiping the maggots out of your eye."

Tom watched as the medic tenderly pulled the fat white worms out of Bark's face. Sullivan wanted to burn them on the spot, to cremate them and torture them for all the feasting they had done on his friend's flesh. He said nothing, concentrating on holding the big man down.

Tully pushed and patted the sides of the wound, oozing still more of the maggots from the deep hole. Bark was screaming now.

"That's it." Tully said to no one in particular. He was draped across Bark's chest, helping pin him as he continued to spread the wound open with his right hand, while his left fumbled with the glass jar he had brought back.

"Need help?" Tom asked.

"No. Hold him." Tully unscrewed the bottle with his teeth, spitting the cap onto Bark's chest. Without hesitating, he poured the antiseptic into the contaminated cavity. Bark bucked hard against them and then lay back against the bamboo as sweat poured off his tortured body.

"Thanks." He whispered before passing out.

"Son-of-a-bitch." Tom squished one of the maggots between his thumb and forefinger.

"Look on the bright side," Tully suggested as he flicked a little pile of them off, and watched with satisfaction as they fell through the wooden slats of the barracks floor to the ground below. "They probably saved him from gangrene."

Tom looked at Bark who was now sleeping deeply, exhausted from his ordeal. "Is he going to make it?"

"I don't know. This is a good start. At least he has the benefit of medicine. That's nine-tenths more than most of these guys have got. I'll try to get more."

"Thanks, Tully." Relief washed Tom.

"I don't think we're going to save his eye though," The medic said gently.

"An eye for a life isn't such a bad trade is it, Tully?"

"No."

"Would he have had to go to Zero Ward without the medication?"

"I don't know. To the hospital probably."

There were two basic wards at the hospital. One for men who had a chance; the other for the goners. Zero ward, where the dead were stacked three deep, was for the goners.

"Tully, may I ask you something?"

"Sure."

"When I was standing in line a while ago the guy in front of me was talking about the medics beating people with sticks. Do you know anything about that?"

"Over at the hospital a guy comes through and whips the patients who are conked out. If they don't respond, then they don't waste much time on them."

"My God," Tom said softly, knowing that it made sense, that care should be extended to those who were willing to fight to live.

"He'll sleep for a good while," Tully observed. "Want to try for some rats?"

They walked to the drainage ditch farthest from their barracks. They were not alone, for here and there along the system there were a score of men perched along the muddy embankment waiting for that propitious moment when a careless rat would run through the ditch.

Tully and Tom, armed with stout sticks, sat quietly, one on either side of the grassy bank with only a foot of slime separating them. They had done this before and had found out that this system worked the best. This way if one of them missed the furry creature, the other was sure to get it.

They waited for an hour and a half, before one of the loathsome rodents ventured down into their section of the ditch. The rats were one of the few fat things in Cabanatuan, feasting on slime, waste and dead bodies.

The animal was wary as he approached them. A veteran. He had been through the ditches before and his caution was apparent.

Tom's arm ached as he held his club in an awkward position, afraid of moving, lest he scare off the animal.

The rat sat on its haunches a minute, sniffing the air. It stared at the men, first one, then the other, before deciding that neither was a threat.

As he ran in front of them, the clubs came together in unison crushing the pudgy body. A blow each was more than enough to do the trick and as the animal jerked spasmodically, Tully lifted it by the tail swinging it hard and snapping its fragile neck.

"That's one!" He grinned, pleased with their catch.

"Five cigarettes," Tom agreed. It was the current black market value for the dead rodent.

"Shall we try for ten?"

Tom nodded.

The medics had started the program. It was serving a dual purpose, that of cleaning up the camp, as well as providing a little more protein in the daily meal.

They waited for another hour before the second rat came along. Within minutes, it was all over.

"You know, Tom, something has occurred to me," Tully said, "do we really want those cigarettes that badly?"

"What do you mean?"

"Why don't we keep them? Cook them ourselves."

"Not share them?"

"No. Not trade them."

"We'd need a pot though," Tom said thoughtfully.

"I think I know where we can get one. Have you got any cigarettes left?" Tully asked. Cigarettes were the camp commodity. A man with cigarettes could get his hands on almost anything.

"A few."

"I'll see what I can do. Stash these someplace safe until I get back." He handed the limp creatures to Tom.

It was not a novel idea. Private kitchens, called quans, were sprouting up all over. The rats, along with trapped birds, lizards, frogs, grub worms, cats and dogs, were finding their way into the quan pots more frequently than into the common kitchen.

※

It was a mixed blessing. They hated it and they needed it, Tom thought as he pushed the hoe back and forth, attacking the clods with as much energy as he could muster. Many of the prisoners were working the farm. At least those who were healthy enough to be on the right end of the short Philippine hoe. Chopping at the clods, bent in an awkward position all day long, gave a man time to think. That, Tom thought, was one of the good things about farm detail.

On the other hand, abuse was common. Guards would stage slapping contests forcing Americans to slap one another for long periods of time. Then there were the endurance tests. Sometimes a man was forced to hold a fifty pound stone over his head for four hours or more in the unforgiving sun. Another favorite Japanese amusement was to force the Americans to kneel for hours with a 2 by 4 placed under their knees.

The three hundred acres had been a farmer's challenge. The raw, virginal land, covered with cogon grass, had fought them every step of the way. The grass itself cut cruelly into their bare feet, and legs, and they soon found these wounds infected with tropical ulcers.

"Watch it! Cobra!" Tully yelled.

Tom jumped back and hacked off the baby snake's head with the dull hoe.

"That's the third one this week," Tom observed. "And that's just us. Ants and snakes. Terrific work."

"On the bright side, more protein." Tully offered, for the baby snake would go into their quan pot.

Tom grinned at the thought. They weren't supposed to be talking at all. Even in whispers. But since there had been so many snakes killed recently, the guards were staying a little farther away. While the cobras were a hazard, they were almost welcome if their presence gave the men the chance for conversation.

"At least we'll eat better when all of this is done," Tully pulled a sweaty arm across his wet forehead and grinned. His optimism would be short-lived for the men quickly discovered that most of the crops went to the Japanese guards. Still, if a man was careful he could harvest a few camote tops and if he was really lucky, he might manage a few onion tops. Either of which was better in their soup than the tough swamp green known as "whistle" weed.

"I think I could even learn to eat eggplant," Tom laughed. While there was not much to be thankful for at Cabanatuan, he was happy this morning. The sun was shining and he was healthy enough to go on a work detail. It was funny how life could be stripped down to the basics in such a short period of time, he thought.

They were lagging a little behind the rest of the men who were breaking up the clods. Almost directly behind them, came another work detail that was raking and smoothing the disturbed earth.

"We better catch up before those vitamin sticks catch us," Tom increased his tempo, not eager to stand out in line.

"Yes. Big Speedo's beginning to pay attention," Tully agreed. The vigilant guard was twirling his wooden club, nicknamed a vitamin stick by the workers for they all maintained that he got more work out of them with that than he would with a fistful of vitamins.

The damned dogs had been at it again. Scratching and digging at the graves when night fell and the darkness obscured their deed. Now, in the morning light, half buried, gnawed bodies were pulled partially out of their common grave.

George Bendetti kicked a severed ear back into the violated pit. He always resented it when the dogs from the nearby Filipino barrio had been digging. It just created more work for the already overtaxed grave detail. Allowing chaplains to accompany the burial details was a new camp policy and for the hundredth time, he cursed his misfortune at being assigned the unenviable task of burying the dead.

It happened his fourth day in camp when a major, his face pitted with pockmarks, had assigned the priest to the detail, suggesting the propriety of the dead having a man of the cloth to say words over them. Bendetti grinned wryly as he thought of some of the words he had said over the departed.

At least he had been lucky enough to be a digger. The carriers really had it tough, collecting the bodies that were stacked outside the barracks each morning. They hauled them out seven times a day. By the time the bodies came to him, they were already stripped, their clothes passed on to the living, their dog tags recorded.

Flies, ever present at Camp O'Donnell, formed a thick shroud for the gruesome corpses wrapped in army issue blankets and brought in strung on poles. While the idea was to unravel the blanket and pull the edge in such a way that its contents would fall into the grave, it seldom worked out that the dead did not have to be touched.

One could poke and pull all one wanted to with sticks to avoid that inevitable moment of contact with dead flesh, but sooner or later there came a snag and the corpse would have to be handled. Usually they had to be straightened out too, for only if they were in neat lines, head to toe, could the maximum number fit into the shallow graves.

Whenever Bendetti had to touch the bodies it sickened him. The rotten flesh seemed to stick to his hands and he could smell the dead on his own body. He shuddered thinking of it, and continued to dig, scarcely noticing the stacks of bodies lined up ready for burial.

The priest had dug down about four and a half feet when he saw water beginning to ooze into the grave. It was a problem activated by the shallow water table. He stopped digging deep and began widening the hole, working steadily around the edges. The effort would have taken a man in good shape an hour at most. It took him most of the morning.

"Over here." He yelled to two men carrying a bundled package of defeated humanity on a bamboo frame.

Working silently, they unrolled the contents of their sling into the grave. Immediately the body began to float up, pushed by the buoyancy of the water that was threatening to fill the grave.

"Better stick him," muttered the smaller of the two carriers.

Bendetti grabbed a long heavy pole and placed it hard against the dead man's chest anchoring the body, as the second carrier shoveled dirt on top of it.

The first man returned from the pile of dead and unrolled another corpse on top of the first one.

"Double decking, it's kind of shallow," the priest said, fearful that the scant foot and a half of cover would offer an invitation to the nocturnal dogs.

"Look at that," the man pointed to the fifty or so dead bodies ready for burial. "Shit, they smell bad enough already. What choice do we have?"

The priest had to agree they had none, if the job was going to be completed. He moved his stick to the third body that had been brought over, holding it down, while dirt was piled on top of it.

They went on stacking the dead in two tiers, always taking care to anchor the first, before throwing on the second body. It was a good day for all of them for they had not seen anyone they recognized.

Bendetti stood at the edge of the grave and stared as the last body was thrown in. He recognized the open mouthed, rigor mortis stiff corpse immediately. It was the pockmarked major that had assigned him to this gruesome detail weeks earlier.

"You can go back now," he said to the carriers, "I can finish this up myself."

Exhausted, they did not stop to argue with him. They lifted their poles and were off down the road.

Bendetti looked to the Japanese guard who was a ways off, lighting a cigarette.

The priest waited until the carriers were several hundred feet away before he turned his back to them, unzipped his fly and urinated in the major's gaping mouth.

30

The stench was almost overpowering, hovering as they were over the open fetid trench. They were not alone, for up and down the ditch men were straddling it, relieving themselves. The trench was never without visitors, for it was as much a part of life at Cabanatuan as the ever present flies, the guards, and the rice sprinkled with weevils and worms.

Sloping gently from five feet down to the open sewer, the foul contents of the channel were constantly increased by the straining, praying men. From the beginning, there had been sights at the ditch that had shocked them all. Conservative men before the war now dug and probed their own anuses in a desperate attempt to dislodge material that was blocking the passage of their body gases, liquids and wastes. There was no privacy here, and the tugging, straining and pulling were taken for granted, having lost their shock value long ago.

Bark strained to eliminate.

"Any luck?" The medic straddled next to him, pouring out a steady stream of brown mucus. He was getting better, for it had been white.

Bark grunted.

"If it doesn't get any better, we're going to have to do something, you know that."

Bark shook his head and concentrated, slowly beginning to feel the easing of the pressure. "No, it's all right."

Tully stepped across the ditch and pulled up his shorts. "I don't see any evidence of that. I think your colon's had it."

Bark strained again, half pushing, half praying that something would pass out of him. He had seen the men with the colons that were gone, eaten with disease. The doctors had worked on them and now they all sported small rubber bags with drainage tubes connected to their stomachs. Vest pocket assholes, they called them. "No thanks."

A gush of liquid came roaring out of him, hitting the ditch and splattering his legs. It was heaven. He felt his prayers had been answered as the fluid poured into the putrid ditch.

"See, Tully! I did it!" The pride in his voice could have been that of a two-year-old boy conquering his first bathroom elimination.

The medic applauded. "You're off the hook, this time." He offered him a hand and pulled him across the ditch.

Barkley patted his now flat stomach. "That feels a lot better, Tully, it really does."

⚔

"Rat's ass!" Tennessee, his bare feet gripping the rugged bark of the coconut tree, scurried down the thirty feet or so he had already climbed, dropping wire to the ground below.

"What's the matter?" Charlie stood at the base of the tree.

"Ants." Parker held out his bare arm, showing large white welts, the size of quarters. "Big frigging tree ants. Those suckers can really sting." He rubbed his swollen arm in an unsuccessful effort to make the spots disappear.

The Navajo began gathering the fallen wire. "Want to try

another tree?"

Tennessee shook his head. "This one's half strung and the colonel wants it done before dark. You got any tuba with you?"

Begay pulled out a soda bottle, its glass mouth stuffed with a rag. Although gasoline acquisition had become a real problem, some clever guerrilla had come up with tuba. Made by combining juice from the palm trees with crushed mangrove bark, the result was a fuel that, with certain automotive adaptations, would give around seven miles to the gallon. On top of all that, the remarkable stuff, sweetened with chocolate or eggs, produced a tasty drink that gave a pretty good kick.

Parker stripped off his shirt and wrapped it around a thick stick, tying it securely. He slowly poured the tuba over the wrapped cloth.

"Got a match?"

Charlie shook his head. Matches were almost as rare as gasoline.

"Hold this for me, will you?" Tennessee thrust the torch into the Indian's hand. "I'll run down and see if any of those guys have one." He pointed to a clearing below, where another crew was stringing wire.

Charlie sat on the ground and after carefully inspecting the coconut bark for ants, he leaned his back against it.

While they were in Manila, Isabel had talked to some of her friends who had introduced them to Primitivo San Agustin and his good friend, Ferdinand Marcos. They were with the underground and had known everything about contacting the guerrilla groups just outside Manila.

Charlie smiled, as he remembered how San Agustin had amused them both with glowing stories of his own death. He swore that he actually had his name inscribed in a granite head-stone in a Manila cemetery. He had even put flowers on his own grave three times since the Japanese had come. San Agustin, Charlie decided, would make a poor Navajo.

Charlie's mechanical skills, and Parker's Signal Corps experience, made them welcome additions to Lieutenant Colonel Guillermo Nakar's growing band of guerrillas. The fact that both men had been raised in the country pleased him too, for the guerrilla leaders were quickly finding that men from the city were having trouble adapting to jungle life. Many of them had already opted for the more structured life of the internment camps.

After the Death March, it was a good feeling to be with reasonably healthy men again. Now the immediate task at hand was putting in a communication system that would not only put the different bands throughout Luzon in radio communication with one another, but one that could contact the outside world. Colonel Nakar was eager to radio General MacArthur and offer him the services of his group.

With their retreat into Bataan, the Americans and Filipinos had sabotaged the communication system. Wires had been stripped and carried off, and now the guerrillas were having to make do with what they could get. In some parts of the system they were even pounding out barbed wire, stripping it of its barbs. The barbs were saved, pounded out and used as small nails. In the guerrilla camp, nothing was thrown out, for necessity would call sooner or later, and even the most insignificant item could become important.

"Got them." Tennessee placed the box of matches between his teeth. "How quick will this burn?"

"Not as fast as gasoline, but you'd better wait until you're on top to light it," Charlie suggested, as he handed the torch back to Charlie.

The radioman was slower climbing the tree this time. He moved carefully, inspecting the bark for ants before he placed his hands on an unfamiliar spot. When he got just below the area where he had been working, he held the torch away from him and lit it with a match. As it began to burn, he waved it back and forth around the tree and charred ant bodies fell to the ground. He moved the torch up above the spot where he had been securing the wire and burned still more of the insects. Finally satisfied, he threw the still burning cloth to the ground and continued stringing the wire.

"Hey, we got any insulators?" He hollered.

Charlie held up an empty soda pop bottle. "Army issue." They quickly found out that, lacking insulators, the pop bottles would do almost as well.

They worked steadily until the end of the day.

"That's the last one," Tennessee slumped against the tree, aching from all of the climbing and twisting. "Shall we give her a whirl?"

"Why not?"

Parker picked up the radio set and began transmitting.

Silence. Parker turned in the clearing and repeated his message.

Still nothing.

He tapped the set before trying again.

"Roger. QRK5." The message was coming over loud and clear. "Come on in."

"You did it!" Charlie slapped the young soldier on the back. "That sounded good. Real good."

"It's better than that Charlie. It's a QRK5."

Begay was puzzled.

"Ham radio talk," Parker explained. "We've just given them a very clear, very powerful, signal."

※

Tom Sullivan stared at his feet as though they belonged to a stranger. They may as well have been, for in their distorted and swollen state they were not doing him any good. He strained to rotate his right ankle, but even as the sweat poured from his brow, there was no movement there. Rigidity had set in. Walking was out of the question.

Tully patted the bridge of his foot. The gesture would have made him scream just days ago but was now hardly felt.

"Beri-beri. That's what you've got," the medic said.

"I know." Tom stared dully at his swollen feet. "I can't walk."

"You'll be able to. We've got a line on the squash scrapings. Bark's out now."

"Tell me about it."

Tully shrugged. Everyone knew about beri-beri in Cabanatuan. Many of them were suffering from it, but it was like anything else, it suddenly became more important when you were the one who was afflicted. When it was your feet that were swollen, then you wanted all the gory details about the disease that was threatening to overcome you.

"Multiple neuritis. You have these protein sheaths on your nerve endings," Tully held up a finger in demonstration. The fingers of his other hand began rubbing down the uplifted digit. "Your body in its starving, unbalanced state is stripping that sheath off and using the protein. Nothing you're experiencing is uncommon. General debility and painful rigidity. It hurts, doesn't it?"

Tom nodded.

"Caused by a lack of vitamin B-1. You can thank your rice diet for that."

Sullivan tried to move his feet again. It was as though they were cast in lead.

"Save your strength." His effort had not been lost on Tully. "We'll see if we can feed you. That should take care of it."

"Could you reach in my bag?" Tom pointed overhead, where a canvas bag hung.

Tully reached for the duffel and handed it to him. Tom fumbled through it and finally withdrew his pocket watch. He snapped it open and handed it to Tully. The medic studied the pretty blonde woman and two cherubic looking children before handing it back.

"Handsome family." He was beginning to worry about the engineer. He had seen it too many times before. Mental attitude, those thoughts that pervaded a man's consciousness, was what made the difference between a man's living or dying. Absent anything lethal.

"Yes," Tom pulled the photograph in close to his heart. "And I'll tell you something, Tull. These bastards aren't going to get me. I'm not coming this far and then dying from fat feet."

"You'll be better next week, Tom. You'll see." Tully tried to keep the relief out of his voice.

While the squash scrapings were slimy against Bark's skin, it was the can of pork and beans, slipping and sliding inside his shirt, that he was worried about. They were all trying to supplement their diets now. Extra rice. Canned goods. Fresh vegetables. All scarce, but sometimes available to those who could pay. A Filipino barrio was not far from the prison camp and many of its pigs and chickens were finding their way in to those men fortunate enough to have money or barter. Japanese guards, as well as regular merchants, were dealing in the black market food-stuffs . One man had set up a regular store inside the prison camp. Canned sardines, sugar, coconut, coffee, all were available to the man who had the means to purchase them.

Even the regular food at Cabanatuan was getting a little better for the rice and *lugao* were now supplemented with some grease and flour.

Bark headed around the corner of the barracks just in time to collide with another prisoner. As the two men hit, the elusive can tumbled out of the gunner's thin cotton shirt and onto the dusty ground. Before Bark could retrieve it, the other man bent and snatched up the rolling container. He held it firmly in his right hand, his eyes straining to read the label.

Bark straightened up, prepared to do battle for the pork and beans. Adjusting the black patch he now wore over his left eye he used his good one to quickly size up the shorter, thinner man. This one, he thought, must have been on the march.

"I'll take that." He held out his hand to take the can, but the other man kept it tightly within his grip.

"Pork and beans. Did you buy it from the darky?"

Bark shook his head. The can had been his first purchase and he had negotiated it through one of the guards. "It's for a sick friend. Beri-beri." He stepped closer to the man and reached for the can. This time it was returned to him.

"Oh, why didn't you say so. I'll come with you," the man licked his full lips. "I can help. I'm a priest."

Relieved that he had retained possession of the precious can, Bark led the man who called himself a priest back to his barracks.

Tom's eyes were closed and Tully was sitting on the slatted floor beside him when they walked in. Bark held up the can.

"There's more where this came from," he whispered, "but I only bought one. I wanted to make sure it was all right."

Tully reached for a homemade, narrow bladed, knife and worked at the top of the can, ignoring the man who had come in with Bark. There were so many men these days that drifted in and out of their lives. It was difficult and discouraging to keep track of them, for the parade of new faces changed constantly.

"He's a priest," Bark explained.

At the sound of his words, Tom's eyes flew open. Maybe he was sicker than Tully thought if they had called in a priest. He squinted towards them but their backs were to the doorway, silhouetted against the sun. Sullivan strained, trying to make out the features on the drawn face of the priest.

"Hello, Father." Tom spoke to the man.

"Hello, my son," the priest knelt beside the stricken man, as much as to get closer to the aroma that was drifting from the partially opened can as to offer comfort.

"George," Tom half rose from his bed. "George Bendetti?"

The priest's eyes narrowed. He was always suspicious of people who called him by both names. He preferred being known as Father George. That was enough. More than that put him in a dangerous situation. One of complete identification and there were certain things he had recently become involved with that could make identification dangerous.

He stared at the man with the swollen legs. It was so hard when the men got so thin. Their features, those things that made them them, faded and took on a kind of homogenous quality. He pressed his memory for thirty seconds or so before it came to him.

"Tom Sullivan." Bendetti patted his old friend with the closest thing to genuine affection that he was capable of showing. "How'd you get here?"

"Corregidor. And you?"

"Bataan. Where are Ellen and Kate?" The priest had all but forgotten his quest for the pork and beans now that he had discovered his old friend.

"Santo Tomas. I don't know about Kate."

A black look crossed the priest's gaunt features. Getting back to the one woman who had meant anything to him was the thing that kept him going every day.

"Have you been here all along?" Tom asked.

"No. Camp O'Donnell. I've been here about three weeks."

"We heard it was bad there."

The priest shrugged. "It's bad everywhere."

Tully pushed the can in front of Tom. "Eat this. It will help you."

Sullivan stared at the opened can, not believing his eyes. Filled to the brim with the brown beans and chunky pieces of pork, it was more food than he had seen in months.

"I can't eat all of that. Let's share it." Guilt was taking over. There was no way he could eat the entire can while his friends went hungry.

Bark pushed the can closer to him.

"Eat, goddamnit. You're the one with the fucking poor feet. If it was me or Tully we'd gobble that up. Next time it might be. But for now, it's you." Bark grabbed Bendetti and pulled him up by his elbow, spinning him in the direction of the doorway as he did so. "Sorry, *padre*, this is a family affair."

"I'll see you later, George," Tom called as the priest left the barracks.

Tully and Bark turned their backs to their friend, giving him privacy in which to devour his feast. Tom tried to eat as quietly as he could, so they would not be tormented with the sounds of his tongue lapping at the contents of the tin.

31

Doc crouched underneath the opened window, waiting.

It wouldn't be long now, he thought, for the Japanese had been meeting for fifteen minutes, and the prizes the young boy sought would soon be thrown through the casement. Just then, the stub of a lit cigarette flew through the window and landed on the dirt in front of him.

He quickly retrieved the spent cigarette, snuffing out the tip in the sand before he stashed it in the front pocket of his shorts. Within minutes, another filterless treasure came flying out and he grabbed that one, too. After an hour, the pocket of his shorts was jammed with the used butts. When he heard the scraping of the chairs against the wooden floor, he knew the meeting was over and he hurried back to the shanty.

The sawali sided, tar paper roofed shack had been a godsend for all of them. It was a place of peace and quiet, of escape from the crowded dormitories and public areas. An entire community of the shanties sprouted on the university grounds. Places where families could go during the day to read, or visit, or sleep. When night came, the internees were all expected back at their assigned places.

Magda sat on a cot, working on a piece of embroidery as Doc walked in. Quickly, he emptied his pockets and lined up the cigarettes in a straight line.

"How grand!" Ellen gave her oldest a quick squeeze, taking care not to lavish too much affection on him. In the last six months, he had taken his responsibilities very seriously. Now he was in that difficult no-man's land, half-boy, half-man. She had seen him gradually withdraw from her hugs and kisses. While it was painful for both of them, it was something they both instinctively knew was a passage. "It must have been a long meeting."

"Yes." The boy watched, as his mother carefully slit the cigarette papers, exposing the coarse tobacco. Expertly, she collected the leaf into an empty can.

"We are out of papers, Ellen." Magda offered, as she continued her stitching.

Ellen paused for a moment before reaching for her Episcopal Prayer Book. Turning to the back pages, she quickly read the last page before ripping it from the well worn book. Tapping some of the tobacco from the tin onto the thin paper, she fumbled for a few minutes before getting the tobacco properly placed. Finally she rolled it up and pinched both ends before lighting it.

"There. That will do." She inhaled deeply. "Yes, that works just fine." She handed the homemade cigarette to the Czech, who put her needlework on the cot beside her.

Ellen picked up the handkerchief she had been working on and read the Japanese name that she was embroidering across it.

"Abiko. That's gruesome," Ellen wrinkled her nose. The scrawling signature of one of the Japanese guards was offensive to her. She could not understand why so many of the women were working on these grim reminders of their stay in Santo Tomas.

"It is a souvenir." Magda took another drag on the prayer book cigarette. "Who knows, maybe I will give you one for your birthday."

The thin blonde laughed. "I can hardly wait. I'd rather have one of those airplane coconuts instead."

"That is getting to be serious. They caught two more drinking. "I understand there is going to be some kind of public display later."

Ellen nodded. She was aware of the liquor problems in the camp. The package line had been opened to facilitate receiving goods from the outside and although the bags were searched, many of the internees had succeeded in smuggling alcohol in.

The Pan American pilots had been particularly clever. Their innocent appearing coconuts had holes bored in them and had been filled with rum. When that ruse was discovered, the pilots had imported bamboo for their shanties. Different sections of the poles had been removed, filled with liquor and replaced. The fun loving pilots and their friends were going to extraordinary lengths to keep the liquor flowing.

But the Clipper boys did not have a corner on the market. The guards had found spirits in the shanties, and a liquor patrol squad had been formed. There had even been threats of increased guards for Santo Tomas.

"Look Mother, there they are." Doc was standing at an open window pointing to the pilots.

Two internees, men they did not know, were being paraded through the camp, their hands tied behind their backs. Apparently sober, they walked in a straight line.

"It could be worse," Ellen said.

"Ya," Magda agreed. "I think we better concentrate on one vice," she suggested as she turned back to the prayer book.

"Mother, where's my gun?" Doc was under the cot reaching for a tattered cardboard satchel.

"It's in there, dear." Ellen knelt beside him, rearranging the things as she groped for the cold metal of the air pistol in the bottom of the bag.

Doc pulled it out and gave it a loving look. It had already been explained to him that he could not play with the toy at all in camp. In fact, Ellen had wondered many times whether or not she should have turned the toy gun over to the Japanese. Magda had talked her out of it, arguing that it was only a toy and could bring no harm as long as Doc did not brandish it about. He seemed to take so much pleasure in it, she had reasoned, in just knowing that it was there.

"Did you hear the doctor last night?" Magda asked.

"No. Was he good?"

"Ya. We are a primitive herd now."

"A primitive herd," Ellen mulled the words over, thinking she had indeed missed an interesting talk.

"The space here. It creates friction. He says we are all jockeying for our positions. More privilege we seek." Magda explained.

"Well, I'm sure he's got something there, dear." Ellen had now torn five pages from the book and five lumpy cigarettes sat on the cot. She was so intent on her work, that she did not notice that Doc had placed the air pistol inside the waistband of his shorts and had covered it with his shirt. Carefully, he closed the satchel and pushed it back under the bed.

"I've got to go to the kitchen now, Mother." The boy tapped his mother's arm. "I'll see you later."

"All right, Doc." She said absently.

❧

The rain was streaming down, pattering against the palm roofs of the barracks and here and there, where the nipa was not quite as thick, or where the rats had loosened it up in making their nests, the water dripped onto the slatted floor. It had been drizzling for three days and the men, who ordinarily did most of their living outside, sat in their slatted beds, sleeping, dreaming, passing time. Although dreary, the rain was welcome in that it killed some of the ever present flies. In Cabanatuan it was impossible to eat without ingesting some of them and their presence contributed greatly to the constant dysentery suffered by the men.

"It was the fourth, wasn't it?" Bark asked.

"No. The sixth," Tom replied.

"You sure?"

"Hell, I wasn't even there and I know it was the sixth," Tully was agreeing with Tom.

"All right. You guys aren't pulling a fast one on me, are you?"

Tom handed Bark his mess kit. There, scratched into the sides were meaningful dates. May 6, 1942 was a prominent one. "Look at it this way, Bark. If we're wrong, these will really be collector's items."

No one remembered who had first come up with the bright idea, but it sure made sense that first rainy day. Now, many of them were carving on their mess kits and cups, creating souvenirs of their time spent at Cabanatuan. Scratching and sculpting with broken glass, crudely fashioned knives, bent nails, anything they could get their hands on, they labored over the kits and cups that were so vital to their existence.

"I'm glad I don't have five kids," Tom said, "I don't know what I could get for all of them."

"They'd just have to share," Tully suggested.

"Tull, it's obvious from that stupid remark that you don't have kids," Bark said. "Kids don't like to share anything, unless there's something in it for them. They're savages."

Tom smiled. He was missing Pete and Doc, and he loved to hear Bark's great expositions on how all children were born savages and how it was up to the parents to teach them right from wrong, civility from animalism. Tom wondered how Ellen was doing in all of those lessons without him.

He labored over his mess kit. This would be for Pete, he thought, the cup for Doc. At least in this way they would have some memento and it was a damn sure bet that the cup and kit would be all that Tom would have for them when this was all over. He sat up and swung his legs to the floor, still appreciative of the effort, for he had no trouble remembering how frightened he had been with the swollen feet that had refused to cooperate with the rest of his body.

The guys had been terrific, channeling as much spare food as they could buy to feed him up and get his body chemicals back in proper balance. They had made him well, he knew that. They talked among themselves about their little group. It was the only way to survive in a place like this. To belong to a clique that would watch out for you, just as you would watch out for them. Sharing. Nothing belonged to one man any more. It was share and share alike. It was a good system and one which was restoring Tom's faith in his fellow human beings, day by day, as they survived in Cabanatuan.

George Bendetti came in, wet hair plastered to his skull, clothes drenched with the monsoon's blessings. He held up two tins of sardines.

"Thanks, George," Tom said. "But I'm better now, I don't need them."

"Take them. You will." The priest said, ignoring Bark and Tully.

"No, really my feet are much better now." Tom rotated his

ankles in unison in a demonstration of the great powers that had returned to him. "I can probably go dancing."

Bendetti threw the unopened tins on the cot next to his friend. "I want you to have these." Without another word he turned and left the barracks.

"Goddamned parasitic bloodsucker," Bark growled.

"You ought to take those sardines and tell him to stick them up his ass." Tully suggested.

"Easy." Tom's voice was strained. "He's doing the best he can."

"Shit," Bark argued, "He's a leech. The worst kind, running around pretending to be a man of God and stealing from all of those poor bastards."

"He's a priest, he really is," Tom offered in Bendetti's defense.

"Then God help the church," Tully said, crossing himself.

"Amen," Bark agreed.

It was now common knowledge that the priest had fallen in with bad companions, including the olive-skinned American, known as the darky. The darky's gang had powerful interests. It had started when they had pawned off pills made of cornstarch as sulfa tablets. No one really knew how many of the little numbers had been sold, and while it was rumored that most of the buyers had been Japanese guards, there had been some Americans who, in their desperation, had bartered for the placebos. The guards, fearing reprimands from their superiors, had kept their mouths shut about the fake tablets. As word had spread throughout camp, the scam had faded and now everyone waited to see what new con would take its place.

The darky's gang had become food brokers almost overnight. If you needed additional rations- sugar, coffee, cocoa- when none were available from any other source, you could always get them from the darky's gang at an exorbitant price. It was a risky business though, for the Japanese had already executed several men for dealing in the black market.

That the gang was powerful was indisputable, for none of the rumored members were ever seen on any work detail and even the guards gave them a wide berth. To belong to the gang gave one a certain amount of protection, along with the enmity of the internees.

"That's the third time this week," Bark said, his good eye staring at the sardines.

The medic took one of the cans off the cot and began opening it with his knife.

Tom watched him open the can. "And this is the same man who suggested we place those treasures in a certain part of a certain person's anatomy?"

"Look on the bright side, it's protein." Tully grinned.

"Tull, you are the eternal optimist. If you found a bag of horse shit in the garage, you'd look for a pony." Bark adjusted the dark patch over his bad eye and reached for Tunes.

He played a few bars before slipping one of the slimy sardines in his mouth.

32

Sky wondered how many was too many. There were over thirty of them now. Fugitives from the Japanese, men preferring to take their chances in the jungle, rather than in the cities and in the internment camps. So far, it seemed to be working.

Although the Japanese presence was formidable on Luzon, the largest Philippine island hosted many guerrilla groups. There were two major companies in the north, one run by Captain Ralph Praeger, the other by Lieutenant Colonel Russell Volckmann. Both groups were sizeable; rumors ran their numbers into the thousands.

Sky had considered joining one of the two military groups, but then as more and more people came into San Alberto, he found that he preferred the autonomy of the smaller band. As long as they didn't become too large or too irritating, the Japanese would probably not consider them threatening enough to pursue. It was the larger groups that offered too tempting a target.

Sky's band, consisting almost entirely of Filipinos, was gradually getting structure. Although run by a civilian, the band was organized along military lines. Some of the men had been recruits before the war and a few, like Tapay, had been civilians. There was an American pilot who had gone AWOL right after Pearl Harbor, and who, for obvious reasons, preferred Berringer's leadership to that of Praeger or Volckmann. While Sky had been leery of the man's willingness to serve under a civilian aircraft instructor, the man from New York known only as Chopper, was working out well.

Weapons were scarce and the guerrillas were dependent on bolos and bows and arrows. Few had guns, and even then, ammunition was rare and bullets had to be produced out of whatever was at hand. Brass curtain rods, stolen gunpowder, coconut shells, sulphur, all had their part in the making of the guerrilla's shells.

Because of their size, as well as their lack of firearms, the guerrilla band was concentrating on intelligence. They were already running a coast watch station, taking careful note of all enemy ships that passed Cape San Ildefonso.

The jungle was fresh this morning, dampened by a light rain the evening before. Sky walked along quietly, Chopper just behind him. There had been reports of a Japanese patrol in the area.

Berringer knelt beside a fresh track on the path. The small footprint clearly showed the recent imprint of the tabby sole of a Japanese boot. He pressed the dampened earth lightly with the tips of his fingers, easily crumbling the sharp edge of the impression.

"Pretty new, Captain." Chopper leaned over Sky's shoulder, his breath hot against the pilot's cheek.

"Uh huh." Sky stood, withdrawing the .38 from his waistband. Slowly, he followed the path, this time moving more cautiously, his ears ready for the slightest variation in the jungle tempo.

They crouched to navigate the narrow jungle path, overhung with vines.

There!

The snapping of a twig just ahead of them. Sky waved the pistol to the side of the path and Chopper stepped into the thicket. He froze in position, waiting for his orders.

Sky was stalking now, his every sense alert with the tension of the hunt. Just ahead, where the path flared out, he could make out the outline, through the dense growth, of a small man squatting beside the trail.

Gathering his energy, much as a wild cat does before it springs, Sky flung his body through the growth, swiping at the man's head with the butt of the .38 just as he landed on him. With a heavy grunt the Japanese, having been too surprised to pull up his dropped pants, tumbled in a heap onto the ground. Before Sky had a chance to collect himself, Chopper was on top of them, a narrow boning knife poised, ready to cut through the jugular.

"No." Sky held up his hand to stop the impending murder. He felt along the carotid for a minute and, finally satisfied the man was living, rolled him over.

It was a Filipino. Sky looked to his feet and felt some relief when he saw the one-toed tabby sole there. He quickly patted down the man's thin body, withdrawing two bolos.

Suddenly, the hair began to rise on the back of his neck. He spun around but the clearing was empty except for the three of them. Chopper straightened. He had seen that look on Sky's face before and it always meant trouble. It was as though the man could smell danger.

"*Neh-hecho-da-nai.*" The steady voice speaking the Navajo tongue drifted across the clearing. Sky stood.

"*Dine.*" He said it loudly. He wanted to be sure the man would hear, for the old Navajo was a better hunter than he. "*Dine.*"

Charlie Begay strolled into the clearing.

Sky hugged the Indian tightly and pounded him on the back in greeting. "How in the hell did you get out here?"

Charlie shrugged. "Long walk. Did you kill my friend?" He nodded to the Filipino.

Berringer shook his head. "Your friend should find a new shoe store."

The Navajo was kneeling beside the stunned man. "We'll carry him back." With little effort, he swept the lightweight Filipino over his shoulder. "You have his knives." It was not a question.

They walked for a mile or so before the Navajo swerved off the path and into the thickest part of the jungle. They were climbing now and had not traveled far when a shrill noise broke the still air.

"Kalow-kalow."

Begay stopped, shifting the weight of the still unconscious Filipino. "Kalow-kalow," he chirped. Within seconds, the call was repeated not far ahead.

Tennessee Parker watched them from high in a tree. After they had passed beneath him and entered the damp cave he waited for a few minutes before repeating the call of the kalow bird.

The Filipino was slumped in one corner, still out. Charlie moved quickly around the small fire, heating water and mixing an herbal tea brew.

They talked of the fall of Manila and of the Death March. Charlie told of their escape from Bataan, while Sky outlined his adventures in San Alberto. Chopper and Tennessee remained silent, listening to the two old friends get caught up. The southern boy and the Yankee eyed each other suspiciously, much like seconds in a duel.

"You were stringing lines near Manila. Why are you up here?"

Charlie shrugged. "Colonel Nakar heard there were some guerrillas up here. He's interested in consolidation."

Sky nodded. He knew it was coming. It was an encouraging sign. They had been hearing rumors all along that there were groups similar to their own, spread throughout the islands. Already a simple pony express system was in its infancy. The runner system was in operation and men were ready to participate in the relay system on an hour's notice. There were even rumors of radio communications being set up. Individually, the guerrilla bands were not much of a threat. But if they could be banded together, working under one umbrella, then they could become a successful extension of any Allied effort in the Philippines.

"He's already made contact with Australia, Sky," Charlie offered. "He's working with General MacArthur."

Santo Tomas
Christmas Eve, 1942

Ellen squeezed the bone even tighter. Pulling and prying with the small knife, she dug at the marrow, scraping it against the side of the tin.

"They haven't arrived," she mused, as much to herself as to Magda.

"Ya. It would have been nice for Christmas."

"Or any time. I wonder what they'll have in them."

"If we get them," the Czech cautioned.

Ellen put the bone down. "Magda! Stop that! You know I've got to believe they're coming."

"Toothpaste. Toilet paper. Cheese."

"Chocolate, clothes, razor blades." She absently felt her legs, soft with matted hair. It had been so long since she had shaved them, it would be like being sixteen again. Then, thinking about it, she knew she would not use the razors for such a frivolous task.

"It's no use torturing ourselves," Magda suggested. "If they come, they come."

"Yes, dear, but it would be nice for Christmas, wouldn't it?"

"Ya."

"Out!" Ellen stamped her foot in the direction of a large white cat. It belonged to Luther Kozalczyk who had the shanty next door. The feline, called Roosevelt, was a favorite with her boys, but today she did not want to take any chance on the beast getting to her bone.

"Irineo brought this." Ellen was on her knees, rummaging underneath the cot. She withdrew a slightly deflated soccer ball. "Won't they love it?"

Magda nodded and returned to carving buttons out of coconut husks. They would be Christmas gifts.

The thin strains of *"Silent Night"* wafted into the shanty, as the chorale group practiced for their holiday performance. Ellen walked to the opening and looked out, tears misting in her eyes as she listened to the familiar refrains of the Christmas classic.

"It's hard to believe it's Christmas Eve." She watched as a broken down truck filled with Japanese soldiers stopped outside the gate, its hood raised as four or five of them gathered around its failed engine. Although fiercely armed, Ellen could see even from the distance that they were just boys.

The singers continued, as the youngsters outside the gates shifted their heavy rifles and fussed with the motor of the disabled vehicle.

"Sleep in heavenly peace," she whispered, wiping her eyes.

"You're thinking of your boys," Magda said.

"Oh, it's not as hard now as it was at first."

Doc and Pete, along with the other boys who were eight and older, had been put in the Education Building under the supervision of B.G. Leake, just three weeks earlier. Although it had been difficult to give them up at first, the system was now working out nicely. The boys were getting the male supervision and attention they so sorely needed, and they still had the benefit of seeing their mother during the day.

"It will be a while," Magda said matter-of- factly, "but we will adjust to all of this."

"Oh God, I hope you're wrong. I just want life to be normal again. To reverse things and have them the way they were."

"But that's not possible."

"You know," Ellen dabbed at her eyes in a rare moment of self-pity. "I heard the other day that the Japanese attacked Missouri."

Magda put her buttons down. Standing and stretching she joined her friend at the shanty's opening.

"Missouri. Is that near California?"

"Oh no. It's in the south, miles away."

Magda closed her eyes for a minute.

"No. Your Missouri is safe."

The Japanese truck had attracted some of the interned boys and they were gathered just inside the gate. Ellen stared at the two cultures, separated by the heavy iron fence. Many of the Japanese boys were not much older than her own Doc. The two groups were taunting one another. She froze, horrified as one of the soldiers jabbed a bayonet through the gate. His target, a gangly redhead, jumped back nimbly, easily escaping the thrust of the weapon. It was a game to them, a dangerous game.

Ellen wondered if Doc was in the group of American boys. He was too far away to hear her warnings. Besides, she thought, he was learning by himself, on a daily basis, how to get along with the Japanese.

"And are we safe, Magda?" She half whispered to her psychic friend.

The woman patted her on the shoulder. "Come, a walk will do us good," she suggested without really answering the question.

33

"What in the hell are these?" Bark picked up the small carved plastic pegs and turned them over in his hand. In the moonlight they were hard to see and he squinted his good eye trying to get a better look at them. Even with the patch covering a good part of that side of his face, the heavy scarring could still be seen.

"Cribbage pegs," Tom grunted, intent on finishing the token he was working on. "There." He put the new peg in Bark's hand. "That makes four blue."

He was carving them from the toothbrush handles that had come into Cabanatuan in the South African Red Cross packages. He pulled a long sleek board out of his pants and handed it to Barkley.

"Carabao horn," he explained, "I got it from one of the guards."

Bark examined the polished board with the carefully executed holes and spaces. Briefly he wondered if someone other than an engineer could have done such a precise job, working with the rough tools they had.

"It's for Doc. For his birthday. I figure he should have something to show for what his old dad did in prison."

Bark handed the board and pegs back. "He'll love it." He stood, walked to the pump, listened to it and then began pacing.

"Something bothering you, Bark, I mean my working upsetting you or something?" Tom set the last peg down on the board.

"It's your friend, the *padre*."

"Is something wrong with him?"

"Yes. No. I don't know. He's going on a work detail in the morning."

Tom laughed. "That's all? I thought that was your and Tully's biggest gripe against him, that he wasn't working. Now you're complaining that he is. I don't get it."

"Do you trust him?"

"Why?"

"I don't know. Tull and I just feel funny about it. The guy's been here eight months now and this is the first work detail he's been on."

"You mean on the outside, don't you? He's done counseling and services in the camp."

"It just doesn't feel right. Something about it."

"You just don't like him. Neither does Tully."

Bark shook his head. "It's not that. I think he's going over the wall."

"He won't. He knows the rule." Tom could not believe that anyone would break the rule. It had been carefully explained to them on their second day in Cabanatuan. Able-bodied prisoners would serve on work details in groups of ten. Some of the details would be outside camp. Some had even gone back to Bataan to clean up there.

Because there were fewer restrictions, fewer guards, on the outside work details, the chance of escape was greater.

To compensate for this possibility, the Japanese had explained the rule. If a man escaped, the rest of his comrades on his work detail, the other nine, would be executed. There would be no exceptions.

Tom shuddered as he thought of three officers, just last week, who had been caught trying to escape. The guards had returned them to camp and left them naked and spread-eagled, baking in the merciless Philippine sun. They screamed and begged for execution, and were only granted that release after they had cooked for well over a day. The Japanese meant what they said about the rule and now examples were everywhere. A man did not have far to look.

They all tried to be careful about the men who served on their work details. A man became suspicious of even his best friends, for you never knew how the outside would affect them, what kind of flight instinct they had. If a detail was gone overnight, as many were, the prisoners kept a closer eye on one another, than did the Japanese guards. Dependence and suspicion had become interchangeable.

"No, I think he'll be all right." It was the strongest defense Tom could offer for Bendetti.

"All the same I think I'll sit his detail out," the gunner said.

"That's moot anyway, Bark. You're on pump duty with me." Two gasoline pumps had been installed and now there was usually enough water for drinking and bathing.

The moon was dropping quickly and clouds were beginning to fill the sky as they padded barefoot through the camp. A Japanese general had come for a visit earlier in the year and had ordered all of the Americans to go without shoes.

"Storm." Bark sniffed the night air.

"Then maybe they won't go out at all tomorrow," Tom said cheerfully, praying for rain. Now that he had thought about it, he realized there weren't any guarantees with any of them.

Changing Woman was visiting him often in his dreams. A floating vision hovering over the Death March, a pure face on the Pacific Ocean horizon beckoning him home. He tried not to think about her. Living from day to day, hand to mouth, ferreting worms out of the rice and keeping shoes on his feet. Those were the priorities.

But still Changing Woman was with him and he reached out for her. Just as she stepped away from him, his hand tangled in a mat of ebony hair. Grasping it tightly in his fist he held on to it, determined to keep his elusive prey.

"Ouch! That hurts!" Isabel pulled his hand with her own smaller one and tugged it gently away from her hair. Rolling over on her back she nudged him. "Hey, are you awake?"

Charlie opened his eyes.

"Yes."

"What were you trying to do, scalp me?"

"No. I was going to make a rug." He rubbed his eyes sleepily. "Navajos. Silver. Rugs."

She traced the line of his jaw sleepily with a thin, delicate finger. "You can't fool me. I've seen those cowboy and Indian movies."

Charlie rolled into a sitting position, swinging his legs off the bed and onto the floor. "Those are the Apaches, not the Navajos. They're the bad ones."

"I knew it was one of those Indians that scalped."

He turned and looked at her. Her long black hair framed her delicate face giving her a childlike appearance. "No, they don't do it much either."

"The Cherokee? That's it." She giggled.

He shrugged. "Beats me."

"What time is it?" She pulled on one of his thick arms coaxing him back into bed, even as she asked.

"Seven-thirty."

In a flash she was out of bed heading toward the bathroom. "I'm late," she yelled as she disappeared into the small room. Minutes later she came out and kissed him lightly on the cheek. "Will you be here later?"

He shook his head. "I've got to get back."

She rummaged in her straw bag and withdrew a folded piece of paper. "It's not much. Tell the colonel it's the best I could do this week."

The Navajo unfolded the paper and saw that it was a schedule of cement shipments. "It's enough."

"Goddamn there's another one," Bark picked a limp white worm out of his mess kit. He smashed it between his fingers as he continued to poke around in his *lugao*.

"You might as well give up, Barkley," Tully offered. "Eat them. They're good protein and not so bad if you don't torture yourself thinking about it."

"Shit." It had never ceased to amaze Bark that Tully could eat the damned things knowing they were there. With some of the men they were just so hungry by the time they were served, that they gulped their ration down, not taking the time to pick out the worms. Bark suspected that they conditioned themselves to not think about what they were eating. But Tully, the fine medical corpsman that he was, not only ate the slimy creatures but he was given to lectures about the nutritional benefits of the goddamned things.

Tom was quietly picking out the worms too. He suspected that Tully was right, that they were good protein, but his mathematical mind convinced him that the few he would get in his cup were not going to make much difference one way or the other. Besides the rice, really sweepings from the warehouse floor, was filled with dirt, sand and gravel in addition to the worms. Several of the prisoners had already cracked their teeth on it and dental fillings had been fashioned out of silver pesos smuggled into camp.

"Powder?"

Sullivan passed the can of tooth powder that had come in with their Red Cross packages. They had long ago realized that the chalky substance did more to sweeten their rice, than it did their teeth. Few were using it for its intended purpose now, preferring to sprinkle it on their *lugao*. The mint taste improved the flavor of their food to some degree.

"Careful, here comes the duck." Tully's eyes narrowed as he watched the short Japanese guard approach them, swinging a stubby two by four. It had been a fun game to nickname the guards and now most of them had American tags, that in some way reflected their personalities or appearances. Donald Duck's sobriquet came from his constant magpie jabbering.

It had been a grand source of amusement when the dumpy guard had been flattered upon learning that his namesake was a Hollywood movie star. The comparison had done a lot to improve his personality and for weeks he had floated through camp, his stubby neck held high, posturing an American film personage. Unfortunately a short time later he had seen a Walt Disney cartoon featuring the famous animated duck and he was now back to his generally disagreeable personality. His revenge was steady, as he took every opportunity to swing the club, cracking heads, arms, legs, whatever was doomed to cross his path.

He had reached their group now and he hit Bark's mess kit hard with the club. Though he tried to catch it before it fell, it was no use and the gunner watched miserably as his just cleaned and powdered rice fell into the dirt. Bark, perhaps because of his size, seemed to attract a lot of the guards abuse. Veins in the gunner's forehead bulged, as he sought to control his temper, a new restraint that they had all learned in Cabanatuan.

The duck poked at him and motioned for them all to get moving. They began walking to the front gate.

"Oh my God." Tully could see nine men lined up just inside the barbed wire. Their hands were tied behind their backs. While he strained to identify the unfortunate, he was flooded with guilty relief that he was not up there.

"At least they're not drying them out," Bark observed. They had all agreed that if a man were to die, a quick bullet was preferable to the sun treatment.

The commandant was now jabbering at them and an interpreter was translating the lecture. They had heard it all before. The rule was in effect and had been broken. Now the work detail comrades of the escapee would suffer for his disappearance.

The observers shuffled uneasily in the dirt, trying not to think about the consequences, even as their eyes were riveted on the condemned.

The nine were in a line with the guards fifty feet or so away from them. The Japanese chatted among themselves.

"Why doesn't the son-of-a-bitch get it over with?" Bark asked.

"He loves it." Bark said.

As if on cue, the commandant barked a command at the waiting guards. They shouldered their rifles. The fire order came and the guns spit their deadly bullets into the line.

But not all of the guards were marksmen. Some were Korean conscripts, who had little military training, and now their incompetence was evident as at least half of the fallen men writhed on the ground, screaming out in pain.

The commandant issued another order and again the rifles were readied. This time the fire was concentrated on the wounded. They did a better job and all but one man appeared dead. The lone survivor, his body gushing blood, twitched in the dust, one bloody mauled arm reaching out for his fallen comrades. He raised his head slightly, elevating it above the earth and tried to say something. It was impossible, for his throat and mouth were inhibited by blood.

Tom closed his eyes. He could not watch any longer. When he heard the final volley, he was relieved the Japanese sideshow was over. At least this time.

That was it. They were free to go. A death detail would soon remove the bodies and throw them into a common grave. Today's lesson was over.

"Well," Tully remarked. "At least I hope the son-of-a-bitch got away."

Tom pulled angrily on the medic's ragged sleeve. "How can you say that? Is one man's life worth what we just saw?"

Tully shook his head. "No. But it's done. At least it wasn't ten men up there."

"But at what cost, Tully, at what cost?"

A scarecrow of a man, very thin and so small that he had been called Tiny all of his life, passed by. Tiny had been the subject of much speculation, for none of them had been able to figure out how such a small man had been inducted into the armed services. Surely he had defied all minimum height regulations.

"You know, Sullivan," he said as he dropped into step with them, "it's enough to make a man give up religion."

"Yes, I know." Tom agreed.

"Religion may be the only thing that will get you suckers through this." Bark suggested.

"Yes but when our spiritual leaders do this, how much more can we take?" Tiny was almost whining.

Tom felt a cold chill grip his stomach. Stopping in his tracks he turned and faced the small soldier. "Tiny, what are you saying?"

"I'm saying, Sullivan, that you don't expect a fucking priest to run out on his fellow man."

"Bendetti," Bark roared. "That was his work detail."

"You got it, mountain man," Tiny confirmed before turning off for his own barracks.

34

The rough surface of the dog's tongue rhythmically licked Kate's leg.

"I think you're right, Faustino. It seems to be working." Kate scratched behind the dog's ear.

She laughed at herself when she thought how horrified she had been when Tapay suggested she let the animal lick her ulcerated leg. That had been before the supplies and medicines had come in, and the wound had festered and puffed, threatening to become badly infected. Now thanks to the mongrel's affection, the cut was slowly beginning to heal.

Faustino stroked his dark, sparse beard. Most of the guerrillas had them, for razor blades were luxuries left behind. "I don't think it will win a place in any of the medical journals. It's an old remedy from Grandmother Rivera."

"At least it's not as bad as the powder some of them are using," Kate said.

Tapay nodded in agreement. Two of their newest soldiers had come in with a yellow, malodorous powder taken from a Japanese mine. Their skin ulcers, common with many of the men, had been smeared with the explosive. While the self-treatment seemed to be working for them, it had caused a great deal of medical speculation.

"Chocolate?" The schoolteacher held out a small wrapped bar. The candy was part of a cache of supplies that Chick Parsons had brought in on the American submarine *Tambor*. The four tons of provisions, including radio equipment, batteries, food, socks, the new malaria drug Atabrine, and even fifty pounds of wheat flour so the Filipinos could make communion wafers, had been carefully doled out to the different guerrilla bands.

"No thanks." Kate picked up the two month old issue of *Time* magazine. It, too, had come in on the *Tambor*. "Did you hear about the Battle of the Bismarck Sea?"

Tapay shook his head.

"We got them there. Eight transports and four destroyers for six thousand troops."

Tapay grinned. "New Guinea isn't that far away."

"Things are definitely looking up." Sky joined them now, sliding down the tree trunk landing next to Kate, his hand resting lightly on her bare thigh. "There are groups like ours all over the islands, just waiting for MacArthur's return."

Kate pulled the new pack of cigarettes out of his shirt pocket. She laughed as she held it up. "I'm beginning to think we're involved in a political campaign, not a war." Many of the supplies had arrived with General MacArthur's "I shall return" on them. "That man could probably beat Roosevelt."

"Not out here, he couldn't." Sky suggested.

"What about Parsons? Are we joining up?" Faustino asked.

"As much as we can. Seems as though we are somewhere between fish and fowl. We aren't under military leadership."

"And he didn't offer you a commission?"

Berringer laughed. "I didn't ask for one. Hell, I was just happy to see him. Those supplies aren't too shabby either."

Charles Parsons had first come to the Philippines in 1921.

Married to a Filipina, he spoke Spanish fluently and had traveled the archipelago extensively. After the war broke out, he collected the names and serial numbers of American servicemen. Narrowly escaping imprisonment, he acted as the temporary Panamanian counsel until he and his family left in June of 1942 on board a hospital ship bound for Formosa. Upon safely reaching American soil, he had volunteered his services to the United States government.

The Intelligence Section of Army G-2 had taken him up on his offer and Chick Parsons became the first member of the top secret group, Spyron, formed by combining the words spy and squadron. Parsons had drawn up the initial intelligence plans and General MacArthur had approved the new network. Early in 1943, the dark, short Parsons, barefoot, dressed in an old bleached shirt and shorts and passing for a Filipino, had returned to his beloved Philippines via a Mindanao beach. Landing in the middle of the night, in a rubber boat launched by an American submarine with only two bare-chested Muslim Moros for protection, Parsons had begun to gather information on what was to become a vast intelligence network.

"Then he's setting up a system," Tapay said.

"Uh huh. He's checking to see who's reliable and who isn't."

"Making a list and checking it twice?" Kate grinned, for when Sky had returned from his meeting with Parsons, loaded down with supplies it had seemed like Christmas.

"Something like that." Sky squeezed her leg affectionately.

"Then things will be easier," she mused.

"Yes and no. There should be more coordination. But we're small fish, very small fish."

"But we've got over fifty men now!" Tapay reminded him.

"They say Fertig on Mindanao has fifteen thousand. Peralta

on Panay has seven thousand Filipinos under his command, Praeger's got over five thousand and God only knows how many Volckmann's got by now," Sky said.

There were other Luzon groups. Colonel Marcus Agustin had Marking's Guerrillas and Marcos and Magsaysay also had their followers.

"As long as you've got candy, I'll stay with you." Tapay bit into the chocolate bar.

"Enjoy it. It may be the last for a while. He's got to throw his stuff to his top priority groups. We better ration what we've got. It could be a long time before another sub gets in."

Kate shook her head. It was amazing to her that even one American u-boat had made it into the Japanese held islands.

"Another thing has been set down," Berringer added. "We're to be an intelligence gathering group only. No fighting."

"That's not going to be too difficult, judging from our past record," Tapay said wryly, for in fact they had had no encounters with the Japanese since coming to San Alberto.

"It's been a problem elsewhere. The Japanese are killing ten civilians for every soldier killed by guerrillas. Oh, there may be good news for you, Katie."

She felt his grip on her leg tighten.

"That sub came in full and is going out a lot lighter. They're taking on passengers for Australia."

Instantly her throat was dry.

"There's no room this trip. Parsons is taking some guys who escaped from Bataan out. If the system works, and Parsons thinks it will, they'll add cargo carrying subs instead of these regular fleet boats and there'll be more room. Eventually he thinks he can get you out."

Kate, not even aware that she had been holding her breath, squeezed Sky's hand. "That is good news," she lied.

※

Ellen put the six ampules of ematine into the shoe carefully, making sure that they were well protected by the shirt she was packing around them. The ematine, along with the sulfanilamide and aspirin, were probably literally worth their weight in gold. She put some cigarettes on top of the wrapped shoes.

"It's raining again," Magda said. Hardly a day had gone by without rain during January, and today was no exception.

"I hope this gets in," Ellen said absentmindedly. She had propositioned one of the guards and felt there was a chance that the package would get through to Cabanatuan.

A handful of outside priests had access to Santo Tomas. While the Visayan priests had been immediately interned, those from Manila and Luzon were still free. No one had heard from the American Jesuits, but it was generally assumed that they had been sent to Fort Santiago, the old Spanish prison taken over by the *kempe-tai,* the dreaded Japanese secret police. All political prisoners, as well as Filipinos suspected of collaborating with the Americans, were sent there. It was a perfect setting for terror with its ancient dungeons and well-used torture chambers and racks. As long as there were priests with access to Cabanatuan though, there was a chance of getting supplies to Tom, Ellen thought.

"What about food?" Magda asked.

Ellen thought for a moment.

"We could send rice flour and some of the canned goods," Ellen said. Although the Red Cross packages had arrived in Santo Tomas the week before Christmas, they weren't handed out until

January. The packages, worth around twenty dollars in the States, were treasured in the prison camp where their going market value was somewhere in the neighborhood of six hundred dollars.

All of the internees had been urged to hold onto their supplies for emergency use, and Ellen had been following that sage advice, although she relished the opportunity to send some of the treasures on to Tom.

"The bouillon or the Spam?"

Magda shrugged.

After debating for a moment or two, Ellen threw in both, along with a bar of soap, two drawings on a scrap of paper by Doc and Pete, and a long letter from herself.

"When is Father Lorenzo coming?" Ellen asked, nervous now that the box was filled.

"Not for another hour. He may be late."

"I wish I could send toilet paper. I know that sounds silly, but it's something that's so hard to do without."

"Ya," the Czech agreed. "But it is impossible." They had been told back in March that the last shipment of toilet paper had arrived and that it would only last three months. They knew supplies were very low.

Ellen studied the cigarettes, marveling at the ingenious design of the package for the American "V" for victory was carefully woven into the border, a subtle reminder from their countrymen so many miles away. They had seen other signs, too, carefully designed pictures that depicted famous American slogans.

"What do you think about the vitamins?"

Magda's dark eyes narrowed. "No. You must keep them for yourself, and the boys." She was worried about Ellen, for although all of them had lost weight, Ellen now hovered around ninety pounds. There was not an ounce of fat on her and Magda suspected that if she got sick that she would not fare well. "Besides, maybe the packages got in to Cabanatuan also."

"Yes, you're right of course. I must think of the boys too." Ellen began pulling string around the package. "Just wrapping this, just sending it makes me feel so much better, I just know everything's going to work out. Why, I bet we're out of here at least by next Christmas."

"Ya." Magda agreed in order to end the conversation. She was exhausted, for she had been tormented all night long with the pictures again.

Horrid, unhappy vignettes of things to come. She had been more tired when she awakened than when she had gone to bed, and now she silently prayed that the taunting visions were in error.

※

The typewriter ribbon was dim. Like so many other things they were getting harder and harder to get. The only thing that seemed to be in abundance, Isabel wryly thought, were the Japanese soldiers.

She corrected a typographical error on the sheet she was working on, catching her mind from drifting too far from her work. She was thankful for her job. When the Japanese first appropriated the factory, she had been both surprised and pleased that she had been able to keep working. So many Filipinos had been thrown out of work that she knew she was lucky to have the job and the pay.

Horrified at the Japanese invasion, she now saw her employment as a means of helping in the fight against the hated aggressors. Although she had heard the stories of sabotage in Poland and Czechoslovakia, she could never do that, she thought. It was too overt. Plus her job responsibilities were not broad enough to allow her contact with any area of the plant where chemical sabotage would be a possibility. As for the receipts, invoices and records, there would be little benefit to altering any of them.

But months ago, it had occurred to her that it might help someone to know just where the cement was being shipped and what construction projects the Japanese were involved in. Carefully she had begun to keep meticulous records of the shipments. Written on tiny pieces of paper she had at first taped them to her small breasts when she left the office. That had come to her, after many nervous days of watching the hated Japanese guards to insure that they did not search anyone. Once or twice she had seen them pat down factory workers, but she had never seen them go further.

Now she had gotten careless. Instead of the tape, she stuffed the tiny reminders in her shoes or in the pockets of her skirts. There was no need, really, to take the time with more concealment than that. At home she stashed the damning records in her coffee tin, and covered them with peanuts for coffee was now impossible to buy. They were picked up weekly.

She was one small cog in the vast machinery of the Philippine underground. In playing her part, for the first time since the war had started, she felt useful, as though she were contributing to the eventual defeat of the evil Hapons.

A small Filipino messenger brought in mail. He handed it to her wordlessly, his dark eyes darting here and there around the office.

"It's all right." Isabel assured him.

"Tonight." The messenger was talking, although his eyes were looking downward through the mail as though he had no interest in her. "Ten o'clock."

"The river?" Isabel continued working, sorting through the envelopes he had just given her, automatically assigning them to wire bins on her desk.

He gave her an almost imperceptible nod and with that was out the door again.

⚹

Doc scrubbed the rice pan as hard as he could, putting every bit of his twelve-year-old energy into it. Scraping and lifting the blackened grains from the bottom of the heavy caldron, he peeled them off with his fingers and dropped the crusted rice into his mouth. The boy next to him was doing the same thing. It had become a ritual with them, this scraping and eating of the burnt rice.

It was one of the benefits of pot detail. The boys considered themselves lucky to be assigned such duty. Anything having to do with the kitchen was prime. From the women who sat at the rough wooden tables under the next open shed, to the sweat drenched, bare-chested men who hovered over the metal pots set in cement kilns cooking rice, everyone connected with the kitchen considered himself fortunate.

At first the charcoal taste of the leftover rice had tasted terrible, but now Doc was so used to it that he found himself actually preferring it over the rice gruel they were all served.

He scraped off another long strip and put it in his pocket for his mother and Pete. He worked quickly, eager to leave his kitchen chores behind him. There was a boxing match tonight, a program really, for the recreation committee would sponsor an actual tournament only when all of the eager contenders had received the proper training.

Petey was scheduled to go three rounds with a freckle faced kid that lived with them in the Education Building. Doc was undergoing training too, but he was not on the schedule this Friday night. The athletic program at Santo Tomas had received a shot in the arm when a couple of sets of ten-ounce boxing gloves, baseballs and bats, soccer balls, and badminton equipment had come in with the Red Cross supplies.

Doc peeled off another long strip and slipped it slowly into his mouth, his tongue rolled across the crust, separating each rice grain from the other. It made it seem as though there was more of it that way, instead of just gulping it down.

Before he went to the match there was another important thing he had to do. He hurried and finished the pan in eager anticipation of sharing an important secret, a riddle that the keepers did not want to share. Finally done, he hurried from the kitchen shed.

Doc crept slowly up the stairs. He had overheard enough of the whispered conversation to know that he had the right location. A bare overhead lightbulb cast an eery glow at the top of the staircase. Just as he reached it, he heard a door open ahead of him. Quickly he stepped into the shadows, edging his way around the corner into the deeper darkness.

He could hear footsteps now and his knees began to shake, as his palms grew sticky with sweat. If he got caught spying on them, it would not be good. Not at all. The only thing that he could imagine that would be worse would be to get caught spying on the Japanese.

But he was saved this time, for the footsteps veered off and Doc could hear them fading down the same stairs he had just climbed. He waited, heart pounding against his thin chest. Finally when his breathing returned to normal, he dared to peek around the corner.

The corridor to his left was empty. So was the staircase. Taking a deep breath, the boy took a few steps away from the protection of the wall, taking care to remain in the shadows. He could make out a dim figure at the foot of the stairs. The man who had come down the corridor was a guard and he was now posted at the foot of the staircase, insuring that no one would come up or down.

The way out was now blocked to Doc. The only other exit was down the corridor, past the mysterious open room. He retreated to the wall again and pressed his cheek against it, weighing his options. He was trapped and he had no choice but to wait until the men were done before he could return to the Education Building, unless he went down the corridor.

He watched the guard for another ten minutes before he could screw up enough courage to dart across the patch of light at the top of the stairs. Once across the beacon, he realized he was now in no-man's land. A commitment was in order, for it was almost as risky to go back across the light and risk being seen by the guard downstairs, as it was to go on ahead, past the open door. His heart began to pound discordantly, as he inched his way down the corridor, straining to hear the voices from within the room.

They were talking quietly inside. Almost whispering. Something about wires. All of his attention was on listening.

"Oscillating detector type," a voice said.

"Amplification of radio frequency."

"UX 210 tubes. We can use them in parallel."

It was like Greek to the boy. They were talking about things that were beyond him. But he had caught one important word. Wire! And he knew that none of them, not even the Executive Committee, were allowed to have electrical wire. His mother had explained it to him once. She said that the Japanese would punish anyone caught trying to communicate with the outside world. It was forbidden. And the penalty was death. Yet the men inside the room were talking about wire.

His mouth was dry. Drawn like a moth to the flame, with the lure of a big secret, he had come. But if he were caught, if they were all caught, then it would be death. And then who would be the man of the family? Who would take over for his absent father and see that Mother and Petey were taken care of? No, he had to go back. Even if he got caught by the men. He just couldn't face execution by the Japanese. His father would never understand.

He took another deep breath and stood just outside of the light pouring from the room. He peeked in and saw three men bent over a tangle of wire on a table. Doc's eyes widened. He had not seen that much wire since they had been interned. As he darted across the light, he was aware of another thing. The man in the middle was a friend of his mother's. He had visited them in their shanty and Ellen had told the boys he had worked with Pan American Airways in Manila before the war. In something called sector communications.

35

The *Alter Christus* dreams had come back a while ago, haunting him. While parts of them were the same with the archbishop resplendent in his robes, and the Latin words recited over him, there were stronger visions now. Stronger than the holy church, stronger than the archbishop's blessing. Dreams of hell and fire and of demons prodding him, taunting him. A voice was filling him up from the inside. Telling him he could be Another Christ, without the church.

When George Bendetti finally sorted it out, he was elated.

He was finally free. Unchained from the shackles of the Army and of Cabanatuan and of the Catholic Church. It was a heady feeling.

He knew in his bones that he had started something new for himself. A new power. It was intoxicating. Without the constraints, he could do anything.

His elation was somewhat dimmed by the steady gnawing in his stomach. Absently, he knew he should be thinking about food for he would need sustenance to keep going.

Now that was a problem, he thought. Going where? What was his destination? What were his choices? They seemed limited. Manila was out. Crawling with Japanese. Scratch Bataan. He did not want to repeat that grim experience.

The hills, that was all that was left. He had heard in camp about the guerrillas and that, on balance, seemed to be his best bet. To find a group.

He began sweating. He'd have to lie. To keep his story straight. For they could never know he had escaped from Cabanatuan or they'd know he had violated the rule. Bataan. That was it. He'd swear he had escaped from the march and had been wandering for months. They'd believe it. After all, this was war and anything was credible.

He stood, patting his wrapped cotton shorts, feeling the moisture of the forest on them. Clothes! He'd have to find some clothes, for anyone who had seen Cabanatuan would recognize the uniform of the damned.

He was totally turned around. He had watched the sun rise that morning and had figured out east. He thought he was heading south now, but south to what? He wished he had paid more attention to the geography, but then who had ever heard of Cabanatuan before this nightmare?

He began walking through the jungle and became worried when he came on a well trodden path. He stopped, hesitated, strained for human sounds. Upon hearing none, he stayed on the well worn dirt, ready to leap into the forest at the slightest sign of human life. He walked for several miles. There was no one in sight.

The path began sloping downward, taking a sharp turn to the right. As he rounded the bend, he smacked right into a young Filipino boy. Legs and arms went flying, as the pair tangled together in the dust. Landing in a tumble on the jungle path, they eyed each other suspiciously as the boy rolled away from the priest and tried to rise.

But Bendetti was too quick for him. Grabbing him hard by one of his small legs he tumbled him back to the ground.

"Do you speak English?" His voice came out in a harsh whisper.

The boy nodded.

"I am a friend. Do you understand?" He shook him roughly. The boy nodded again.

Bendetti held him tightly by one thin arm.

"Is there a village near here?"

"Yes. Down below." The Filipino child pointed down the path. "Maybe three kilometers."

"Japanese?"

The boy shook his head. His luminous brown eyes held terror of the American. He couldn't have been more than eight.

Bendetti stood, pulling the boy to his feet. "Will you take me to your village?"

The boy nodded and headed slowly down the path.

They had gone maybe another kilometer when the boy broke from his captor running as hard as his small legs would take him down the path.

"Joe, Joe, 'cano!" He was yelling now.

Hesitating only an instant, the priest tore after him and even in his flight he marveled at the speed and strength he had. He quickly overcame the child and tackled him hard. Wrapping his arms around the boy, he dragged him once again to the ground, cupping one hand over his screaming mouth.

It was instantly quiet, save for the nagging voice that had returned to the back of Bendetti's brain. As they wrestled together on the ground he groped inside the cotton shorts for a piece of jagged glass he had brought with him from Cabanatuan.

Working swiftly, the priest jerked the glass hard against the soft throat, feeling the boy's warm blood gush out over and across his hand. He held the small body for a few minutes before it stopped twitching.

Satisfied the child was dead, he pulled him off the path into the undergrowth. He shuffled around in the dirt, trying to obscure the blood as much as he could.

Only when he turned back into the jungle did he realize that the voice was now silent.

⚔

"You can damned near see his penis," Tully observed.

Tom strained his eyes and twisted his head in an effort to get a better shot at Bark's groin. "Nah."

"You're right," Tully laughed, "it's not big enough to see!"

Bark made a playful lunge at the medic, who dodged him, ducking around the wooden picnic table just outside the barracks. This was their living area, for the barracks was used for sleeping only.

"You'd think you were an Igorot," Sullivan said. Bark's preferred mode of dress, the g-string that the Japanese were issuing and that many of the men were now wearing, had been the subject of a lot of good natured teasing.

"It's cool," Bark said in his own defense.

"So are these," Tom pulled the cotton fabric of his shorts away from his thin legs. It had taken him a while to even get into the short pants, much less a g-string.

"I thought they gave you movie stars better clothes than that," Tully poked at him.

"Shut up Quack." Bark growled. It was a sore point with him. He had been included with a group of POW's that had been sent into Bataan thinking it was a work detail just like any other, but when they reached the peninsula they discovered that the Japanese planned to make a war propaganda movie using Americans in the film.

And so *"Down with the Stars and Stripes"* was born. The star was a Filipino. Bark and the others all received new uniforms and helmets and empty Enfields. It had felt strange to many of them to hold one of the American guns after such a long period of time. In the slack moments of the film making, they sabotaged the rifles as best they could. Pulling pins and dropping grains of sand in the works, they rendered many of the old guns useless. It was a movie experience most of them would prefer to forget, although some of them did get new uniforms out of it.

"I've got a new one for you, but you're not going to get it if I have to listen to this crap," Bark threatened.

They did not have to ask what "one" was for it had to be rumor. Forbidden from discussing the war, or passing news on to one another, it was, of course, the favorite subject of conversation.

"Cabanatuan is being abandoned."

"What?" Tom almost dropped the duck egg he was holding. "When?"

"By the first of October. That's why they're shipping out the work details." At least a thousand men had already been sent to Japan.

Tom broke the duck egg into the pot, thinking of what the rumor could mean. Civilians were already on some kind of a special status with the Japanese. Just what kind had not yet been determined by any of them, but so far they had not been assigned to any of the details bound for the enemy land. Maybe the news would work in his favor and he would be sent to Santo Tomas and be reunited with his family.

"That's a pile of shit if I ever heard it," Tully grumbled. "Take us from our happy home?"

They laughed. Cabanatuan was not a country club by any means, but they had learned the ropes over the last year and the death rate also seemed to be dropping.

"It's just a rumor, maybe there's nothing to it," Bark offered. Rumor was so much a part of their lives that they were like sea sponges, letting the news drift into and out of themselves, waiting for the one morsel that would stick. There was always rumor, rarely fact.

Tom cracked another egg into the jar. Things weren't so bad here now that they had the pot. It had taken a considerable amount of their resources at the time, but now the quanning was easier. Pooling their assets, including the funds Tom received from the Benguet mining officials in Santo Tomas, had brought them such luxurious quan as eggs, fruit, peanuts and cassava flour. Occasionally they had been able to round up native sausage and ham. Coffee beans, a luxury, were one thing they tried to keep on hand, for the black liquid had quickly become their treat of the day. It had replaced the cocktail hour for them and they guarded it just as carefully as they would a bottle of one hundred year old bourbon.

Tom threw the shells on the table. "It's the uncertainty of the whole thing that drives me crazy."

They all nodded.

"That and this," he waved his hand around, "fantasy land. God, I traded my watch for a sack of sugar the other day and I actually think I got the best end of the deal. It really makes you think."

Tully shrugged. "It's all relative. Maybe someday we'll thank the Japanese for this. At least it's changed our thinking about money."

"That's true," Tom said, "it's a means. To an end. And that's all it is."

"It's not everything," Tully agreed.

"Hey, speaking of sugar, did you write Ellen about that new stuff?" Bark scratched himself under his g-string, not bothering to think if it was appropriate behavior for the dinner table.

"Yesterday," Tom replied. "I checked with that industrial chemist in the next barracks. He says it won't hurt us."

They had all been excited when they had heard of saccharine. Their elation stemmed from the fact that the substitute was three to four hundred times as sweet as sugar, and they could use less of it. When they also learned they could buy it for eleven cents a gram, they immediately set the wheels turning for a purchase.

"I told her we could use twenty grams." Tom dished out the contents of the pot, an ersatz stew made with the eggs, mongo beans and a tiny piece of pork. They ate quietly, thankful for the quan pot and its contents.

⚚

The white, mite ridden rooster was hurt. Red flecks mottled his coat and there was blood flowing from his wattles. His head, which had been held erect, now sagged and threatened to disconnect from the rest of his body. There was no rest for the weary bird, for the smaller fiery bantam kept coming at him, darting and ducking and spurring his larger adversary at every opportunity.

There was another hit and the white went down on one leg. It was enough, for the bantam charged in, spurs high as he thrust into the soft undercoating of the Leghorn's neck. Even as the larger bird flopped in his death throes, the victor set his beak to the ground, pecking at the blood of the conquered bird.

"Dinner!" Tapay yelled, for they had all agreed when Chopper brought in the chickens that they would serve as entertainment before they were eaten. It was a small celebration for in the morning they were splitting up for a few weeks.

The chicken meat, cooked up with some pork, would make a fine *adobo*. There would be rice and camotes. Faustino had even scrounged some *sinnoman*, a coconut juice cake made from cassava flour and wrapped in banana leaves. They were celebrating their leave-taking in style.

Sky handed the dead rooster to Chopper who had volunteered to make the *adobo*. Of all of them, the pilot was becoming quite the cook. He could take almost any combination of food and make it palatable, sometimes even good.

"Where's Kate?" Berringer asked.

"With the gorilla," Tapay said walking away from the corral.

Sky fell into step beside him. "He's not cooking again, is he?"

"Uh huh. Decided to make his own dinner. Guess ours wasn't good enough for him." Tapay sniffed the air.

They could smell it long before they reached him. The charred, rotten meat of the python was roasting over a little fire, which the stout Mindanaon carefully tended.

"Hello, Gorilla," Sky said, although his eyes never left Kate as she sat on a log sketching the cooking pagan.

The Mindanaon grunted. It was a joke in camp for when the man had first joined them he had fooled them all with his English. "I shall return" he had said and they had all been impressed with his command of the language. Unfortunately that was all he could say as far as any of them knew. It had given the Americans pause, as they thought of the efficacy of General MacArthur's advertising campaign if a pagan from Mindanao could repeat the famous slogan.

Quickly dubbed the Gorilla, a moniker that amused them for he was now known as the Gorilla Guerrilla, the native fit right in. Through a combination of pantomime and merged dialects he also took orders fairly easily.

But his personal habits had both fascinated and repulsed most of them. While the others had slept outside on the ground or in huts in the village, the Mindanaon had constructed a crude platform high in the trees. Barefoot and climbing a knotted rope, he scurried up the trees. The Gorilla's dietary habits had been yet another source of amazement. He would fast for days and then gorge on rotten monkey or snake meat.

"Jesus, that's bad," Faustino held his nose as he sat next to Kate, "how can you stand it?"

"Stand what?" The full sun caught the blonde highlights in Kate's long brown hair and picked up a few freckles scattered across her face. Even without makeup, Tapay thought she was the most beautiful woman he had ever seen. They were all in love with her.

"You're telling me artists don't notice, or pretend not to notice, these things."

"Whatever," she smiled at him. "Who won?"

"The banty. Chopper's putting him in the pot now. Should be another hour or so."

"Some winner."

The Mindanaon began dancing around his fire. He deftly pulled the stick with the thick roasted python on it off, and waved it in the air in an effort to cool the sizzling meat. He came over to them and proudly displayed his prize, his grin exposing broken, black teeth.

SINCLAIR BROWNING

"At least the flies are off it now," Sky observed, shaking his head in refusal of the native's offering.

"The eggs are still there. I can see them," Tapay gagged, pointing to little crusted bumps on the snake. "Man, I've had it." He got up quickly and headed off in the direction of the larger group.

"Want to go for a walk?" Sky held out his hand as Kate put her pad and pencil to one side.

The jungle was noisy this afternoon. A good sign, Sky thought, for when the animals and birds were quiet it was almost always a clue that something was disturbing them.

"It seems sort of unreal, doesn't it?" Kate asked as they walked.

"Uh huh." Sky reached for her hand.

"Yet in a frightening sort of way it's almost normal. If I sat down at a formal dinner party now, I'm not sure I could even remember which fork to use."

"You'd remember. Maybe you should have gone with Ellen."

"No. I made the right decision. But it seems so long ago."

"Almost two years."

"And how many more I wonder. Still," she cocked her head listening to the birds, her painter's eyes on the patterns of the shadows ahead as the bright sunlight filtered through the overhead brush, "it is a beautiful day."

"Yes." He loved her for being so positive through all of it. "Charlie's coming back."

"Before we leave?"

"No, he'll be here when we get back. There's bad news about Colonel Nakar."

"What is it?"

"The Japanese tracked down his radio signals. They got him."

In spite of the heat, she shuddered. "Was it awful?"

He nodded. "Torture. They finally beheaded him."

"Oh!" Her hand flew up to cover her open mouth. "Charlie!"

"No, he'll be all right. He may be joining us."

Her face brightened.

"We're not sure yet about Tennessee. They may not let him go, there's some talk about his being a communications liaison."

"We could use that here."

"Yes."

They walked on in silence for a while.

"Are you sure you want to go in the morning? You can stay in San Alberto with some of the others." He asked.

"I thought you said it wouldn't be dangerous."

"It shouldn't be. Could be pretty uncomfortable though. We need to go and get back as quickly as possible so the pace will be tough."

"And you don't think a woman can keep up?" The steady turquoise eyes challenged him.

"No, no," he put his hands up in mock defense, for he had seen her outwalk many of his men. Her only routine left over from her formerly civilized life was her early morning devotion to a strenuous calisthenics program. There was not an ounce of fat on Kate and, in her shorts, her calf muscles were the envy of many of the men. "I'm not worried about your keeping up."

"I'll go. The change will do me good. Besides, maybe there will be something of value I can sketch."

"Captain!" Chopper came running up behind them. "You better take a look. It's the suak trap, it's been tripped."

Sky and Kate ran after Chopper, quickly covering the mile to the trap.

The pit had been caved in. The native grass entwined with

sharp little barbs, carved from the poisonous bagakay bamboo, was now flattened. The idea behind the trap, was if a Japanese patrol came along, someone would yell or fire a warning shot. The enemy would drop onto the barbs and while there was no immediate danger of anyone dying from the wounds on their bellies and chests, they were nasty things, festering and weakening their hosts.

The trap had been a diversionary tactic and was entirely dependent on the warning shot for its success. If the Japanese stepped on the suak, it would do little damage to their boots.

Sky had thought little of the system when Chick Parsons had told him about it. He thought it would make more sense in a heavily patrolled area. But Faustino and Chopper had been bored one week and had dug the pit and carved the barbs, almost as a lark. Now they had been tripped and not by one of their own, for all of them, as well as the villagers, knew the location of the suak pit.

"What does it mean?" Kate asked.

"I don't know," Sky shook his head. "Have you checked the village?"

"Faustino did," Chopper said. "Nothing. No one is sick. They all knew about it."

"Yes."

"And if it was a friendly stranger, seems like they would have come in for care." Chopper speculated.

"Double the guards and send down to the other villages. See what you can find out."

"All right." Chopper kicked at the flattened barbs.

"Katie, you'll be coming with me to San Ildefonso tomorrow." There was no longer any question of his leaving her behind.

The mosquitoes were horrible tonight. They usually never bothered Isabel but she had been constantly swiping at them for the last fifteen minutes. She knew that the grassy, marshy bank was a breeding ground for them, and that her invasion of their territory would only result in a hearty meal for the biting insects. The others were bothered too, for although none of them were talking, she could feel them squirm and fidget as they waited.

Isabel had lost count of the nights they had spent at the river waiting for the Japanese patrols that never seemed to materialize. Tonight, she was sure, would be yet another disappointment. She squeezed a mosquito, rubbing her fingers against the tall grass. It was late, and she was at least an hour from home. But they had all agreed to give it until midnight before forfeiting. It would be worth the wait, the late hour, the mosquitoes, the months of planning, if they could gain their prize.

She stiffened as she heard the far off drone of a small engine. There was a movement in the brush, a signal, for they could all hear the boat now. Tense and eager, Isabel prayed that Rubita was doing her job. There was no way of knowing, until the boat drew closer. As her breathing quickened, the sounds of the boat's motor grew louder and louder.

At the bend of water just above them, she could see the first rays of light as a searchlight swept across the water. Now the vessel turned into their stretch of the river and she pulled out the gun stashed in the waistband of her skirt. The boat was not traveling as fast as they had been told. Maybe that was bad. Perhaps they had heard of the plan and it was all some kind of reverse trap.

The light swept the shore just in front of her and caught Rubita in its bright beam. Beautiful young Rubita with the firm, full breasts and long silken hair. She was kneeling by the bank pounding a pile of clothes with a smooth river stone, appearing as any ordinary woman doing her laundry but for the fact that it was close to midnight and that she was stark naked.

When the lights hit her she stood, in rehearsed disbelief, and fumbled for her clothes, taking care to posture her flawless body so all of the boat's occupants could have a full look. The throttle was turned down as the ship glided into shore, yet the searchlight never left Rubita's body. There seemed to be no suspicion, so enchanted were they by their capture of the eccentric laundress out after the midnight curfew.

They yelled to her in Japanese.

She replied in Tagalog.

They chattered among themselves. Rubita, playing her part beautifully, struggled to pull a white dress over her head, tugging and stretching even as she lifted her breasts high for their inspection. The wet garment plastered her body, doing little to cover her nakedness as her round brown nipples pulled against the tight wet fabric. She gathered the rest of her laundry as quickly as she could, giving every impression of an innocent maiden caught in an awkward situation.

The soldiers in the boat were arguing. One of them called out to Rubita but she ignored him, turning to leave the shore. He jumped out of the boat, grabbing her roughly by the arm as he chattered in Japanese. She tried to pull away, but his grasp was too tight. He pulled on her, trying to get her into the boat, as she dropped her basket of clothes and kicked him. He shook her and her arms flailed against him, raining his torso with fist and claw. Soon it became evident that there was no way that one man alone was going to get the angry Filipina into the boat.

The rest of the soldiers were laughing now, taunting their companion. He struggled with her, pulling her through the water as her wet dress hiked up above her curvaceous thighs. She broke from him and ran back to the shore but he was too quick for her. He tackled her about the legs and pulled her down to the wet sand. Quickly he rolled her over and straddled her, his knee pushing hard between her legs, forcing them apart.

She was still struggling with him and he slapped her hard across her face. Whimpering now, she submitted as the enemy fumbled with his pants, withdrew his engorged penis and mounted her.

The soldiers were cheering encouragement from the boat as they watched their companion ride the woman. Soon their amusement turned to lust, as one by one they climbed over the side of the boat. As the last of the six soldiers started to climb down, the oldest of them barked something in Japanese and the sixth, clearly unhappy, stayed in the boat.

The soldier on top of Rubita was thrusting faster now, nearing his climax, as she twisted and bucked beneath him. The waiting men began to argue among themselves as the first rapist stood.

The guerrillas opened fire, cutting the Japanese soldiers down in the first volley. Too late, the remaining soldier in the boat reached for his Type 100 machine gun. A bullet tore into his forehead as he spun and slumped over the side of the vessel.

Working quickly the guerrillas moved in, checking each soldier carefully to insure he was dead. They rolled them over and began stripping them. Isabel struggled with one, pulling off his boots first, then the socks and pants. They had earlier agreed that the under garments were unimportant. Within minutes the dead soldiers were stripped.

"There are a few holes," one of the men said, holding up the Japanese officer's jacket and tugging on a small red bar which had torn loose.

"We can take care of that," Isabel answered, "the blood too." She hugged him. "I can't believe we finally did it!"

"Yes," he shook his head, "The colonel will be happy to see these. Rubita, you all right?"

For the first time since they had killed the soldiers, Isabel thought of the naked nymph.

"I'm fine, Marco." Her still wet clothes molded her fine body. "After all he was only a man, like any other man. Maybe we are wrong to be so afraid of them." She laughed, despite the swelling that was growing on her face.

Before the war Rubita Moreno had been one of the highest priced whores in Manila.

36

Outside, on the picnic table, Bark had set out their mess kits. It was a day of celebration, for it was Ellen's birthday and they were observing it in her honor.

Tully leaned over the quan pot. "Smells like chicken."

"Right-o!" Bark grinned. "We are having chicken a la king tonight." It was a feast he was thrilled to prepare, for he was fond of Ellen. They all felt they knew her from the letters that Tom so generously shared with them. Vicariously, they were all married to one another. "Sit down. It's ready." He spread his hands, enjoying his role as host.

"Wait," Tom said, "I'd like to offer thanks." He bowed his head, clasping his hands together. "Dear Lord, watch over and protect those loved ones who are not with us this evening. Give them the courage and the wisdom to know that this war will soon be over, that our uncle will soon be here. Thank you, oh Lord, for this food we are about to receive. In Christ's name, amen."

"Amen," Tully and Bark said in unison.

The high roar of an airplane overhead, distracted them. They looked to the skies, straining to make out the high flying craft.

"Zero." Bark was the first one to break the spell. It would have taken almost an act of God to see an American airplane.

It took them a few minutes before they were back up to their usual camaraderie. Toasting Ellen with cup after cup of coffee, they dawdled over the meal, enjoying each other's company and the treat of an occasion.

"When I get back," Tully offered, "I will never stand in a line again. If someone so much as mentions that I should fall in or out, I think I'll kill him."

"No, no," Bark waved his hand, "Crowds, that's it for me. Crowds. Anything more than two people will be a crowd that I will avoid like the plague."

"Ah," Tully grabbed Bark's neck and pulled him over. "Which one of us, Bark, makes the crowd?"

Bark grinned good naturedly before pulling away.

In the dusk, Tom could barely make out the outline of Mount Santo Tomas rising out of its mountain range. Although he could see the mountain every day, there were some times, such as tonight, when the sight of the majestic peak bothered him more than others. It was a constant reminder of happier times, of drives and picnics with his family.

Tears welled in his eyes as he thought of his wife, struggling to be both mother and father to his boys in an alien place, run by alien people. He rubbed his eyes in an effort to dispel the tears that were gathering there. Doc and Pete were now twelve and ten, and it had been almost two years since he had last seen them. Doc was on the brink of manhood, leaving his boyhood behind.

"Soft voices," Tom whispered, in as much of an effort to calm himself as to emphasize his point. "Soft, well modulated voices, that's what I miss."

"Besides Ellen and the boys," Bark added.

"Of course, you asshole." Tully jabbed him in the ribs, for Tom's melancholy had not gone unnoticed. "Come on, I'll help you clean up."

"I don't think so," Bark's voice had lead in it, "it looks like we've got trouble."

Donald Duck and another guard, nicknamed Air Raid, were approaching the barracks. Both were eagerly swinging their heavy clubs.

"Air Raid!" Bark yelled at the top of his lungs. It was a warning they all used whenever the guard in charge of the gardening detail came around. "Air raid!" He yelled it out again, this time breaking into song as he continued scrubbing and picking at the pan.

But his charade had not escaped their attention. Air Raid wasted no time in covering the ground between them, and laying the stout club up against the side of Bark's head.

Tom leapt forward to catch his falling friend, but was stopped by Donald Duck's club which caught him just beneath his rib cage. As he collapsed, it was with some relief that he saw the quan pot was still intact.

Tully stood waiting. But the guards ignored him, as they charged into the barracks and tore it apart. Personal belongings, bedding, clothing, all were searched with a vengeance, as contraband piled up on the wooden slats. Tully knew the treasures would soon be carted off.

"How bad is he?" Tom asked, as he and Tully knelt beside the unconscious Bark.

"He'll live." The medic's hands quickly explored the side of the gunner's head. "Too bad it was this side though." Bark's patch still covered his left eye, but the right side of his head was turning an ugly purplish-blue in color. Already the swelling threatened to cover the remaining good orb.

"It won't affect his sight, will it?" Sullivan asked.

"I don't think so. He may have a hard time for a day or two." Tully patted Bark's shoulder. "I wish I could give him something when he comes to, but it's too dangerous with them right inside."

"Yes." Tom knew of the dangers. There had been a lot of shakedowns and the men had finally taken precautions to bury what medicine they could lay their hands on. Their cache of the tough ones to get, the sulfanilamide, the ampules of ematines, the quinine and the aspirin, was hidden in the Cabanatuan soil. They had left a bottle of Yatrens and some Ematine out, for they did not want to be too suspect. Besides, there had been strong rumors that the Japanese would soon be supplying the camp with the last two drugs.

The Japanese were loading a bag with their prizes. They hauled the heavy bag off and the barracks was safe again until another day. It was always like this, the quick hit and then the shakedown. There was no rhyme or reason to the pattern, although they rarely hit two barracks close to one another on the same day.

Bark groaned, and slowly awakened.

"Air Raid. Air Raid," he whispered the name with a little less verve.

"All right hero, shut up." Tully ordered. "Tom's gone for the aspirin."

Bark looked dazed, as he grabbed Tully hard by the shoulders.

"Tull, am I gonna be able to see? I'm having trouble here." He rubbed his swelling eye.

"You'll be fine in a couple of days. Might have a shiner though."

"We'll find you a steak to put on it," Tom joked, as he returned with three of the precious aspirins.

"Like hell," grumbled Bark. "God, that is a mean son-of-a-bitch."

"So tell us something new, Theodore." Tully agreed. If a popularity poll had been taken in Cabanatuan, the guard known as Lance Corporal Kazutane Aihara, nicknamed Air Raid, would have come out at the bottom.

"Goddamn, I am losing it!" Bark frantically patted his good eye but to no avail for the tissue there was rapidly swelling the eye cavity shut. There was barely a slit peeking out now, and Tully and Sullivan both knew that there was no way he was seeing much out of his right eye.

"Trust me, Bark," Tully reassured him. "You're going to be all right in a couple of days. It's swollen, that's all. There hasn't been any permanent damage done, I promise you."

Tears were rolling out of the slit and down the purple side of Bark's face. "All right, Quack, I'll give it a couple of days, but I'm telling you here and now I'd rather be dead, than a blind man." He reached for Tom and caught his arm.

"Sullivan, is that you?"

"Yes, Bark," Tom answered quietly.

"Promise me something."

"Anything."

"That if I can't see, if it doesn't get better that you'll bring me something so I can do what has to be done."

"You're going to be all right, Bark. Trust Tully, he knows what he's talking about."

The grip tightened, pinching and squeezing Tom's thin arm. "Promise me, goddamnit!"

"All right."

"Because I won't be able to do that for myself. If I can't see and all how could I ever get around to find something, you know what I mean?" Bark's voice was very low now, as his mind raced through the grim possibilities ahead of him. "I'd do it for you, Sullivan, I swear I would."

"I know."

"And, Tull, for you too." Bark released his death grip on the engineer.

"Well the whole thing's stupid," Tully said, "because you're going to be fine, just fine." His voice was cracking a little, for Bark had gotten to him with his talk of suicide pacts. He wiped his eyes.

"Tull, if I'm going to be so friggin' fine, then why are you crying?"

"Here she comes!" Chopper yelled, as they all froze in position, their eyes riveted to the skies, searching for the airplane that had eluded them for two days.

She was due Tuesday afternoon. Now, on the third day, their last real hope, the Lockheed Hudson was in view.

"Right on target," Sky mumbled under his breath, as he watched the aircraft drop for a good look at the clearing. The plane gained a little altitude before coming in on it's final pass. Wordlessly, they all watched as the cargo door opened and a cache of packages came floating down, not a half mile from where they were standing.

They ran for the supplies, oblivious to the Hudson's wing dipping goodbye.

Tennessee reached the teleradio package first. Like a kid at Christmas he tore into the webbing and carefully removed the radio. The parts-transmitter, receiver and loudspeaker- were all there, safely ensconced in their metal boxes.

"I've got batteries and benzine, Captain." Chopper hollered, having inspected the package at his feet.

"Looks like you're really in business now, Tennessee," Sky patted the young boy's shoulder. "See, we didn't bring you all the way up here for nothing." Berringer had been surprised, and pleased, when Tennessee had arrived the morning they were leaving for San Ildefonso. He had been a logical choice to man the new coastwatching post.

"No sir, that's a fact." Parker grinned from ear to ear. "Those Japs won't know what hit them when we get this station set up. Ehah!"

Codenamed "Ferdinand", the coastwatchers were to become an integral part of the intelligence effort in the South Pacific. Originally organized by the Australian Commonwealth, the system was being expanded throughout the Solomons, the Marianas, the Gilberts and the Philippines. Set in tactical outposts, away from mechanical disturbances, the coastwatchers kept track of enemy shipping movements. Working at their lonely tasks, they were in immediate contact with their Allied Intelligence link the moment they had news to report.

Commander Parsons had already given Sky all of the necessary codes and the instructions on what to report, and how to report it. Berringer had then briefed Tennessee, and the two other men who were going to man the station. There would be other posts, but they would lack teleradios and their communication with the main station at San Ildefonso would have to be by runner, a clumsy system at best.

"Let's get back to the point and sort this stuff out," Sky ordered. He was uneasy at having this many men so far from San

Alberto but the manpower had been necessary for the small gasoline engine alone weighed over seventy pounds.

The hut, simply constructed of native palm fronds, was set up on a cliff overlooking the Pacific ocean. They had made it as waterproof as possible although one of the beauties of the 3B teleradio was its seeming indestructibility. From the rocks below, the hut was indistinguishable.

By late afternoon, the radio was set up. All the supplies had been gone through and put away but for two bottles of whiskey.

"This one," Sky handed a bottle to Tennessee, "is yours. You're in charge here and there may come a time when you'll need it. But this one," he said, as he took the cap off with a flourish, "we'll all share."

Some of them considered that a bottle of whiskey split among fifteen people would not go very far. But it was enough, as they all toasted each other and their day's good work.

"Cheers." Kate held her mess cup up to Tennessee who grabbed her around the waist and pulled her close to him. As he did so, a dizzy feeling swept over her and she swayed against him as she sought her balance.

But her vertigo went unnoticed by the signal corpsman.

"To Katie," he said raising his cup high. "For being such a damned good trooper. Pardon me." He was blushing at his profanity in front of her.

"Here! Here!" The men were all toasting her.

Kate waited an appropriate amount of time before drinking, feeling some guilt in the relief she felt that inside of three, four days at the outside, she would be in the comfort of San Alberto.

The gulls were up before any of them, gliding on the air currents and scolding the intruders in their world. Sky sat close to the drop of the bluff, watching the waves pound the weathered rocks below.

"It's not such a bad place to get stuck, is it?" Tennessee said as he joined Berringer.

"No. Is there anything else you need from me?"

"No, sir. I've got the codes and the instructions. As for the radio, well I guess I'll just have to figure it out if anything goes wrong."

Sky nodded. Parker was a long way from help out here.

"You'll be on shifts."

"Eight hours on," Tennessee grinned. They had been through all of it many times before.

"I won't need to know what's going on up here unless it affects us in San Alberto, or unless there's something I can do for you. Your reports will go directly to naval intelligence through your link."

"Yes sir." That, too, had been explained. How the Allies had finally gotten together and formed the Allied Intelligence Bureau, sharing funds and resources so that all concerned countries would have access to the coastwatcher reports. His supplies would also come from the AIB.

"You've got the Playfair code. Remember, there are none for aircraft."

"Yes sir. News is cold on planes. Takes too long to decipher."

"Right." Sky stood and extended his hand. "From here on in you're on your own. It's your brains that will call the shots. You'll know how long you can stay, and what to report."

"I'll bury the radio, sir, if anything goes wrong. In that place we talked about."

"You'll be fine. You're pretty remote here so I doubt whether you'll see any action. If this thing gets off the ground you could be really busy. Although I suppose there's always a chance they'll come for you."

"Yes sir." There was no fear in Parker's voice.

"Charlie will let the AIB know you're set up. There'll be no need to contact them until you have something."

"No."

"And remember Ferdinand."

"Yes sir. Sit quietly."

"Fight only if you're stung," Sky added.

CHANGING WINDS

37

"Eight percent is just too high." Ellen was pacing the floor of the shanty, weighing the pros and cons of borrowing money.

"Ya. But as your husband says, 'it is all relative'. It is only money," Magda offered.

"But eight percent! Why, why that's robbery."

Magda silently worked on her embroidery, knowing full well it might be her last piece as thread was getting scarce.

Ellen paced in silence. Finally she stopped in front of the Czech. "All right, I'll do it. I'll talk to the twenty percent boys."

"Costs are going up, Ellen. You cannot fight it."

"You're right, of course. Things are changing a little too fast now, aren't they?"

The redheaded woman said nothing.

"And now the scraping and the bowing. I wish our uncle would hurry up and get here."

The Japanese were getting stricter. Internees were now expected to bow in respect whenever they encountered one of the guards. Classes had even been held to show them the proper way to do it.

Santo Tomas was rife with rumors, fed by the smuggled letters coming in from Cabanatuan and the other POW camps. Always couched in ambiguous terms, uncle was mentioned frequently. Uncle was doing well in Italy. Uncle was in the Solomons, Uncle was in Rabaul, Uncle was in Borneo, hang on, Uncle was on his way.

That there was some truth to the rumors was evident, for tensions were rising in the camp. Once jovial guards now clammed up, going about their duties with a minimum of conversation. Before the rumors, they would occasionally let the internees listen to Tokyo broadcasts on the radios, now even this questionable favor was withdrawn. Food scarcities were troubling again, and many of them, like Ellen, were juggling assets to prepare for the inevitable squeeze.

Ellen reached in her satchel and pulled out the latest of Tom's letters. As always it was in a tiny square, having been folded many times, reduced to its smallest possible size so that the mailman-priest could hide it in his cassock along with many others. Gently, she unfolded the thin, folded paper.

"Tom says they're disbanding Cabanatuan. Maybe they'll come here." Her blue eyes sparkled and for a moment she almost forgot that she had already read, and reread, the letter to Magda many times. "That would be good news."

"Ya."

Something in Magda's voice caught Ellen.

"Is something wrong?" she asked.

Magda shook her head.

"You don't believe it, do you? You don't believe he's coming here at all!" She sat on the cot next to her friend with her eyes boring into her face. "You don't want to believe it, that's all. You're jealous."

Magda put her sewing to one side.

"You're afraid, aren't you? You're afraid that if Tom comes you'll have to move out of the shanty, that there won't be room for you," Ellen was beginning to cry now. "You're afraid there'll be less food."

Magda waited, stiff with tension, as Ellen sobbed. The Czech, cautiously at first, put one arm around her thin friend. When she met no resistance there, she pulled her to her still ample bosom, comforting her as she cried, her tears spilling onto, and blurring the beloved words from Tom. Gently she pulled the letter from Ellen's grip and put it on the cot.

Great sobs racked the American's body, aggravating the cough she had had for weeks. Gasping and gulping for air, she was trying to regain control of herself. Magda handed her a well crumpled piece of newspaper. They had been using them for tissue and toilet paper for months.

Ellen heartily blew her nose into the front page. "He's not coming, is he?"

"The future, Ellen, it is very difficult. You know that. There is so much free will."

"But there are too many people involved in this, aren't there? You said so yourself. That if there were a lot of people involved then it was more difficult for something to change, that if there are only two or three people then the possibilities are greater. You said that, didn't you, Magda?"

"Ya."

"And you see something now, don't you?"

Nothing.

"Don't you?"

"It is so hard, Ellen. I am wrong sometimes. You yourself have proof of that."

"He's not coming, is he?"

Magda sadly shook her head. The pictures had been haunting her for months and she knew they were not wrong.

Surprisingly there were no more tears. Ellen reached across the Czech and retrieved her letter, folded it carefully and returned it to the satchel. Wordlessly she closed the clasp, and pushed the baggage back under the cot. She stood and dabbed at her splotched face a last time, before patting her skirt smooth.

"I'm sorry, Magda, but this time you're wrong. Tom's coming to Santo Tomas. He'll be here soon and you're just going to have to live with that." She turned on her heel and left the shanty.

Wearily Magda picked up her embroidery and slowly began pushing the needle in and out of the handkerchief.

❧

Kate's clothes were clinging to her, soaked through with the sweat from her body. Was that why she felt so clammy, she wondered. Her head was pounding, throbbing, aching all over. God, how she just wanted to lay down for a few minutes, to rest and still the shaking in her limbs. She knew it was impossible. They were almost home. Sky had told here they'd be there by late morning tomorrow. She could make that.

There was no denying the trip had been a rough one. There had been no path and they had blazed their own through the unforgiving jungle, hacking at grass and brush, slapped by the relentless branches. They were all covered with mosquito bites, and two of them had even been bitten by spiders.

The salt from her perspiration was dripping into her eyes, biting and stinging them, and she closed them while she wiped at her face with the tail of her dirty shirt. The rag she had thought to tie around her forehead was soaking wet, offering no resistance to the moisture that was pouring from her. Dimly she was aware of a stream dripping steadily from her hairline down her spine.

She had never felt more tired or dirty in her life, but still she kept walking, plodding one foot after the other, not daring to think of the sweating or the shaking. She looked ahead to the others and vaguely wondered why they were so far away. She must think now, concentrate on where they were going, on getting there. Her head was down. Maybe if she kept her mind on the dust in front of her she could do it. Of course she could. She was in good shape, she could handle this little jaunt. After all, she had made it up here, hadn't she? No, she just had a little bug, maybe the flu.

A sudden chill caught her and it was as though she were a bystander, watching her own body twitch and shake uncontrollably as the shivering overcame her.

"Are you all right?" Sky was beside her now, holding her elbow. She turned and squinted, trying to focus on him, but he wouldn't stand still. It was strange but there were two of him there.

"Me? I'm fine," she said, even as she reached for his blurring image. "Really." It was her last word as she collapsed in the dust.

They were late for boxing practice because the pot watcher had gotten distracted and let the rice burn. There had been plenty of complaints and cleaning the kitchen pots had taken longer.

Now Doc and Pete were running across campus to make up for their lost minutes. Coach would not be happy if they were late.

Hurrying as they were, eyes glued to the ground, they did not see Lieutenant Abiko come around the corner. With a dull thud,

Pete crashed into him, throwing the stunned Japanese guard off balance. Even as he tottered, he grabbed Pete hard and shoved him from him.

"What are you doing?" He screamed. "Where you go in such a state?"

Pete stood erect, scared to death, for he had seen Abiko's sadistic temper before. The guard slapped him hard across the face and as his head returned to its original position, Abiko backhanded him.

"I'm sorry sir," Pete stuttered, "I was going to boxing practice."

"Boxing practice!" The Japanese spat. "And they teach you no respect at boxing practice?" The tiny eyes seemed to be on fire.

"No sir. That is, yes sir." Pete was confused now. Although they had all been present at what had come to be known as the lecture on respect, and although his mother explained to them the importance of it all, he was now at a complete loss as to whether he should bow, or scrape, or just what it was he was supposed to do.

"Honorable sir." Doc went into a deep bow. "My brother meant no disrespect, sir."

Pete caught on. He went into a deep bow. "Please forgive me."

The camp commandant had been strict in insisting on the outward polite formalities between the guards and the internees. Abiko gave the boys a very slight bow.

"In future, you watch your steps," he ordered.

"Yes, sir," the boys answered in unison as they watched him walk away.

"Shitface," Doc offered, as he looked at Petey's reddening face.

"Hail Mary, full of grace, the Lord is with thee. Blessed art thou amongst women and blessed is the fruit of thy womb, Jesus. Holy Mary Mother of God, pray for us sinners now and at the hour of our death." There, Bendetti thought, that was ten, or was it only nine?

He paused for a moment before deciding that one Hail Mary one way or the other didn't make any difference. He carefully replaced the worn rosary beads back into his pocket.

Over two months had passed since he had met the first young boy on the jungle path and there had been two more children since then. While something buried deep in his tormented brain tried to send out warning signals, Bendetti pushed it aside, knowing he was involved in a war greater than man had ever known. The children had all been enemies. They had all wanted to turn him into the dreaded Japanese, and for that they had deserved to die. Surely God would understand that, would want His teachers to protect themselves. Surely He, in His wisdom would forgive, nay condone, that protection. Wasn't that why He had given him the voice? To instruct him?

The sun was warm, beating against him as he rested against the thick tree trunk. Although his watch had been lost on Bataan, he knew he was early. Morning had not yet passed, judging from the placement of the sun, and we was not to meet the contact until two. He probably had hours.

The meeting had taken some doing. He had made the proper contacts in Manila and now the rendezvous would take place. He was going into an arm of the growing guerrilla army. He had given serious thought to staying in Manila but there were too many Japanese there, the risk too great. Speaking none of the Filipino dialects hadn't helped either.

None of them in the Manila underground had known him. It had been easy enough to lie about his military status, and now, luck of luck, he was being connected with one of the few groups, if not the only one on Luzon, that was led by a civilian.

Bendetti closed his eyes as his mind drifted back to the children. He hadn't even known their names, any of them. They had all been boys. They had all been, he thought, under ten, although sometimes it was hard to tell with the tiny Filipinos. Curiously they had all spoken English. The last two, in fact, had spent a considerable amount of energy trying to convince him that they were really on the Americans' side. Lying little bastards. You could see it in their eyes. In those dark cesspools, that was where the truth lay.

The priest laughed to himself when he realized he had an erection. The telltale bulge pushed and strained against his shorts, begging for release. Bendetti opened his eyes. It was quiet and still, nothing had changed. He thought about it for a minute. There was time, plenty of time, for his contact would not be here for another hour. How long would it take? What was a few minutes out of an entire day? He smiled before closing his eyes again and returning his thoughts to the dying children.

He opened his shorts laying his engorged member out, his eyes still shut. Starting slowly, he began to fondle himself while the macabre daydreams danced in his head. He began to chant as he slowly stroked himself.

"If I were hungry, I would not tell thee: for the world *is* mine, and the fullness thereof," his hand was moving faster now, "will I eat the flesh of bulls, or drink the blood of goats?"

His hand was trying to match the racing tempo of his chant. "Offer onto God thanksgiving; and pay the vows unto the Most High," he chanted the 50th Psalm, fully aware that he could not long continue. "And call upon me in the day of trouble; I will deliver thee, and thou shalt glorify me." With a shudder he fell back against the tree, his shorts soiled with the remnants of his forbidden fantasies.

He kept his eyes closed, not yet wanting to face what he had done. It wasn't the first time, nor would it be the last. It had gone on for almost as long as he could remember. But still, afterwards, there was the awful dealing with it. The admission that he was less than perfect. That he had to so treat himself in order to get release. It was humiliating. He hated that part of it. The other, before, had been an act of self-love and that he could stand.

In the seminary it had been different. There had been another who had helped him. Actually they had helped each other. But since then there had been no one. Until the last child.

The priest fumbled to close his pants even as he opened his eyes. He stood and stretched, patting the front of his shorts, eager for them to dry. He unscrewed his canteen and drank from it, sprinkling a little water on his hands and rubbing them together. He pulled the material of his pants away from his skin, and tried to shake it dry. Then he turned around and saw the man standing quietly behind him.

"You!"

"They sent me for you. Do you have everything?" The Navajo's dark eyes divulged nothing.

Bendetti screwed the top back on the canteen. "Where are we going?" His mind raced, wondering how much of his performance the man had seen.

"To the village. He's up there, waiting to meet you."

"Berringer." The single word came out like venom. "I should have known. He's the leader, isn't he?"

"Yes." Charlie's eyes never left Bendetti's face.

The priest vacillated for a minute. He could return to Manila. He could ask for another group.

He had choices. He did not have to go with the Indian. He did not have to work with a man he detested.

"I'm going back to Manila."

"Suit yourself," Charlie turned to go.

"Wait!" Another thought had occurred to the priest. "Is she with you?"

Charlie had seen it before. This lust for Sky's woman. He did not have to ask who he was asking about. Neither would he lie about it.

"Yes." He said simply.

Without another word, Bendetti collected his belongings and numbly followed the Navajo up the hill.

※

It had seemed so easy. That was the one thought that kept coming to Isabel in her brief lucid moments. Most of the time she was delirious, swept into the past with little or no recollection of the present. Mercifully.

She had lost all awareness now of whether or not they were hanging her by her heels again, or burning her body with their cigarettes. There had been more. Much more. Her fingers were still useless for they had jammed .25 caliber cartridges between them and then squeezed. She could vaguely remember the wet floor, and the electric sticks they had run inside of her. And the pain. Was she capable of feeling pain any more?

There was nothing left to feel, for she had run the gauntlet. The tree. That's where she was now. Tied naked to the tree. She tried to shake her head to clear the cobwebs there, but was unable to move either right or left for they had lashed even her head to the sturdy trunk.

How many times was it now? Five? Six? It was impossible to keep track. There had to be some kind of rhythm to it, of that she was sure. For she was never tied to the tree for less than twenty-four hours.

She tried to lick her lips, but there was no moisture in her mouth for the sun had baked it out hours ago. Her tongue, swollen nearly double, felt like a wad of cotton. She tried to speak, even a whisper, but nothing came out. Surprisingly her eyes were still good. She could see the guard thirty yards or so away, sitting in the shade of the building, smoking a cigarette. God how she hated them all.

There was nothing to her posture now. Had they released her from the support of the tree, she would have collapsed in a heap on her native soil, for her body had been so wracked and lashed and abused that there was nothing left of it. Never large to begin with, her diet of bread and water had taken its toll on her over the last month.

Month? Could it be that long? Yes. The others were now long dead. All of them. Even laughing Rubita. But Isabel had endured all of it. The rapes, the beatings, the torture.

She remembered her mother saying long ago that women were the stronger of the two sexes. That they had the physical stamina to take more than the men. The way her mother had explained it to her had been good. She had said it was the way God had intended things. For if the men had been the carriers of the babies, there would be fewer babies. They could not take it, she had said. At the time it had seemed so nice to have this extra strength, this ability to endure. Now Isabel wasn't so sure.

She closed her eyes. It took too much effort to keep them open. Somewhere, back in the recesses of her barely conscious mind, she dredged up a prayer and recited it over and over again in her mind. Was this a sin? Would God forgive her for asking for death? There must be a reason in all of this, she thought. There must be.

In the beginning, she had tried to faint. Had willed herself to lose consciousness. But it hadn't worked. Her body had refused to obey her. So she had done the next best thing. She had pretended to faint. But her captors would have none of it. They were professionals. They had lit matches and held them to the soft instep of her foot until she had begged them to stop.

Her thoughts were drifting from the prayer now. Back to the river and to Rubita with her taunting breasts. That time had been so easy. The guerrillas had been so grateful for the enemy uniforms. It had been for such a good cause. And it had given Isabel's group courage. Confidence. Maybe too much of both. Was that not also a sin?

Then the soldiers had come to the factory wharf. Isabel had known they were coming, had seen the message in the front office. It had been so easy to organize the group, to get the naked Rubita to volunteer once more, under only slightly different circumstances. They had gotten four uniforms from that escapade. Four. But the colonel would never see them, would never know what they had done for their country. For they had all been caught.

Isabel was remotely aware of the tugs at her ropes as she opened her eyes. They, too, were now fading. Was that how death came, she thought. The guard was handling her roughly. There was no love there, no care, she thought, dimly aware of a heavy sadness coming over her. We are both eastern people she wanted to cry out. We are brothers, you and I. But no sound would come from her throat.

The ropes were loose now. He was pulling on her, trying to get her to follow him. She wanted to cooperate, she really did, but her legs would not listen to her. A wetness slithered down the inside of her thighs, triggered she did not know by fear or need.

The guard twisted her around, and pulled at her long black hair. Once it had been so pretty. Now it hung in filthy uneven clumps, knotted and torn. Pulled back from her forehead as he dragged her by her hair, the bruises and burns on her once flawless face stood out more clearly.

This was nice, she thought, I cannot even feel the pain from the roots of my hair. Is that right? Shouldn't I feel something? Am I still alive?

The guard grunted and pulled her across the dirt into the shed where they had been keeping her. An example. That's what they had said in the beginning. She was to serve as an example to the factory workers, to the guerrillas. Spies of the Imperial Japanese Army would not be tolerated.

The officer was inside the room. It was so nice and cool here. Almost like coming home, she thought. She tried to smile at him. They had been through so much together, were they not as close as friends? But her eyes were closed. How could she know he was there? She tried to smile again. Smell. It was still there. Her eyes and body had failed her but her sense of smell was still intact.

The officer poked and pinched her, and got no response. He lifted her eyelids, one by one, staring into the glazed orbs that disappeared into the back of her head. He slapped her hard several times across the face, watching in disgust as her head rolled limply around on her neck. He grabbed her right nipple and pinched it hard, but there was no resistance to his assault.

His lit cigarette roamed across her nakedness, touching here and there to leave yet another mark on her already scarred body. Finally he held his index finger to her neck. The pulse was barely discernible.

"She is gone." He barked to the man who had brought her in from the tree. "Take care of her."

And so, on the thirty-second day of her captivity, Isabel Fajardo, Filipina patriot who had never left her country in her twenty-seven years, was shot in the back of the head.

Her mother had been right about her strength, for she had not talked.

38

Charlie Begay had been talking for ten minutes, although it was a conversation that only the Indian and a fellow Navajo could follow for they were talking in code. In Navajo.

The whole program had been briefly explained to Charlie by Sky, who had learned about it from Chick Parsons. Hoping to thwart the Japanese, who were experts at code breaking, the Marine Corps, prompted by a Los Angeles engineer who had grown up on the Navajo Reservation, had begun the Navajo Code Talkers. Started well over a year ago with an initial group of twenty-nine men, the code talkers, now known as the 382nd Platoon of the United States Marine Corps, were growing by leaps and bounds.

While Indians of many tribes, among them the Comanche, Creek, Hopi and Chippewa, were used in communications in all of the war theatres, they were talking to one another in their native tongues. The Navajo code talkers had taken their cryptography a step further. In addition to speaking Navajo, a complex language not only to master but to speak properly, they had created a Navajo code. Thus battleships became whales; dive bombers became chicken hawks; mine sweepers, beavers. Or in code *Lo-tso*, *Gini* and *Cha*. Hitler became the "moustache smeller" and the Japanese became "narrow eyes". Words were chosen based on their familiarity to the Navajos. Clan, wind, yucca, fire builder and running water all stood for something in the new code.

Charlie, while not a code talker, had been given a few of the code names. Armed with this information, as well as his fluency in his native tongue, he was able to communicate in a code of his own.

He signed off with naval time.

"I hope he got that right. I'm not sure I've got this new thing yet."

"You're doing fine," Sky reassured him. "I couldn't understand a word you said."

Begay laughed and took off his earphones. "Let's hope he did."

"They're going to have one hell of a time cracking this one." Charlie nodded.

"We won't use you all the time," Sky said. "Just for the critical ones." They had used the transmission to tell Australia that San Ildefonso and several other stations were now in operation.

"You saw the man."

"Yes." Sky had met with Bendetti and the meeting had not gone well.

"He stays?"

"For a while. Until I can figure out what to do with him."

"He wants your woman."

"I know."

"That makes him a dangerous enemy."

"He's a priest," Sky shrugged. "There's nothing he will do about it."

The Navajo's dark eyes narrowed. "Keep the sun to your back."

"Relax. Bendetti's the most ineffectual man I've ever met."

Charlie was not so sure. "She is not any better."

"No. We have to wait for the quinine to take effect. I wish we could get our hands on some more Atabrine." The new antimalarial drug that Parsons had brought in to them was now gone.

Begay nodded. They were all worried about Kate. They had been back from the mountains for two weeks and she seemed to be getting worse. Confined to her bed, thrashing with alternate spells of chills and fever, her malaria attacks rather than abating, were recurring with alarming frequency. Food was almost out of the question, and although they had all sat by her bedside with bowls of broth, their success in that area had been limited. Her illness was having a staggering effect on Kate. Shadows had set in under the sunken turquoise eyes, and her weight loss was dramatic.

"Speak of the devil," Sky muttered under his breath, for Bendetti was coming at them at a fast clip.

"We've got to get her to a doctor. She's getting worse," the priest insisted.

"The doctor's seen her. She's getting quinine. There's nothing we can do but wait for it to take hold." Berringer's eyes turned the color of steel.

"Doctor? Witch doctor you mean. There isn't a doctor in this village."

"Amazing how they make it through the ravages, Father. Don't you think?"

"She's getting worse. Any fool can see that."

"It always does. She's close to breaking it."

"You mean it's getting close to breaking her," the priest spat.

"She's tough, Bendetti. A lot tougher than you are. She'll make it." There was no way he was going to share his worry with a priest he did not trust.

"We can take her into Manila. I'll go. Say I found her wandering in the mountains or in a hut. I'll think of something."

"No. Katie's not going anywhere."

"You're crazy. She's dying, and you want to keep her to fulfill some kind of Robin Hood fantasy."

"I'm not even going to acknowledge that remark." Sky was trying hard to keep his anger in check. "You take her into Manila and her life's worthless anyway. You know what they do to guerrillas."

"Goddamnit she's not a guerrilla!"

"Try explaining that to the Japs."

"You've seen those notices. You know they'll put her in a camp where she'll get better medical care than here."

Sky walked off, leaving him alone in the radio hut.

He had seen the notices all right. The Japanese Military authorities had insisted on papering the country with glowing testimonials from internees up at Camp Holmes in Baguio. The internees had written a letter urging all civilians who were not interned to turn themselves in. They had even suggested that they would be better off in the camp than they would be on the outside. The Japanese were also sending groups of civilians out in an attempt to lure their friends in.

Kate was alone on her perspiration soaked bed when Sky went in. Her light brown hair was dull and wet, clumped around her drawn face. Sky sat in the chair next to her. She was sleeping. He reached over and lightly felt her forehead, pleased to find it cool. The light sheet that was covering her was also soaked.

"Sky."

"I'm here."

She reached for his hand and pulled it weakly to her chest.

"Thank you."

"How are you feeling?" He squeezed her hand.

"Better I think. Tired."

"That's normal. You need to rest."

"Yes," she placed his hand against her damp cheek. "Are you sorry I came?"

"God no. You're not the first one to get malaria you know."

"No," she smiled weakly. "George came to see me. He thinks I should go to Manila."

"I know. It's ridiculous."

"Is it, Sky? Is it really? I wouldn't be a burden there."

"Sssh," he held his fingers to her dry lips. "You're not a burden here. Besides, malaria's not going to kill you."

"They'd torture me, wouldn't they?" It was one of her more lucid moments.

"No, hush. You're safe here and you're going to get well. Faustino's gone for a medic now." Although Sky would not admit it to the priest, he too, was eager for a second medical opinion.

Chopper knocked on the door. "Captain, we have a problem out here. I think you'd better come." There was an urgency in the pilot's voice.

"You'll be all right, Katie darling." Sky bent over and kissed her wet forehead. "Get some sleep."

It was bright and humid outside. Sky squinted as the sunlight assaulted his focusing eyes.

"Over here." Chopper led him away from the houses, toward a large communal garden. They marched through the talinum and sayute beds. Halfway into the camotes, Chopper stopped and pointed.

Crumpled in the damp earth was the body of a young boy

nestled into the fetal position, his small knees bent and almost touching his lifeless chin. Blood stained the round knees and a pool of it collected beneath him soaking into the ground.

"Jesus Christ," Sky knelt and felt the young body. It was cold, very cold. "When did you find him?"

"Ten minutes ago. One of the guys was out walking with a dog. The dog really found him. No one else knows."

Sky rolled the small boy over on his back, his knees, frozen with rigor mortis, were still in the chest high position. The child's neck was laid open.

"My God," Sky's fingers traced the edge of the torn skin and he shivered as he did so. He patted the camote leaves around the body, brushing and picking them up off the ground.

"It's clean, Captain. I already looked. I think the kid's been killed." There was little emotion in Chopper's voice. "There aren't any dogs around here that would do that."

Sky lifted the small, stiff body in his arms, juggling and shifting it, for it was difficult carrying the unyielding corpse.

"That's the way you want to handle it?" Chopper asked.

"It's the only way, far as I can see. We tell the village and they'll come out and trample all the crops. God knows they need those."

"Whose kid is it, do you know?"

Sky shook his head.

Together they walked back to the sleepy village with the dead child.

☙

The metal of the pellet gun felt cool against Doc's flat belly. He had been up here now so many times that he had lost count, but he always tucked his secret weapon in the waistband of his shorts. It had become a game with him, this business of spying on the men with the radio. He had it down pat. The eavesdropping and the mad dash to the building before the guard or the men arrived.

From that first time he had torn across the open door he had found another way out. There was a little storage room just off the landing. Although it had probably once held mops and buckets and other cleaning supplies, it was now empty except for one small window. Doc found that it opened on to a large acacia tree. Since the building was only two stories high, the twelve-year-old reasoned that he could climb down the tree and even if he fell the risk of injury was not too great. Now he had an almost foolproof method of leaving whenever he wanted to.

He crouched, yawning in the dark. It was almost time to go. He could see the back of the man posted as guard and, deciding it was safe, he took one last look in the radio room.

The men were excited tonight. After working for months on the equipment, they had completed the construction of two receivers and two transmitters.

"Until we need it," a man's voice drifted into the hall, "we'll dismantle them until then."

"Too risky," a deeper voice agreed.

"At least on transmissions. Break them down."

"Receivers too."

"No. Keep them in component parts, we can receive if necessary."

They were dismantling the equipment they had worked so hard to build! It didn't make sense to Doc. He stopped just short of running into the room and begging them not to do it. But the game was serious business to the men inside the room. No, they would not think kindly on a boy who presumed to tell them their business. Doc crept back down the hall, around the corner and into the supply room.

His spy missions, it looked like, were coming to an end for a while. Sadly, Doc pried the window open, checking the ground below to make sure the coast was clear before climbing out and down the tree.

Pete came tearing into the shanty, his little wheelbarrow skidding across the dirt floor, kicking up puffs of dirt.

"They're here, Mother!" His little round face still, miraculously, held much of its innocence. "The Red Cross   packages. I saw them."

"Thank God." Magda said. "I was beginning to wonder if they would ever come."

Ellen scowled in an effort to silence the Czech. They had agreed long ago to shelter the boys from any apprehensions they might have regarding Santo Tomas, or the problems connected with feeding so many people.

"Does this mean milk and sugar?" Pete asked. Although he had never said anything when the camp had run out of them along with bread, oil and meat, it was clearly on his young mind.

"We'll see, darling. It will probably be like last time." Ellen said a silent prayer for meat and other protein items. Rations had been cut days earlier and again, food was the uppermost subject on everyone's mind. All of them were thinner now. The adults had been generous with the children and they were the only ones who seemed to be maintaining their weights. "Run along and find your brother for me, won't you?"

"Right-o!" Peter was playing with the British children and picking up their speech patterns.

"I wonder how long it will be before we see them this time," Ellen mused.

Magda shrugged. She was not going to say anything, for the two of them had agreed after their last argument over the disbanding of Cabanatuan that if their friendship were to survive, it must not include any talk of clairvoyance. Ellen had apologized to her. An apology prompted by bitter disappointment when, in October, the commandant at Santo Tomas had instructed all of them that under no circumstances were any prisoners of war coming into camp.

"It's been a long time since there was anything in the pot." Ellen's hands caressed the old tin pot that Luther had made for them. When they could get extras, they went into the pot. It had been a link, she thought, with Tom at Cabanatuan. Many times she had tried to imagine him standing over his quan pot.

The two women sat very still. Things were getting even tougher in Santo Tomas. The attitudes of the Japanese guards were deteriorating. American canned goods were unattainable now at any price. The morning rice mush, coupled with black beans for lunch, were meager nourishment to carry them through the day. By late afternoon, most of them were exhausted and more than ready for the evening meal.

"Even the plants are beginning to look good to me," Magda said. "We are going to have to be more experimental."

"You're right of course," Ellen twisted her wedding ring round and round her finger. The diamond solitaire was still stuffed safely away in the satchel. "If we can make vinegar out of bananas, anything's possible, isn't it?"

The clear notes of Doc's whistling came into the shanty before he did.

"Hello, Mother." He pecked Ellen on the cheek. "Happy anniversary."

"Thank you, dear, but that was last month."

"No, it's everyone's anniversary. Don't you know what day it is?"

In truth most of them only occasionally kept track of the exact day. There was no need to do more than that. There were no checks to write, no appointments to keep, no newspapers to read.

Ellen thought for a moment.

"Why, it's the eighth. December eighth."

Even given the International Date Line, it had been two years since Japan attacked Pearl Harbor.

39

"Will Tully make it?"

Tom stared into Bark's good eye. "I don't know. God I hope so." Tully had been gone a week now, sent to the makeshift diphtheria ward with hundreds of other prisoners. "I just don't know what the odds are without serum."

"Tiny says they've got some but not enough for all of them."

"Did he try to arrange a buy for us?"

Bark nodded. "He didn't get very far. They're dispensing it this afternoon."

Tom put down the letter to Ellen he had been working on. "I think I'll walk over and see if there's any change."

"I'll come too." Bark slipped Tunes into the pocket of his shorts. He had become ingenious in hiding his harmonica from the Japanese guards and took great pains to keep it with him at all time.

The ward was crammed with patients. Although Tom visited the medic earlier in the week, he had a little trouble finding him among the row after row of cots since so many new men had been added to the ward.

Huge blue-black flies crawled across Tully's face as he slept. The ward, constructed of woven bamboo over bamboo frames, had no windows or screens and the flies were feasting everywhere.

Bark and Tom stood by his cot, reassured as they watched the thin wall of his chest heave up and down in labored breathing. His neck was swollen with the fibrinous pseudomembrane that had formed there. In the next cot, a man wheezed through a tube that had been placed in his cut throat. Throughout the ward there were men who were already dead, whose hearts had given out, or who had choked to death, before anyone could reach them.

"There's a doctor." Tom nudged Bark. The two left Tully and began following the man through the ward. The doctor was carrying a tray with the precious serum and needles on it. Followed by a soldier with a list, the medic would check the dog tags against the slate and the soldier would check off each name as the recipient was injected with the serum.

"Say, Doc." Bark approached the man as he was giving an injection. The doctor did not look up. "We have a friend over there who really needs a shot of that stuff."

"They all do, soldier." The doctor was an older man. And he was tired, very tired, from treating the men with inferior drugs. Now that the diphtheria serum was here he was eager to administer it as quickly as possible.

"Then there's enough. We heard a rumor there wasn't." Relieved, Bark turned to leave.

"That's right," the doctor stopped long enough to face him. "There are over five hundred men in here. I've got serum for two hundred." A young soldier followed him with a list. The doctor tapped the list with the spent syringe that would be boiled and used again. "The two hundred whose names are on this list."

"Jesus Christ! What the hell kind of treatment is that?"

"I don't make the rules, son. I don't have anything to do with it." The doctor brushed past him and walked down three cots before checking the patient's dog tags against the list. Satisfied that the man was the same whose name appeared on the yellowed sheet, he prepared another injection.

Bark stomped after the doctor. Tom caught his arm. "Let me," he urged.

"Excuse me, sir." Tom waited until the needle was withdrawn from the soldier's frail arm. "Where did the list come from?"

"The Japanese drew names."

"Names of the sick?" Tom was incredulous.

"Uh huh. There are two hundred injections. They drew two hundred names. That's the way they do things here."

"What will happen to the others?"

The doctor looked him squarely in the eye. "They'll probably die."

"All of them?"

"That's my best guess. Fact is, some of them who get it will probably die." The doctor was off, trying to locate his next patient.

Tom followed him. "Excuse me sir, may I ask one last question." He didn't wait for an answer. "Our friend, he's a medic, Steve Tulliver, is he on your list?"

The doctor was swabbing an unconscious soldier's arm. "Don't know. The names are written down as drawn. They're not in alphabetical order. You'll have to wait and see." The man was not going to relinquish his list nor did he want to take the time to search through the names looking for one that began with "T".

They withdrew to Tully's cot. Although he was barely conscious he licked his lips trying to put moisture there, but there was none in his mouth to give.

"Water," he whispered faintly.

"I'll get it." Bark reached for Tully's mess kit and withdrew his canteen cup.

Tom felt a dry scratchy finger rubbing against his arm. "Tom?"

"Yes Tully, I'm here."

"There's medicine." His voice was barely audible.

"Yes, there's some serum." Tom hedged.

"But not enough." Tully had seen it time and time again at Cabanatuan. He had shared that frustration more than once.

"No."

"Is it all gone?"

"No, they're doing it now."

Bark returned and held a spoonful of water to Tully's parched lips, cradling his head in his arms as the man tried to drink. It was a slow process for the lump in his throat threatened to close it entirely and only a few pitiful drops could get down.

"There's a letter in my things," Tully strained to tell them. "If I die, see that it gets there, will you?"

They waited forty minutes.

The doctor was next to them now, cleaning a soldier's arm. "This will help you son." The doctor's voice was low and calm, but loud enough for them to hear.

Tom looked at Tully nervously. He had watched the doctor work through the ward and he knew the odds of his coming to two beds in a row were not good. Still he prayed.

Tully's eyes shot open.

Bark and Tom could not watch the doctor's progress, their eyes were frozen on Tully's own, so mesmerized were they by the fear and hope they saw mingled there. As though watching a reflection in a mirror, they studied his tired hazel eyes as they tracked the doctor.

"Hello, son." the man was at the cot now, reaching for Tully's dog tags. "Tulliver, Steven P."

Tom held his breath.

"Tulliver, Steven P." the young soldier replied, scratching Tully's name from the list as the doctor injected him with the priceless serum.

☆

Charlie had been missing for a day and a half when Sky finally found him. He had taken to the hills, climbing miles above San Alberto before settling in next to a waterfall. Berringer had actually heard him before he had come upon him, for the sounds of the Navajo chant were caught on the mountain breeze and carried down to him as he climbed through the thick brush and tropical ferns.

Begay, clad in a g-string and nothing else, had been dancing around a small cleared area, making guttural sounds strung together in some type of mysterious chant. The range of his voice did not even stretch an octave but hovered around four or five notes, leaving the listener with an eery, haunted feeling.

Sky walked into the clearing, saying nothing as he took a seat against a huge rock outcropping. He stayed throughout the night, watching Charlie dance and sing and although he was sure the Navajo was aware of his presence, he had not interrupted him, knowing that he was witnessing some kind of pagan ritual.

And so he sat. Drinking water occasionally and watching his old friend dance with the vigor of a man half his age. By noon of the second day after finding him, Sky watched as the Indian placed spent bullet casings, a lock of Asian hair, a few pieces of bone and a Japanese fan into a piece of cloth. Charlie wrapped the items carefully up and then placed the bundle in the middle of the clearing.

Suddenly it was clear to Berringer. Remembering a story the old Navajo had told him years before, Sky rose from his resting place and reached for his rifle. He checked to insure it carried a full clip. Releasing the safety, he walked to the dancing Indian. He aimed the rifle carefully and slowly fired four bullets into the bundle of Japanese memorabilia. The curing ceremonial was final now. Charlie was free from his past experiences with the Japanese. The Enemy Way ceremonial was complete.

As Charlie dressed, Sky remembered the story he had heard from him about a Navajo who had visited a white prostitute in Gallup. He had needed purification after that occasion and his friends had performed an Enemy Way ceremony for him. Taking some of the prostitute's belongings, they had wrapped them in a bundle and then had fired four shots, the lucky Navajo number, into the possessions. Enemy Way. Good insurance, Charlie had called it. Very important when one was dealing with enemies outside.

Sky was troubled as he watched Charlie gather the rest of his things. Enemy Way was done when the contact with the outside forces was done. Why was he doing it now? Surely they would have more opportunity to deal with the Japanese.

Halfway down the mountain they spoke for the first time.

"Why?" It was all Sky asked.

"Changing Woman came again on the night of the full moon. Why did you come?"

"The battery came in for Parker's radio. It's got to get up to him and I thought you might want to be the one to take it."

"Yes."

It was late in the day when they reached San Alberto. The medic that had come in from Volckmann's group was waiting for them.

"Bad news, I'm afraid. Blackwater fever."

Berringer sat heavily on the wooden steps.

"Blackwater fever," he repeated wearily.

"You've been treating her with quinine, haven't you?"

"Yes."

The medic nodded. "We're going to Atabrine now. Of course it's not in supply yet the way the quinine is. There's some suggestion that the quinine can occasionally lead into Blackwater."

"Then it's a form of malaria."

"Rather a complication. We see it in cases of chronic falciparum malaria treated with quinine." The medic was very serious. "It's an acute intravascular hemolysis."

"Which is what in plain English?"

"An infusion reaction."

"To the quinine."

The medic nodded.

"How long has she been bleeding?"

"She's bleeding?" Sky was visibly shaken.

"It comes with it sometimes. That fellow, Marcos."

Sky nodded. He knew of Ferdinand Marcos, one of the guerrilla leaders working in Manila.

"He had Blackwater fever. Bled from all his body orifices. Almost died before they got him to the Philippine General Hospital."

"It's serious then."

"Very. I would encourage you to get her into Manila but under the circumstances I don't feel good about making that recommendation."

"No." The medic did not have to explain to him the consequences of bringing in an American who had been at large for over two years. It wouldn't take the *kempei-tai* long to get to Kate.

"But I think it only fair to tell you that the odds aren't real good."

"Like?"

"Fifty-fifty at best. Under optimal conditions. I'll leave you some medicine for her. Is she a strong woman?"

A hint of a smile crossed Sky's face as he thought of her morning workouts and her recent hike with them to San Ildefonso. "Yes."

"That will help. That and her will to live. Oh, it's important to keep her quiet. Avoid moving her if you can."

"That won't be hard. It's pretty quiet up here."

Sky watched George Bendetti cross in front of the village well. He was going to be a real problem, he thought. Simpering and fluttering around Kate, he had tried to keep them all at bay, preferring to tend to her himself. While Sky had gone looking for Charlie he was sure that the priest had only gotten more vigilant in his role as Kate's caretaker.

"She's got to go to Manila." The priest was on them now.

"She's staying."

Bendetti grabbed Sky's collar and shook it as hard as he could. "Staying? Are you mad? She's going to die in there. Wrapped in her own sweat and blood she's going to die, can't you see that?"

Sky threw the priest's hands from his collar. "Shut up. She's not going to die."

"You sorry son-of-a-bitch." Venom had replaced any pleading in Bendetti's voice. "Do you really believe that?"

"She's staying, Bendetti. You believe that. If you can't accept it or live by the rules up here then go back with the doctor."

"Your rules," the priest spat at him.

Berringer's eyes narrowed dangerously. "That's right," there was a low, almost indiscernible growl in his voice, "my rules."

Without a word Bendetti turned, leaving behind an uncomfortable silence between the medic and the guerrilla.

"He's probably right, that's the hell of it," Sky offered.

The medic shrugged. "It's like the fever. Fifty-fifty. When you die it doesn't much matter much how it happens. They're identifying too many of us. There would be a great risk in taking her in."

"Yes," Sky agreed.

"You know Chick Parsons?"

Sky nodded.

"They're offering fifty thousand dollars for him. Dead or alive."

Sky shook his head. "I'll pray they don't pay it."

"You won't be alone," the medic extended his hand. "I'll be praying for the lady there."

"Thanks, Doc. I'll have the gorilla show you back to the trail."

"Hello." The Navajo's deep voice drifted across the twilightbreeze, just catching Tennessee's ear as he sat on the bluff watching the waves pound the rocks below.

"Begay." Parker ran to the Navajo hugging him in a rush of emotion. "You came."

"Couldn't miss an opportunity to see you, Tennessee Parker. I come bringing gifts."

Tennessee grinned. "Isn't that supposed to be my line?"

"Only if you're buying Manhattan. How are you doing?"

"It's picking up. I used the teleradio three times last week before the batteries went. We're getting a lot more traffic up here."

"Ours or theirs?"

"Funny man." They both knew it had been years since American aircraft or ships had been seen in that area of the Pacific. "Guess some of my Ferdinand brothers are getting even more action. You've heard?"

Begay nodded. The good news, as well as the rumors, spread fast on the bamboo telegraph. They had all heard of the campaign on the Marshall Islands. They had also heard that the Japanese had lost over sixteen thousand men to one thousand Americans. If losses like that could be sustained, the war in the Pacific could be over very quickly.

Admiral Mitscher's task forces were busy throughout the area. Truk on the Carolines was under great attack from the Allies, due to her hosting the largest Japanese air and naval base in the Pacific. If they could break Truk, the pieces would fall into place. Campaigns were also being waged in the New Guinea group. Surely it was only a matter of time before the forces of good would come for the Philippine archipelago.

"Hey, I'm glad you came. It's good to see you," Tennessee, in his isolation, had thought a lot about the Indian who had saved his life on Bataan. "It gets pretty lonely up here."

"You're not missing much down there," Charlie assured him as he pulled a bottle of Jack Daniels out of his bag. "Sky sent this up."

They drank most of the evening, sitting right there on the oceanside bluff, watching the waves crest and fall. There wasn't much news to be shared, only the anticipation of things to come. By ten o'clock the bottle was almost gone.

"Charlie," Tennessee was slurring his words badly now, "I will never forget you. You saved my life, goddamn you, you saved my life."

"You saved yourself," Begay said quietly.

"No goddamnit," the boy was insistent. "It was you who did it. I'd have been a goner for sure. I was piss poor scared."

The Navajo smiled, remembering his first meeting with Parker in the corral. "I can't argue that."

"But you gave me something that day. Something that I can hardly even talk about. You gave me courage." He reached for the bottle. "Do you have any idea, any idea at all, how goddamned important that is?"

Charlie remained silent.

"I looked at you and I listened to what you were saying and I thought, goddamn this man knows what he's talking about. It was the most important thing anyone has ever done for me, I want you to know that." Parker grabbed the larger man and pulled him to him. "I will never forget that day or you, so help me God." He was maudlin now. "I only hope I can pay you back."

Charlie reached for the Daniels. "There are no debts."

Parker slumped against his side. Charlie righted him but the young Signal Corpsman's eyes were closed now and he slumped again. He had passed out, watching the ocean and talking of obligations. Charlie arranged him comfortably and sat quietly finishing the bottle.

It had been important to come see Parker, he had known that instinctively. He had thought about telling him about the Enemy Way cleansing but something had held him back from that confession. There were few men outside the Navajo Nation who would understand it.

The one thing that nagged him as he sat watching the rise and fall of the sea was why he needed to do it so soon. Why hadn't he waited until he had gone home or until the war was over?

He stood unsteadily and walked to the edge of the cliff. The moonlight gave a phosphorescence to the pounding waves below, outlining them as they crested against the massive boulders. For a moment as Charlie stared, he thought he saw the face of Changing Woman below, her hair spread around her flawless face in the water, beckoning him to join her.

Angry, wanting her to leave him alone, he threw the empty Jack Daniels bottle on the rocks below, taking some satisfaction as he watched the bottle shatter into a hundred pieces.

40

The crackdown had come earlier that month. There had been all sorts of changes in the rules and regulations and order of daily life in Santo Tomas. The camp had lost its civilian buyer and she had been replaced with Japanese authorities. The package line, which handled six hundred packages a day, mostly containing food, had been ordered permanently closed. Now the food lines had grown longer since many of the internees could no longer rely on outside supplements. The commandant ordered a ten foot space around the camp wall cleared. All vehicles, even the garbage trucks, were now forbidden camp entry. Construction, whether for individual shanties or for communal projects, had been ordered to a grinding halt.

"I've looked everywhere Magda, are you sure you can't help me?"

"Sorry." Magda had already racked her brain but the lost object would not come to her. Psychometry was not one of her psychic skills. "Did you try to trade?"

"Yes. I've got a notice posted but it seems no one has one they want to part with."

Three days earlier they had discovered their loss. The queen of hearts was missing from their tattered card deck. Replacement decks were out of the question and since card playing was one of the few camp pleasures, no one was willing to break up his own deck by releasing his queen.

"We will have to keep playing with the paper queen."

"Oh I suppose so but it's not much fun knowing who's got her." Ellen walked to the edge of the shanty and looked toward the wall. "So many changes."

"They are closing down the blacksmith and plumbing shops."

"And no more sheet metal. I heard they want all electrical cords turned in now too."

"Ya."

"And the lists." The Japanese had demanded a list of all the room monitors and shanty superintendents. They were obviously taking a census of some sort.

Ellen squatted beside the cot, reaching way up under it feeling for a treasure she had hidden there.

Slowly she unwrapped the bright silk scarf until she got to the ring inside. As she held it up, the light from outside caught the faceting of the perfectly cut diamond solitaire.

"Well, at least the insurance policy's still here." She held the ring up for Magda's inspection.

"You cannot eat stones."

"No, but it will bring a lot of food."

"If there is food."

"You think I should get rid of it now?" Ellen had considered trading the ring many times. Every time there was a food crisis, or the threat of one, she had run to the shanty and felt under the cot.

"I do not know."

"No. The time's not right. We still have plenty of our relief supplies. They're still safe. We'll be fine, just fine. This will wait." She wrapped the diamond ring carefully back up in the Japanese scarf and returned it to its secret spot.

"Mom! Mom!" Pete ran into the shanty at full speed. "The doctors just came in. They're here." He was jumping up and down in front of her, his blue eyes crystal clear, excitement shaking his ten-year-old body.

"The doctors?" Ellen asked absently.

"From Dad's place. One of them knows him!"

Her composure now visibly shaken, Ellen Sullivan followed her young son out of the shanty.

In January, 1944 the medical board had recognized the shortage of doctors in Santo Tomas. They suggested to the Japanese authorities that several physicians, including a tuberculosis expert and an eye, ear, nose and throat man, be transferred over from the War Prisoners Camp. Although they had made the recommendation, few of them really thought that the needed medical men would appear. Now they were here, from Cabanatuan.

There was a large group milling around the three arrivals, two doctors and a dentist, by the time Ellen got to them. Internees pushed and pressed to get news of their loved ones.

"Please, please," a short bald man held up his hands, his voice rising above the din. "There will be time for everyone. There are letters." He waved his hand showing a fistful of the cherished mail. "I will hand these out and then you can talk to the doctors later. They cannot possibly talk to all of you at the same time."

Ellen was ecstatic. Soon she would be getting firsthand information on the dreaded Cabanatuan. And Tom.

※

George Bendetti knew that Kate had lost weight yet he was still surprised at how feather light she was. Picking her up and carrying her had been no problem. He had had to pull some strings and pay a lot to get the narcotic but it had been worth it, knocking her out so that he could do what needed to be done without her protesting. They had been through it all before and she had stubbornly refused to listen to him. The large doses of quinine had affected her mind, he was sure of that. She wouldn't, couldn't, think clearly and was therefore not in any position to judge what was best for her.

It had been a simple matter to get two of the villagers to help him with his mission. He had been smart in waiting until Sky and Chopper and most of the others were out scouting. The village had been bereft of American guerrillas and leaving had been a simple matter.

Bendetti looked behind and watched the two Filipinos carry the light litter. Blood spots were showing up on the sheet covering her, he noticed with disgust. That had been the clincher for him. Kate was still bleeding and there seemed to be no stopping it. She would die if she were left in the village, of that he had been sure.

They were getting close to the road now. He knew there would be villagers coming down very soon, for he had already made arrangements with a man in Baler who was going to meet him with an oxcart.

He motioned for the men to put the litter down. They rested it under a spreading Banyan tree and scurried back to San Alberto, their lips sealed with silence, and money.

It was quiet as he watched Kate, her brow damp with sweat. He was glad she was out, for he did not want to argue with her again. He would put her on the cart and the man would take her in for him. It was all worked out. She would soon be in a hospital where they could take care of her properly.

He closed his eyes entertaining dreams of her regaining her health. Of a better time when the war was over. Maybe they could start over again. Forget the past. Yes, he was sure of it. They would marry. Settle down. Have children. At the thought of children he could feel his body begin to betray him. No, he forced those thoughts from his mind, he wouldn't do that with his own children. With white children. This, this was different.

Charlie was exhausted. The trip north had been wearing and he had only stayed one night, preferring to return to San Alberto as quickly as possible. He crossed the road carefully after having watched it for several minutes.

He was climbing the hill now, puffing, out of breath. He had been pushing himself too hard in his eagerness to get home and the effort was beginning to wear him down. Just as he crested the hill, he saw them. The priest, asleep against the tree and a body wrapped in a white sheet resting on a litter. Bendetti. But what was he doing so far from the village?

He approached them carefully, putting a wide distance between himself and the priest until he had time to analyze the situation. Sure now that the man was alone, save for the bundle, the Navajo was quiet as he walked closer to them, taking care that he was to their backs. He was close enough now to see the pale face sticking out of the top of the sheet. Kate! She too was asleep.

"She's going to the hospital." Bendetti's harsh voice surprised Begay for he thought him asleep. "I'm taking her there."

The Navajo remained silent. There was no need for words for he knew the priest was acting alone. Sky would never agree to such a thing.

"You didn't see us." The priest had newfound courage. "I didn't see you."

"She is going back." The Navajo looked Bendetti in the eye knowing he was crazy.

Kate moaned and the sound caught Begay off guard as a knife flashed from the waistband of the pants the priest wore. In one swift movement the man slashed at the Navajo's belly. Charlie jumped backward, leaving the knife with only a slice of fresh air. There was no stopping it now, he thought, as the priest lunged forward again slashing at him. The Indian dodged backward away from him, half stumbling, half falling over a felled log, gaining his balance just seconds before the boning knife came at him again.

Charlie's right hand flew down the side of his pants just in time to retrieve his own weapon, hidden snugly in the side of his boot. Something was wrong though, for Bendetti was backing off, walking backwards toward Kate. Charlie began his advance. It would not be a contest, he thought, for there were few men who could match him with a knife. Briefly he considered wounding Bendetti but he dismissed the thought, knowing he must kill the man. He was evil. He would bring evil down on all of them.

Charlie began circling as the priest knelt beside his pack. Charlie lunged for him and as he did so Bendetti withdrew an old .45 automatic and fired it pointblank into the Navajo's stomach.

Charlie's eyes rolled wide in amazement. A gun! As far as he knew Bendetti never had a gun. The Indian looked to the spreading stain on his white shirt. Funny, it looked so brown, not red, was his thought as he crumpled to the dust, dropping his knife as he clutched his stomach. He could feel no pain there, just pressure, as his innards begged to be released from their confines. Maybe if he held them in it would all go away, he thought.

But now Bendetti was beside him, breathing his hot stale breath into the Navajo's face. He reached across him, grabbing the Indian's knife and throwing it far from his downed body.

The pain was there now and although it was not in him to beg the Navajo had to ask.

"Finish it." His throat was dry, closing.

The priest shook his head and stared at the dying man, taking care not to touch him.

Charlie gasped as a new wave of pain hit him and a trickle of blood dribbled from the side of his mouth. He would not ask again.

Bendetti had a light stick now and he was whittling the sucker branches off it, making it smoother and sharper. He worked for a moment or two until the branch was the dimension and shape that he wanted.

He began rubbing Begay's arm with it slowly, almost sensuously. Up and down the brown arm. Recognition flickered in Charlie's brown eyes.

Slowly, deliberately, Bendetti began poking the stick into Charlie's stomach. At first the invasions were soft, well above the gaping hole. They were close enough, as wave after wave of additional pain hit the Navajo. The stick was dropping lower and lower and by the time it reached Charlie's hand that was holding his entrails in, it was an easy matter for the barrier of flesh to be brushed aside.

Grunting with pleasure, the priest poked and prodded inside the gut wound, only slightly discomforted by the brown eyes that never left his face.

He felt something slick and mushy and pressed the green stick into it, flicking it out as he did so. The large intestine gushed forward onto Charlie's shirt, hesitating there only a minute before dropping onto the dirt.

Charlie watched in disbelief as his betraying tissue pulsated and unwound as it gained release from his body. Still the priest poked and pushed with the pointed end of the branch.

Another rush of intense pain gripped the Indian and blood

now poured from his mouth, merging with the blood from his stomach. The brown eyes closed. Bendetti continued his invasions but there was little point now as life drained out of the Navajo.

41

"I'd bury that son-of-a-bitch so fast it'd make your head spin," Bark volunteered.

"Really?" Tom held the tiny sheets of paper in one hand. "You think it's that bad?"

"All I know is I see a lot of guys ditching those things. It's not worth the risk."

Tom folded the tiny papers even smaller. "I'm hoping to get it into Ellen."

"Shit." Bark stopped stirring the quan pot. "She gets caught with that stuff and she's going to wish you'd never written her a letter."

"You're probably right."

"God, Sullivan, a diary's a diary. There's enough guys in here that none of this is going to be forgotten. Your words or someone else's, what difference will it make? Besides, if you find a good spot for it, you can always come back after the war."

"Yes." Tom knew the logic, he had heard it from some of the soldiers who had already buried their journals. Still he wondered whether any of them would come back to retrieve them. "I'll take care of it this afternoon."

Bark picked up Tunes and began playing *"Yankee Doodle"*.

He knew how important the diaries were to Tom. He had kept them on the Rock too, but that record had been lost. Now, in the years they had been in Cabanatuan, Sullivan was the only one of the three of them who was keeping track of the major events in their imprisoned lives.

Another thought occurred to Bark as he stopped playing.

"You can tell Tull and me where it is. We'll remember." The minute he said it, he wished he hadn't. There was no need to infer that any of them would not make it through. After all, they'd come this far, hadn't they?

"All right."

Tully came up and pulled out the bench. "Tell me what?" he asked wearily.

"Where the treasure's hidden." Bark said.

"Oh." They had been through it all before. "That's a good idea, things are getting a little hot around here."

They had all seen it. The work details were going out all the time. Many of those without civilians were not coming back, but were being shipped out to Formosa and Japan. The transferred men were an indication of the war's toll on Japanese industry, as the Cabanatuan prisoners replaced those positions left vacant by the young Japanese soldiers. The Americans had become fodder for the mines and factories of the enemy land.

"They're on to the tablets," Tully offered.

Instinctively, Bark and Sullivan moved in closer.

"Oh shit," Bark said.

It had been a good gimmick. Tablets, made of salt and rice flour, and poured into plastic molds fashioned from the handles of the Red Cross toothbrushes, were passing for sulfathiazine. Many of the Japanese guards, suffering from gonorrhea, were desperate for the phony little pills. Ashamed and scared to confess their sins to their own doctors, they had been eager to get the medication from the American medics. The pills were good forgeries, too. Uniformly round and stamped with a pharmaceutical "w" they were easy to barter.

"Carson's ditching the molds now. Each of us took some of the tablets."

Tom stirred the pot. "You've got them with you?"

Tully nodded. "I didn't get a chance to unload them." He reached into his pocket and withdrew a fistful of the white placebos.

"Here comes Air Raid," Bark looked across Tully's shoulder as the angry guard charged toward them. "Give me those." He held out his hand, protected as it was by Tully's body. The medic dropped the pills into the gunner's outstretched palm.

"Sullivan." Bark held the full hand behind his back as Tom took the tablets from him. Air Raid was twenty feet away and gaining fast as Tom slipped the capsules into the quan pot, taking care to stir them to the bottom.

Air Raid grabbed Tully by the shoulder and swung him around clobbering him up along the side of the neck with his stout club. As the medic wavered, he yanked him by his collar, spreading him against the wooden table. The club hung loosely from his waist, fastened there by a leather thong as he quickly patted Tully down. Angrily he pulled out his pockets, shaking them out. But there were no pills to be found. The guard's tiny eyes bulged with anger as he swung the club up and into the medic's stomach.

As Tully fell, Air Raid came around the table and faced Bark. "The pills. Where are they?" He screamed.

"I'm sorry sir, I don't know what you're talking about, sir." Bark stretched his g-string out as far as it would go to demonstrate to the outraged guard that he was not carrying contraband. Air Raid screamed and cracked the club against Bark's forearm.

Tom set the spoon against the edge of the quan pot, waiting for his turn. The guard patted him down quickly before whacking his kidneys with the bludgeon. The blow was strong enough to send the engineer reeling to the ground. With a disgusted grunt, Air Raid stomped off.

"Guess that makes it unanimous," Bark was the first to speak. "Tull, you OK?"

Tulliver grunted. "That sorry yellow-bellied son-of-a-bitch." He straightened up slowly, hoping the slower motion would calm his churning stomach. Carefully his hands sought the side of his head. "Am I bleeding?"

"No," Bark diagnosed, "just sweating."

Tom was standing now, stirring the pot. He fished around in it for a minute looking for evidence of the tablets. Satisfied they were all dissolved, he put the spoon to his lips, shuddering as the accumulated grams of salt hit his tongue.

"All that and we had to ruin supper too," he said.

Dimly Ellen was aware of a screeching as she fought through the cobwebs of her sleep to a state of awareness. Her eyes opened to darkness as the alarm continued to wail.

"Magda?" She was fumbling for her clothes and in the dim light she could see the Czech sitting on the edge of her cot.

"Ya?"

"What is it?"

"I do not know."

The women hastily dressed and went into the main corridor which was quickly filling with the other women as they filed through it and on to the outside.

"Is it an air raid?"

"No, I don't think so," Ellen's ears strained for the sound of airplanes, but there had been none so far, although they had had a practice air raid alert weeks earlier.

"Damn!" A frail Canadian walked next to Ellen. "My son is in the Education Building. I feel so helpless."

Ellen had already thought of her own Doc and Pete cut off from their mother in the middle of the night when the piercing sirens awakened them. "Mine are there too," she squeezed the woman's arm warmly. "Mr. Leake will take care of them."

"Yes, I suppose he will," the woman agreed.

On the ground below, the internees were wandering aimlessly. Someone said that the members of the Internee Committee were looking for an explanation from the commandant, but their trip to the main building had been in vain, for he was now walking quickly toward the assembled group. The Japanese guards were there too, dressed neatly in their uniforms pushing and instructing all of the sleepy internees to stay in front of the building.

"Back, back to your rooms." It was as though they were herding cattle, "do not talk to one another. Do not leave your rooms."

"What is happening here?" Magda asked the closest guard who ignored her.

The Japanese were poking and prodding with their sticks. "Back, back. To your rooms." Slowly, the internees began filing into the building and up the stairs. They walked in silence.

"Maybe it's the Yanks," an Englishwoman offered.

"Probably just a faulty system."

"Japanese efficiency."

Back in the dark confines of their room, Magda and Ellen

quickly undressed.

"It's strange, isn't it? Usually there's a reason." Ellen said into the darkness.

"Ya. I think it is encouraging."

"You do? Really?"

"The Americans will come. That is why our captors are on edge. They are afraid. Men who are afraid are not always rational."

Ellen thought about it. Of course she was right. The Japanese always operated with startling efficiency and the raid that was not a raid was unusual.

"It is twelve-thirty. I saw Mrs. Damron's watch," Magda said. "The hour is late."

"Yes." Ellen rolled over and faced the wall, her mind racing with the events of the day. Things were getting tighter in Santo Tomas, there was no denying that. There was now a new bamboo fence two meters from the old one. The electrical repair shop and the soap making plants had been closed. Fresh fruits and vegetables were no longer available. The camp broadcasting system had been closed down, although there were rumors it would be reopened under strict supervision.

"Magda?"

The Czech mumbled.

"Do you think it's time I sold the ring?"

There was a heavy pause.

"No, Ellen. Not yet." The woman said as she drifted off to sleep.

⚞

Gorilla and Chopper trotted into the clearing, happy to be back in San Alberto. Although exhausted and thirsty, they headed to the open ramada where Sky was seated.

"Any luck?" He asked, not really expecting a positive reply for Kate had been gone for over a month now. Still every time there was a chance, or a report of a sighting of an American, the men would go out and check it out.

The priest, too, had disappeared.

"We met with Compadre. He had this for you." Chopper handed Sky a dirty piece of paper. "From Manila."

Sky quickly unfolded the message and read it.

"Kate in Philippine General. Recovery seem imminent. High-Pockets." Sky read it three times.

Claire Phillips, code-named "High-Pockets", a *nom de guerre* stemming from the valuables and messages she frequently carried in her brassiere, was an American singer who owned the Club Tsubaki in Manila. Phillips, and her nightclub, served as an information center for the guerrillas. Plying Japanese officers with liquor and entertainment, Phillips was able to receive information on ship schedules, cargos, ammunition shipments and a host of other data, all helpful to guerrilla operations. She also smuggled needed supplies into Cabanatuan and served as a vital communications link between the prison camp and the guerrillas.

"She's safe," Sky told them. "At least for the time being. In Manila."

Chopper groaned. He and Sky had talked about getting her back if the opportunity ever came up, but Manila was in the heart of Japanese territory.

"Captain, better Cabanatuan," the pilot offered.

"No," Sky disagreed. "Maybe Faustino can get in to see her." He sat down heavily, debating in his own mind the wisdom of sending the Filipino schoolteacher into the capital. Kate was gone and Charlie Begay had also disappeared. It was a growing puzzle and one that was costing him his closest friends. Could he risk another?

"Of course I can." The teacher flashed his clean white teeth. "No problem, I am but a poor peasant man." He bowed his head and shuffled his slumping posture through the dust. "I love honorable Japanese. So pleased to meet you, kind sir. You like my country, take her." A hardness edged into his voice.

"It's too dangerous." Sky made up his mind. "God only knows where she is or what has happened to her. The *kempei-tai* could have her by now."

"I can get her out. I know I can."

Sky shook his head. "It's too risky."

"Then perhaps we should just go in and kill her." Chopper suggested.

Sky gave him a dark look.

"Captain, I like Kate as much as the next guy but we've got to look after our own skins. If she becomes a threat than we ought to eliminate her."

"Hey man, I think you just talked yourself out of a trip to Manila," Faustino joked.

"No. No one's going," Sky's voice was resolute. "For any reason."

Kate drifted in and out of consciousness so many times that it became one continuous nightmare. Vaguely she was aware of an opened window and a slight breeze. People had been around her for some time now, shielded by the diaphanous mosquito netting, stopping momentarily to check her bedside table or to invade her body yet again with some manner of injection, probe or catheter. If it was a dream, it was a bad one.

The Japanese had been there too, in her greater moments of consciousness she could dimly remember that. They had come and tried to ask her questions, but the voices of the Filipino doctors had come drifting in to her as they told the Japanese that she was unable to be interrogated, that she had almost died and that they could have her when her health was up to it.

Even in her barely stirred consciousness, she had to laugh at the irony of it all. To get healthy so the Japanese secret police could break her down again. There was no sense, no sense at all, to any of it.

She awakened and wondered, not for the first time, how sick she really was and how much she was bringing on herself to avoid inquisition. It was a question she could not answer.

"Feeling better?" A man's voice was very close to her left ear.

She opened her eyes slowly, afraid of the vision that would greet her. For the moment she was safe, for the man seated next to her bed was a Filipino.

"Are you a doctor?"

"Yes. Welcome back." The young man smiled at her.

"I'm in Manila?"

"Yes. General Hospital. You've been here over a month."

"A month!" She tried to sit up but her weakened body failed her.

"Relax." His hand was soft and warm against her skin. "You're very weak. We almost lost you."

"How did I get here?" Even the conversation was straining her exhausted resources.

"Some peasants from the north. Said they found you wandering by the side of the road, although in your condition I doubt if you were doing much wandering." His hand slid down her wrist as he took her pulse. "Good." He muttered his approval, placing her arm gently back on the sheet.

"How long do I have?"

He gave her an intense look. There was no sense in asking what she meant, for they both knew.

"Maybe a week. They're not easy to stall."

"No." She could not ask for special favors for him, she knew the risks were too great, the favors to be saved for those who meant something to him.

"When will I be strong enough to travel?"

"Two, three weeks. If you are talking backwoods, then longer."

Kate bit her lip. "Well then, Doc, it looks like I'm in one hell of a situation, doesn't it?"

"Maybe something will work out," he leaned very close to her now, dropping his voice to a low whisper. "We are in contact with the underground, they know you're here."

A brief smile played across her white lips.

"In the meantime," he leaned back in his chair, returning his voice to normal. "Eat, get some rest. Regain your strength. I'll check on you every day."

Fear clutched Kate's stomach. "Will you know before they come?"

"Sometimes," he patted her arm. "But you're safe for at least a week."

She gave him a forced smile. "Thank you," she said weakly as she watched him gently swab the inside of her elbow before piercing her skin with yet another needle.

The days passed quickly. As each dawn came, Kate convinced herself that she was getting stronger, a belief that was reinforced by the young Filipino doctor. As the days ticked off, her fears deepened and as she awakened in the early morning hours to her own anxiety, she would struggle out of bed and force her tired body to perform. Pacing barefoot back and forth to the bathroom while the rest of her ward slept, she pushed herself to exercise her lower body. For she would need to be stronger to slip away from the hospital before the dreaded *kempei-tai* came.

On the fifth day she was roused from her afternoon nap by a Japanese interrogator.

"Your name?" The man snapped at her.

She told the small man with filthy fingernails and he began firing questions at her. She tried to answer them the best she could, all the while watching his blackened fingernails record her answers in a tidy little notebook.

She smiled at him as she tried to convince him, that she was a misplaced Englishwoman who had been living in the hills.

He leaned over and placed a vice grip on her upper arm, pinching her uncomfortably.

"The hills?" His fishy breath blasted against her cheek. "You eat well for lazy, pampered woman living in hills."

Kate froze, afraid to pull away from him.

"You had help." He twisted her flesh until a whimper escaped from her throat. "I want to know your friends. You will tell me," the man stood. "It is better for you here, but if not," he shrugged, "then in Fort Santiago. In some ways we are more sophisticated there."

In spite of herself, Kate winced.

"Ah, you are familiar with Santiago." He reached for her hand and began caressing her thumb, his filthy fingernails in sharp contrast to her own clean white ones. "We pull you to your feet by these." He pinched her thumb hard until she thought her nail would pop off. "Then higher until you hang by your thumbs. It is not pleasant." Abruptly he dropped her hand. "Think about it. I will return in morning. We will have your doctor's release."

Without another word he spun on his heels and left the ward. In spite of the stifling heat, Kate shivered as she crawled deep beneath the sheets, drawing the worn linen up over her head.

"Water, missy?" A Filipina was taking her pitcher. It was the time of day for all of that. Dinner would not be far behind.

Kate rolled on her side out of bed and slowly stood. Her legs trembled, threatening to betray her. Walking slowly she made it to the bathroom, huffing as she closed the door behind her. She was in lousy shape, there was no denying that.

She doubted if she could get as far as the hospital's front entrance on her own. Maybe, she thought, she could arrange for a wheelchair or a cart of some kind. She immediately dismissed that possibility, for she had no resources here. Although the doctor had told her he would know before they took her, she hadn't seen him all day. By tomorrow morning it would be too late. No, her escape, would have to be tonight, when everyone was asleep.

She took advantage of the offered dinner before falling fast asleep.

They were trying to string her up by her thumbs but she was biting and fighting them, refusing to cooperate with their willingness to torture her. She lashed out at them, but her hands were powerless weapons against their assault. Just as they slipped the first leather thong over her wrist she awakened, her heart pounding wildly as she huddled under the sheets.

She lay there a moment, collecting herself, relieved that she had only been dreaming. She remained under her bedding until her heart slowed. Gradually she pulled the sheet away from her head, gasping as she saw a dark shape hovering over her bed. They were there! Instantly her heart was thrashing again, adrenaline pumping through her veins as she rolled away from the shadow, collecting her strength for flight.

But her assailant was too quick for her, bolting around, throwing his body against hers, shoving her back onto the rumpled sheets. As his body blocked her, his right hand shot out and covered her mouth and his body collapsed across her own, pinning her to the bed.

"Sssh," he hissed.

Kate's turquoise eyes widened as she recognized him.

"Are you all right?"

She was unable to speak for his hand was still across her mouth.

"Do you know who I am?"

She nodded, tried to smile but only succeeded in wrinkling the corners of her eyes.

He dropped his hand from her mouth, relaxing his body as he rolled off her. "We haven't got much time."

"Faustino!" She whispered. "How did you get in here?"

He held his fingers to his lips to silence her this time. Working quickly, he rolled a laundry cart around to her side of the bed. He pulled a stack of pillows out of it.

"Can you get in?"

"Yes, I think so." Kate stood, damning the weakness she felt. Holding on to the edge of the bed, she draped one long leg over the wire rim of the canvas laundry cart. Tapay held it steady, helping her in with his free hand. Mustering all the strength she had, she vaulted over the side and into the cart.

No sooner had she nestled in the laundry, then Faustino was piling linen on top of her. Satisfied that she was well hidden, he took the pillows and shaped them as he placed them carefully under the sheets. He pulled the top sheet over the pillows and punched them again, rearranging the shape until it resembled a sleeping body.

Finally satisfied with his subterfuge, he wheeled the heavy laundry cart out of the sleeping ward.

42

Out after the midnight curfew, hidden under the cover of night, they navigated the Manila streets safely. There was no moon this evening of the Emperor's birthday.

They had crossed the Pasig River earlier and Faustino was glad for the cover of darkness so that Kate would not see the headless bodies floating there. They were becoming more and more common in Manila, along with the looting. Japanese soldiers thought nothing of entering a civilian's home and taking services and goods without pay. Allied food, refrigerators, radios, even bathtubs, had made their way to the enemy ships anchored in the bay and were now on their way to Japan.

Kate had rested and regained her strength for almost a month. While stronger now, they had been walking briskly for over a mile and she was panting, her body aching with a side stitch.

Faustino ducked into an alley and she followed him, relieved when he stopped for rest.

"You all right?" He whispered.

She nodded, not wanting to use her labored breath for conversation.

"It's not much further."

"It's OK." Her response came out hard on an exhalation.

Tapay dropped the *bayong* bag he had been carrying. "We can sit for a moment if you like."

Kate sat on the hard cobblestones, her back supported by the brick wall of the nearest building.

"You sure you're all right?"

"What choice do I have? With horses you shoot them."

"Yes."

"God, I hope this works." She was breathing easier now and the side stitch was almost gone.

"It will."

In his heart, Faustino was not at all sure the plan was going to work. It had never been tried before, for as far as he knew no one had ever been smuggled into the University of Santo Tomas.

"I wish I had your confidence."

"It's got to work. The dwarfs are always looking for people to get out. Who in their right mind would want to get in?"

"I can't imagine. I still can't believe there's not a way I can go back with you."

"It is impossible. You are not strong enough."

"Then let Claire Phillips find a place for me. I can draw! I'm reasonably intelligent. There are all sorts of things I can do." Kate's eagerness to go along with the plan of voluntary incarceration was fading fast.

"There's too much of a risk. The *kempei-tai* will be looking for you." He had heard from the underground just how displeased they were. They had already arrested the Filipino doctor and were questioning him at Fort Santiago. Tapay had prayed every night that smuggling Kate into Santo Tomas, placing her right under the noses of the Japanese along with thirty-seven hundred others, would be successful.

"You know where to go." Once inside, there was no way Faustino or the underground could help her. While they had their contacts within the university walls, Santo Tomas was off limits now even to the Filipinos.

"The dormitory building. Someone will meet me inside."

"Right. What will you do for roll call?"

"Stay in the building." That was their one big fear, that during roll call, a head count actually, the Japanese would figure out that they had one extra person. Meal tickets would be taken care of, a place to stay had been arranged, but there was still the danger of the roll call.

"Are you ready?" Faustino stood, lifting the heavy bag. It had been carefully prepared for Kate to insure she carried no items that were not readily available to the internees.

Kate stood and grabbed the startled Tapay around the neck, kissing him on the mouth. "Thank you for saving me."

He stared at her. Although thin and pale, she was as fresh and clean as the day he had first met her.

"Thank you." He said strangely, setting off down the alley toward the quiet Manila street.

It was eerily quiet along the campus. They crossed Calle España and went along a side street coming in behind the large garden. It had been dry for the last three days and the ground was not as muddy as it might have been, a blessing, for there would be no telltale footprints leading through the vegetable plot.

They stood next to the wall for a long time as Faustino pressed his ear against the thick structure in an attempt to pick up any sound on the other side. But there was none. Finally satisfied, he nodded to Kate. Cupping his hands he hoisted her up, pushing still higher until she gripped the top of the wall. She struggled and clawed her way to the top, pulling her body up and over the edge of the wall.

He watched her disappear into the garden and waited, holding his breath. If there was going to be a problem, this was probably where it would occur. Quiet. Not a sound.

He felt a tug on the rope connected to the bag and knew that Kate was now trying to pull the heavy *bayong* over the masonry wall. He lifted it, feeling her pull the slack out of the rope. There had been no rehearsing this part of the plan, and Tapay held the bag high over his head, trying to give Kate as much help as he could.

The *bayong* was well above him now, being tugged along with jerky pulls. It was a heavy chore, he could tell, by its slow progress of jerking for a few feet, then stopping, jerking, stopping. As it got to the top of the wall there was a long pause, as though Kate were gathering her strength on the other side. Faustino waited.

Finally with a great tug the *bayong* went sailing over the top and even through the thickness of the wall he could hear it hit the inside bamboo fence. Still he waited. He could hear nothing. There were no sounds, no alarms, coming from the other side. If the plan was still uncovered, Kate would be looking for the entrance cut in the bamboo fence now.

The schoolteacher stayed for thirty minutes before he sadly headed out of Manila. Kate was now inside Santo Tomas. There was nothing more he could do to help her. It was April 29, 1944, two years to the day that Faustino Tapay had met her.

꩜

The food line was long, and Ellen and Magda were toward the end of it. They had gotten a late start this morning for a new letter from Tom had come in, and they had gone over it carefully before coming for their cereal.

Everyone was so thin now, Ellen thought. Clothes hung like sacks off the emaciated bodies. Just ahead, she noticed a woman whose clothes hung a little better than most. Still thin, the woman held herself in erect posture and there was something vaguely familiar about the back of her head. Questions began nagging at Ellen.

"Magda, that woman up there, do we know her?"

"The one in the brown dress?" The Czech had also noticed her.

"Yes."

"No, I cannot tell from here. Probably. Why do you ask?"

"I don't know." Ellen shook her head. "Just going batty, I guess. Still," she stepped out of the line in the hope of seeing the woman's face, but as she did so, the woman turned away also and she was again stuck with the back of her head.

The line was moving quickly. It was easy when there wasn't much food to serve. Just a scoop full of rice cereal, that was it. No sugar, no coconut milk. It didn't take long to send hundreds of people through.

Ellen's eyes riveted on the woman in the brown dress. But she never turned around.

As the woman was getting her rice she turned back to the man behind her, a man Ellen recognized as a member of the Executive Committee.

Kate! It was Kate! It was all Ellen could do to restrain herself to keep from running to her old friend, but instinct told her to keep still, to wait until the moment would not cause notice.

Eagerly she got her cereal and followed the woman with the brown dress to a table.

"Hello, Kate."

Kate spun in the direction of the familiar voice. Tears clouded her eyes as she recognized the scarecrow form of her old friend.

"Ellen!" Her arms went around Ellen's neck as she fought the sobs that were gathering within her. "Of course!" Even as she hugged her, her eyes darted nervously around, searching for Doc and Pete.

"They're all right." It was as though Ellen had read her mind. The two women clung to each other for a long moment, wordlessly, as tears streamed down their faces.

"I think you had better save some of that," the man with Kate suggested gently, "we don't want any unnecessary talk."

"No." Ellen looked around, but there were no guards in the immediate area. Still, it would not do to have the internees talk either. "You're looking well," she said. "But how on earth did you get in here?"

Kate tasted the cereal. It was awful and she shoved it away from her, a fact eagerly noted by Magda.

"We'll talk later," she suggested gently, hating to let Ellen down but not eager to share the circumstances of her entrance with any but her closest friend.

"You remember Magda, don't you?" Ellen quickly changed the subject. "You met her that last summer at the Pines Hotel."

"Yes, yes I do." Kate studied the Czechoslovakian woman, amazed at the changes she saw there. The once voluptuous woman was now scrawny, her tight proud breasts hanging in the loosely draped cloth. Magda's brown eyes kept dropping to Kate's bowl.

"Magda, I'm not hungry, would you like my cereal?" Kate pushed the bowl in her direction.

"Thank you!"

Kate watched in fascination as the Czech hungrily lapped up

the tasteless cereal. It never occurred to the newest internee that her untouched cereal was a priceless treasure in Santo Tomas.

※

"Forgive me, Father, for I have sinned," the man began, kneeling on the hard packed earth.

George Bendetti shifted his weight, aware that another soldier had come to confession. There had been a constant stream of them all morning, generally all confessing the same transgressions with very little variety. While most people were fascinated with confession, Bendetti considered it a tiresome, monotonous chore.

"Oh, my God, I am heartily sorry for having offended thee and I detest all my sins because I dread the loss of Heaven and the pains of hell." The soldier continued with his act of contrition, as the priest looked away from him, staring into the jungle.

There were no barricades here, no confessionals, and they were doing the best they could. The priest sat on an uncomfortable wooden chair while the penitent knelt in the dirt beside him. The arrangement elevated him too far above the soldier, and the intimacy of the whisper in one's ear was lost.

The sins were spilling from the soldier's lips now. They started with missing Mass and irreverence to God. Cursing. The soldier started to stumble.

"What is it, my son, you can tell me," Bendetti offered his encouragement automatically.

The man continued. Masturbation. Neglect of home. Murder.

"And how do you feel about taking a life?" George prodded.

"It was a Japanese, Father." The soldier offered.

"Yes."

"He would have killed me."

Bendetti was silent. There was nothing he could say. The rules were all gone now.

"And how do you feel about it now?"

"I am ashamed and frightened."

"Give penance to absolve your conscience. Say ten Hail Marys and five Our Fathers. And think about what you did."

"Thank you, Father," the boy stared into the dirt before crossing himself.

Bendetti straightened up, crossed himself and began, "*Dominus vobiscum...*"

Getting into another guerrilla band had been relatively easy after leaving Kate. It seemed there was always room for a Catholic priest, and the commanding officer had been genuinely glad to see him. This was not always the case at the front, Bendetti knew, for he had heard an officer say once that the chaplain was just another goddamned man to keep from getting hit.

The priest had been relieved to hear that Kate had made it safely into the Manila hospital. Visiting her was too dangerous, but the peasants had promised to keep him informed. Now that the deed was done, Bendetti had had an uncomfortable moment or two thinking of the Japanese secret police. But what good would a single woman do them? He prayed a lot and in his heart he was sure that his God would not let him save her so the *kempei-tai* could kill her. That could not happen.

He still wanted her. He could not deny that, although marriage was now out of the question. He had seen the blood from her body orifices and she was no longer pure in his eyes.

In a way releasing Kate had been a release for himself also. There had been no children for over two months. His religion was coming back to him and he was reveling in this renaissance. God would provide for him. Of that he was sure.

Only occasionally did he think of the dead Navajo. He held no remorse, the man would have killed him, given the chance. As he thought back to the death, it was almost as though he were watching someone else through inverted binoculars. There was so much distance involved.

As he waited in the bright sunlight for the next soldier, George opened the worn leather bound bible his new leader had given him. The pages fell open to Deuteronomy. Bendetti's eyes fell on a passage and he began to read.

"Honor the father and thy mother, as the Lord thy God hath commanded thee; that they days may be prolonged, and that it may go well with thee, in the land which the Lord thy God giveth thee.

"Thou shalt not kill."

It was like a brand on him. He gasped and quickly closed the book. *Thou shalt not kill.* Yet he had. As had the soldiers. They had all sinned. He hung his head in an effort to clear the doubts gathering there. Breathing deeply for a moment or two, he sorted it out. No, it was different. This was war. They were not children. They were the devil's disciples.

Once his breathing returned to normal he opened the volume again. This time his eyes fell to the 102nd Psalm. He began to read again.

"Hear my prayer, O Lord, and let my cry come unto thee.

"Hide not thy face from me in the day *when* I am in trouble; incline thy ear unto me: in the day *when* I call answer me speedily.

"For my days are consumed like smoke, and my bones are burned as an hearth.

"My heart is smitten..." he stopped, opened his eyes to the bright day. There was a message here, he thought, his God had not forsaken him. He understood. About the Indian. About the children.

☞

The traps were set again. Although the commandant had ordered the rodent control ceased, he had recently permitted the rats to be trapped as long as no poison was used. The traps were set with precious foodstuffs and the new system seemed to be working well.

Pete carefully drew back the heavy metal bar, releasing the rat into his bag. It was an extra job for him and he was proud of it. Rats and messages.

The ground was still soggy from the heavy storm the day before. It had rained so hard that he had not gone on his rat patrol, and now he was eager to free the traps so they could be reset and he could get to the decoration day services that had been post-poned once already because of the rain.

Most of the internees were gathered in the front plaza as a member of the Executive Committee stood on the steps, reading names.

"Charles Eiseltein, Adolph Elmer, Valerie Fahnestock, Walter S. Farnes," the man's voice was steady, unyielding.

"Thomas H. Fletcher, Albert H. Flunker, Oliver Fong," the voice droned on, calling out the names of those who had died in Santo Tomas since the war began. Before the day was over, two hundred and forty-nine names would be read.

Ellen sat on top of the blankets on the wet lawn quietly, lis-tening as the names were read. She was ashamed at the relief she felt at not having been close to any of them. What was the law of averages, she thought? How long before someone she knew and loved was going to be on the list? She shuddered at the thought.

Things were getting a lot tougher now. Sugar and cereal rations had been cut drastically, and just last week it had been impossible to purchase milk or eggs. They were all getting thinner. Clothes were hanging on all of them, even the children, although they were faring better than most. The adults saw to that. Even those without children shared their rations in a community effort to keep meat on the bones of the young.

Pete snuggled in next to her, draping her arm around his own thin body. Ellen hugged him, sad that he had to witness the horrors of war firsthand. Still, she hoped her boys would be stronger for the experience.

"Where's your brother?"

Pete shrugged. He had not seen Doc since morning.

Ellen tried to concentrate on the names again but fear kept pervading her thoughts. Food was constantly on her mind now. the Executive Committee was meeting more and more frequently to discuss the impending food crisis. It was imminent, they were all sure of that. The commandant had even called them all to gether in a special meeting to urge them to grow their own food. Gardens were now being tilled.

"There! There he is!" Magda nudged Ellen.

Ellen looked up to see a slight, barefoot Chinese man dressed in torn pants and an old tattered shirt.

"That's him?" Somehow she had expected the man to be more heroic looking. "That's Tun Yun Lee?"

"Ya." Magda sat back, her eyes following the movement of the Oriental man until he sat down on the far side of the gathered group.

"I'm surprised he's not in jail," Ellen said.

"Ya."

The Japanese authorities had drafted an oath in April and had insisted that all of the internees sign it. The oath pledged that they would not, under any circumstances, attempt to escape. Conspiracy against the Japanese was out of the question. The Executive Committee had turned in a letter along with the signed oaths, saying they were signed under duress. When this was deemed unacceptable by their Japanese hosts, many of the internees had simply signed their names and then the words "under duress." They had all signed them but for one holdout.

Tun Yun Lee.

A Chinese-American, born in New York City, Lee had been a seaman on the *President Grant.* The unexpected sailing of his ship when war broke out had left him stranded in Manila, and shortly thereafter he was thrown into Santo Tomas. Even before the oaths, they had heard his name for he had refused all Red Cross packages and clothing.

After his refusal to sign the conspiracy oath, they had all waited for the Japanese to take action against the lone holdout. But so far nothing had happened.

"I should not have signed," Magda whispered.

"No, dear." Ellen patted her arm gently. "You had no choice." Many of them were tormenting themselves over signing the oaths and the Chinese-American had gained a great deal of their respect with his defiant act.

"Hey there's Roosevelt!" Pete jumped up from the damp blanket and ran to the side of the group, collecting the big white cat in his arms. He returned to his mother stroking and scratching the big tom. "Nice Roosevelt," he crooned, while the cat arched and stretched his back in appreciation.

Ellen's eyes caught Magda's. They had talked about it before. There was little protein in their diets. Fish and meat were getting scarce. While neither of them would eat domestic cat, there was no denying there were some in camp to whom the animal represented a substantial meal. Luther Kozalczyk, was also aware of this risk and had recently been tying his pet in his shanty.

"Peter, let Roosevelt go," Ellen whispered, eager to disabuse him of his affection for the animal.

"Mom!" Pete drew his lips into a pout.

Ellen gently freed the cat from his arms, but Roosevelt was having none of it. Immediately he was back against the boy rubbing against his side and purring loudly, begging to be petted.

Pete reached out and scratched the big cat behind the ears.

"Peter." There was clearly a warning in Ellen's voice.

The boy dropped his hands from the animal but Roosevelt was persistent. He batted at his young friend wrapping his arm in his own furry paws.

"Meow."

Ellen watched as Pete sat, trying hard not to pet the insistent beast. She noticed with despair as the cat climbed into his lap, curling up contentedly on the outstretched legs of the boy who was not allowed to pet him.

SINCLAIR BROWNING

43

Tennessee Parker glassed the sea slowly, counting to himself as he did so. There had been a lot of traffic in the past few days, all dutifully reported to his Australian link. Now there was a Japanese aircraft carrier out there. Something big was brewing. Parker made a few more notations on his pad before standing and brushing the dirt from his shorts.

The carrier was reason enough to break radio silence. He would report her right away.

✈

Air Raid was in good form today. His club had not rested all morning as he hit any prisoner who crossed his path. He was not alone in his ill humor; it was shared by many of the Cabanatuan guards. Constant beatings were now taking place. What little easy banter that captor and captive had indulged in earlier was now gone. It was not worth the risk. Tempers fueled by Allied victories across the Pacific were not to be tampered with. Rumors flew among the prisoners, none of them substantiated by fact. But the facts were easily obtained by their Japanese captors and they did not find them pleasing.

The Battle of the Philippine Sea had raged for days with the Japanese vice-admiral Jisaburo Ozawa sending in over three hundred and seventy airplanes against the American Task Force 58. Two hundred and forty of them had failed to return. The carrier *Taiho* had been lost, and the *Shokaku* badly crippled. Iwo Jima and Chichi Jima had been under heavy attack by the Allied forces and in July, six Japanese ships had been sunk in their own waters by the United States submarine *Cobra*. In the Mariana Island group alone, the Japanese had lost over twenty-seven thousand troops to the Americans' thirty-four hundred.

In the midst of the turning trend, there had been a shakeup in the Japanese government. The Navy Minister Shimada had been replaced with Nomura, and General Hideki Tojo, the architect of Japan's entrance into the second World War, had resigned his combined position as Prime Minister-War Minister- Chief of Army Staff after Saipan fell to the Allies.

He had been replaced by co-premiers General Kuniaki Koiso and Admiral Yonai with General Yoshijiro Umezu becoming Army Chief of Staff. The Japanese command, which had been chiefly the responsibility of one man, was now split and fragmented.

After Tojo's resignation, the Americans headed for Guam. They had already taken much of her Orote Peninsula and battles were ranging there, none of them being decided in favor of the Japanese. As the Allies blazed across the Pacific, the Cabanatuan guards became so skittish that the slightest infraction would send them into a crazed fury.

Bark and Tom were on pump duty this morning, happy to be out of sight of Air Raid, Donald Duck and the others. It was bright out here, removed from the sounds and squalor of the rest of camp.

"It's got to be coming soon now," Bark said as he watched

the water pour through the irrigation ditch.

"Yes," Tom agreed. They had all been optimistic since their first internment but still the months dragged on and on. They had both seen the work details that had left Cabanatuan bound for Formosa and Japan. It had not been a bad sign, for it was generally agreed that the war was turning around if the Japanese were taking the prisoners closer to home. "I wish we knew what was going on."

"Tully says we can tell by their treatment. The war's turning. Kind of hard to believe isn't it?" Bark picked a weed and chewed on it, grateful for any taste he could glean from it. "You figure we're gonna be shipped out, Sullivan?"

Tom drew circles in the dust with the tip of his finger. "Don't know. I worry about it."

Bark laughed. "You worry, most of the guys are dying to get out of here. You're safe, Sullivan, the civilians haven't been going."

"Yet."

Bark considered that. It could change at any time. There were rumors, always rumors. "You're right. God, wouldn't that be the shits to sit here for two and a half years, and then end up in Japan?"

"It wouldn't be for long. If we really are winning this thing," Tom offered. It was little consolation, for they both knew that if they were shipped to Japan or Formosa their liberation would just take that much longer.

"I can't figure out what they're doing with all of them."

"Fodder," Tom explained. "They're filling gaps left by their soldiers."

Bark groaned. They had all heard of the infamous Japanese mines with their foul treatment of their conscripts and prisoners.

He grabbed Tom's upper arm almost, but not quite, encircling it with his thumb and middle finger. "They're going to get a lot out of your body."

Tom pulled away from him. "Right, fatso."

Bark, although much taller, was now as thin as he was. All of them were walking skeletons, their faces all looked alike- thin, drawn, sunken, stripped of any individual features by the hunger that tormented them. "Somehow I don't think it much matters to them as long as they can get some work out of us."

"No."

They were silent for a time, each wrapped in his own thoughts.

"Catch the pump there, will you?" Tom was standing now, shovel poised, ready to divert the water into the next area as Bark fiddled with the pump valve.

That was one of the nice things about the pump job, he thought, you could always get a drink of fresh water.

"I can't believe they'd do it!" Kate paced the tiny shanty. "Using the tower to signal their military, I just can't believe it! God, we'll all be bombed. And by our own planes."

"Kate, dear, the committee has registered a protest about it," Ellen offered.

"The Committee? What good is that? They complained about the rice cut too, and we're not getting any more. I can't figure out if the committee is here to really get things done, or just to placate us."

"Well, I'm sure it won't happen again. And it's not as though we're actually being bombarded."

"Ya," Magda agreed. "There has not been an American airplane in years."

"But they're coming," Kate insisted.

"Yes," Ellen agreed.

Food was constantly in their prayers now. The first of the month had started with a grim announcement over the loudspeaker. All money, regardless of whether camp or private funds, was ordered turned over to the Japanese. The money had been collected, and was now on its way to the Bank of Taiwan. Individuals were allowed to keep a scant fifty pesos which, with wartime inflation and black market prices, would not carry any of them very far.

There were few extras now. When food arrived it was often rotten and moldy. One fish shipment had been so bad that it had been fed to the Japanese ducks while the internees went hungry.

There had been a bright light in all of it when the Japanese military authorities had agreed to let the committee paint a red cross on the roof of the Santa Catalina Hospital. That act had made the Americans arrival seem real.

"Corned beef's here." Pete pushed his wheelbarrow into the shanty, removing a can from the top of the pile and handing it to his mother.

"Thank you, dear." Ellen clasped the can to her breast. The cans were gold. Rations had been so reduced that the committee had dipped into their hoarded reserves to supplement the camp diet. They were now given a twelve-ounce can twice a week for four people. At the rate of dispersal they were currently following, one of the men on the committee had told Ellen that the food reserves would be gone by mid-October, less than a month away.

"Are you all hungry?" She asked. It was a rhetorical question for they were always hungry. Really it was a matter of degree. *How* hungry are you? is what she meant for they had just finished their evening meal.

"How about tomorrow morning?" Magda suggested.

"That's a wonderful idea. We'll have an elegant breakfast here in the morning. Tell Doc, won't you Pete?"

"Yes, Mother." He leaned across the wooden wheelbarrow and reached up to kiss her cheek. "Goodnight." He was off making the rest of his deliveries before curfew set in.

Kate wrapped the silk shawl around her shoulders. It was cooler this morning with the sun blocked by gray clouds.

"Anything I can do?" She was standing at the open side of the shanty as a soft breeze blew her long brown hair away from her thin face.

"No. I've just got to get this darned thing open. Is Magda here yet?"

"Don't see her." Kate's eyes were drawn upward to the circling Japanese airplanes, the red circles apparent on their wings, as they dipped and teased one another across the gray sky. They had been practicing dogfights for weeks. From some distance, the popping of anti-aircraft guns could be heard. "They're practicing again," Kate muttered.

"That noise does get tiresome, doesn't it?" Ellen still struggled with the can.

Kate watched the Japanese planes in morbid fascination. She wished it were in her power to make them disappear. Almost from the moment she was conscious of that thought, one of the planes plummeted to the earth.

"My God," she said softly, not believing it. She rubbed her eyes. As she watched, another Japanese airplane fell from the sky. "They're shooting down their own planes!"

"What?" Ellen was beside her now, craning her neck toward the sky. A third plane dipped, its wingtip flipped heavenward as it began a dizzying spiral, its fate evidenced by thick, black smoke.

The sky was filling fast with airplanes, white stars apparent on their sleek silver bodies.

"My God, Katie." Ellen dropped the unopened corned beef as she reached for her friend. "They're ours, thank God, they're ours!"

Tears streamed down their faces as they hugged one another.

All around them now people were pouring from their shanties watching the American pilots come in again and again for their targets. Their skill was evidenced as the northern and eastern skies of Manila filled with black smoke.

"They're all ours," Kate said in awe for the skies were now clear of the aircraft with red circles. A rainbow of colors shot across the heavens as the Japanese sent tracers to mark spaces for the anti-aircraft gunners. Suddenly an American plane was shot down.

"Jesus!" The enormity of what they were watching finally hit Kate.

They watched in silence as more of the white stars plummeted to the earth. But still the American airplanes kept coming, wave after wave, out of the northern sky to drop their cargo on their prey. Although the Japanese had camouflaged their military supplies, the underground intelligence knew their locations, and now the persistent Americans zeroed in flawlessly on their targets.

"Attention!" The loudspeaker was crackling, a male voice

struggling to be heard above the Pandemonium. "This is not an alert. I repeat, this is not an alert. This is an air raid. Take cover! I repeat, take cover!"

Kate couldn't move. She was oblivious to the cramping in her neck as her eyes stayed riveted to the skies.

"Come." Ellen had already collected the beef and she was pulling at her friend's shawl. "We'd better go to the main building."

Numbly, Kate followed Ellen, walking slowly as she bent her head backward to stare at the silver airplanes with the beautiful white stars.

The Americans, after two years and almost nine months, had returned to Manila.

44

"Won't be long now, Captain, will it?" Chopper was cleaning his .45 the best he could without the proper chemicals.

"No." Sky agreed. He had been in contact with some of the other guerrilla groups, and they had all agreed that their roles would soon be changing.

"How long you figure it'll take?"

"Couple of months." It was a wild guess, but then again it hadn't taken the Japanese that long to capture Manila in the first place. "Maybe more."

"More, nah. I still like that bounty idea."

Berringer flinched. He was sorry the pilot had ever heard about Fertig's operation in Mindanao. Down there they were exchanging twenty centavos and a bullet for each pair of Japanese ears. It was a system that held particular appeal to the Muslim Moros, a group of Mindanaons known for their fighting and piracy skills. There were other methods of head counts, notched *pakos* or fighting clubs, and Japanese souvenirs brought in as proof of kill. It reminded Sky of a perverted sort of wild game hunting, only the prey was human.

Faustino came into the ramada. "Man is this an exclusive group," he said, for Chopper and Sky and few of the others had firearms. There were rumors that General MacArthur had sent the *U.S.S. Nautilus* in with weapons, M1 carbines, Browning automatic rifles, Thompson submachine guns, for Major Robert Lapham's guerrilla group, but the San Alberto men had seen none of them.

"I guess when the Japanese come you'll have to feed them to Ernest head first," the schoolteacher said as he pulled out his bolo and kissed it.

"Right." Sky polished his .38.

"When are we getting our orders?"

"Soon."

"And then we'll go after the dwarfs."

Berringer laughed. "Don't count on it. We'll probably go after the bridges and roads. Make their lives a little more difficult. If a few get killed in the process," he shrugged.

"Are we going to Manila?"

"If we can." Sky's voice was grim, for there had been few days that he had not thought of Kate in the capital city. "Although I don't think we're in any position to storm Santo Tomas."

"Well," Chopper suggested," maybe we can count on a little help. Them fly boys has got friends with feet."

October 11, 1944

Sweat streamed off all of them, dressed as they were in the heavy Japanese army clothing. It had been a change for the captured barefoot Americans, going from near nakedness to shirts and pants and shoes.

"Goddamn," Bark was scratching frantically at his crotch. "There's lice in these things."

Almost as he said it, the doors to the pier shed were pulled open, exposing the bright light of day. The prisoners squinted and blinked, adjusting their eyes to the sun.

Air Raid and Speedo prodded the front prisoners of the group, pushing them out on the dock. Slowly, the men began filing out of the shed and down to Pier Seven.

"Jesus!" Tully was the first to speak, "The *President Polk* she ain't."

"What did you expect after our fine hotel last night?" Bark asked. They had all spent the night in Bilibid Prison in Manila, a hellhole that served as a holding place, a prison and a hospital. They had received the uniforms and shoes there.

"My God," Tom whispered.

The rusty Japanese freighter sat high in the water, the letters and numbers on her encrusted hull barely discernible, even in the bright sunlight.

"*Arisan Maru*. 2209." Tully read out loud. "She can't be more than five or ten tons." He looked grimly at all the men assembled on the dock. There were close to eighteen hundred of them.

"Maybe we aren't all going," Tom suggested.

"I'm afraid we are," Bark said.

"Well," Tully stopped long enough to scratch. "Look on the bright side, at least some of us will probably get to sleep on deck."

The guards were jabbering in Japanese as the first prisoners began to board. In the sweltering heat the deck was soon crawling with the Americans. It was like a line of ants disappearing into a hole, Tom thought, as they got to the edge of the hold.

"Jesus Christ!" The stalwart Tully almost collapsed as he

looked inside.

The ship had been used to transport Japanese troops, and the main hold was on two different levels. Now in a space that had been planned for a hundred men, more than nine hundred were already standing, pressed tightly against one another, their newly issued clothing drenched with sweat. The stench in the hold was already unbearable, and the trip had yet to begin. Many of the men were stripping off their clothes in an effort to cool themselves in the sweltering quarters.

Bark froze at the top of the hold.

"Come on," Tully, halfway down the rope ladder, urged.

"I can't." Fear froze his face. He had always been claustrophobic, and the thought of climbing into the hold to spend God only knew how many days with the rest of them, packed together with no room for standing or moving around, was unbearable.

But Theodore Barkley had no choice as Air Raid came up from behind him and booted him square in the middle of his back. Bark struggled for his balance but lost it as he fell backward into the hold without benefit of the rope ladder.

Instantly Tully was on him, helping him to his feet. "You all right?"

Bark rubbed his back. "I think so." His good eye was wild as he looked around at the men. "I can't do this."

"Yes you can. You've got to Bark. It won't be that bad."

Bark gave him a disbelieving look.

"Take a deep breath." Tully was breathing with him as he guided him over to the side of the hold. There were no portholes, only narrow bunks, shelves really, tiered three high without any room to sit or raise one's knees. "Would you feel better up there?" He pointed to a bunk.

Bark shook his head.

Tom was in the hold now and wasted no time in finding his two friends. They had already discussed it last night in Bilibid. The same principles applied here as in Cabanatuan. If they were going to survive, they would have to stay together.

The men were packed in, shoved against one another, able to stand erect and little more. Already the smell of feces and vomit pervaded the hold as the sick, lacking latrines or the strength to get to them, defecated and threw up where they stood. No one sat. They were all afraid to, for fear of being trampled.

"Christ, they're going to close the hatch!" Bark screamed for his good eye had never left the patch of sunlight, his last remaining link to the wide outdoors. As they watched, the Japanese guards drew the heavy tarpaulins across the hatch, securing it from topside.

The heat quickly soared as more and more men jostled and squirmed to get out of the heavy Japanese clothing. They dropped the garments where they stood, neither caring nor trying to retrieve them. Temperatures nudged one hundred and ten degrees.

"Sirens," Tom whispered to Tully, not wanting Bark to hear. But above the din of the men and the sea lapping at the *Arisan Maru*, the Manila air raid sirens could be heard. The boat began to move slowly as it was pulled away from the dock by a pair of tugboats.

"Sayonara," Tully said softly, but neither friend heard him. Bark was concentrating on his breathing, and Tom was praying for the wife and children he was leaving behind.

※

"One teaspoon soda, two tablespoons shortening, one teaspoon vinegar, water." Kate talked to herself as she threw the ingredients on top of the rice flour. While many of the work details had been laid off, she had a new job now. Making the bomber bread kept her busy most of the mornings when she was not in the shelters.

The air raids had increased to the point of becoming an accepted part of camp life, generating none of the wild enthusiasm they had all felt on the twenty-first of September.

The bomber bread had come from the raids, and that had been a good thing, for it had created a job for her, something to do to pass the time until the Americans, and Sky, could return. The bread provided sustenance during the eight to ten hour raids. Uniformly tasteless, it would not spoil and could easily be carried into the main building or the other air raid shelters. That too, had been a laugh, for the trenches that had been dug for shelter last August quickly filled with water during the rains. They were useless for their intended purpose.

"Hi, Doc." Kate looked at Ellen's oldest boy as he came in.

"Good morning." His blue eyes twinkled with his secret. It was impossible not to share it. "I heard a new rumor," he said as casually as he could.

"Oh?" She did not look up from the bread. Rumors had been flying fast and furiously. The Americans would be here in a week. In a month. The Germans were committing suicide and dying like flies. Rumors.

"We beat the hell out of the dirty Japs in Formosa."

"Doc!"

"Sorry." In his enthusiasm he had forgotten his mother's ban against profanity. He was thirteen now and he wondered on which birthday he would be allowed to say hell. "Anyway, they lost over three hundred planes."

At this Kate stopped her mixing. "Three hundred planes, really, Doc, where did you hear this?"

"Oh, just around." Doc helped himself to a pinch of the dry bland dough before walking out of the kitchen.

This war was really getting exciting now, he thought. Why the Americans were all over Luzon, everyone knew that. Information coming into the camp was closely guarded, and on the few occasions when it was released, there were always intentional distortions. The Japanese were already suspicious, arresting and questioning anyone found to be passing rumors. Although the radio had not been started up again, the guards had torn apart the electrical repair shop, and confiscated everything of an electrical nature in an attempt to keep Santo Tomas in isolation.

Quickly Doc hurried to the family shanty. He would not share the rumor with them, for his mother had forbidden him from talking about the war. She had seen too many people go in for questioning and it was not a fate she wished for her boys.

"Good morning, Mother." Doc was bored this morning, eager for something to happen. He was ready for the fireworks and the shooting. He smiled, thinking about the pellet gun safely tucked away. There had been a few uneasy days when he had convinced his mother, lied to her, that he had not taken the gun. He had even gone so far as to suggest that maybe another kid had stolen it from them. No one knew he still had it. Not even Pete.

Magda took a simmering pot, for nothing ever really boiled, from the small tin burner and dumped the bubbling water just outside, taking care not to let the canna bulbs drop on to the ground.

"They'll be ready in a little while," she said as she poured water over the flower roots for the third time.

"Good." Doc tried to be polite. Although he was hungry all the time, he had yet to develop a taste for the cannas. Even with the garlic added to them and fried, the plants didn't taste like much, but still he found himself eating them, as they all did.

Ellen came up from behind him and gave him a big hug. He was getting thinner and thinner now, and she worried about both her children. Tom's letters had been so explicit about that. He had written her to spend every penny on keeping them in food and in good health. He had encouraged her not to despair over any foodstuff, but to buy what she could so they would all be healthy and strong when their ordeal was over.

She feared, not for the first time, that she was failing her absent husband as there was no more money, and the committee would fast be out of the reserved foods. Soon she would sell or trade the diamond solitaire, but as long as there was rice she had to hold on to it, for what would happen when the rice, too, was gone?

"The cannas are better than the hibiscus leaves, aren't they?" She tried to joke with him.

"Of course, Mother." He humored her. Actually he preferred the hibiscus leaves when they were chopped up and served with vinegar. They had stopped eating them though when they began causing stomach upsets. "I have to go now," he pulled gently away from her hug and was off.

"I wish we could have gotten our hands on one of those puppies," Magda complained as she watched the cannas boil for a third time.

Ellen shuddered. She knew many people had eaten them. Even Luther, in order to protect his beloved pet, had told everyone that Roosevelt had died, although Ellen knew he was alive and well, still safely tied in the Russian's shanty.

❧

They had it worked out now. Half of them would sit at one time while the other half stood. It had helped when, on the third day, the Japanese officer in charge had taken five hundred of the prisoners and put them in the #1 hold, which also held coal. The men quickly found that every time the ship rolled the coal would cover quite a few of them. It was also impossible to get any rest sleeping on top of the anthracite.

Upon leaving Manila, after the air raid on Luzon, the *Arisan Maru* sought shelter along one of the other islands. The ship returned to Manila on the twentieth of October for supplies. The next day she headed out to sea.

The men left in hold #2 had enough room to sit down. Laying down was out of the question, and even sitting was only possible if a man's knees were drawn up to his chest. Tom, Bark and Tully sat frozen in this position, hours on end, talking, when they had the energy to do so, only to the back of each other's heads.

There was yet a third hold, which in spite of the overcrowding, remained empty.

"Sorry, Tom." Tully had dysentery, and there was no containing it as he passed the watery substance and felt it slosh in front of him. There was no way the vile substance could avoid hitting Sullivan.

Tom nodded. They were all sitting in feces and vomit and sweat and it didn't make much difference any more whether the liquids came from the man behind you, or from your own body. At least the Japanese had taken the hatch covers off during the day.

"Bark," Tom looked at the back of Bark's greasy hair. "You doing OK?"

"Yeah." Bark, while never adjusted to the jammed hold, concentrated on his breathing during his bad times. "But the guy in front of me hasn't moved in two days. I think he's dead."

"How can you tell?" Tom asked wryly, for indeed there was no way to tell. They were all frozen in the same position.

Some of them, the medic knew, had certainly gone mad, but again there was no way of telling, jammed up against one another the way they were, heads resting on knees when sleep, death, or insanity came.

"Can you get his canteen or mess kit?" Tully asked.

"I already got the cup," Bark replied. Actually it was a rusty tin can.

There was a mad scramble on both sides for the man's mess kit. Bark lunged for it, but could not reach it in time. Oh well, he thought philosophically, it had been too far away anyway. In fact he had tried for it earlier when he had gotten the cup.

The Japanese provided a half a canteen cup of rice twice a day and three ounces of dirty water per man. If a man died, and you inherited his utensils, you got double servings. It was enough to kill for.

Tully struggled to his feet, his legs crusted with feces, his body dripping bloody mucus.

"Don't bother," Tom urged.

But the medic was up, carefully weaving his way through the sitting bodies to take his place in line, waiting for a turn at one of the five gallon latrine buckets.

The buckets, once full, were passed up to the Japanese guards who dropped the slop over the side before returning the empty pails.

Tully tugged at his pants just as a bucket was passed up to one of the guards. As the medic bent over the can, he was unaware of the taunting look on the Japanese face as the guard grabbed the heavy pail and laughingly turned it over, dumping its foul contents on the men below.

Tully was covered with the excretions of dozens of men.

"Son-of-a-bitch!" The man waiting behind him in line had

seen his way to duck clear, and he made no effort to help Tully clean the excrement and vomit from his body. Tully used his hand to scrape his body off. There were no towels, no water that could be squandered for such a purpose.

Numbly, the medic made his way back to his place, squirming and pushing to get the same amount of space.

"Don't know why I bothered," he said by way of apology.

"Bark?" Tom asked.

"Yeah."

"Guy next to me is gone too." There was no scramble for his possessions. He had been dead for two days, and the struggle for his mess kit and canteen cup had come late last night.

"You know," Tully said, "look on the bright side, it's probably a good thing our rations are light, otherwise we'd be swimming in this filth."

"Fuck your bright side," Bark said. "I'm praying we get bombed."

It was the last thing he said for six hours as he rested his head on his knees.

OF LOSS AND HONOR

45

The dreams were there again, teasing him, licking at the darkest recesses of his mind. Stroking his subconscious with forbidden visions, encouraging him to participate in them.

He no longer called them his ordination dreams for the glory of the Roman Catholic Church, the resplendent archbishop, the Latin words, all had been stripped away. Replaced by pictures of thirsty hell flames and dancing demons prodding him, daring him. Instructing him once again.

Rationally he knew that it was too risky for there were too many professional soldiers in this group. At first he worried that the trained killers would recognize him, know him for what he was. But that had not become a problem, for they continued to come to confession spilling their sins to him like so many seeds upon the earth.

Bendetti had taken the day off, and was hiking in the thick forest, eager to leave the guerrillas behind him and sort out the thoughts that once again threatened his holy vows. It was hot and sweat was pouring off him as he came upon a small glade.

Framed by ferns and jungle vines, a small pool blossomed at the bottom of a waterfall and it was in this water that a group of

Filipino children played. Their clothes hung from the jungle plants as they frolicked their naked bodies in the cool mountain water. Giggling and splashing one another, they were oblivious to the man in the bushes who secretly watched their play.

Bendetti stood for a long time, trying to center in on each of the male children. Slowly, deliberately he counted them. Five, no six, that one had been under water. Six pure, smooth bodied little boys.

As the priest watched, he was acutely aware of his own clothed body. With that awareness came the realization that nothing was happening to him. There was no erection this time. No surge of heat. No welling of desire. He closed his eyes and directed his attention back to the children. Mentally he began singling them out, wondering what it would be like with each of them. He closed his eyes and imagined slitting their throats and feeling the warm gush of blood run over his hands. The blood of Christ.

Only a small tingle went through him now. He was forcing it though. What had come naturally before was now gone. He opened his eyes and in that instant it all became clear to him. Perfectly clear.

The children were gone, not in fact, but from his attention. They would not come back. They had been replaced by the one thing that threatened to take his manhood. Threatened *alter Christus*. The one man who stood between him and the woman who would make him whole. Sky Berringer.

He would have to find the pilot. That would be a difficult mission, he thought, in the vast Philippine archipelago. His thick lips curled tightly around his teeth as he instinctively knew where to find him. He would go to Manila. The Americans were on their way there now. Sky would go for Kate. Slowly, oh so slowly, it was beginning to come together.

Could it actually hurt to breathe, Tom wondered. He wanted to ask Tully who would surely know, but he no longer had the energy. Sweat poured off him, clogging his skin, his pores, his mind. It was all he could do to sit, waiting. For water. For rice. For land.

The *Arisan Maru* was bucking and rolling in the choppy sea as it fought the edge of the typhoon. Sullivan had lost track of things now, but he could only remember good weather for the first three or four days.

The hatch cover was on, had been for days, and the few times it was removed to pass the honey buckets or the rice and water, the sky outside had been dark and foreboding. The lurching of the ship was just another thing to put up with. Another obstacle to survival. Tom thought of Ellen and his boys and made yet another vow to himself that he would survive, that he would live to be with them again.

It was a little cooler today and he was thankful for the bad weather for bringing a drop in temperature. The engineer tried to stretch his cramped muscles, but his legs only went out inches in front of him before they hit Bark's back. When and if they ever got off this ship, he thought, they would all have to learn to walk again. They had been sitting, knees to their chests for almost two weeks now and it would probably take days for their bodies to return to normal upright postures.

Sullivan shifted his weight, conscious of sitting in filth, wearing filth, struggling to keep filth out of his mess kit and canteen cup. The floor sloshed with a nasty blend of bloody mucus, vomit and excrement.

The Japanese had allowed them to remove their dead twice.

The medical personnel had stripped the bodies of their dog tags, a military procedure for later recordation, and then the burial ceremony had consisted of dumping the corpses over the side of the aging freighter. There were still some lifeless bodies, frozen in their curious "n" position, mixed in with the living in the crowded hold.

They were all struggling to breathe the putrid air. It seemed as though there was so little of it now. It hung over them, threatening to smother all of them if they didn't keep on breathing. In and out. In and out. Deep breaths or gasps were out of the question. They took too much energy and hurt too much.

"Tom?" Bark's voice was raspy. It had been almost twenty hours since they had water.

"Yes?" Tom hated making the effort but he was thankful that the claustrophobic Bark was keeping his wits, while all around him men were quietly going insane. The living dead, Tully had called them.

"We're not gonna make it."

"Sure we are, Bark. This part's just a little tough, that's all." In his own mind Tom wished that he could be as sure as his words. He tried to lick his swollen lips but there was no moisture on his tongue. It must be getting close to rice time, he thought. And water. The men were getting restless.

"You figure we're on a regular shipping lane?" Bark asked.

"I don't know."

"Yeah." Tully's voice came in behind Tom.

"Good." Bark was quiet again, praying.

The restlessness was increasing as men shifted in their positions and jostled one another. Like wildfire it took over the hold, and simmering animosities exploded as men bit and punched one another in a feeble effort to gain more space from the men who had been touching them for weeks. Swinging canteens, their only weapons other than their emaciated bodies, they fought one another bitterly.

A man stood, cupping his hands as he urinated in them. Tom watched in horror as the man eagerly lapped his own urine. Suddenly a canteen crashed into the man's knees, knocking him on top of three men.

The fighting was widespread and it was only a matter of time before the Japanese would come and open the hatch and yell, or worse, fire their guns into the quarreling men.

Bark stood. He held Tunes to his lips, and although his mouth was parched and covered with fever blisters, he blasted a long shrill note. It was enough.

"My daddy was a sharecropper," he began in a stronger voice than he had used in days. "My momma took in laundry." He was practically shouting now, and the sound of his loud, strong voice so caught the attention of the men that they stopped their fighting to listen.

"And I'm an American. Not a rich one, not a poor one. Just a country boy from Oklahoma. And I'll tell you something," he held up an emaciated, filthy finger. "You are Americans too. You come from the north and the south, the east and the west, but it doesn't matter because we're all from the greatest country on this earth, and we'll get out of this hellhole, the Lord willing."

There were a few feeble cheers.

"And if we don't," Bark said softly. "Then, by God, let's die like Americans." Without another word, he sat down. Miraculously the fighting and bickering stopped. The men sat quietly, waiting for their evening rations as Bark played "*God Bless America*" on his beloved Tunes.

"I didn't know you knew that one, Bark." Ton said softly, as he wiped the tears from his eyes.

Half of the rice had been served when the Japanese guards went crazy. Through the opened hatch Tom could see them running around on the deck above. First to one side and then the other.

"Fish!" Someone yelled.

"Go, Navy go! Don't miss!" A sailor screamed.

"Bracketing," Bark said softly to himself as he tucked his head in silently as tight as he could between his knees. There was no use in saying anything more. His prayers had been answered.

The torpedoes from the *USS Shark II* were indeed bracketing their target. After picking up the Japanese freighter, they fired the first torpedo which passed the forward part of the ship, a deliberate miss. The Japanese had run to that side while the *Shark* fired a second torpedo aft.

A guard stood at the open hatch, screaming at the rice crew on deck. Other guards quickly drew the hatch covers across the holes, pulling them down tight.

"Torpedoes!" One of the cooks yelled.

The third torpedo now hit its carefully bracketed target, exploding the front part of hold #3, the empty one, ripping the steel hull apart as the ship rocked against the assault, its bow tipping skyward.

The American prisoners in the other two holds, trapped inside, were tossed and thrown against one another, acting like cotton, absorbing the sound of the explosion and the blood of their comrades as hundreds of men absorbed flying shrapnel.

Tom grabbed Bark and pulled him to his feet even as he groped for Tully behind him. But Tully was not there. They were all wearing bits and pieces of each other now.

There was no time for searching as Tom and Bark punched

and shoved their way to the latched hatch covers.

"The rope's been cut!" A soldier held up a piece of the severed rope ladder which was the last act of the Japanese before they evacuated the ship.

"Get 'em open." A gruff voice demanded. The voices were all louder now, the bodies stronger, as the adrenaline rush urged them all out of the hold before it became a watery tomb.

"Can't. It's fastened."

"Goddamn Nips."

Those closest to the hatch worked and struggled with the cover until they were finally able to pry it open. Hundreds of men scrambled to the deck above, leaving behind them in hold #2 nothing more than the howling wind.

The ship was listing. And burning. Although it would be hours before she actually went down, many of the men were diving over the side. A lifeboat, bearing the Japanese officers, was bobbing its way toward a Japanese destroyer that had been in pursuit of the American submarine. Some of the prisoners started swimming for the Japanese boat.

"Let's go, Bark." Tom nudged his friend.

"Wait. Are there any life preservers?"

"I don't know. Hell there are those kapok things. They're only good for a few hours." Tom pointed to one on deck and Bark quickly ran to it, fitting it around his body.

They ran toward the Japanese kitchen and filled their canteens with water. Still there was no sign of Tully.

"Rice!" Bark pointed to the steaming cast iron cauldrons, the *couwas*, and they dipped their hands into the hot rice, stuffing it into their mouths.

"Not too much," Tom warned. He leaned against a steam wench giving his stomach time to adjust to the amounts of rice he had just eaten. "My God."

"What's wrong?" Bark mumbled, his mouth gorged with rice, grains dripping out between his lips.

Tom pointed to a brass plate on the steam wench. The raised letters identified it as having been made in a ship yard in the United States in 1923.

"Full circle," Bark agreed.

"Let's do it." Tom headed for the side of the ship. Down below in the oily water he could see pieces of the ship, broken boards, oil cans, crates, and other pieces of flotsam bobbing below. "We'll grab onto some of that stuff. That'll keep us up."

"Sullivan," Bark's fingers clutched his arm. "Is it OK with you if we go over together?"

"Sure."

The two men climbed up on the side of the ship, perching there on top as they considered the distance below.

Tom reached out for Bark's hand. Taking it securely in his own, he gave it a squeeze.

"Ready?"

The Oklahoma gunner nodded.

They were able to slide down stool cables leading to the ocean below. Cold water rushed at them as they hit. Tom was forced down deep. His ears were popping, his eyes stinging from the saltwater. Holding his breath and clawing the water he fought and stroked as best he could to break the surface of the sea.

He came up fighting and gasping for air, and as he treaded water he searched for Bark, but there was no sign of him. He spotted a broad plank of floating wood and swam to it, eagerly clutching the weathered lumber as he gasped to catch his breath.

There! A flash of orange as Bark too, came bobbing up, huffing and puffing for air.

"Over here!" Tom yelled, but his voice was lost on the screaming wind. They were at least in the same area of the ship, which was a godsend he thought, as he half pulled, half swam with the floating board.

The waves were high. Ten to fifteen feet and if one or the other of them got out of the swell they were sharing, they would be unable to find each other, Tom thought.

Bark had seen him now, and was limply kicking over toward him. Finally he reached Tom and the board and he clung to it, his fingers almost imbedded in the surface. He took in enormous gulps, fighting for his breath and his voice.

"You all right?" Tom asked. Bark's eye patch had been taken by the ocean and Tom was trying hard not to stare at the hollow scarred cavity which had once held his friend's left eye.

The exhausted Bark barely nodded. "How long did you say these things last?" He pointed to the life preserver he was wearing.

"Couple of hours. Don't worry though, we've got this board."

"Guess I never told you. I can't swim." Bark, in spite of his exhaustion, gave him a lopsided grin. "My momma always told me I'd be sorry."

"You're going to be fine. She'll keep us afloat until help comes."

They rode the cold waves with their floating board, clutching and hanging on to it for life, as dampened splinters pierced their bloated flesh. Great gigantic waves pulled them high on their crests, and then sent them crashing fifteen feet. Up and down. Ascent and plummet. They vomited rice and sea water as they clung to the life sustaining wreckage.

As they rode the sea, it was by accident that they came within visual distance of the Japanese destroyer. She had come over for a closer look at the sinking *Arisan Maru*. As Bark and Tom squinted in the fading light, they could see the Japanese seamen scurry about on deck with long bamboo poles. They were honed to a sharp point and used as fishing spears but now the fish had been replaced by drowning Americans struggling for assistance in the water. As the prisoners floated close to the destroyer and tried to board her, the Japanese poked and stabbed them with the lethal poles.

"Jesus. They're drowning them." Bark watched as a laughing Japanese sailor held the end of a pole between a prisoner's shoulders, forcing him beneath the surface of the sea.

The wind and the ocean current was taking their board closer and closer to the Japanese destroyer.

"We may be next."

"No," Tom said. "It will be dark soon."

And it was. Blissfully, darkness fell, quickly as it does in the tropics, where it is light one minute and dark the next.

Through the night they talked only occasionally. Just enough for each to comfort the other that he was still there. Screams drifted across the water as darkness shrouded them and they clung to their board and to their fading dreams.

As the sun tried to rise through the black clouds, it cast a hellish light on the South China Sea. The *Arisan Maru* was barely visible as her passengers clutched fragments of the ship. The sea was littered with the dead and dying, and with those struggling to live. The Japanese destroyer, so close at dusk, along with a companion ship, was now just a shadow against the horizon. Rain, no longer howling but soft and steady, poured down on all of them.

"Sullivan?" Bark's voice was hoarse and weak.

"I'm here." Even in the light it was hard to make out definitive shapes for their eyes had been tortured and battered all night by the salt water. Things were looking fuzzy, not clear at all.

"The jacket's had it."

"Hang on to the board, Bark. You'll be all right."

"Do you think Tull made it?"

"I don't know."

"Maybe he's on the bright side now."

"Maybe."

"Sullivan, would you do me a favor?"

"If I can."

"Tell me about Ellen and the boys again."

Tom began talking, straining his sore, salt rubbed throat while clinging on to the board. It was even soggier now, saturated with the sea water. His legs were numb, dangling in the cold sea. He talked about Doc's soccer games and of Ellen's knitting, of Pete's grades and of Putt Putt the cat, of bridge games and picnics past, of his beloved Catalina Mountains and of dogs whose names were all but forgotten. He talked on and on, not even aware that mingled in with the saltwater and the rain were his own tears.

"Did you ever figure it would end like this?" Bark asked.

"It's not over. That submarine will send help."

"Why? They think they've sunk a Japanese freighter."

Tom was silent. Bark was right. The United States would not be likely to send help for drowning Japanese seamen.

"Funny, my fingers look like they're about eighty years old." Bark tried to laugh but the noise came out a squeak, as he held one hand out in front of him, his flesh swollen and wrinkled with the effects of the water. "Prunes."

They floated on the waves until noon before speaking again.

"Sullivan, do you believe in God?" Bark's voice was weaker now.

"Yes."

"I'm not sure I do, but I guess I have to now, don't I?"

"It would probably help."

Tom was so tired. The wind was picking up, and it was taking more effort to hang on. He had thought several times about letting go of the board and each time a vision of Ellen and his boys had come to him. He had promised them he would fight to live and if he let go, that promise would be broken. He had to hang on. He owed them that.

A huge wave crested and crashed into them, wrenching the board from their weak grasps. The wood flew up, away and out of their hands as both men were thrown under water.

Tom surfaced first.

"Bark!" He yelled, spitting sea water from his mouth. "Bark!"

To his right he saw flailing arms, and as he made his way toward the struggling figure, he saw the gunner go under the surface. He swam as fast as his tortured, aching body would allow to the spot where he had last seen Bark and began diving.

Again and again he went down, his eyes stinging from the salt, his hands and legs reaching wildly out in the chance of making contact with his friend. But it was hopeless.

Finally, his body wracked with exhaustion, Tom surfaced for a last time. This time he panicked as he searched for the board that had held them afloat for so long. He treaded water weakly, trying to conserve his strength as he caught his bearings.

A hundred and fifty feet or so away he could see the board, bobbing on the waves, sweeping away from him on the ocean current. He began to swim, slowly, steadily toward the evasive wood even as the rain pounded against his back. Pain wracked his bones, wrenching every stroke he made toward the floating timber.

He had almost reached it when the wave hit, tumbling him under the surface yet another time. This time when he came up for air, the board was not in sight.

He could not breathe now, he was suffocating although his head was still above the water. The rain pounded him. He tried to breathe but could only take in water. Water from the sea, from the rain, from his tears. There was nothing left for him. He knew that now. Bark was gone. The board was gone. His strength was gone.

"Please, God," he whispered as he again saw the vision of Ellen and his children. Doc was reaching out for him now, pleading with him to stay.

As Tom Sullivan reached out for his oldest man child, he went under the South China Sea for the final time.

SINCLAIR BROWNING

46

Although the stone had not been cleaned in over three years, the sun caught its faceting and created sparkling prisms in the bright sunlight. Ellen held it up, looking through the platinum prongs and admired it for a last time. With tears welling in her eyes, she slipped it onto the third finger of her left hand, nudging it up against her plain gold band.

She stretched her hand out in front of her, admiring the sparkling diamond solitaire. Pulling it easily from her finger she held the stone to her mouth and kissed it, feeling the hardness of the diamond against her lips. There would be another one, she thought, another time.

Tightening cramps jerked across her stomach, a cruel reminder of the task at hand. She slipped the ring into her pocket and went in search of Teijiro.

He was at the guard station near the front gate listening to his radio. When he saw her approach, he turned down the volume as a look of irritation crossed his face. Still, he knew she had the ring and he wanted it.

This time, he was sure, she would sell it to him, for all of them were now walking scarecrows. Sunken faces, arms and legs that were bony knobs and little else, they all had the look of starving animals. He could see it in their eyes.

He beckoned her into the shack, hiding his greed as she flashed the large diamond at him. Taking it roughly from her fingers he held the stone to the light and checked its clarity. Teijiro knew nothing of diamonds but the ring had caught his eye from the first and he wanted it. Casually he shook his head and handed it back to her.

Tears welled in Ellen's eyes. "You don't want it."

"No. There is no money."

"But food. You have food. I will trade you for it." She knew that throughout the prison camp internees were trading their most precious personal items for food. Hamilton gold watches were being swapped for kilos of sugar, Esterbrook pens bartered for tobacco. It was happening all over with the desperate prisoners getting the short end of the trades.

He took the ring back. "Sugar. I will give you a kilo of sugar for it."

Ellen's stomach knotted as she considered what Tom must have paid for the ring. She shook her head. "There's no protein in sugar. I must have meat for my children."

Teijiro considered this for a minute before reaching under a stack of Japanese papers and withdrawing a twelve-ounce can of Spam.

Ellen's eyes darted to the can. She could see the picture of the beef and pork shoulder on the face of it and her mouth drew wet with desire.

"I need more."

The guard covered it back up.

"No!" She cried. "All right. I'll take the can." Sadly she took the tin of meat.

She tucked it under her blouse as she returned to the shanty.

"Wow, Mom, where'd you get that?" Pete's eyes grew wide when he saw the tin.

"Ssh," Ellen took the Spam to the far reaches of the shanty, away from prying eyes, and turned her back to the open side as she quickly opened the can. Spilling out the greasy contents onto a plate, she carefully cut two thin slices.

"This is for today."

"Oh." Disappointment flooded Pete's voice.

"Ssh, not a word. This is going to last for a few days," she hesitated, "and you must not tell anyone we have it here. Do you understand?" Her heart was torn as she watched her hungry children stuff their mouths with the tender meat.

"Aren't you going to have any?" Doc had taken time off from his eating to notice that his mother was trying none of the meat.

"No, not right now. I'm not hungry," she lied, trying to avert her eyes away from every bite they took.

They were done quickly.

Carefully she wrapped up the remaining Spam. If she could hide it well, it would serve them for another four days. "Run along now," she said, waiting until she was sure they were gone.

She turned away from the open side of the shanty again and faced the bamboo wall, the lid to the tin in her hands. Slowly, savoring every taste, she licked the inside of the lid before replacing it on the tin.

General MacArthur was back. The news had come over the bamboo telegraph and over the radio sets. Although the Battle of Leyte Gulf had raged for days, he had managed to wade ashore with the third assault wave on October 20th on the east coast of

Leyte, onto a sandy stretch dubbed "Red Beach". Carlos Romulo and President Osmana (President Quezon's successor after his death from tuberculosis in the United States in August) had accompanied the general.

The ever accommodating Signal Corps had set up a mobile broadcasting unit on the sandy beach and the general had given an emotional speech.

"People of the Philippines, I have returned," he had said. "By the grace of Almighty God our forces stand again on Philippine soil- soil consecrated in the blood of our two peoples."

Although the speech was short, lasting only two minutes, in it General MacArthur had managed to call upon the resources of the various guerrilla bands scattered throughout the archipelago.

"Rally to me. Let the indomitable spirit of Bataan and Corregidor lead on. As the lines of battle roll forward to bring you within the zone of operations, rise and strike. Strike at every favorable opportunity. For your homes and hearths, strike! For future generations of your sons and daughters, strike!"

Rise and strike! The orders were passed, like an Olympic torch, throughout the communications network of the islands as guerrilla groups collected their hidden weapons and plans and began hitting Japanese targets after three years of restraint. The phantom guerrilla units suddenly became visible to the Japanese. And to the Americans. For upon their return they found 250,000 insurgents supporting their effort to retake the Philippines.

Sky's duffel bag was stuffed with his possessions. Although he was restricting himself to only those things he deemed essential, the bag bulged and stretched with each addition.

"I'm all ready," Faustino said as he entered the room.

Sky stopped, his maps in hand ready for the bag. "I didn't think you were going."

"Why not? I like a little fun as much as the next guy," he fingered his bolo. "Besides, Ernest's bored."

"There's no need for you to go. San Alberto's your home, stay here."

"And the Philippines are my country," the schoolteacher said softly. "You guys are cleaning house on Leyte. The beaches are secure and all you're doing is mopping up the ground forces."

"That could take some time."

"And that's why everybody's packing, right?"

Sky grinned. There was no denying the excitement in the air now they knew the Allies were getting close to Luzon. A landing would not be far off.

"We'll be more helpful closer to Clark."

"Yes." Tapay swung his feet easily off the bed. "I'll get my things."

Kate pulled the weeds as quickly as she could, sorting them out as she went along. The larger stack she would clean and take back to the shanty. The smaller group contained the poisonous rejects. There were a few strangers in the take home pile and they would be treated with deference for she had learned weeks ago that not all of the garden weeds were edible.

She had been lucky to get the job weeding. She was allowed to keep the weeds and they came in handy in salads and soups, giving precious little added nutrients to their starving group. She had really wanted a job as a vegetable peeler, but that had been impossible. The peelers had their rewards too, they took home the shavings.

She had just collected the stack of weeds when the air raid siren sounded. Trotting quickly, stopping at the shanty only long enough to dump the weeds on the table, she hurried to the main building and joined the others.

They sat in their regular positions, waiting for the all clear to sound. It was eight hours before Kate was able to return to the shanty and prepare her weeds.

Magda was already firing up the tin stove, carefully stoking the papers underneath and blowing on them to get the flames going.

"Happy Thanksgiving, Magda," Kate offered the greeting without thinking that the American holiday would mean little to the Czech.

"Ya, same to you, Katherine," she said as she poured water into the pot.

"What are you cooking?" Kate asked for it had been a long time since the pot had been used.

"A surprise. A Thanksgiving surprise for everyone." There was a glint in the brown eyes. "Dinner." She reached for some cubed white meat, an effort not unnoticed by the American.

"That's meat. Where on earth did you find that?" Kate was amazed as she admired the chunks and strips. Even the pigeons that had perched and nested and raised their families for so long on the Main Building had disappeared weeks ago.

"A little secret," she smiled mysteriously,"but this night I am fixing a great Czechoslovakian meal. Curry!"

"I thought that was Indian, or maybe Hungarian."

"No, no." Magda shooed her away from the meat. "Curry tonight will be Czechoslovakian. If you like you can think of it as turkey dinner."

"Some turkey!" Kate smiled. She had never seen turkey meat quite like that. "Where's Ellen?"

"Resting. She'll be here later." They were all concerned about Ellen. She was down to eighty pounds now. Throughout camp the weak and the elderly were beginning to die in alarming numbers as food became more and more scarce. Signs of starvation were apparent everywhere. Hollow eyes rested in sunken, drawn faces. People were refusing to go on their work details, preferring to go to bed and sleep or rest, so exhausted were they by the lack of food. Skin infections were rampant, and many were also displaying the bloated appearance symptomatic of beriberi and the other deficiency diseases.

Posture had suffered too. Even the younger people were stooped and slow moving, giving them the appearance of being more than twice their chronological ages.

"And the boys?" Kate asked.

"Doc's over trying to catch rats and Peter's begging at the food processing shed," Magda offered matter-of-factly, not commenting on the irony of the two boys who before the war had maids, a cook, a houseboy and an *amah*, now begging for food.

The children were discouraged daily from hanging around the sheds but they always returned, hoping for a handout. Even the garbage was gone through time and time again by industrious people looking for any way in which to supplement their meager diets.

Magda plunked the meat into the simmering salted water, watching it turn and bubble. Although the meat would not be ready for a couple of hours she stayed there, beside the pot and the tin stove, watching it cook, insuring that the pot would not run dry or, worse, that the meat would disappear.

After a while she began the sauce, mixing in garlic and cinnamon with the red curry powder. The condiments were the only thing left available to buy and she was using them liberally, hoping to cut the unknown taste of the meat.

Although the holiday had no special significance for Russians, they had invited Luther to join them. It was almost dark now and curfew would be called shortly. Magda had waited almost to the last minute before calling them to the curry. She had wanted the meat to stew as long as it could and the long air raid had prevented her from cooking it any earlier in the day.

"Doc," Ellen began, smiling at her eldest son, "would you offer grace please."

Doc bowed his head and the others followed suit.

"Dear Lord, thank you for the blessings we have today, for the food on our table and for our good friends and family and help our soldiers beat the dirty Japs. Especially Lord guide and protect Father so that he may come back to us in good health and spirits. For these gifts we thank you, in Christ's name, amen." The boy had offered a daily blessing for his father for almost three years.

Luther's head remained bowed, despite the reference to Christ.

"Shall we eat?" Magda suggested, as she began dishing up the steaming curry, pleased with the spicy aroma wafting from the tin pot. Carefully she ladled it over the rice on each plate, handing her prize to the pleased diners.

"Only a very little for me, please," the Russian said quietly. Magda did not argue with him as she gave him a spoonful of the meaty dish.

"Delicious!" Kate dug into her plate with gusto. Of them all she was the only one that still looked healthy. None of the ulcerous sores had yet afflicted her and she was still ramrod straight. She had been doing her calisthenics daily since coming in to Santo Tomas.

"Better than corned beef!" Doc proclaimed as he held out his plate for a second serving.

"What is it?" Pete finally asked the question they had all been avoiding.

"Meat." Magda answered, not looking at Luther who tinkered with the curry on his plate, pushing it around and eating the rice under the sauce.

"I know," Pete pressed. "I mean what kind of meat is it?"

"Oh. goat."

"Boy I bet Roosevelt would love some of this, wouldn't he, Luther?" Pete said as he finished his second plate.

"Ya, he would." The Russian said quietly.

There was no way any of them were going to tell the excited boy that his splendid Thanksgiving dinner was given courtesy of Roosevelt himself.

47

As they closed in on the Japanese they were exchanging hand signals and pantomimes, instead of oral instructions. The enemy were a few hundred feet in front of them as they fanned out in their predetermined assault plan. Moving silently, and quickly, they paused only long enough for the signal to be given before they fired on the surprised Japanese.

They had risen and they were now striking.

✈

For the three previous holidays there had been a great deal of planning and excitement. Now, in the Christmas of 1944, the enthusiasm for the Christian day had waned. The thought of food burned in everyone's mind, distracting all thought of holiday parties. Listless and weak from malnutrition, the internees opted not to have the large decorated Christmas tree that had put up in front of the Annex in previous years.

There were no organized toy making parties and the wooden, handcrafted treasures of the past, the scooters and stilts, cars and puzzles, all crafted from scraps of lumber, were not seen this year. The ice cream, cake, nuts and fruits of former years were also long gone. Santa Claus, escorted by the traditional nimble figure clad in black, did not come in from the outside with his entrance pass as he had done in Christmases past.

Kate was the first one back to the shanty after church services and she filled the pot with water. There was nothing to put in it, but they had long ago realized that steaming water assuaged their empty stomachs.

"Merry Christmas, Katherine." Magda was next in.

"Same to you." Kate smiled at the redheaded woman. She was so stable, she thought, so unflagging in temperament. She had been good for all of them.

"Merry Christmas." Ellen walked slowly in. She was moving more stiffly now. Although Kate had tried to get them all interested in her early morning calisthenics, Magda and Ellen had demurred. Doc and Pete had thought it great fun, and on the mornings when they were around, they had happily joined her in the exercise routines. The stiffening of Ellen's joints came, Kate was afraid, not from her hesitancy to exert any extra effort, but from beri-beri beginning to set in.

"The boys and Luther will be over shortly," Ellen offered.

Kate nodded as she poured simmering water into their cups. Their group, since Thanksgiving, had grown to include the generous Luther, for he had shared with them his most precious gift.

"Merry Christmas everyone!" The boys came running in to the shanty hugging their mother, and greeting the other women. Doc accepted the cup of hot water offered by Kate. "Mother are you going to tell us about Christmas in America?"

"Oh, Doc, no, not this year," Ellen tried to get out of the tradition begun three years earlier.

"Please, Mother," Pete begged, his troubled blue eyes riveted on Ellen. "Please?"

"All right," she capitulated. "What would you like first?"

"The food!" Cried Pete.

"No. Dad. Tell us about Dad," Doc insisted.

Ellen held up her hand, her already long fingers accentuated by her loss of weight. "No. That is a rule today. No food. No tales of Christmas dinner. You've heard them before, and I'm afraid, my darlings, that you're just going to have to make do with your imaginations."

Kate thought Ellen was right. There was no sense in torturing the starving children with tales of steaming turkey, dressing and creamy mashed potatoes.

Slowly Ellen began talking, telling the boys about the Arizona they had left behind. A land that Doc barely remembered, and Pete had hardly known. She talked of the funny saguaro cactus that had to live many years- some said eighty- before it grew its first arm, and of the thousand year old creosote bush and of the howling coyotes and the clear blue skies, and of roadrunners devouring lizards. She talked about Christmas mornings waking up to face the Santa Catalina Mountains and the smell of citrus heavy on the trees. She told them, not for the first time, of the bright *luminarias*, brown bags filled partially with sand and candles, a custom borrowed from the Mexicans, lining the paths and roads and walls of the churches and homes.

She told of the Posada de los Niños where children carried lighted candles through the Tucson streets, singing Christmas carols while re-enacting Joseph and Mary's quest for lodging on their way to Bethlehem. She told them about the desert Christmas wreaths, made of red chile peppers and garnished with shredded corn husks, and she reminded them of their own creche back in Baguio, made from Mexican clay with its clay and straw figures.

"And," she continued, "at San Xavier del Bac the Papagoes celebrate a beautiful midnight mass."

"That's what Charlie is, Mom, isn't he?"

"No dear. Charlie's a Navajo," she corrected. "At the Papago mass the Christ child is at the altar."

"The real one?" At eleven, Pete couldn't resist the joke.

"A statue. After the mass the people are allowed to kiss it. Some people even hold their babies up so they can kiss it too."

They were all silent now. Ellen was tired from the strain of talking.

"Mother, you forgot the most important part," Doc said gently.

"What's that, dear?"

"'and next year, my darlings, we'll all be home for Christmas,'" he said softly, for it was as much a part of their Christmas tradition as all the rest.

Tears welled in Ellen's eyes as she stared at her hands, folded in her lap. "Yes, Doc, of course we'll all be home for Christmas next year."

The drone of a plane coming in low caught their attention.

"Another low one," Luther observed. There had been many of them in the past few weeks. At first the internees had jumped up and down and whooped when the American planes had come in that low, but now it almost took too much effort. They were happy the Americans dominated the skies, but they were eager to have it behind them before they all starved to death.

The plane made another pass and Pete ran outside.

"I feel kind of bad for the little kids this year, you know, without Santa Claus," Doc said.

"Yes, but I imagine many of their parents have individual things planned," Ellen said.

"Santa's come!" Pete said gaily, waving a piece of paper. "Listen!" He began to read the paper that had fallen from the skies. "The commander-in-chief, the officers and men of the American Forces of Liberation in the Pacific, wish their gallant allies, the people of the Philippines, all the blessings of Christmas and the realization of their ferv, ferv," he stumbled.

"Fervent." Kate was reading the message over his shoulder.

"Fervent hopes for the new year."

"Merry Christmas!" Ellen hugged Pete with more enthusiasm than she had mustered in a long time. "Merry Christmas everyone!"

The map was difficult to read in the failing light, and its creases and bends attested to the fact that it had been pored over many times before. As Sky checked it, his fingers were automatically drawn to the route they were taking to Clark Field.

"Ready?" He asked Tapay as he carefully folded the map and replaced it in his pocket.

"Yes. Chopper's getting the rest of the guys up."

They had been sleeping during the afternoon, getting rested for the last leg of their journey, the one in to Clark Field. Coordinating with several other Luzon guerrilla groups, escort carrier operations, and with Task Force 38, an American fleet carrier group, Berringer's guerrillas were eager for action.

"We're almost ready," Chopper joined the two men. "Gorilla's packing the rest of the stuff right now."

Sky looked at his watch. "We have time."

"Clark Field," Chopper reached for a cigarette. "It's been a long time."

"Three years." Sky said.

"Did you fly out of there?"

"Uh huh. Trainers. You too?"

Chopper nodded.

"And now we're going back."

"On foot," Chopper wryly agreed.

"Well at least you flew for the right side. You could have been kamikazes," Tapay said.

Chopper and Sky were both silent. The thought had occurred to both of them before, for the Japanese suicide missions both fascinated and repelled them. While they had yet to see an actual kamikaze, the tales of their missions had hit the bamboo telegraph and now all of them knew of the fearless Japanese pilots.

Flying alone in their Zero fighters, laden with bombs weighing in at five hundred and fifty pounds, the Oriental pilots would crash to their death as they flew their airplanes into their American targets. They had first surfaced during the Battle of Samar in October when they hit the *USS ST LO*. She had sunk hours after the hit.

That success fueled a hunger for the American ships, and soon the kamikazes were after the big ones, the carriers. They hit the *Intrepid,* slightly damaging her in October, and badly damaged the *Lexington* the following month. The battleships *Maryland* and *Colorado*, and two destroyers had been seriously hit in December.

Task Force 38 retaliated by hitting some of the Japanese-held airfields on Luzon, knocking out one hundred and seventy of the enemy airplanes. Still the kamikazes kept coming, flying in groups of three, with a few escort planes to fend off the American fighters. They hit the carrier *Ommaney Bay* so badly she had been abandoned. Two more battleships, the *USS New Mexico* and the *USS California* had also been hit.

"They're at Clark. Along with just about everything else the Japs have got." Chopper said. "How long do you figure this is gonna take?"

"I wouldn't make any dates for the next few days," Sky offered.

Just as it had served the American and Filipino forces, Clark Field was now the bastion of Japanese air strength in the Philippines. If she could be knocked out and retaken, it would be a serious blow to the enemy forces. The taking of Clark was part of an overall plan known as Mike I, which would come to fruition when the Americans landed in Lingayen Gulf in two more days. Having secured Leyte on Christmas Day, the Allies were now moving on Luzon.

"I'd rather be up there," Chopper pointed to the darkening sky.

"You're probably too good for the kamikazes," Sky said. Flying was the common bond between the two of them. It was the one thing Sky was looking forward to when the war was over. That and Kate.

"Probably not good enough," Chopper said in a rare moment of self effacement.

Sky shook his head. "How good do you have to be to hit an aircraft carrier? They'd be fools to send their best pilots up there." His wisdom as a training instructor was accurate, for the Japanese were sending young, inexperienced pilots up in the most obsolete airplanes that would serve the task.

"You know," Chopper drew circles in the dust with his forefinger. "It honest to God is one thing to say you're gonna die for your country, I mean, I suppose we could any day. Any time. Maybe there's a Japanese patrol scouting us right now. But to go up in one of those and really know you're gonna die, that there's no turning back, my God, that's incredible."

"Yes," Sky agreed, "but they're not going to win the war with it."

"No," Chopper said. "They'll run out of guys." He was wrong, for the Japanese had three volunteers for every available plane.

"They're not going to win because we don't have to send our kids on suicide missions. That's the difference," Sky argued.

"It's not quite that brutal," Faustino interjected. "More like a religion. Suicide doesn't have the stigma it does with us or with the Americans."

"No, I don't imagine there are too many priests running around Tokyo telling those guys they're about to execute a deadly sin." Chopper said wryly.

"No," Faustino agreed, thinking of the difference in cultures. Years later in his English classes he would teach about the kamikaze, the Divine Wind, telling his students of the rituals that preceded the death flights. He would teach the poetry that many of the pilots had left behind, and talk of their ritual farewell parties and the toasts eagerly shared with their commander. He would show them pictures of the bright, young men, lined up with their samurai swords and the flags, pictures and mementoes they carried with them as they proved their willingness to die for their Emperor. And he would read a poignant passage, written by a Japanese airplane mechanic, that told of preparing the Zero's cockpits, much as one does a funeral coffin, shining and polishing the aircraft's metals so the airplane would become a pure funeral pyre worthy of its pilot.

"I hate to break this up," Sky stood, brushing the dirt off his pants, "but it's time. That is unless you have some moral dilemma about attacking the noble Japanese self-sacrificers?"

Tapay pulled Ernest out of his shirt and swung the bolo quickly, taking slices out of the invisible air. "I too am brave, most honorable gray eyes," he gave a mocking bow.

The two Americans and the Filipino were off gathering their forces for the fight for Clark Field.

48

Maybe it was because it was off-limits that the grounds in front of the Main Building held such fascination for Doc. After the first American planes had been spotted in September, the Japanese had turned the area into a military camp. Soldiers pitched tents, and carted in box after box of military supplies. Rations, guns and bullets were all rumored to be in the cartons and the commandant had given strict orders for the internees to stay away from the area. Those choosing to ignore the order would be shot.

Protected by the edge of the building, Doc peeked around the corner. He'd been watching them from the time he had been let out of school. Skipping down the steps from the roof of the Main Building, he raced to the vantage point so he could watch the troops load the heavy army trucks. His eyes widened as they freed the boxes from their camouflaged tarpaulins and loaded them into the empty beds of the transport vehicles. They were loading personal items, too. Trunks, clothes, even an occasional piece of furniture went into the heavy trucks.

Luther was right! He said the Japanese would be leaving.

As Doc watched, he saw something fall from a carton one of the Japanese soldiers was carrying. He waited for the man to retrieve the lost item, but he was apparently unaware of his loss as he took the carton to the truck and handed it to a man inside. Doc's eyes remained glued to the place where the fallen object lay.

Finally everything was loaded and the soldiers jumped into the remaining space in the beds. Without fanfare, the tents, boxes, and the soldiers were gone.

Surely, Doc thought, there would be no danger in going into the forbidden area now that all the troops had left. He inched his way around the building, walking slowly toward the front gate. With every step he expected a warning, but none came. After what seemed an eternity he was in the area where the object had fallen. He casually kicked the dirt with his foot, hoping to uncover whatever it was the Japanese soldier had dropped.

Feeling something hard under his thin, worn sole, he stopped and retrieved the item. A bullet! An undetonated Japanese bullet! He placed it carefully in his pocket before quickly walking away from the area.

The acacia tree was his secret. He had found a hole low on its trunk and this had become his special hiding place. Glancing around to make sure no one was watching, Doc sat next to the tree, his hand behind his back as he dislodged a piece of protective bark he had placed there. He pulled out a leather pouch, its weight reassuring him that the air pistol was still safe. He placed the bullet inside, along with one of the leaflets dropped from the American planes Christmas day. He had traded Petey his football for the paper. If his treasures were ever found, he would be a dead duck, for sure, he thought. The Japanese commandant had forbidden them to keep the leaflets, insisting that they all be turned in to his office.

He was on his way to the shanty when the dogfights started. Japanese and American fighters were ducking and dodging each other across the expanse of sky. A heavy American bomber was coming in, heading east. She had barely crossed overhead when she was hit by the anti-aircraft guns. Struggling to keep her altitude, black smoke poured from her left wing as she took a reckless tilt and began plummeting to the earth. Horrified, Doc watched the dying American plane. His horror changed to relief as he saw tiny objects, with floating white clouds around them, jump from the downed bomber.

Luther sure was right, he thought. It won't be long now.

※

He left the last group under the cover of night. There was no sense staying. The end was near, even a fool could see that, for the fires and destruction raged throughout Manila. The Americans had executed a successful landing at Lingayen Gulf, and were now fighting, point by point, town by town, to secure Luzon.

Having also landed at Subic Bay, they were now involved in a fierce pincer drive to retake Manila. Clark Field, after ruthless fighting, was close to being an American conquest. Once the air field was in the Allies hands, there would be no stopping the liberation of the Philippines.

It was risky, the priest knew, coming in this close to Manila. He was still an American, and he knew that would mark him for a Japanese bullet.

※

Kate was waiting in the food line with their tickets clutched tightly in one hand. She was the logical one to do it now for she was by far the strongest. Ellen was shrinking almost daily and she had just begun to play with her rice, pushing it this way and that around her plate. Soón, she would not eat at all, Kate thought, as she shifted the empty tin pail to the hand that held the tickets. Magda was quieter too. And the boys were less active. They were less physical now, complaining that it hurt to run.

"Quiet, eh?" A gnarled old woman in front of her turned to talk.

"Yes, yes it is."

"I remember when we used to chat in these lines. Now folks are so busy worrying about food seems they don't have time for conversation."

Kate nodded. The woman was right. The skeletons standing in line were quiet. There was no casual joking and none of the banter that had graced the food lines for so long. When had it stopped, she wondered.

"I hear the Executive Committee is going to ask for Mr. Duggleby and others," the woman said.

"Yes." Kate had also heard the rumor. Four men, including Carroll Grinnell, C.L.Larsen, E.E.Johnson, as well as Duggleby, had been taken away by the Japanese military police. No one had heard a thing about them, although they had been gone over eleven days.

A man, not ten ahead of her in line, stepped out and hurriedly headed in the direction of the men's latrine.

"One down," the woman said.

"Maybe he'll be back," Kate said.

"You know, I used to weigh a hundred and forty pounds before the war," the woman said proudly. "I never thought I'd see a size six again."

"How do you know?" Kate asked. All of their clothes it seemed were patched and ragged and homemade. She hadn't seen a label on anything since she had come to Santo Tomas.

The woman grabbed her free hand and placed it on her

scrawny wrist. "That's how I know," she said triumphantly. "Why, I've bones I never even knew I had. Sometimes at night, just to amuse myself, I lie there and count the darned things! Actually count them."

The line was moving slowly, for tickets had to be checked, rechecked and punched before any of the rice was put in pails. These tasks were executed by undernourished, exhausted people and it all took time.

"God, how I'm sick of smoke," the woman continued.

"We all are." Kate looked to the east at the heavy black smoke hanging over Manila. The smell of the burning city was everywhere, in the latrines, in the dormitory rooms, even, she heard, in the convent. It was an acrid heaviness from which there was no escape.

"Lookit that old man over there." The woman pointed to a wasted, drawn man walking slowly and stiffly away from the pot of rice. His knees were like baseballs, attached to the two thin sticks that were passing for legs. Hunched over, the concavity of his stomach cavity seemed close to touching his spine. In truth, he could have been an old man or a young one, for starvation was the great equalizer in making everyone look ancient.

"He's going to die."

Kate stared at him. He was not well, that was apparent, but he didn't look much worse than the rest of them. "How can you tell?"

"His eyes. You can always tell if you look in their eyes. My first husband was a doctor, he told me that."

"The eyes?"

"Uh huh. You get this milkiness that creeps in. Right before you die. He's got it. I know, I stood behind him last night in line."

Kate unconsciously rubbed her own right eye. She would

look in the mirror the minute she got back to the shanty. In fact, she would inspect all of them for the telltale milky film.

The woman was gnawing on her fingers now, stripping off little sections of skin and chewing on them. For the first time, Kate noticed her hands. The sides of her fingers were red and raw. She had apparently been chewing on her own body for some time.

"Something to do." The woman dropped her hand in embarrassment. "Since I quit smoking."

There were few cigarettes in camp these days.

"Fact is, it doesn't taste so bad either." She went back to peeling off the skin with her long yellow teeth. "Some of em's vomiting."

"Yes, I know." Kate had been horrified when she had first heard that some of the internees were vomiting so they could get a new taste in their mouths.

She handed the kitchen worker her ticket and he carefully inspected it before punching it. She proceeded to the man standing at the steaming cauldron, his tin scoop filled with rice. He leveled the scoop before dumping it into her pail.

"How's tricks?" Kate asked, winking at the older man.

"Lots of them today, they're all floating up there on top." The man smiled back at her. It was an old exchange for them. Looking into the pail, Kate saw the white worms, struggling and swimming in the thin, wet rice. At least the stones had sunk to the bottom.

Roll call the next day turned out to last most of the morning. Kate, always nervous during the count twice a day, waited in the dark shelter of the stifling broom closet for hours.

Sitting on the floor, sweat streamed from her body as she tried to pick lice off her skin. Her body was stiff and cramped now and fright began to set in. What if the Japanese had carried out the worst rumors and massacred the entire camp? She waited, her mind ticking off the minutes.

Terrified to leave, afraid to stay, she slowly eased the door open a crack, holding her breath as she listened for sounds in the empty room. Nothing.

She opened the door another few inches and waited, but still no one came to jerk open the closet the rest of the way.

She walked gingerly from her cramped quarters into the large empty room. Heart pounding, she approached the window, standing to one side as she looked out on the ground below. It was littered with internees, standing in lines as the Japanese officers passed among them, counting heads. Here and there in the heat a few had passed out, their inert bodies stretched out in the hot, drying sun. Why, she thought. Why were they doing a count that should have been done hours ago? Relieved that a massacre had not taken place, Kate touched her toes and stretched high to the ceiling before returning to the musty broom closet.

Forty minutes later Magda was at the door.

"What happened?" Kate asked, blinking as she stepped out into the bright light.

"Roll call. Three times," Magda said glumly.

"Where's Ellen?"

"Lying down. The heat," Magda shook her head. It would have been an ordeal under the best of circumstances, but with weakened, exhausted people, it had been inhumane. "I wish I could get my hands on that man."

"Who?"

"Joe Eisenberg. He's missing from the gym. They are looking everywhere for him."

Kate's stomach jerked spasmodically. She could have easily been found out.

"Are you all right?" Magda grabbed her arm to steady her. Kate nodded.

"Oh," Magda added, "they are going to execute anyone trying to escape."

⚚

Sky's body was aching. They had been crawling for over a mile on their bellies, across the flat rice fields in front of Cabanatuan. Just ahead, Berringer could see the eight foot high barbed wire front gate of the prison camp, its heavy padlock barely discernible in the fading light. He followed the man ahead of him into the drainage ditch as he waited for further orders.

They were an odd assortment, Sky thought, this group that had already snuck in twenty-five miles into enemy-held territory. The liberating forces consisted of the 6th Army United States Rangers and the Alamo Scouts. Less than a hundred and thirty soldiers in all, against a hundred Japanese guards and another 1,100 enemy soldiers camped less than a mile from Cabanatuan at the Cabu Bridge. Yet another group of Japanese soldiers of division strength was three miles away in Cabu City. Led by the twenty-seven year old Lieutenant Juan Pajota, a thousand guerrillas were holding all those soldiers at bay, keeping them from crossing the bridge and helping out the small garrison at Cabanatuan. The guerrillas had also knocked out the telephone lines, and would provide rear support for the mass exodus.

A roar startled them all. Sky looked to the sky as the P-61 Night Interceptor Pursuit Airplane, fondly known as the "Black Widow", flew in on a low pass. Berringer had been at Platero barrio last night, just a few miles away, and there had been a big party thrown for the Americans. Plenty of food, dancing and singing. The Rangers had told him all about the Black Widow then. The new Northrop airplane could fly equally well at thirty thousand feet or a hundred, circling at slow speeds without danger of stalling. They had said nothing, however, of her presence here tonight.

That she was a performer was evident now as the sleek, black airplane passed the camp, distracting the guards enough to give the Rangers time to move in closer.

Sky smiled, thinking of last night's festivities. The Filipinos had thought nothing of slaughtering their prized livestock to fete the Americans. Their cooperation, as well as that in the other barrios along the route, was complete when, after the party they put their dogs and chickens inside their homes so none of the animals would sound an alarm when the Americans started out for Cabanatuan.

It was late. Briefly Sky wondered if something had gone wrong with the mission. It was dark now as he peered over the edge of the ditch. Just on the other side of the road, inside the wire, he could see the buildings they had been told were the officer quarters. Through the little yellow squares of light, Sky could see the shapes of the Japanese soldiers getting ready to settle in for the night.

A shot rang out as Lieutenant Murphy, stationed at the rear of the camp, fired the opening signal. Bedlam broke out as a grenade shattered the gate house, the two Japanese guards inside blown to smithereens along with the wooden structure.

They were pouring out of the ditch now, M1's and Browning automatic rifles in hand as they ran to the front gate. Sergeant Richardson reached it before Sky. He battered at the lock with the butt of his Thompson submachine gun, but the heavy metal refused to give.

"Watch it!" Sky yelled as he fired at a Japanese guard who was coming at him. But the Rangers behind them had seen the man too, and his bullet ridden body now lay slumped in the dust.

Richardson leveled his .45 at the stubborn lock and fired. Half of it fell to the ground as they poured in through the front gate.

Sky kept his eye on the tin shed ahead as the bazooka team rushed past him. Intelligence had warned them about the trucks and tanks inside the sheds and it was now imperative that the Weapons Section demolish the shed before the enemy had the opportunity to get any vehicles out. As Sky watched, the first building disintegrated under the bazooka's rocket. The second shed also exploded, taking with it Japanese soldiers and trucks.

Sky was with the First Assault Section of the Second Platoon now, and he ran with them to the prisoner compound in the northeast corner of the camp. Again, the lock that held the barbed wire gate closed was shattered with a bullet. This time by an M1.

Sky ran to the nearest barracks and took the steps two at a time, unprepared for the sight he would find inside. At the sight of the Rangers, a loud cheer went up from the cadre of men who were able to stand. Others, dying and weak, lifted their heads from their cots and attempted to smile.

Sky blanched. These had been men. Strong American soldiers who were now reduced to skeletons with drawn, sunken eyes in tiny, surreal bodies. Their features were almost indistinguishable, eyes uniformly sunken, knees swollen and painful, many with their hands and ankles swollen from beri-beri. Others, drenched with their own sweat and wastes could only wait on their cots for help.

"Where are the rest?" Sky asked a withered soldier.

"The rest?" He was puzzled for a moment. "Oh, they were shipped out months ago."

Sky shook his head. Only the weak, the dead, the dying, had been left behind.

The Rangers worked quickly . Sky went to the closest cot and looked at the scarecrow of a man lying there.

"Can you get up?"

"I don't think so." Tears sprang to the man's dull eyes. He was eager to help, but he knew his limitations. "I haven't walked for two months."

Sky scooped him up, amazed at his light weight. It was like carrying a child. The man, clearly embarrassed, draped his arms around Sky's neck as he carried him out into the night air.

"Put him on your back, the strain will be easier there. Meet at the front gate," the Ranger in charge barked efficient orders.

Sky plodded toward the gate, his burden hardly noticeable, his mind consumed with rage. He had heard that things were bad in Cabanatuan, that food was scarce and the prisoners weak, but to actually see the shriveled human beings was almost more than he could take. His rage turned to fear as he thought of Kate in Santo Tomas.

The Rangers took their precious human cargo back to Platero, protected by the guerrilla troops who held the enemy at bay. Loading them onto carabao carts they were then transported twenty-five miles to the Allied lines.

And so, on January 30, 1945, of the 6,000 prisoners originally interned at Cabanatuan, 516 were liberated.

49

"They're just goat turds, really Petey, you make such a big deal out of everything." Doc was getting angry at his younger brother for making such a big scene, insisting that he had stepped on one of his precious marbles on purpose.

The marble game had broken up anyway, the boys bored with their luck and discouraged by the disintegrating marbles. That was one problem with using the goat droppings, for while they lasted they made pretty good marbles, but they fell apart when they got too old.

"Look at that!" Pete pointed to the sky and the boys stared as six planes came in low over Santo Tomas.

"Pursuit planes," Doc said in awe for the planes were very low. They watched in fascination as they could see, actually see, the face of one of the pilots. "Hey, he's smiling!" Doc waved frantically at the departing airplane.

Pete was running now, running for something that had been dropped from one of the airplanes. Now he had it, and he returned to the group.

"Oh boy! Look at what I've got!" He held up a pair of pilot's goggles. A piece of paper dangled from the well worn protective glasses. Carefully, Pete undid it from the leather strap.

"What's it say?" The boys were crowding around now, eager to hear the pilot's message.

Pete unfurled the paper and read the message out loud. "It says 'roll out the barrel.'"

⚓

The priest was kneeling at the altar, his black robes gathered on the floor while his knees ached with the unaccustomed posture. The Filipino priests had given him the cassock and with that gift he was beginning to feel, for the first time since the war had begun, that he was back in the fold.

The church was almost empty. A few parishioners were in the back and occasionally one would come to light a candle, but it was the dinner hour and most were home with their families. The building was quiet as its stained glass altar windows framed the fading light. The Christ child, with his ancient, cracked face, stared down in wonderment on the empty pews.

Bendetti had been lucky to find the church and the Filipinos willing to take him in. They had kept him under wraps, back in their quarters and only in the very quietest hours had they allowed him into the chapel.

It was against their wishes that he was in the church now, but he had felt an uncontrollable urge to pray. For the first time since he had arrived, he was beginning to think about the children again and now, sheltered in this sanctuary, he could ill afford to indulge himself. Overcome by the need for guidance from his Lord, and he truly believed that His presence was in the chapel, he had come in to pray.

The jeep slowed in the street outside the chapel, stopping just in front of the heavy mahogany doors.

"I'll only be a minute," Sky said as he hopped over the side of the vehicle.

"Take your time. We have plenty," the captain said, not

bothering to look at his watch.

Sky crossed himself before going inside. Upon seeing the church, the first outside the tiny chapel at San Alberto he had seen in over three years, he had felt an almost uncontrollable urge to pray. Somehow the fear of what he could find ahead had gotten to him, and now he was in God's house to ask for forgiveness and guidance and, most of all, for mercy for those he loved.

He bought a candle in the back and slowly approached the altar. He stared for a moment at the *milagros* pinned to the cloth there. Miniature arms, legs, homes, heads, animals, children, every manner of facsimile was represented, gathering dust. All implanted with the giver's fervent hope that one's arm, leg, home, head, animal, child would receive a blessing.

Taking a taper, Sky lit his candle.

George Bendetti raised his head and studied the man at the altar. As the man turned, his profile was to the priest. Berringer!

Slowly, so as not to cause attention, Bendetti gathered his robes and made for the closest exit from the altar. But he was not fast enough, for as he walked quickly to the door he heard Sky's voice ring out.

"Father!" The guerrilla had seen something familiar in the back of the departing priest. "Wait, Father."

Berringer was quickly closing the space between them, but Bendetti had his head down, eager to get back to the priest's quarters. As long as Berringer was not sure of his identity, then perhaps he would not pursue the fleeing black robed figure.

Bendetti was at the door now and as he closed it behind him he broke into a run, passing through yet another portal. The garden lay ahead, a broad expanse of green. That would take too long to cross, he thought, turning off to the left through another wooden door.

An office was to his right, small and cramped and through the opened door he could see Father Espinosa there, poring over the church books. Bendetti hesitated a moment.

He ran down the corridor and opened the outside door at the end, purposefully leaving it ajar. Turning back, he entered a small door inside the corridor which led to the church's bell tower. Taking the steps two at a time, he climbed quickly to the top and fumbled with the door. Once inside, he stood, panting and gasping for breath, and waited. He checked the doorknob looking for a way to secure the door, but there was none.

As he looked around the small space he realized he was trapped. There was no way out, other than the narrow staircase he had just ascended. The heavy iron bell, its rope tied to the side stood quiet and still. Quickly Bendetti looked around for a weapon but there was none. Still, he thought, maybe Berringer would fall for the door he had left open, thinking he had run outside. If he did follow him up to the bell tower, he would be winded when he hit the top of the stairs. That in itself would be a considerable advantage.

He listened.

Nothing.

He strained his ear toward the bell, hoping the acoustics would allow some noise to waft upward. Still nothing. The priest began to breathe easier. Perhaps Berringer had decided he was mistaken.

With a crash the door flew open and the guerrilla came barreling in. "Bendetti!" He roared.

As he advanced, the priest retreated toward the rear of the small platform. Suddenly he stood straight and still. There was no reason to fear Berringer. He had done nothing wrong, save take a sick woman to the hospital. That was all Berringer knew.

"Easy," he held up his hands. "I understand your anger, but she was sick, you know that."

"You took her against her will!" Berringer's fists hung clenched at his sides, veins popping out on his forehead as he strained to control himself.

"She was delirious, not capable of making a decision."

"And you made it for her!"

"Yes." A smug look crossed the priest's face. There was nothing, he was sure of that now, nothing to fear. He was in control and would remain so.

"What have you done with Charlie?" Sky's words spilled out through clenched teeth.

"Charlie?" The priest feigned puzzlement.

"Begay. You know goddamned good and well who I mean."

"Oh yes, the Indian. Is he missing?"

The innocence was not convincing and something, a glint, an intuitive knowingness came over Berringer.

"You've killed him," he said woodenly.

"You've no proof of that. I'm a priest." In spite of his resolve, beads of perspiration were beginning to stand out above his heavy upper lip. He fanned his hands in front of him. "Priests don't kill people."

Enraged, Sky flew across the space separating the two of them, his hands lunging for Bendetti's throat. But the priest expected the charge and he easily blocked it with an uplifted knee, catching Berringer squarely in the groin. Sky collapsed to the floor, curling into a fetal position, his hands clutching his wounded scrotum as Bendetti kicked him sharply in the ribs.

"You've no cause to be angry," he said softly as he uncurled the bell rope, aware now of the excitement surging through his body. "No cause at all."

The voice was back, taking over for him, telling him what to do. The rope was now free of its anchor, and he placed his knee in Sky's back and wrapped it twice around his neck. As Sky struggled, Bendetti jerked the rope hard, catching his wind.

"I didn't want it to be this way," Bendetti crooned to his trapped prey. "I really thought you'd be more of a challenge. This is so easy."

Sky jerked against the rope, struggling for freedom but Bendetti had the advantage and he pulled it even tighter. Berringer could not breathe now and his elbows flailed helplessly as he tried to make contact with the errant priest.

"Your friend was more difficult. Maybe it's the Indian blood. You're soft, Berringer."

Sky's eyes were bulging and his face blued from lack of oxygen. His hands clawed at the constricting rope but Bendetti used the leverage of his knee to keep it taut.

"Father, what is happening here?" Father Espinosa, in spite of his eighty years, had climbed the belfry stairs.

It was enough to throw Bendetti off balance and as his grip on the rope slackened, Sky elbowed him hard in the stomach, rolling away from him as he did so. But the rope was still around his neck and as he struggled to his feet, Bendetti grabbed it, jerking him along like a reluctant marionette.

Sky grabbed the rope, giving himself slack as he loosened it from around his neck.

"Father Bendetti!" Espinosa was dancing around the two men now, trying to get the priest's attention. But Bendetti was having none of it, as he shoved the frail father out of his way and lunged again for Berringer.

They were wrestling now, wound up together in the rope and each other as they struggled. Bendetti had Sky against the belfry railing, pushing and shoving in an effort to throw him over, but Sky's right foot wrapped around Bendetti's left, causing him to fall to his knees as Sky eased back from the probable fall.

The priest was on his feet, quickly lunging for him again and this time as he came, Sky waited for the last moment before dodging to one side. The force of his charge, timed at a now non-existent target, was enough to send Bendetti hard into and over the railing. He fought to stop himself as he plunged over, hitting the heavy bell as he fell.

Sky unwrapped himself from the rope and looked over the railing to the ground below.

There, spread-eagled against the cool red tiles, was the broken body of the aberrant priest.

"Holy Mother of God!" Father Espinosa was beside Sky crossing himself as he looked below.

Berringer ran down the stairs, pausing at the bottom only long enough to feel for Bendetti's pulse. There was none. Quickly, he left the church.

Captain Colayco started the jeep's engine. "All set?"

"Yeah. Thanks Manny." Berringer did not look back as they left the neighborhood church.

They did not have far to drive and again the Filipino captain stopped the jeep. They waited in the fading light. Sky said nothing, knowing that the captain and his Guerrilla Intelligence Unit had everything under control.

"Not very pretty, is it?" Sky asked, pointing toward Manila. The smoke was hanging over the torn city, casting an eery red light in the dusk.

"No and I'm afraid it's going to get worse before it's over." He leaned forward, resting his arms on the jeep's steering wheel. "Now there's a pretty sight."

In the dusk, Sky could make out a column of American tanks. The United States First Cavalry, with its armored "flying columns" had arrived. They had penetrated the enemy lines, ahead of the 37th Infantry and the 11th Airborne Division, to liberate Santo Tomas.

"This is the big one," Sky said, settling back in his seat as Captain Colayco guided the columns through Manila and onto Rizal Avenue, weaving in and out among the mine fields and other Japanese booby traps.

Colayco knew the streets like the back of his hand and that knowledge, coupled with the guerrilla intelligence, was taking them unharmed to their final destination.

☙

The two women stared out the window at the angry red sky. Fires, deliberately set by the Japanese demolition crews, blazed across Manila as history repeated itself. Materiel and warehouses, ammunition dumps, fuel supplies, the very items the Americans had been so eager to dispose of over three years earlier, were now being torched by the Japanese Imperial Army. Flares shot up to the north. Santo Tomas was blacked out tonight and that made the color of the sky all the more dramatic.

"Do you think we'll ever get used to that sound?" Ellen asked. The popping of gunfire from the southern part of the city had not let up.

Magda came into the room and joined them at the window. "They have been burning records all day," she said softly.

"The end is near," Ellen shook her head, "It must be."

"Yes," Kate agreed, "whatever that is."

"Do you think they'll kill us?" Ellen whispered, afraid to let her fears have a stronger voice.

"No, not really," Kate said. They had all heard the rumor. The men would be killed, women and children would be taken to Japan and held as hostages. It was only rumor, although the Japanese had made a list of all the males over eighteen years old.

The loudspeaker crackled. "Attention. All internees. Keep away from the windows."

It crackled and buzzed its static message a second time before dying out.

The three women sat together on Ellen's bed. Kate reached out for each of them and held their hands. They were silent, as their eyes stared at the windows, their ears straining for some sound, some clue as to what was happening outside their prison walls.

Suddenly light filled the room, streaming in through the window.

"Listen." Kate whispered, and as she did they could all feel the rumbling and shaking of the building.

"Is it an earthquake?" Ellen asked.

"I don't think so," Kate replied as they sat.

And waited.

50

Santo Tomas was ahead, her hulking tower with the gigantic cross on top, barely discernible in the darkness.

Running ahead of the tanks and jeep, a select force of one hundred men were busy scaling the fence that had imprisoned the Americans for so long. They would surprise the Japanese guards from the rear, taking as many of them as they could.

Captain Colayco pulled the jeep to one side of the road, allowing *Battling Basic*, the first of the tanks, to pass him. He looked at his watch.

"Almost nine o'clock," he said to Sky.

Without hesitation, the heavy lumbering tank charged through the locked main gate of the University of Santo Tomas, ripping and wrenching the large iron gates as it passed through the portal, its searchlight seeking out the buildings and guard towers of the Japanese. Four more tanks followed.

Colayco's jeep fell in behind the last tank. As the vehicle passed through, Sky jumped from the side, withdrawing his .38 from the waistband of his pants.

"Good luck, Manny," he said as the jeep pulled away from him. He began running toward the Woman's Dormitory building. Flares shot up all around now, illuminating the blacked out camp.

A Japanese soldier in the gate's guardhouse lobbed a grenade, missed the tank and hit the jeep. It exploded on impact, and within seconds Captain Manuel Colayco of the Guerrilla Intelligence unit lay dead.

The battle for Santo Tomas was over in minutes.

Suddenly the internees came pouring out of the buildings, filling the front plaza.

"Are you real?" Ellen stared at the tall Texas soldier in front of her, his skin yellowed from taking Atabrine. He was so big, she thought. Tall. It was like looking at a giant. Then she figured it out. The man had real flesh on his bones, there was none of the gaunt, haunted look about him that so many of them had.

"Yes ma'am, I'm real all right," he drawled. He handed her a flashlight. "You use this until the lights come on."

There were photographers everywhere, clicking, snapping, recording. The headlights from the tanks and the flares illuminated the patio and cast an eery glow on the cheering, dancing people.

Internees were rushing by Ellen. As Magda passed, she reached out and grabbed her.

"Come. They have Lieutenant Abiko."

Caught up in the frenzied crowd, Ellen followed Magda to the front of the main building. Profanity and threats were flying through the air, all of them directed at the hated Japanese guard.

Magda pushed and pummeled her way through the crowd until they stood at the edge of it, facing the downed Abiko. He was curled up on the floor, his hands clutching a bullet hole in his stomach as his blood oozed and spilled into the dirt. His left ear was dangling from the side of his face, slashed nearly off.

"Filthy Jap!" A woman spat on him, while another poked him with the lit end of an American cigarette. A man worked quickly around the dying guard, slashing the buttons off his uniform for souvenirs.

The crowd was pushing and shoving now, yelling at him, spitting on him as he lay in dying agony, soiling himself with his own urine and blood. Human sounds escaped him as a series of wild animal whimpers came from his crumpled body.

"I've seen enough," Ellen turned, leaving Magda to appreciate the last agony of the dying Lieutenant Abiko. She struggled to contain the bile that was rising in her throat.

"Ellen!" Kate ran up. "I've been looking everywhere for you." She grabbed Ellen's arm. "The Japanese have taken the Education Building!"

"What?" Ellen stopped walking, her hand a death grip on Kate's own.

"The Education Building. There are about sixty soldiers in there. Commandant Hayashi's trying to make some kind of deal."

"My boys?" She asked, fear gripping her fine features.

"I don't know. No one's seen them. They've got about two hundred hostages in there."

A cold chill spread through Ellen's stomach as she raced to the Education Building.

Its face was pocked with shellfire and it was ringed now with American sharpshooters. An interpreter was standing outside yelling at the Japanese.

Suddenly shots rang out, and an American tank, parked a couple of hundred feet away, turned on its headlights and opened fire.

"No!" Ellen screamed and began running toward the building. She was stopped well short of it by an American soldier.

"You can't go in there," he said gently, walking her back to the sidelines.

"My boys, my babies," Ellen was sobbing now, frantic for Doc and Pete.

"I'm sorry, ma'am. We're doing all we can," the soldier explained kindly. "General Chase is negotiating now." Actually Lieutenant Colonel Charles Brady was handling the negotiations for the general.

Kate gently pulled Ellen away from the young soldier. "It's going to be all right," she said trying to soothe the distraught woman.

Now more women were coming, screaming, trying to run for the building. They were desperate and unbelieving that they could come through the war this far to have their children and husbands held hostage by the Japanese. Everywhere, comfort and restraint was given to the terrified women.

"Oh God, no!" Ellen collapsed again into Kate's arms. Barely aware of the strong man that came up and encircled both women with his powerful body.

"Sky!" Kate yelled, throwing her arms around his neck. Now she too broke into tears as she pulled Sky and Ellen to her.

"The boys are in there," Kate pointed to the building and Sky nodded.

"They're working on it now, Ellen," he said. He did not tell them he had overheard the American soldiers talking about the Japanese commandant's opinion that surrender was not compatible with Japanese military doctrine.

"Yes, I know," she was trying to get under control, dabbing her red eyes with the tail of her blouse. "God, how I wish Tom was here."

Sky was silent, not wanting to tell her that they had not found him at Cabanatuan.

"Katie, take her back to the dorm, let her get some rest."

"No." Ellen's feet were firmly planted, her posture straight.

She would not leave the area until her boys were safe.

It was a long night for all of them as they huddled in the darkness, waiting for word that the hostages had been released. As dawn broke, negotiations were still deadlocked.

"There's Doc!" Kate pointed up to the third floor where several young boys were smiling and waving to the people down below.

Ellen blew her oldest son a kiss and pounded her flat hand to her heart. She pointed to herself, pounded her chest and pointed at him. It was an old pantomime they had used for years. *I love you.* Doc repeated the gestures and then held up his fingers, the second one wide from the third, in a clear victory sign before disappearing from the open window.

"So far, so good," Sky muttered, happy to see at least one of Ellen's children. "All right, let's get you something to eat." He steered them away from the building. "We can come back right after." Like zombies, the two women followed him through the maze of waiting relatives and soldiers.

The liberating troops had set up on the front ground, roughly in the same spot the Japanese troops had occupied just weeks earlier. Tents were pitched, trenches and foxholes dug, campfires burned, as soldiers slouched against trucks and tanks named *San Antone* and *Georgia Peach*.

The strong smell of coffee, absent for so many months at Santo Tomas, was back, along with the aromas of cooking oil, bacon and tinned ham. It was assaulting all of their exhausted senses at once.

Sky led them to a group of soldiers cooking under the trees. Fluffy scrambled eggs shared their skillet with ham, "Have you got any breakfast to spare?"

"Yes, sir." A soldier quickly collected three mess kits and

filled them with the army rations, adding canned tomatoes, the first the women had seen in three years. He handed the kits to them before filling the canteen cups with the strong, steaming coffee.

"It's so much," Ellen stared at the pile of food.

Sky walked them over to a stack of wooden boxes and they sat down and began to eat. After the third bite, Ellen knew she was in trouble.

"Excuse me," she said, putting the mess kit down.

She ran from them, only making it a few yards before the scrambled eggs came up again. The food was too rich. She could not handle it, she thought, as she stared at the sad mixture of eggs and worms that had come out of her stomach.

Soon Kate, too, was beside her, disgorging her first real breakfast in months.

⚔

"We can do it, I tell you we can," Doc was using every ounce of persuasion he could muster on his younger brother.

"I don't know. If we're wrong, Mom will kill us."

"I'm right, Petey, I know I am." Doc tugged and pulled on him, drawing him up to the window. "Look at that! That lady over there is eating food, Petey, real food! And look at the soldiers."

Doc did not have to tell him to look at any of it, he had been watching all day, and was as eager as any of them to join the happy people down below.

"Aren't you hungry?" Doc goaded. Although food had been sent in for all of them, the Japanese had wasted little time in eating it.

Pete nodded.

"OK, then follow me."

Doc crept down the hallway, clutching the Benjamin air pistol to his chest as Pete followed him. They had been captives for a little more than twenty-four hours and now, after hours of begging, bribery and threats, Doc had finally convinced his younger brother to follow him on this daring freedom mission.

They were in luck, for there were no guards in the hall. Moving quickly, they dashed to the back staircase and slowly started down, pausing and listening every few steps. But the building was quiet due to the late hour.

"Almost home free," Doc whispered words of encouragement to Pete. "We're almost there."

The Japanese guard looked up in time to see the two boys on the landing above him. He scowled and brushed his hand at them, indicating they were to go back up the stairs.

Doc hesitated and then raised the empty air pistol, aiming it straight at the Japanese guard.

"Move away from the door," he said in his deepest voice.

A look of surprise crossed the guard's flat features. He turned to the side, just enough so they would not see his right hand drop to his holstered belt. Mumbling in Japanese, he spoke loudly even as he cocked his own weapon.

"We're coming down," Doc's voice was shaking slightly, betraying his flagging confidence.

The guard twisted his body and faced them full again as he drew up his cocked gun. He took careful aim, sighting in on the largest boy, the most likely target in the dim light. The boy's head was centered in the sight now. Just before he pulled the trigger, he reconsidered.

"Go up there." he growled in broken English as the boys disappeared from the landing.

✈

"It's set," Sky walked up to them. "The deal's been made."

"Thank God," A wave of relief passed through Ellen. "When?"

"The Japanese will be coming out at first light."

"Alone?" Kate asked.

"American soldiers will escort them to their front lines. The hostages will be left behind."

"Are they keeping their guns?" Kate knew that the Japanese had insisted upon "safe conduct with honor" which meant they intended on keeping their weapons.

"We're taking the grenades and machine guns. They're keeping their personal weapons."

Slowly the contingent began exiting the Education Building. The first ones out were the hundred American soldiers who would provide the escort. The sixty-five Japanese followed them, and once outside they all fell into formation, the Japanese marching three abreast, guarded by American soldiers in columns of twos. They walked quickly through the camp and although it was still early morning, small groups of internees followed them, yelling and hooting at their defeated captors. It was a moment of glory for those who had been under Japanese rule for so long.

✈

"Oh, I don't know. Don't you think this one?" Ellen held up a tattered floral print, long-sleeved blouse in front of the one she had on.

"I can't tell. Magda?" Kate turned to the Czech woman who was already wearing a dress.

"Either is fine," the redhead said. "They both have the right sleeves, ya."

They had all discussed it. The occasion was a grand one and they wanted to look their best. While the American soldiers had brought in food and some medicine, clothing was still at a premium and they had to make do with what they had brought into Santo Tomas.

"The sleeves are important," Kate said tugging self-consciously on her own long-sleeved dress. It had been one point on which they had all agreed. Long sleeves. To cover their scrawny arms. Even the men were wearing long sleeved shirts to cover the embarrassingly thin upper arms, many of which resembled those of ten year old children.

The army doctors had looked many of them over and when the statistics were finally in they would show an average loss of twenty-seven percent of body weight for the internees. The women were averaging a hundred pounds with the men a scant twelve pounds more.

"Ready, Mother?" Doc stood in the door, wearing his only pair of long trousers, his hair wet and plastered to his skull, evidence of his having slaved over combing it. Pete stood beside him, clean in his tattered cotton shirt and well-worn shorts.

"My, don't you boys look handsome!" Kate clapped her hands together. "We should have a picture."

"Yes, if we had a camera," Ellen said.

Magda laughed. "I do not think that will be a problem. Have you not seen all the photographers and newsreel men?"

The media had been at the camp since its moment of liberation. Even Carl Mydans, the *Life* photographer who had been interned with them for nine months before being repatriated on a prisoner release program, had come back to capture their liberation on film. Soon his pictures would grace the magazine.

"Well, your father is going to be sorry he missed such a grand occasion," Ellen said with forced gaiety. "Maybe we can twist someone's arm to take a shot of you two if you promise not to break the camera!"

Magda stared out the window, tears in her eyes.

"There." Ellen finished folding the rejected print blouse. "Now we're ready. How about Sky?"

"He's meeting us downstairs," Kate said as they left the room.

"Beautiful! Beautiful!" Sky put an arm around both Kate and Ellen. "The three of you are enough to turn any man's head and I'm the lucky soul who gets to serve as your consort."

"Please. Escort!" Ellen protested, laughing.

"Chaperone will be more likely. There are some pretty eager soldiers here."

"Ya!" Magda's eyes shone gaily. She already knew about that. Quickie romances had already been formed and now many of the people were complaining about the rum bottles and used condoms found every morning on the university grounds.

The internees were all walking toward the Administration Building. Crowds of them, dressed in the finest clothes they could muster together, their hair combed, faces shining, and, for some, their skin slowly returning to a somewhat normal shade.

Cameras were snapping everywhere and newsreel men walked backwards in an effort to preserve the liberated people on film that would be shown not only back home, but around the world.

The internees were alive! Santo Tomas was freed!

The front of the Administration Building was packed with people of all ages. Women, men, soldiers, Americans, British, Dutch, Poles, the old and the infirm sat on the ground, or on chairs, while small children played tag, oblivious to the occasion.

The doors to the balcony hanging above the entrance were opened now. Soldiers stood at attention on the sides of the entrance while military men and members of the Executive Committee walked in and out of the building.

An American soldier came up to Magda.

"Hello there." His eyes never left her face. "Mind if I join you?"

She hooked her arm in his. "I can not think of anything nicer than to be with you Americans on such a day!"

They worked their way to the edge of the crowd, angling for a place on the side where they would have a good view of the balcony. Now there were two soldiers standing at attention beside the opened balcony doors.

"Here she comes!" Someone yelled and a hush fell over the crowd.

Two more soldiers, crisp in their fresh uniforms, clean for the occasion, walked steadily across the balcony. They were carrying something between them, carrying it with great pride and respect.

"God bless America," a lone voice said.

It spread throughout the crowd. "God bless America. God bless America."

And then the singing began.

"Land that we love. Stand beside her, and guide her,"

Voices were cracking, people crying, spines filled with chills and hearts with love for their homeland so far away.

"Through the night with the light from above."

The soldiers were to the edge of the balcony. They knelt and positioned their treasure, securing it to the balcony's edge.

Assured that she was safe, with no danger of falling, they slowly unfurled the American flag.

"From the mountains," they sang.

"To the prairies," the stars and stripes were now clearly visible.

"To the oceans, white with foam," a breeze rippled the flag giving her the motions of the living.

"God bless America. My home sweet home."

The Americans *had* come home.

AFTERWORD

I can still remember that day. Seated on the floor of a public library, I was looking at a March 5, 1945 edition of *Life* magazine studying the photos of the liberation of Santo Tomas taken by the photographer, Carl Mydans.

As I looked at a blonde, curly headed boy in the second story window of one of the buildings held by the Japanese, chills assaulted me and tears flooded my eyes. The boy, who looked so much like my own son, was my husband.

I had heard the family stories and I had come to the library to learn a little more about this chapter of American history. Little did I know that day that I would be hooked on a project that would take years to complete.

America's Best is the kind of novel I like to read, a blend of fact and fiction. When I read a book of this sort, I often find myself wondering, what *was* true? Fiction?

In the case of this novel, most of it is true. While I have a fairly wild imagination, it could not begin to compete against many of the war vignettes I encountered while doing my research. The story was there, I just implanted a few fictional characters against the backdrop of the Philippines during the second World War.

The Sullivan family in **America's Best** is loosely patterned after my husband's family. His father, Horace Benjamin Browning, known as Mike, like Tom Sullivan in the book, was the chief engineer for the Benguet Consolidated Mines in Baguio. Like his fictional counterpart, he was asked to go to Corregidor by General MacArthur, was interned at Cabanatuan, and was killed on board the *Arisan Maru*.

The spotting of airplanes by Kate and Ellen, the bombing of Camp John Hay, the Brereton party and Pearl Harbor is all true. In fact, other than a few minor skirmishes the characters are involved in, all of the military history is true, including the massacre of the owner of Good Joe's and his employees, although the name of the tavern is fictional. It is thought that the Filipino tavern owner was largely responsible for the Japanese success of the Clark Field air raid, including the loss of the majority of our Flying Fortresses.

The Clark Field bombing, and the evacuation of the Baguio people to Manila is true, as is the blowing up of bridges and roads to Baguio, the camouflaging of the gold mine and fuel supplies there, and the razing of supply depots and destruction of anything that might be useful to the Japanese. The shooting of the Alhambra cigar sign outside Manila really took place.

All of the events dealing with the major historical personalities, including Presidents Franklin Delano Roosevelt and Manuel Quezon, Ferdinand Marcos, General Douglas MacArthur, Major Generals Jonathan Wainwright and Edward King, and their Japanese counterparts: Generals Masaharu Homma and Hideki Tojo, Vice-Admiral Jisaburo Ozawa, Colonel Motoo Nakayama, and Carlos Romulo and Tokyo Rose are true.

The exodus into Bataan, and the blowing up of Calumpit Bridge is all factual, as is the fighting (including the obsolete weaponry used by the Americans and Filipinos) that took place on the Bataan Peninsula. Pat Casey is real. And, although it grieved him to do so, General Wainwright did order his beloved horse, Joseph Conrad, to be the first horse of the 26th Cavalry to be shot to feed the starving men on Bataan.

The Japanese surrender tickets, the dropping of beer bottles and the *"Dugout Doug"* song are all true.

The dumping of silver in Manila Harbor and the burning of currency all took place. It is estimated that $16 million in silver was dumped into the bay. During their occupation of the Philippines, the Japanese used American sailors and Moro pearl divers to recover as much of it as they could. After the war the U.S. Seventh Fleet returned to Manila and recovered even more of the treasure. While it is anyone's guess as to how much of the precious metal still lies embedded in the wet rock and coral, some estimate that $8 million is still there, waiting to be recovered.

During the writing of the book, at times I felt as though I were there. While there are those who will call me sentimental, I believe that the spirit of Mike Browning, the father-in-law I never knew, was with me when I wrote **America's Best**.

As I struggled with the story, I would receive affirmations that I was meant to write this book. The first, and perhaps strongest of these, occurred when I read the actual names of the first three men to escape from Santo Tomas.

Fletcher. Weeks. Laycock.

Fletcher, my grandfather's first name.

Weeks, my mother's last married name.

Laycock, the name of the obstetrician who delivered my younger sister, my younger brother and my only child.

With this affirmation, I not only had to keep writing, but I knew there would be other signals along the way.

My husband Bill, his brother Mike, and their mother Mary Louise were all interned in the University of Santo Tomas. Many of the pre-war and Santo Tomas segments of the novel are taken from their memories. The fly contests, boxing matches, embroidered handkerchiefs, smuggling in of liquor by the Pan Am pilots (among others), and secret radio conversations are all true. The Episcopal Prayer Book was used on more than one occasion to roll cigarettes from the leavings of the Japanese.

The Santo Tomas guard Tejiro was real as was the sadistic Lt. Abiko (nicknamed "Shitface").

Even the trading of the Leica camera took place. As a curious aftermath, the camera was actually tracked down after the war and returned to the family. After Mary Lou traded the camera for food, the Japanese guard took his new treasure to a camera shop in Manila. The proprietor recognized it, as he had made the custom case which looked like an overnight bag. The shop owner saved the camera for the Brownings but couldn't locate them when the war was over. He then gave the camera to one of Mike's friends who went to South America after the war. He later gave it to Mary Lou who sold it for $900, money which helped in lean times. Before she sold the camera she had the film in it developed and found pictures of the Benguet men camouflaging the mine and fuel supplies.

The Bataan Death March was infamous. Horrifying as it may seem, the incidents related in the book- the casual torture and shooting of American and Filipino soldiers, burying them alive, running over hospital patients with tanks, the Japanese insistence on the marchers drinking from contaminated carabao wallows when fresh water was available, and the lack of food all happened. On a happier note, so did the strong support of the Filipinos including women who hid Americans beneath their skirts.

The Cabanatuan and Camp O'Donnell segments are drawn from history, including the Japanese refusal to honor the terms of the Geneva Convention, the high daily death rates at O'Donnell, the death details, the darky's gang, the work detail rule, and sadly, even the lottery for the diphtheria serum.

In Cabanatuan the rat hunts along the drainage ditches, Zero Ward, the vest pocket assholes, the food, worms, latrine ditches, black market and quan pots are all true. As are the salt tablets manufactured by the Americans and sold to the Japanese as medicine to treat their gonorrhea. The movie *"Down with the Stars and Stripes"* was filmed. The guards Donald Duck, Big Speedo and the most hated, Lance Corporal Kazutane Aiharo, known as "Air Raid", were real personages.

The carving of mess kits took place, and one of our family treasures is the cribbage board and a pair of dice made by Mike Browning, while in Cabanatuan, for his oldest son's birthday. The bases are carabao; the pegs and insets are made from the plastic handles of the toothbrushes sent into the camp by the Red Cross. Many men kept diaries and buried them in the soil of Cabanatuan.

The Corregidor and Malinta Tunnel scenes were also drawn around real events. Irving Strobing was a real soldier, and his last radio broadcast from Corregidor before it fell, is reproduced here as it was actually recited. Wainwright's men, even the weak and the dying, standing to salute him as he left Malinta Tunnel is also true.

The Filipina patriot in the book, Isabel Fajardo, is modeled after Trinidad Diaz, a real Filipina who was a cashier at a cement factory in Luzon, who helped the guerrillas, and who was caught by the Japanese. Diaz was tortured for thirty-two days before dying with honor. She died without ever revealing any of the guerrillas. It is to her memory that I dedicate this part of the book, perhaps one of the most difficult scenes I have ever had to write.

Over one hundred books on America's involvement in the South Pacific were read, as well as dozens of magazine and newspaper articles. Personal letters and unpublished manuscripts were also researched for this work. The most painful of those were the love letters written by my father-in-law to his wife. Folded into tiny packets so many of them could be carried out at one time, letters were smuggled out of Cabanatuan and into Santo Tomas by Catholic priests and guerrillas. The sentiments expressed in them are as moving fifty years later as they were then. One of Mike Browning's actual letters is presented in Chapter 28 as a letter from Tom to Ellen, although the paragraph about Bark is fictional.

There were many guerrilla bands in the Philippines, most of them consisting of Filipinos. They were not well armed and in many cases had to rely on bolos and bow and arrows. The following guerrilla leaders in the book were all real: Colonels Marcus Agustin and Wendell W. Fertig, Lieutenant Colonels Guillermo Nakar, Macario Peralta Jr., and Russell W. Volckmann, Major Robert Lapham, Captain Ralph Praeger Jr., and Lieutenants Ramon Magsaysay and Juan Pajota, Primitivo San Agustin.

Chick Parsons lived in the Philippines for years before war broke out. After getting his family out, he volunteered his services and began Spyron. Not only was he an emissary to the guerrilla groups, but he was able, over the years, to get 450 Americans out of the Philippines on Spyron submarines, in spite of the Japanese occupation.

Clare Philips, the nightclub owner known as "High Pockets", was also real, and an important communication link for the guerrillas in the Philippines.

The Coast Watchers and the Navajo Code Talkers were active groups in the South Pacific.

When I decided that my Navajo character Charlie Begay was going to be a code-talker for this book, I began to research the group. I finally found a book that dealt with the code-talkers. Although the group eventually ran into the hundreds, in the beginning there were only twenty-nine of them. As I looked at the picture of the initial group, and read the names below, imagine my surprise to find one Charlie Begay looking back at me!

Bingo. Another affirmation. I kept writing.

And while the fictional Begay has no basis in fact from the actual Begay (a common Navajo name), I'm sure that many of our code-talkers were every bit as heroic as their fictional counterpart. As far as I know the Navajo code-talkers were never in the Philippines, although twenty-two Navajo men were in the New Mexico National Guard. They were on Bataan when it fell and were on the Death March. Two or three of them were interrogated and forced by the Japanese to listen to the code, but since they had not been trained as code-talkers it sounded like gibberish to them.

The Enemy Way ceremony is accurate as I know it. Legend has it that in May of 1944 such a ceremony was held for 150 Navajo warriors who were still in active service. The ritual lasted all night. Ornate prayer feathers were planted on American soil to insure the return of the men. Many Navajos who served in the second World War, upon returning to the United States, engaged in similar curing ceremonials.

George Bendetti, I am happy to report, is a novelist's creation, thrown in, just in case the war was not giving the reader enough emotional tension.

The dreaded Japanese secret police the *kempei-tai* were real, and carried out their torture in Fort Santiago.

As far as I know, no one was ever smuggled into Santo Tomas.

Tun Yun Lee, the Chinese man who refused the Red Cross packages and who refused to sign the escape oath, was real.

Other real Santo Tomas characters included Alfred F. Duggleby, Carroll C.Grinnell, Clifford L. Larsen and Bertram G. Leake. Duggleby, Grinnell and Larsen were actually taken from Santo Tomas right before liberation. Their tortured bodies were recovered the following month by the Americans.

The Japanese used the Santo Tomas tower to signal their military. All of the segments relating to the Americans returning to the Philippines are based on actual accounts.

The hell ships were just that. There were many of them, and our men were herded into crowded, sweltering holds where many went crazy and died.

While numerous personal interviews were done for this book, probably the most spectacular among them was my interview with Calvin Graef, first sergeant of Battery 8 of the 515th Anti-Air-craft Coast Guard Artillery. Not only is he a survivor of the Bataan Death March and Cabanatuan, but he was one of nine men, out of 1,782, who survived the sinking of the *Arisan Maru* by the *USS Shark II*. Graef, along with four others made it to mainland China in a life boat. Three other men were picked up by a Japanese destroyer and one floated on a wooden raft for four days before being picked up by a Japanese merchant ship bound for Formosa.

Today we hear of casualties and fatalities due to "friendly" fire. Most of us have heard of the *Titanic* and the *Lusitania*. Yet fifty years ago we had a ship carrying almost 1800 Americans that was torpedoed by an American submarine and no one has ever heard of it!

Calvin Graef graciously shared with me his recollections of his time on the *Arisan Maru.* He remembers seeing the plate that identified the ship as being American made. I am grateful to him for also sharing those last minutes before the *Arisan Maru* was hit, and what happened after. He told me that in the midst of all the death and despair and fighting in the hell ship, that an American got up and gave a speech about dying like Americans. And while I do not know who that inspiring man was, I have modeled Bark in his memory, and his speech as it is given in Chapter 45 is patterned after the encouraging speech that American gave to his heartsick comrades so many years ago.

On the 24th of October, 1944 the *USS Sea Dragon* received a message from the *USS Shark II* stating that she was going to attack an enemy freighter. In a naval diary it was reported that "after the *Arisan Maru* was torpedoed the Japanese escorts counter attacked. Seventeen depth charges were dropped, bubbles, heavy oil, clothing and cork came to the surface of the exploding sea." The *USS Shark II* was never heard from again and it is assumed that she went down either during or after her attack on the *Arisan Maru.*

The drowning of the desperate Americans by those on the Japanese destroyer is true.

Mary Lou Browning actually traded her one carat diamond solitaire for a can of Spam so her children would not go hungry. And, while the Brownings did not have cat for Thanksgiving dinner in 1944, one of the families did. In fact, as food became scarce, puppies, pigeons, even toads caught in the latrines, were all eaten.

Joe Eisenberg was a real Santo Tomas internee who escaped.

The liberation of Cabanatuan by the U.S. Rangers and Filipino guerrillas is presented as it actually happened.

The Christmas message that Pete found was dropped into Santo Tomas by an American flier on Christmas day.

Captain Manuel Colayco of the Guerrilla Intelligence Unit was real. He was killed by a grenade while guiding the American troops to Santo Tomas.

The liberation of Santo Tomas is also based on history. The flying columns of the First Cavalry Division raced ahead of the U.S. 6th Army to free the Americans and their allies.

The Japanese held 220 men and boys in the Education Building for a tense thirty-six hours, finally bartering their release for safe passage to their own lines.

And finally, the closing passage in the book, again, one of the most moving, actually happened. In early February of 1945, the American flag was unfurled from a second story balcony as members of the allied nations sang *"God Bless America"*.

Veterans of the Bataan Death March still meet every year. I was thrilled when Calvin Graef invited me to a convention in Las Cruces, New Mexico. There I conducted personal interviews with men who were on the Death March, who were on Corregidor when it fell, and who were interned at Japanese POW camps including Cabanatuan, Quezon City, Davao and Bilibid Prison in the Philippines, Kenose, Japan, Kyushu, Formosa and Mukden and Manchuria in China.

I talked to the "regular" guys. Men who served on death details at Camp O'Donnell, who were 37mm anti-aircraft gunners on Bataan, and who were survivors of the hell ships *Nagata Maru* and the *Benjo Maru* (the Americans name for the hell ship whose name they never knew).

Corregidor nurses and army personnel who were personal friends of Generals MacArthur and Wainwright were also interviewed.

Over the course of three days, I laughed with, drank with and cried with, the most amazing group of people I have ever met. These Americans, caught in a war and circumstances not of their own choosing, really exemplify what is best about our great country.

While in New Mexico, a third affirmation came to me. On a bright Saturday morning we all stood in a hotel parking lot. A makeshift altar carried candles representing the men who had died on the Bataan Death March, and the men who had survived but had since died. The American flag flew proudly on a standard. As it was lowered and replaced by a white flag signifying the surrender of Bataan, a twenty-one gun salute was given.

Then all of us began singing *"God Bless America"*.

It was unnerving. I found myself re-enacting a scene I had written only a month earlier.

It was a great finale for the most memorable writing project I have ever tackled.

When what was left of the Browning family finally came home, they landed in San Francisco on the day that President Franklin Roosevelt died. Dressed in oversized Army fatigues, they ventured into a department store. While there, Mary Lou asked a clerk for a box of Kleenex.

The clerk's unwitting reply was ironic, "Lady, we don't have any. Don't you know there's a war going on?"

I have tried to be true to the history and to the personalities of the era. I have also tried to be true to those who shared with me their stories and feelings about this compelling chapter in their lives.

For in the end, **America's Best** is not my story.
It belongs to all of us.

Sinclair Browning
Tucson, Arizona

**TO ORDER ADDITIONAL COPIES OF
AMERICA'S BEST WRITE TO:**

**AMC PUBLISHING
A DIVISION OF AMERICAN METRO COMPANY, INC.
P.O. BOX 64185
TUCSON, AZ 85728
OR**
ISBN: 1-887037-00-4
SEND CHECK OR MONEY ORDER FOR
$24.00 + $4.50 POSTAGE. (PER COPY)